Sixty Years of Boom and Bust

The Impact of Oil in North Dakota, 1958–2018

Edited by
Kyle Conway

The Digital Press at the University of North Dakota
Grand Forks, ND

Book Design: William Caraher

Library of Congress Control Number: 2020944021
The Digital Press at the University of North Dakota, Grand Forks, North Dakota

ISBN-13: 978-1-7345068-3-9 (paperback)
ISBN-13: 978-1-7345068-4-6 (PDF)

Cover photo is by James N. Holter, courtesy of Janet Zander.
Back photo is by Kyle Conway.

Sixty Years of Boom and Bust:
The Impact of Oil in North Dakota, 1958–2018

Table of Contents

Section V. Social Change

Section VI. Conclusion

Section VII. Appendices

Preface
How to Read this Book

2018 | *Kyle Conway*

In 1958, the University of North Dakota published *The Williston Report: The Impact of Oil on the Williston Area of North Dakota*. Written by four UND professors, Robert Campbell, Samuel Kelley, Ross Talbot, and Bernt Wills, the book described the dramatic changes brought about by the discovery of oil on the western side of the state in 1951. They wrote about the impact of oil, from its discovery until 1954, on the region's physical geography, politics, economy, and social structure, providing a methodologically rigorous analysis, rich with statistics, maps, and photographs.

Sixty Years of Boom and Bust: The Impact of Oil in North Dakota, 1958–2018 reproduces the five chapters and two appendices of *The Williston Report*, which have now entered the public domain. It also adds chapters about the same themes as they relate to the boom that the region underwent from 2008 to 2014. The book has two goals: first, to provide a historical perspective for citizens and policy makers in the state, and second, to provide a longitudinal study useful to others wishing to understand resource booms. No study of resource booms, it should be noted, has looked at as wide a range of impacts over as long a period of time.

There are at least two ways to read this book, from beginning to end or selectively and strategically. Readers who take the first approach will discover that the first chapters on physical geography, politics, and economics are data-rich and provide a solid contextual foundation for the final chapters on social change. Those who read strategically might start with the final chapters about social change, the topic most discussed in accounts of the boom in newspapers such as the *New York Times* or on websites such as Buzzfeed or HuffPost. These chapters are more focused on narrative, in contrast to the more technical examinations offered in the first chapters. Rick Ruddell and Heather Ray's chapter "Social Impacts of Oil Development" (chapter 10) would be an especially propitious starting point, as it provides an even-handed overview of the effects of the boom, in contrast to the sensationalism of many of the articles in the popular press.

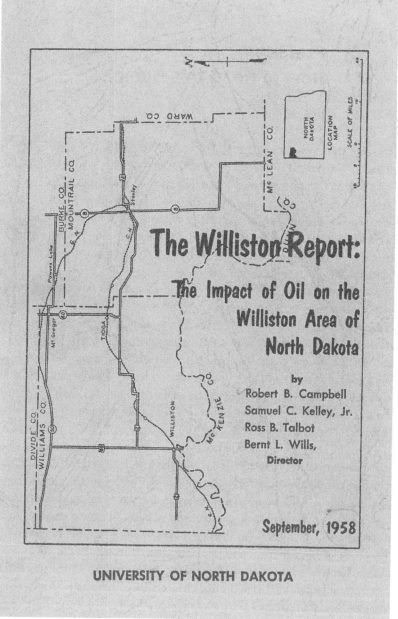

Figure 0.1. The cover of *The Williston Report* (source: author's personal collection)

Figure 0.2. Clarence Iverson No. 1, the first successful commercial well in North Dakota (source: James N. Holter, Williston, North Dakota)

A couple of explanatory notes are necessary here. First, with respect to the beginning and end points of the most recent boom, for the sake of consistency and readability, I decided in my capacity as the volume's editor to treat the boom as beginning in 2008 and ending in 2014, despite the changes (all minor) that this decision necessitated in certain chapters. These years are heuristically useful bookends: the contrast between North Dakota's prosperity and the recession in the rest of the United States began to be felt in 2008 (the country having officially entered a recession in December 2007), and the price of crude oil dropped below the threshold necessary to make drilling new wells profitable in 2014. But the dates are somewhat arbitrary. As certain chapters show (for example, the 2018 introduction and David Flynn's chapter, "The Economic Consequences of Oil Development"), oil production was growing before 2008, and both the number of active wells and the number of barrels produced continued to climb for several years after 2014. The number of barrels of oil produced even rebounded in 2018.

Second, although the 2018 chapters all update the 1958 chapters, some also consider the older report as an object of historical concern. This is especially true of the narrative-oriented chapters at the end of the book. Whereas the 1958 chapters about the physical geography of the region, its politics, and its economy each have only one 2018 counterpart, Campbell's 1958 chapter "Social Change in the Basin" has four, and they, more than those that precede them, are critical in their historiographic approach. This fact, I think, is due at least in part to the attention paid by the popular press to the social changes in western North Dakota during the most recent boom. It reminds us that we should ask how we know what we think we know, both as we read the 1958 chapters, whose unacknowledged biases the 2018 chapters work to reveal, and as we read those from 2018, whose unacknowledged biases we as contemporary readers might be inclined to share.

Sources and Acknowledgments

The task of recreating the 1958 *Report* involved quite a few people whom I wish to thank here. First, I would not have discovered the book if the HathiTrust Digital Library (https://www.hathitrust.org/Record/001313629), working with Google Books, had not made a scanned version available and discoverable. Second, although HathiTrust's e-book included a text version derived from an optical character recognition (OCR) scan, it was only one source—and not even the primary one—for the reconstructed text. Instead, I worked with an international team of researchers to recreate the book manually. I focused on the text, the first draft of which Dave Haeselin gave to his students to proofread and copyedit during a course on digital publishing at the University of North Dakota. My research assistant Raphaela Nehme, a master's student in the Department of Communication at the University of Ottawa, painstakingly entered—by hand, and with exceptional accuracy—all of the data from the report's charts, of which there were more than one hundred. Roxanne Lafleur, a media librarian at the University of Ottawa, scanned all of the images from my paper copy of *The Williston Report*, demonstrating an unrivaled level of technological wizardry and aesthetic judgment. Finally, Shane Gomes copyedited the final, revised manuscript and fixed the details that I, having read it too many times, could no longer see.

Beyond the technical aspects of recreating the book, there were administrative tasks that made its production possible. Kelly-Anne Maddox in the Faculty of Arts at the University of Ottawa helped me prepare an application for a publishing grant, which I received from the University of Ottawa. Finally, Bill Caraher, my former colleague at the University of North Dakota and founder and director of the Digital Press at the University of North Dakota, championed this book from the very beginning.

A sincere thank you to every one of these collaborators. A sincere thank you, also, to all of the contributors, whose goodwill and attention to detail made this book possible.

A Few Final Technical Notes

First, the book is being published in 2020, meaning the "2018" in the updated chapter titles is a symptom of wishful thinking. (I began work on the book in 2017.) During the revision process, the authors and I updated certain statistics past 2018, leading to a slight incongruence between the title and the chapter content. Second, I have made a few minor changes to the text of the 1958 *Report*, largely to correct typos, add missing information, or standardize the presentation and layout from one chapter to the next. None of these affect the content of the report. Likewise, the 1958 *Report* numbered all of its figures and tables consecutively, from one chapter to the next. I maintained this system in the 1958 chapters, but used a different system restarting the count at the beginning of each of the 2018 chapters.

K.C., Ottawa, December 2019

Chapter 1
Introduction and Summary

1958

Bernt L. Wills, Ross B. Talbot, Samuel C. Kelley, Jr., and Robert B. Campbell[1]

From the time of its earliest permanent occupance until 1951 the area of this study had been an agricultural area. Directly or indirectly, almost every resident had relied primarily upon the thin cover of soil, upon the vagaries of a capricious weather and upon the biological rhythm of plant and animal life for his livelihood and for his welfare.

The people there were products of this land. Several generations in that place had brought about a pattern of living, an adjustment of man to land which was established and mature. It was a way of life based upon neighborhoods and communities where major problems were common problems, where not only rancher and farmer, but banker, lawyer, doctor, school man, storekeeper—almost everyone there—knew this way of life, understood it and was a part of it. By most standards these people were well off, and evidence is lacking that they were less content with their lot in life than were those in other areas.

That this area was a possible source of oil had been known to geologists and oilmen since the 1920's. The people of the area were quite familiar with the sight of oil derricks and drilling rigs, for numerous unsuccessful attempts to find oil had been made.[2] Most of the people had become quite inured to talk of oil by the winter of 1950–51 and few really expected that anything so unusual as the discovery of oil in their area would upset the even tenor of their lives.

In January, 1951, Amerada Petroleum Corporation reported the recovery of a single pint of oil on a test of its Clarence Iverson wildcat well on the Nesson Anticline of the Williston Basin. That recovery, small

---

[1] The first section of this chapter is by Bernt L. Wills. The summaries are by the authors of the chapters which follow.

[2] It was in 1920 that the Pioneer Oil and Gas Company drilled North Dakota's first dry hole, township location 154 N, R 100 W. The Amerada successful effort of 1951 was at nearby T155 N, R 95 W. So near but yet so far!

though it was, stirred oilmen throughout the United States. To them it indicated the probable opening of a new oil province, the Williston Basin.

On April 4, 1951, Amerada Petroleum Corporation brought in its discovery well, Clarence Iverson No. 1, with an initial production of over 300 barrels in 17 hours, and the oil boom was on.

The onslaught of the boom activity disturbed the established patterns in the impact area. What seemed to be multitudes of strangers invaded and over-ran the town and rural areas alike. The influx included not only members of the oil fraternity—the oil operators, oil scouts, oil well promoters, the geologists, drillers, lease buyers, royalty buyers, brokers, etc., but also many people whose coming was related only in a secondary way to the oil activity itself. These ranged from unskilled workers willing to work at anything to an instructor in aesthetic dancing, and from persons who would cheerfully work outside the law to professional welfare and religious workers.

Demand for housing far outran supply. All available space was pressed into service. Garages, granaries, and sheds were converted into living quarters and business places. Improvised shacks, as well as substantial structures, were constructed and utilized. Hundreds of house trailers were brought into the area.

Community services were jammed; schools were clogged and put on a shift basis, transportation and communication systems were strained, roads suffered damage from the heavy truck traffic. Repair work could hardly keep up with the rapid wear. Thus the permanent residents of the area found that costs of public services rose sharply while the services declined.

Business activity in the towns soared. The newcomers brought both capital and demand for goods. Dozens of new establishments came into being, from small lunch counters and service stations to large oil-field equipment supply houses. In some instances these establishments extended well beyond the towns, as along the three-mile highway from U.S. Highway 10 into the town of Tioga.

In the oil producing area itself the cultural landscape changed as steel derricks rose in ever increasing numbers, as drillers and geophysical crews sought and found the limits of the pools. Pipe lines were laid to sidings. Loading racks were erected. Storage tanks went up at wells and at local terminal points. Warehouses, company offices, and "camps" were built at desired locations. As gas pressure weakened at producing wells, the wells were put on pumps and the enormous jacks (for these are deep wells) became distinctive features of the landscape. At night

OIL WELLS AND PIPELINE NEAR TIOGA, N.D., SUMMER, 1954 —
This is a representative scene of the major North Dakota oil producing area. The pipe line is the 24-inch line being laid to the Tioga refinery. Note that farming operations generally continue throughout the field. **COURTESY GNDA**

the oil fields literally sparkled with the lights of the burning gas flares which dotted the area like so many torches.

To these landowners on whose property oil was found, or who received high payment for mineral rights, the oil development meant increased wealth and opportunity for "the more abundant life." To many of the others it yielded little more than bitterness. Often the original residents found themselves in the position of a minority group. The newcomers often had markedly different backgrounds from the older residents; often they were of different political or religious persuasion. When the earlier residents sought employment in the oil development program they found only the lower paid, less skilled jobs open to them, for the big oil concerns commonly brought their own trained labor supply into the area.

The almost frenzied activity of the boom gradually subsided and by 1955 conditions could be described as quite well stabilized or settled. The conditions, however, were not those of 1950, for the effects of oil development are long-lasting. To all, new or old, the oil development meant readjustment and change. To the state it meant increased wealth and a partial check on the declining trend of the state's population. To the oil producing area it also meant release from almost complete dependence upon an agricultural economy.

AMERADA'S FIELD CAMP AND TIOGA, N.D, SUMMER, 1954 — *In the foreground is the Amerada Camp, first its supply dump (largely pipe, or casing); in the center of the camp are warehouses and offices followed by 30 company houses. About a mile to the north of the field camp is the town of Tioga.* **COURTESY GNDA**

Summary

The effects of the oil development have invaded every aspect of life in the "Basin." They have influenced the demographic structure, the political balance, the social organization, employment and standards of living, and the physical attributes of the area.

These impacts are considered in summary form in the following paragraphs. The chapters which follow treat of them in greater detail.

Physical Impacts

The area of this study, the "impact area," consists of much of eastern Williams County and western Mountrail County in northwestern North Dakota. The principal oil fields comprise an area about 35 miles long (north-south) by 5 miles wide, located about 40 miles east of the city of Williston, North Dakota. (FIGURE 1)

Geologically, this is a portion of a filled basin—the Williston Basin. The most important oil trap is the Nesson Anticline, and at the time of this study most of the producing wells are located on that structure. Topographically this is a plains area, largely overlain by glacial drift.

This region has a semi-arid continental type of climate, with relatively cold winters and hot summers. The average annual rainfall at Williston is slightly less than 15 inches.

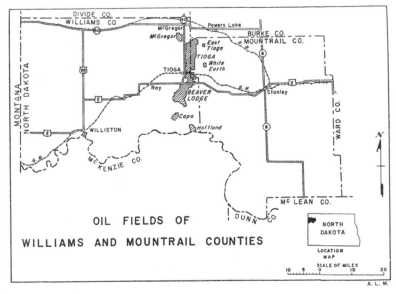

FIG. 1—*Oil Fields of Williston and Mountrail Counties*

Transportation Network Impacts

The major routes of supply of this area are the main line of the Great Northern Railway, Federal Highway No. 2, and State Highway No. 40. (FIGURE 1) Very little change in the pattern of the major routes of supply occurred outside of the oil fields as a result of oil development, but within the oil producing areas the changes were marked. In those areas approximately 200 miles of all-weather roads were added between April, 1951 and July, 1954. This added mileage consisted of township and county roads and of "well-access" roads. The latter type were built by the petroleum companies, of which the most active was the Amerada Petroleum Corporation.

A direct consequence of the oil development activity was the additional wear and damage done to road surfaces by the increase in vehicular traffic (this increase was in both number and weights of vehicles), and by the attendant increases in maintenance costs. The exact amount of the road wear and cost which can be attributed to oil development is difficult, if not impossible, to measure, but that it was considerable is certain.

Demographic Impacts

The impact of the oil industry on population numbers and characteristics in Williams and Mountrail counties was of varying significance. In general, notable effects were experienced in the rural non-farm centers (Ray, Tioga, and Tioga Environs) and in the urban center (Williston) which were ideally located to serve as residential, service, and focal points in the oil field and associated developments. The remainder of the two counties, including the rural impact townships and Stanley, was noticeably less affected.

The following basic changes in population characteristics seem to be especially significant.

1. Williams County had a percentage population increase of 26.8% between 1950 and 1954, whereas Mountrail County had a decrease of 5.5%. Rural non-farm settlements and urban Williston showed marked increases due to the direct influence of the oil industry; the remainder of both counties maintained the downward trend characteristic of purely rural North Dakota counties.
2. There were changes in the proportion of younger persons relative to other age groups in those significantly affected centers, with a trend towards a generally younger population.
3. A relatively large number of people in Ray, Tioga, and Tioga Environs occupied trailers, illustrating the migratory nature of a fairly large sector of the labor force.
4. Large numbers of workers and families were attracted to the area from considerable distances. In each of the rural non-farm and urban centers a rather large proportion of the population has been drawn from noncontiguous states.

5. The great increase in workers engaged in the mining and construction, service, and trade classifications reflects the nature of the development and the increased requirements for various services and facilities.

6. The fluid nature of the population and frequent population fluctuations have resulted in a trend towards a lower but more stable population level. This trend became evident in late 1954.

Social Impacts

The large increase in population, particularly as it represented an influx of "alien" people to the Basin, was expected to create social problems, situations for which there would be feelings of dissatisfaction and around which would develop conflicts in attitudes. It was anticipated that these attitudes would be readily observable in the opinions of the inhabitants of the area and in the actions of their organizations and agencies. Only to a limited extent were these expectations borne out by the observations.

It was true in Williston that the already existing organizations did not make general efforts to embrace the newcomers into their memberships; but it was also true that there were no overt antipathies toward the newcomers on the part of organization leaders. There were conflicts in Ray and Tioga about specific issues, but the participants in the conflicts were not identified by background and length of residence as much as by "conservatism" or "backwardness" and their opposites. The most general negative attitude about the people involved probably was that held by the rural residents toward the town merchants, who were considered to have "sold out" to the oil people. The nearly complete absence of negative categorical attitudes of "natives" and "newcomers" regarding each other in Williston is indicated by the latters' opinions about the former and the opinions of both groups as to whether or not the newcomers had been accepted. Both attitudes were positive to the extent of 99% and 96% respectively.

There was a surprising absence of social problems arising out of the changed situations. The housing situation was the one most clearly considered problematic, although it appeared that housing in general (rather than specific residences) was most often the situation opined about. There were very few comments about small, dilapidated, dirty residences in the area, despite the general awareness of a "tight" housing situation. (Apparently no plans for low-rental housing were being made either by public agencies or private building firms; all construction appeared to be aimed at high-rental levels, thus creating what turned out to be a new problem rather than a solution.)

Criminal and immoral behavior did not develop to the level of general problem conditions, and there was a virtual absence of comment regarding it. There were a few expressions of negative attitudes about the oil people, but they were limited primarily to rural residents' comments about the bad-check writing of oil field workers.

The really apparent changes, some of which took on the nature of social problems, were to be found in public agency requirements. The school systems and the post office (in Williston, at least) were seriously taxed to keep abreast of the changes. Building could not be accomplished at sufficient speed, thus a series of makeshift arrangements had to suffice; schools had to operate on a split day in the small towns and the Williston post office had to reorganize its operations and to remodel its working space. (Other agencies encountered less startling and less pressing changes with the possible exception of government road construction and maintenance agencies).

In general, the change was widespread in the circumstances of the Williston Basin residents, but the definition of these circumstances as problematic was not sufficient to bring about even more sweeping changes. Conflicts appeared to be local and confined to specific issues, which were resolved with so little lasting prejudice that negative attitudes about the "alien" inhabitants were not apparent to a noteworthy degree.

Political Impacts

The discovery and development of an important natural resource is almost certain to involve the phenomenon of political power. In Bertrand Russell's words, "power may be defined as the production of intended effects."[3] When a new oil field is opened there is tremendous activity by those who desire to produce certain "intended effects." Such was the case in the Williston area. First, some of the major oil producers moved into the new boom area to secure legal authority to develop the oil field. Then it became necessary to protect investments through the passage of favorable legislation and the creation of a sympathetic public opinion. This strategy was not novel on the part of the oil companies but constituted what has been called the utilization of "anticipated reactions." The large oil producers formed an association called the North Dakota

---

[3] Bertrand Russell, *Power—A New Social Analysis* (London: George Allen and Unwin, Ltd., 1938), p. 35.

Oil and Gas Association; some landowners and businessmen organized the Williams County Landowner's and Royalty Owner's Association and other like interest groups. At the state level, the State Legislative Research Committee delved into the problem of proposing oil legislation that would be in the interests of the State of North Dakota. Out of the crucible of the legislative process came oil legislation which was a mixture of the efforts of pressure groups, legislative committees, lawyers, research directors, prominent politicians, and influential citizens. The unstable power situation in the North Dakota legislature meant that compromise was a necessity but the oil companies were successful, for the most part, in securing tax and conservation features in oil and gas legislation that were compatible with their best interests.

In the administration of the oil laws new frictions and contentions arose. The issue of well-spacing was threshed out but the decisions reached did not always meet with the concurrence of some of the land owners. The role of the State Geologist became more complex and confusing as scientific judgments and political and economic interests became intertwined. The importance of the North Dakota Industrial Commission in the field of oil policy was soon apparent and, more recently, the role of the Public Service Commission became increasingly important due to the construction of pipe lines and the wholesale price of natural gas products. The value of state-owned land in the oil areas assumed a new significance as its revenue-producing capacity increased very considerably with the discovery of oil.

The public's role in this new venture was interesting and perplexing. The results of a questionnaire survey, which was conducted by the authors of this study, strongly indicated that most people in the Williston area actually did not understand even the main features of the legislation pertaining to oil. Also, in an effort to create a favorable climate of opinion for their activities, the oilmen created a local unit of the Oil Industry Information Committee in order to "educate" the youth and, to a lesser extent, the adults about the production and distribution of oil. Their efforts were well-planned and intelligently executed but there is some question as to whether the techniques constituted education or propaganda. This study attempts to analyze that issue.

What might be termed the "power elite" has not changed notably since the advent of oil. The executives of the major oil producers have been added to the existing power structure in the Williston area composed primarily of prominent bankers, lawyers, and businessmen. Thus a new and dynamic element was grafted onto the already existing power structure within the local communities and principally within the city of Williston.

As one would expect, the rapid influx of population caused some disruption and overburdening of the local governmental and non-governmental facilities in the Williston area. The public schools were particularly hard pressed; the cities had to increase their municipal services for considerable numbers of new customers. The changes in the "old way of life" and the increases in taxes caused the demand for a different form of city government in Williston, the election of a new city council in Ray, and some intra-community conflicts in Tioga.

Neither politics nor public administration, of course, stand alone. The economic basis of politics in the Williston area was quickly apparent. Much of the political controversy centered around the ancient question of who was going to get what, and how. Social changes in terms of in-migration, the interaction of different cultures, the increased public welfare burdens, etc., were not as vast as expected, but these changes may have a rather substantial long-run effect upon voting patterns and habits. The geography of the area is certain to have an impact upon future political events. If the oil fields are considerably extended and increasingly productive the changes in voting patterns of the electorate may again be modified.

As of the end of this study (1955), it appeared that oil had not caused any political revolution in North Dakota. The picture should be somewhat clearer after the counting of the ballots that will be cast in the November election in 1956.

Economic Impacts

The economy of the Williston Basin is characterized by agriculture. The peculiarities of climate and rainfall limit the agriculture of the area to dry-farming and grazing. Nearly 80 percent of the value of farm products sold in 1954 were derived from field crops, mainly cash grains and the remainder from livestock and livestock products.

This type of agriculture, which is characteristic of the Great Plains, requires extensive farming on a very large scale. Average farm size in Williams County is over 830 acres, yet the typical farm is operated on a family basis with a large capital outlay for mechanical equipment and little outlay for hired labor. Nearly 90 percent of all farms in Williams County were operated by full or part owners. Only 60 percent of all farms employed any hired labor in 1954 and only 15 percent spent more than $500 for farm wages.

The non-agricultural sector of the area's economy is engaged exclusively in the distribution of goods and services to the farm sector. It produces, locally, almost nothing that is consumed by the area. Prior to the development of petroleum extraction, manufactures and mining were limited to printing and publishing, domestic food processing and the extraction of lignite on a limited scale. Nearly all private employment and income was derived from occupation in trade, service, and transportation.

In this type of economic situation, extensive agriculture tends to evict people from farms in an area where the number of other employment opportunities is dependent upon the size of the farm population and farm income. The out-migration that results produces a population decline and a consequent reduction in income and employment.

The discovery of oil in this area has had two primary effects upon the economy of the area. First, it has created supplemental income to farm families through the sale of mineral leases and mineral rights, and to a smaller number of persons through royalty payments on land with producing wells. This supplementary income has permitted the repayment of mortgage obligations on farm land, the purchase of new farm equipment, and general farm improvements. In many cases it has provided the capital outlay necessary to eliminate the farm from sub-marginal status.

Second, it has provided additional job opportunities directly and indirectly as it has employed individuals in well drilling activity, in the servicing of oil extraction, and in the impact of an expanding population upon the trade and service industries. Between 1947 and 1954, manufacturing employment in Williams County increased by nearly 90 percent and value added by manufacture nearly 300 percent. Employment in retail and wholesale trade increased by 30 percent and sales by 70 percent. The major expansion in indirect employment was in the service industries. In this industrial sector, employment increased by more than 60 percent and service receipts had a gain of 226 percent over 1947.

As these values suggest, the oil development has stimulated the local economy to levels of activity in excess of that expected under the economic condition existing prior to 1951. However, it is apparent that the initial impact of the development has acted as an autonomous factor inducing change that is not warranted by the long-term potential of petroleum extraction in the area. The local economy is beginning to feel the effects of the induced over-investment in business inventories, in land, and in extended credit. A favorable combination of factors such as winter climate had, however, acted to reduce the rate of growth induced by the discovery and thus to decrease the magnitude of the adjustment below that which has been observed in other "boom" areas. It appears quite likely that oil will provide a sustaining factor in this economy in the future and that much of the adjustment to the altered economic structure is already accomplished.

2018

Chapter 2
Introduction: Sixty Years of Boom and Bust

Kyle Conway

It is a disorienting experience, in light of the western North Dakota's 2008–14 boom, to read the 1958 *Williston Report* six decades later. In many ways it is unexpectedly current. "Community services were jammed," the authors wrote, "schools were clogged and put on a shift basis, transportation and communication systems were strained, roads suffered damage from the heavy truck traffic" (p. 8, as reprinted in this volume). Their observation is not too different from one made by the *New York Times Magazine* in 2013 when it wrote, "[The boom] has minted millionaires, paid off mortgages, created businesses; it has raised rents, stressed roads, vexed planners and overwhelmed schools" (Brown 2013).

In other ways, the report is surprisingly different. For instance, during the recent boom, human trafficking and drug use both increased (Ruddell 2017; Berg Burin, current volume). In contrast, the authors of the 1958 report wrote, "There were no indications available to the researchers that there had been a notable increase in, or even the presence of, organized criminal or immoral activity—gambling houses, theft rings, 'protection' or houses of prostitution" (Campbell, p. 262). Where drugs were concerned, they wrote only about alcohol, saying, "drunkenness was prevented from developing to the problem proportions it might have reached by a combination of already existing circumstances" and strategies, including "a system of quick pick-ups in the 'skidrow' section" near the bars in downtown Williston and the tendency by judges to "[penalize] to the maximum offenders of the drinking laws" (p. 261).

Perhaps the key difference between the two booms is the way people relate to historical events. People affected by the 1951 boom (which lasted until 1954) did not have other boom experiences to refer back to—they had to figure things out as they went along. In contrast, many people affected by the

2008–14 boom still remembered the region's boom from the 1980s, and some even remembered the one from the 1950s. In the 1950s, most people did not feel that history was repeating itself. In the 2000s, many did. Thus, reading the 1958 *Report* feels uncanny because it is simultaneously familiar and foreign. We have been down this path before, even if it looks a bit different this time.

Sixty Years of Boom and Bust explores the similarities and differences between the booms from 1951–4 and 2008–14 and asks what sixty years of history can teach us about North Dakota today, where the vicissitudes of the oil market keep the region constantly on the edge of a new boom—or a new bust. The biggest difference, as these chapters show, is scale, in two senses. First, the 1950s boom affected only two counties, but the most recent boom affected the entire state and surrounding region. Second, hydraulic fracturing (or "fracking") made it possible to extract an ever-greater amount of oil from the ground: 6 million barrels in 1954 compared to about 400 million in 2014 (North Dakota Industrial Commission 2016, xiv). Of course, these factors are related: improved extraction tools increased output and allowed oil companies to expand the geographic reach of their operations.

After an overview of the history of oil in North Dakota, this introductory chapter examines the question of scale, describing both the rates of oil production and the industrial logic behind them, which can be characterized as high-risk, high-reward. It also describes, in broad strokes, the social impact of this industrial logic, or the way it influenced interactions between newcomers and longtime residents. It shows how both production and its social impacts are shaped by contradictory forces. With respect to production, these forces are observable in the logic of the built-in contraction: one driver of the need for new wells was the technology of the wells themselves, which quickly lost capacity. With respect to social interactions, they are observable in forces related to class and to how long residents have lived in the region. This chapter ends with a consideration of what it means to read *The Williston Report* sixty years after it was published through the lens of twenty-first century concerns, a theme that the book's conclusion will develop more fully. As the preface mentions, no study of resource booms has looked at as wide a range of impacts over as long a period of time, and in this respect, the 1958 chapters and their 2018 counterparts hold up a useful mirror for North Dakotans (and others) today who wish to examine the situation in which they find themselves.

History of Oil in North Dakota

Western North Dakota sits atop the vast Bakken oil formation or play (as people in the industry call a group of oil fields), which stretches across two states, North Dakota and Montana, and into two Canadian provinces, Manitoba and Saskatchewan. The oil—more than 7 billion barrels of it (USGS 2013)—is contained within layers of shale, which workers frack by injecting a slurry of water, chemicals, and sand at high pressure to open cracks through which oil and natural gas flow more freely.[1]

Although the first boom began in the 1950s, geologists and "oilmen," as the vocabulary of the era would have it, had known there was oil to extract since the 1910s. The Pioneer Oil and Gas Company drilled the first well—which was dry—in 1916, an effort that was reproduced many times over the next four decades (Robinson [1966] 2017, 457). It was only in 1951 that a well was finally successful, on a farm near Tioga that belonged to Clarence Iverson. A few months later, a number of successful wells were drilled on the farm of Henry O. Bakken (Dalrymple 2012). The formation was named after him, but not immediately. In fact, the name Bakken does not appear at all in the 1958 *Report*. Instead, the area was referred to simply as the Williston Basin, as it had "the general shape of a basin or dish. The bottom of the 'dish' [lay] under western North Dakota for the most part" (Wills, p. 36). (As Brad Rundquist and Greg Vandeberg show in their chapter in this volume, the Williston Basin and the Bakken Formation are not identical, although they do overlap quite a bit. See their map on p. 69.)

The 1950s boom was followed by another in the 1980s. Rundquist and Vandeberg attribute the first to the discovery of oil itself, and the second to the spike in oil prices due to the embargo by the Organization of the Petroleum Exporting Countries (OPEC) in the 1970s (p. 82). Both were hampered by technological problems that fracking would eventually solve. Oil companies had to drill vertical wells and hope to hit an already fractured vein in the shale. If their guess was off, they might miss the vein and the well would be dry. Technologies developed in the early 2000s, such as steerable rotary bits, multipad drilling (where "multiple descending wells from a single surface location eliminate the need for rig transfers between locations"), and zipper fracking (where "two or more parallel wells are drilled by perforating each at alternating intervals") made it possible to drill wells faster and extract more oil from them

---

[1] Russell Gold's (2015) *The Boom* is perhaps the best description of the history and technology of fracking.

(Maugeri 2013, 8), leading to the 2008–14 boom. Oil companies could direct their drills toward oil-rich shale and create fissures within it to release the different forms of petroleum.

As a result, the differences between the 2008–14 boom, which Rundquist and Vandeberg describe as the "technology boom" (p. 83), and those of the 1950s and 1980s were dramatic. Rick Ruddell and Heather Ray, in their chapter in this volume, characterize the first two as "minor" (p. 272): the 1950s boom lasted forty-eight months and affected two counties, while the 1980s boom lasted sixty months and affected four counties. In contrast, they describe the most recent boom as "major." By their estimation, it began in 2007 and had not ended as of 2019, lasting 152 months and affecting seventeen counties. The relative scale of the two booms is clear: the most recent one was of an entirely different magnitude, so much so that "the findings of research about rapid growth communities prior to 2000 provide limited insight about contemporary booms" (Ruddell and Ray, p. 272).

Scale of Change: Geography

The difference in scale is observable in at least two places: the area in which drilling took place and the amount of oil produced. The 1958 *Williston Report* focused on just two counties—Williams and Mountrail—and within those, just four towns or regions—Williston, Ray, Tioga, and what the authors called the "Tioga environs," an area near Tioga that had been undeveloped until the boom (Wills, p. 52). Of these towns, Williston was by far the largest. It was the commercial center to which people would travel from the other towns, even if they could buy what they needed closer to home (Kelley, p. 192). In 1950, before the boom, it had about 7,400 residents, a population that grew to 9,700 by 1954 (Wills, p. 56). About 30 percent of its new residents came from outside Williams and Mountrail counties, and about 10 percent from farther away than North Dakota's neighboring states (Wills, p. 61; Kelley, p. 214)

Ray and Tioga, in contrast, were much smaller, although they grew at faster rates. By the end of the boom in 1954, Ray had about 1,500 residents, twice its population in 1950, while Tioga had about 1,600, more than three times its population in 1950 (Campbell, p. 246; *Williston Report*, Appendix B, p. 371). Whereas many of the new residents in Williston worked as managers (the town became a center of operations, according to Campbell, p. 250), those who came to Ray and Tioga were more likely to work in the oilfields, and they were more likely to come from farther away. Tioga attracted "the more nearly permanent oil field workers—the better paid, supervisory field personnel"; 20

percent of its new residents were from farther away than a contiguous state. Ray attracted "the transient and temporary employees" who worked the rigs; 45 percent of its new residents were from farther away than a contiguous state (Wills, p. 60; Campbell, p. 250).

Direct comparisons with the 2008–14 boom are difficult because people studying the affected areas have measured different things, but demographic estimates and analysis of the geographic distribution of jobs still reveal the magnitude of change, both between booms and in the years of the most recent boom. Williston, where most of the oil-related jobs were (63 percent near the height of the boom in 2011), grew dramatically. Before the boom, it had about 13,000 residents. In 2013, its population was between 30,000 and 38,000, depending on which demographic model researchers used and whether they counted the surrounding townships. Before the price of oil began to fall in 2014, demographers were even predicting a population of 42,000 (or 54,000 with the surrounding townships), although only about two thirds were permanent residents (Hodur and Bangsund 2013). People came from farther away than during the 1951–54 boom, as a number of indirect measures show. Between the 2011–12 and 2013–14 school years, for instance, the Williston Public School District #1 had students transfer in from almost all fifty U.S. states, in addition to Cameroon, Ghana, Indonesia, the Philippines, Honduras, Turkey, Nigeria, Taiwan, China, Russia, Mexico, Canada, and islands in the south Pacific Ocean (Conway 2016, 38–9). Similarly, the North Dakota Department of Transportation registered 255 prequalified contractors from twenty-eight states: ninety-seven from North Dakota, fifty-eight from Minnesota, eighteen from South Dakota, and between one and seven from most of the western U.S. states (Nowatzki 2014).

Also in contrast to the 1950s boom, oil jobs were distributed more widely across the state. About 20 percent were in Dickinson, two hours south of Williston, and 15 percent in Minot, two hours east (Hodur and Bangsund 2013, 9). Similarly, the economic effects were also distributed more broadly, in something of a ripple effect. Within one hundred miles of the Bakken, there was an increase in wages, although not as large as within the Bakken itself, and within two hundred miles, there was a decrease in unemployment (Batbold and Grunewald 2013, 14). As a result, Williston's role was different than in the 1950s. Although its importance grew during the boom (it generated more sales tax revenue than Fargo, the state's biggest city), it was not as economically central to the Bakken because the effects of the boom stretched so far into the rest of the state (see Flynn, current volume).

Scale of Change: Oil Production

The difference in levels of production can be explained in large part by the different technologies oil companies had at their disposal during the two booms. "Throughout the area of this study the oil producing formations are relatively deep," explain the authors of *The Williston Report* (p. 36); "most of the wells find 'pay depths' at below 8,000 feet and some at below 11,000 feet. This factor of depth is very important, for it constitutes a critical cost factor in the production of oil." The problem was that the technology was such that there was "no way to prove the presence of an oil reserve except to drill for it" (Kelley, p. 195). Still, despite the risks, the potential rewards were enough to attract a large number of speculators:

> Well drilling is an expensive operation, in particular when drilling depths are great. The cost of an exploratory well may range from 50,000 dollars to twice or three times that amount.[2] The probability of success for a wildcat well is probably about 10 percent for the nation as a whole. On the other hand, the potential rewards are sufficient to induce many gamblers, large and small, to join the game. (Kelley, p. 195)

The rates of oil production from 1951 to 1954 reflect the limits that technology and risk placed on exploration. Williams County, of which Williston is the seat, produced 25,000 barrels of oil in 1951 and 6,025,000 in 1954, as shown in Table 2.1 (adapted from Kelley, p. 200).

TABLE 2.1.
PRODUCTION OF CRUDE PETROLEUM, NORTH DAKOTA AND SELECTED AREAS, 1951–4 (THOUSANDS OF BARRELS)

	1951	1952	1953	1954
Williams County	25	1,481	4,248	4,135
Mountrail County	0	91	900	1,253
Other	0	26	218	637
North Dakota (TOTAL)	25	1,598	5,466	6,025

By the time of the 2008–14 boom, technology such as steerable bits (which could be directed toward oil-rich shale) and fracking (which could force the oil

---

[2] Roughly $430,000–$1,200,000 in 2018 dollars, assuming an annual inflation rate of between 2 and 2.5 percent. As a point of comparison, in 2012, individual wells cost about $8–11 million to drill (Reddall 2012). The success rates made possible by fracking have also made it possible for oil companies to take greater financial risks.

out once the drill had cleared a path to it) had advanced in ways that diminished some of the earlier risk. As a result, the state produced more than fifty times as much oil as during the 1951–4 boom. In 2012, it produced a little more than 240 million barrels of oil. In 2013, that number rose to about 314 million. In 2014: 397 million. In 2015: 432 million (North Dakota Industrial Commission 2016). (See Figure 2.1.) Production declined in 2016, but by 2018, it had increased again, breaking records for monthly production in August of that year (Dalrymple 2018; Brady 2018).

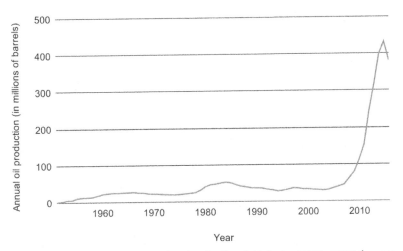

Figure 2.1. Total annual oil production in North Dakota, 1951–2016 (source: North Dakota Industrial Commission 2016)

These numbers bear further scrutiny, however. For production to increase at this rate, companies needed to drill wells at a furious pace because they quickly became inefficient. In a sense, the bust that started in 2014 was built into the boom from the very beginning: it had merely been hidden by the accelerated rates of drilling. In other words, the boom was premised on a contraction.

What exactly does this observation mean? Fracked wells produce oil most quickly during the first month after they come on-line. After a year, their production drops as much as 50 percent, and after two years, as much as 70 percent. As a result, during the height of the Bakken boom, oil companies had to drill about ninety new wells a month just to hold production steady (Maugeri 2013, 1–3), and the number of active wells ballooned from about 4,200 in 2008 to more than 13,700 in 2015 (North Dakota Industrial Commission 2016, xiv).

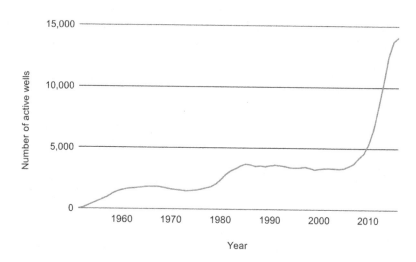

Figure 2.2. Total number of active wells per year in North Dakota, 1951–2016 (source: North Dakota Industrial Commission 2016)

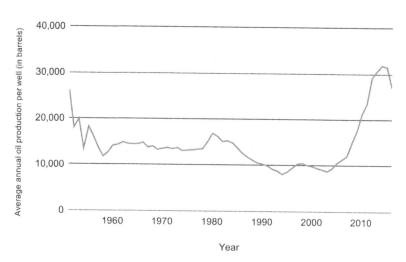

Figure 2.3. Average annual oil production per well in North Dakota, 1951–2016 (source: North Dakota Industrial Commission 2016)

(See Figure 2.2. For a useful point of comparison, note that there were about three and a half times as many wells in 2015 as there were at the height of the 1980s boom, and nearly thirty times as many as during the 1950s boom.) In other words, many of the jobs created during the most recent boom were those of the people who worked the drilling rigs. Their work was in demand because oil companies knew the wells they drilled would slow down in a relatively short time.

At the same time, however, the technology for extracting oil from shale was becoming more efficient, making it possible to drill wells faster and extract more oil from them (Maugeri 2013, 8). In the Bakken, these improvements translated into wells that produced twice as much oil annually as those from the 1980s boom (North Dakota Industrial Commission 2016, xiv). (See Figure 2.3. Note that the statistics from the 1950s are thrown off by the fact that there were very few wells, which has the effect of inflating the annual average production per well.)

Although new technologies helped mitigate the risk oil companies incurred, the rates and tendencies of employment remained relatively volatile. Because production in shale-based fracked wells declines so quickly, oil companies feel drops in the price of oil acutely. As Maugeri explains, "starting production when the market is down means selling the bulk of a [well's] total production for cheap without possibility of recovery" (2013, 11). At the same time, drilling new wells can be done quickly: "it takes only a few months from obtaining a drilling license to bringing a well online" (Maugeri 2013, 11). Thus, companies stop and start as oil prices fluctuate, the break-even point during the 2008–14 boom being about $85 a barrel (Maugeri 2013, 14).

It was during the drilling stages that the fastest population growth occurred in the Bakken "as a greater number of workers were required to drill the wells and to construct the infrastructure, such as plant structures, railways, and pipelines that move these commodities" (Ruddell and Ray, p. 276). To hedge against the volatility of oil prices, companies relied on "fly-in, fly-out" (or "FIFO") workers, who could quickly start wells when called upon to do so but go elsewhere when production slowed. In this way, the new technologies for fracking shale made it possible for companies to treat their workforce as flexible. In effect, they could hedge against risk while maximizing gain by transferring the burden of the risk onto their workers, whose fortunes rose and fell with the price of oil.

Social Impacts

As both the 1951–4 and 2008–14 booms showed, this high-risk, high-reward logic had impacts on the communities within whose bounds oil was found. During the most recent boom, the reliance on FIFO workers, for instance, which solved problems for oil companies while creating them for workers, had destabilizing effects on the boomtown communities "by reducing informal social controls, which in turn [increased] disorder and crime" (Ruddell and Ray, p. 276).

But the booms also revealed the complex, sometimes ambiguous nature of social integration. To give an example, on the one hand, respondents to the surveys administered for the 1958 *Report* thought that newcomers had been welcomed: "a total of 96% of the old residents and 95% of the new residents thought that newcomers had been accepted" (Campbell, p. 252). In a similar vein, the perception that booms were places characterized "a general laxity of law enforcement or, at least, of a greater incidence of loose spending for illegal and barely legal pleasures" proved to be wrong, as Williston increased its police budget during the boom (Campbell, p. 259).

On the other hand, according to the 1958 *Report*:

> Conflicts on the personal level in Ray and Tioga were more apparent than in Williston not only in ... political issues but also in general attitudes about people of one sort or another. One woman, whose son was a leader in the fight for the water system,[3] reported that her neighbor had not spoken to her for a year as the consequence of the fight. Others referred to the "backwardness" of the native residents, to the "riff-raff" who came in to work the oil fields, and to the destruction of the close friendly relations between town and country since the business had begun to cater to oil workers, such statements reflecting an outspoken but numerically small group of people. (Campbell, p. 250)

Studies of the 2008–14 boom reveal similar contradictions. On the one hand, a recent, survey-based study showed that a range of demographic characteristics, including gender, race, and years of residency, were not statistically significant predictors of longtime residents' attitudes toward newcomers

---

[3] The dispute in question took place in Tioga and concerned whether the town needed a municipal water and sewer system and, if so, who should pay for it. See Talbot, p. 133.

(Huynh, Robinson, Mrozla, Dahle, Archbold, and Marcel 2019). Instead, significant predictors included longtime residents' perceptions of crime: those who thought it had increased were less likely to perceive newcomers positively. Conversely, longtime residents who "viewed their community as a friendly place, believed that most people in their community can be trusted, and ... [attempted] to interact with new residents in their community were also more likely to have positive perceptions of new residents" (Huynh et al. 2019, 1003).

On the other hand, there is ample evidence to suggest that the boom produced anxiety for longtime residents in the region (see Ruddell and Ray, current volume). Frequently that anxiety focused on specific places, such as the Walmart on the north end of Williston. When the boom began, the store's "parking lot became an informal campground" and then grew "increasingly crowded and rowdy, which resulted in safety concerns" (Caraher and Weber 2017, 75; see also Caraher, Weber, and Rothaus, current volume). Many women felt they could not go there without men following them around (Eligon 2013). Whether the perception resulted from a statistically significant increase in crime is difficult to determine, for reasons related to challenges in measuring the region's population and the scant records of crime before the boom. Still, as Rick Ruddell (2017, 48) writes, "a 20% increase in crime may not be statistically significant, but that change has a substantial impact on the operations of the police, courts, and corrections."

How to interpret these apparent contradictions? For one thing, it is likely that longtime residents felt—and feel—anxiety in some situations, but not all, and that the way researchers asked questions influenced what they said. It is entirely possible that respondents thought outsiders were welcome in a general sense but still felt anxious when they walked through the Walmart parking lot. For another, these contradictions hint at the complexity of the impact of oil on the region, as companies and governments have hedged against the risk of the bust that is always on the horizon. The Williston Report and the follow-up chapters in this volume have only just begun to unravel this complexity. Consider the points where the 2018 chapters go beyond those from 1958. Andrea Olive, for instance, describes how new technologies have meant more exploration and, consequently, more environmental impact and more agencies involved. The 1958 Report describes the role of the Industrial Commission, which formulated conservation regulations, the North Dakota state geologist, who directed the State Geological Survey, and the Public Service Commission, which regulated public utilities. Also involved, but to lesser degrees, were the Tax Commission, the Board of University and School Lands, and the Bank of

North Dakota, the latter two having lands under lease (Talbot, p. 120–3). Olive expands this list to include the Water Commission, the Department of Health, the Department of Labor, the Game and Fish Department, and the Parks and Recreation Department (p. 164). The addition of these agencies attests to the boom's reach and the need North Dakotans felt to address the impact of oil extraction on their lived and natural environments. Consider, too, the healthcare-related needs in the Bakken in the 2000s. While *The Williston Report* mentions hospitals only once (to discuss their economic impact [Kelley, p. 213]), Karin Becker, in her chapter, provides a clear picture of the workforce shortages and need for mental health services at seven sites across the state. Finally, consider the increase in human trafficking that occurred during the 2008–14 boom. As noted above, the 1958 *Report* claimed that prostitution was not a problem in the Williston Basin. As Nikki Berg Burin argues in her chapter, not only was it a problem during the most recent boom, but there is reason to think it was also a problem six decades prior, the claims of the 1958 authors notwithstanding.

Reading the 1958 Report *Sixty Years Later*

The Williston Report reveals as much about its time in what it does *not* say as in what it *does*. Contemporary readers bring a set of expectations to the text that its authors did not share, as the final chapters of this book demonstrate. For instance, the authors of the 1958 *Report* defined social problems as "any situation which is reported by people involved in it as undesirable and, therefore, about which they express a negative opinion" (Campbell, p. 254). Not wanting to impose their own sense of what constituted a problem, they relied instead on their informants. This choice had the effect, as Bill Caraher, Bret Weber, and Richard Rothaus (current volume) point out, of reproducing the basic assumptions underpinning the region's broader social structure, for instance by ignoring structural issues affecting the scarcity of adequate housing, which the authors treated as an individual, rather than social, problem. Similarly, as Nikki Berg Burin argues, there is reason to be skeptical about the authors' claims that prostitution was not a problem. Although contemporary scholars do not have the same direct access to the situation as the authors of the original report, the laws passed in Bismarck about prostitution suggest that there was a problem to which lawmakers were reacting. Thus "we have to be careful consumers of [this] research" in reading the 1958 *Report* now, as Ruddell and Ray write (p. 272).

Hence the value of the updated chapters, which reveal a number of patterns that remained latent in 1958. Such patterns relate to the logics that support the oil industry, in particular the way it has shifted the burden of risk onto workers (who fly in and out, contingent on companies' needs) and onto the communities where they operate (which have to invest in infrastructure and housing in ways that obligate them well beyond the likely end of the boom) (see also Conway 2018). The concluding chapter examines these things left unsaid, related to social problems and risk. It also examines two of the most conspicuous absences from the original report, Native Americans and the environment, as well as a point where they intersect in current debates, namely the conflicts about oil pipelines. In this way, given the perspective provided by the passage of time, the mirror *Sixty Years of Boom and Bust* holds up is—one hopes!—broader and more revealing than that of the book that inspired it.

References

Batbold, Dulguun, and Rob Grunewald. 2013. "Bakken Activity: How Wide Is the Ripple Effect?" *Federal Reserve Bank of Minneapolis FedGazette*, July. https://www.minneapolisfed.org/~/media/files/pubs/fedgaz/13-07/bakken_ripple.pdf.

Brady, Jeff. 2018. "After Struggles, North Dakota Grows Into Its Ongoing Oil Boom." NPR.org, November 23. https://www.npr.org/2018/11/23/669198912/after-struggles-north-dakota-grows-into-its-ongoing-oil-boom.

Brown, Chip. 2013. "North Dakota Went Boom." *New York Times Magazine*, January 31. https://nyti.ms/XdD1yf.

Caraher, William R., and Bret A. Weber. 2017. *The Bakken: An Archaeology of an Industrial Landscape*. Fargo: North Dakota State University Press.

Conway, Kyle. 2016. "Notes from the Global Hinterlands: What It Feels Like To Be Global In North Dakota." In *The Bakken Goes Boom: Oil and the Changing Geographies of Western North Dakota*, edited by William Caraher and Kyle Conway, 31–49. Grand Forks: Digital Press at the University of North Dakota.

Conway, Kyle. 2018. "Passing Through: Migration, Class, Crime, and Identity in the Oilfields of North Dakota." *Great Plains Quarterly* 38 (4): 425–32.

Dalrymple, Amy. 2012. "Famous Bakken Formation Named for North Dakota Homesteaders." *Oil Patch Dispatch*, November 25. https://web.archive.org/web/20150120202822/http://oilpatchdispatch.areavoices.com/2012/11/25/famous-bakken-formation-named-for-north-dakota-homesteaders/.

Dalrymple, Amy. 2018. "North Dakota Oil Production Sets More Records, but Limited by Gas Capture." *Bismarck Tribune*, October 12. https://bismarcktribune.com/bakken/north-dakota-oil-production-sets-more-records-but-limited-by/article_07378c45-1265-50d7-b292-8238b538da75.html.

Eligon, John. 2013. "An Oil Town Where Men Are Many, and Women Are Hounded." *New York Times*, January 15. https://www.nytimes.com/2013/01/16/us/16women.html.

Gold, Russell. 2015. *The Boom: How Fracking Ignited the American Energy Revolution and Changed the World*. New York: Simon and Schuster.

Hodur, Nancy M., and Dean A. Bangsund. 2013. "Population Estimates for City of Williston." Agribusiness and Applied Economics Report 707.

Fargo: North Dakota State University, Agribusiness and Applied Economics. http://purl.umn.edu/157412.

Huynh, Carol, Chloe Robinson, Thomas Mrozla, Thorvald O. Dahle, Carol A. Archbold, and Alexandra Marcel. 2019. "New Faces in a New Place: Long-Time Residents' Perceptions of New Residents in an Oil Boomtown in the Bakken Oil Shale Region." *Deviant Behavior* 40: 992–1006. https://dx.doi.org/10.1080/01639625.2018.1456689.

Maugeri, Leonardo. 2013. "The Shale Oil Boom: A U.S. Phenomenon." Discussion Paper 2013-05. Cambridge, MA: Harvard Kennedy School, Belfer Center for Science and International Affairs. https://www.belfercenter.org/sites/default/files/legacy/files/The%20US%20Shale%20Oil%20Boom%20Web.pdf.

North Dakota Industrial Commission. 2016. "Oil In North Dakota: 2016 Production Statistics." Bismarck: Department of Mineral Resources, Oil and Gas Division. https://www.dmr.nd.gov/oilgas/stats/AnnualProduction/2016AnnualProductionReport.pdf.

Nowatzki, Mike. 2014. "Contractors Flocking to N.D. for Work." *Grand Forks Herald*, February 23. http://www.grandforksherald.com/business/2346007-contractors-flocking-nd-work.

Reddall, Braden. 2012. "Analysis: North Dakota Oil Drilling Costs Have Peaked—For Now." *Reuters*, October 3. https://www.reuters.com/article/us-bakkenoil-costs/analysis-north-dakota-oil-drilling-costs-have-peaked-for-now-idUSBRE89216D20121003.

Robinson, Elwyn. (1966) 2017. *History of North Dakota*. Grand Forks: Digital Press at the University of North Dakota. https://commons.und.edu/oers/1/.

Ruddell, Rick. 2017. *Oil, Gas, and Crime: The Dark Side of the Boomtown*. New York: Palgrave Macmillan.

United States Geological Survey (USGS). 2013. "USGS Releases New Oil and Gas Assessment for Bakken and Three Forks Formations." https://www.usgs.gov/news/usgs-releases-new-oil-and-gas-assessment-bakken-and-three-forks-formations.

Chapter 3
Physical Attributes of the Area

1958 *Bernt L. Wills*

Geographic Location

The oil producing area is relatively small. For the most part it consists of a field about thirty-five miles long (north-south) and about five miles wide (east-west) located astride much of the common boundary between Williams and Mountrail counties in northwestern North Dakota. Several smaller fields lie nearby. A surrounding area of considerably larger size felt the impact of oil development very strongly, however, and is included within the area of this study. The oil field, the additional major impact area, and other significant features are shown on the map, Figure 2. It will be noted that the oil field lies about forty miles east of Williston, the county seat of Williams County, and about twenty-five miles west of Stanley, the county seat of Mountrail County.

Topography

This area constitutes a part of the Missouri Plateau, a sub-province of the Great Plains, and for the most part is a region of undulating plains. Toward the southern portion of the area a change of slope conditions occurs and the topography becomes much more rugged. There relatively high escarpments overlook deep coulees and valleys and finally face upon the broad floodplain of the Missouri River. Glacial drift blankets most of the area except in the bluff section in the south where underlying formations are exposed. These formations consist chiefly of shales, some sandstones, and occasional layers of "scoria."[1] Gravel deposits are quite common throughout the area.

---

[1] This "scoria" is not that of most geologic literature, but is the term applied locally to a naturally baked clay bed.

Geologic Situation

The Williston Basin is a geologic basin, although, as indicated above, it is a plains region topographically. It is a filled basin whose upper sedimentary formations encompass more than half of North Dakota, plus parts of Manitoba, Saskatchewan, Montana, and South Dakota. This large areal extent is shown in Figure 3.

As the name implies, the Williston Basin has the general shape of a basin or dish. The bottom of the "dish" lies under western North Dakota for the most part, and in its thickest sections the sedimentary formations in that area have a total thickness of over 15,000 feet. This dipping of strata and depth situation is graphically illustrated in the diagrammatic geologic cross-section of North Dakota, Figure 4. This drawing represents the eastern portion of the dish or basin. Westward the basin and its structures incline upward upon the geologic extensions of the Rocky Mountains.

Within the basin are structures which serve as oil traps. Of these the important one, for the purposes of this study, is the famous Nesson anticline. This structure lies east of Williston, North Dakota, trends roughly north-south, and is the present site of the producing wells of this area.

Throughout the area of this study the oil producing formations are relatively deep; most of the wells find "pay depths" at below 8,000 feet and some at below 11,000 feet. This factor of depth is very important, for it constitutes a critical cost factor in the production of the oil.

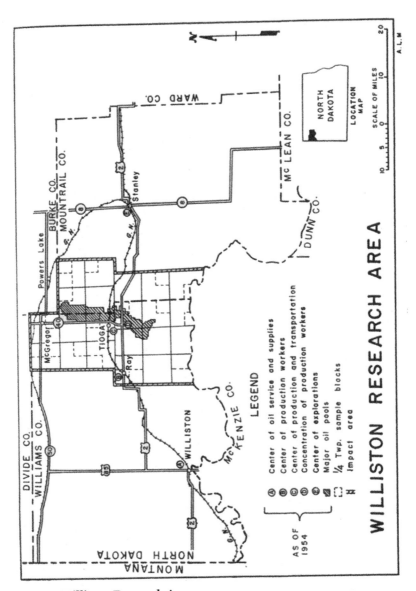

FIG. 2—Williston Research Area

38

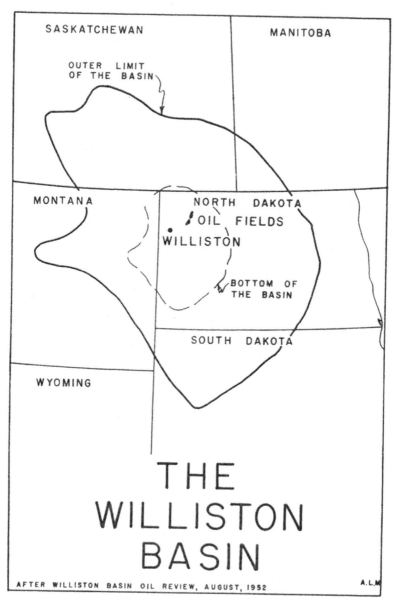

FIG. 3—The Williston Basin

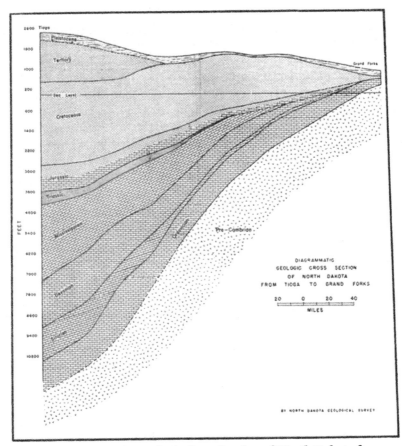

FIG. 4—Diagrammatic Geologic Cross Section of North Dakota from Tioga to Grand Forks

Climate

The climate of this area, as of any area, affects not only the agricultural pursuits, but the efficiency and economy of men and machines in virtually all fields of endeavor. It affects the comfort and the cost of living of the labor force. It affects the cost and convenience of transportation of men and of goods. In this last regard crude oil transportation is no exception, for climate affects depths to which pipe lines must be laid, as well as cost of laying and maintaining road beds for trucks or trains.

Because of its location near the center of the North American continent, Williston and vicinity has a semi-arid continental type of climate with relatively cold winters and warm to hot summers. During the long hot summer days readings of 100°F are not uncommon, but nights are usually cool and conducive to rest and sleep. Sunstroke is virtually unheard of in this dry region, and because of the dryness of the air even the hottest days are not as uncomfortable as they would otherwise be. The record maximum temperature of 110°F occurred in July of 1936. The average temperature for the month of July in Williston is 69.4°F. In winter temperatures below zero are common. The record minimum –50°F also occurred in 1936. When temperatures are low, however, the air is generally dry, with little or no wind, and the weather is clear and invigorating. The average temperature for the month of January in Williston is 7.9°F. Variable weather characterizes this area for it lies in the track of cyclonic air masses which move eastward across the continent.

This oil producing area is the driest part of the state of North Dakota. The weather station at Tioga, with an annual average precipitation of 14.3 inches, has the lowest average reading of any station in the state. The average at Williston is 14.66 inches. Winter is the dry season. Few places so far north in the United States receive so little snowfall. Spring and early summer is the time of maximum precipitation.

The wind blows much of the time, usually from a westerly direction, and with an average hourly speed of about eight miles. The absence of violent windstorms in this area is indicated by the fact that the highest wind speed ever recorded at Williston was 60 miles per hour. However, blizzards are not uncommon in winter, and when they occur outside activity is brought to a halt. Fogs are infrequent and cloudy days are few. It is therefore, healthy, invigorating climate, favorable to physical and mental activity.

Transportation Patterns and Oil Developments[2]

Major Transportation Routes

Figure 2 shows the major routes of supply of the area of this study. This pattern was not altered by the discovery and development of oil. It will be noted that the area is crossed by a single railroad, the main line of the Great Northern Railway, which serves, in order from east to west, the towns of Stanley, Ross, Manitou, White Earth, Tioga, Ray, Wheelock, Epping, Spring Brook, and Williston, each a focal point of local trade in the area. A branch line of the Great Northern Railway extends northwestward from Stanley through Powers Lake and thence north of the major oil producing area (FIGURE 1). This branch line is of minor significance to the oil producing area but the main line is very important.

The area is crossed only one federal road, U.S. Highway No. 2. This is the only continuous, first class road which crosses the area. It, like the railroad, connects Williston and Stanley and crosses essentially the same territory but follows the lines of the township and section surveys, therefore nearly always running straight north-south or straight east-west, consequently being of somewhat greater length than the rail line. It misses several of the towns of the area, including Tioga.

Similarly the area of this study is served by only one state road, State Highway No. 40. This road runs north from U.S. Highway No. 2 through the town of Tioga and thence northward through the Tioga field. It became a very heavily used road following the discovery of oil, and as a result had much increased maintenance costs including additions of gravel. It was hard surfaced from the junction with U.S. Highway No. 2 to Tioga in 1953; thus for three and one half miles it is a first-class highway.

The remaining roads shown on Figure 2 as being major routes of supply are gravelled county roads. The first of these, in importance, is the so-called Ferry Road, which extends north-south across the Beaver Lodge Field from U.S. Highway No. 2 to the ferry on the Missouri River. The other is called the Scenic Highway. It runs eastward from Williston through the southern portion of this study area and is of particular importance to the Cafce and Hofflund Fields. It is rather fittingly named, as it skirts the breaks of the river and crosses small bad-lands areas.

---

[2] Most of this section on transportation is condensed from the exhaustive work done on this subject by Donald H. Poole, "The Impact of Oil Upon the Road Patterns and Road Surfaces which Serve the Tioga-Beaver Lodge Oil Pools" (unpublished research paper, Department of Geography, Northwestern University, 1954). The maps shown in Figures 5, 6, 7, 8, and 9 are also by Mr. Poole.

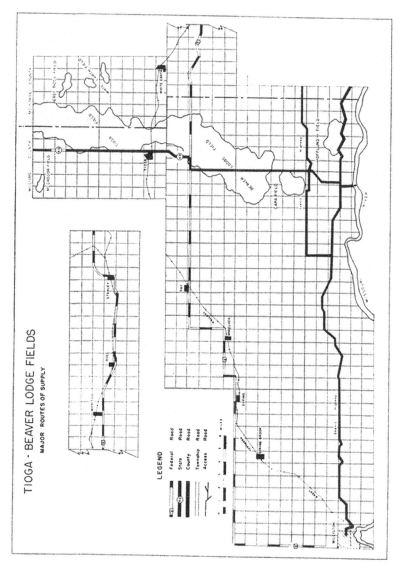

FIG. 5—Tioga Beaver Ledge Fields: Major Routes of Supply

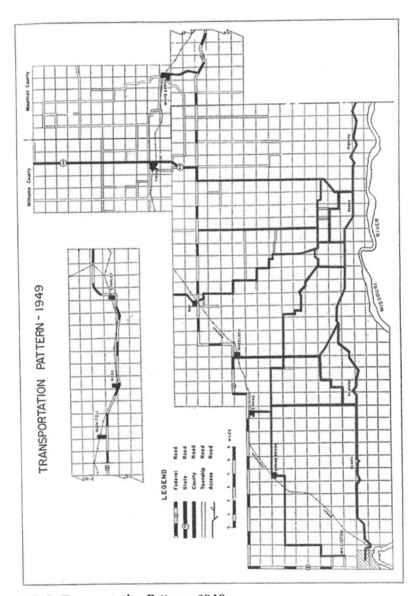

FIG. 6—Transportation Patterns, 1949

Comparison of Road Patterns, 1949 and 1954

A comparative study of the road systems of 1949 and 1954 as shown in Figures 5 and 6 point out three significant facts: (1) as previously stated, the basic road patterns remained unchanged, (2) most of the construction occurred within the oil producing districts, (3) most of the construction consisted of well-access roads, although there was some extension and improvement of township and county roads.

It may be noticed that the maps in Figures 5 and 6 show certain patterns which are identical on each of those but which are omitted from Figure 4. Figure 4 shows the major arteries, and the additional roads shown on Figures 5 and 6, while very important locally, are tributary to the major routes.

One relatively minor change in road pattern occurred south of the Beaver Lodge Field. Here new construction in 1954 resulted in the re-routing of the Scenic Highway two miles northward, in that area, and thence eastward along the southern boundary of Dry Fork Township. The older road was abandoned to the backwaters of the Garrison Dam project.

Road Patterns Within the Oil Fields

Figures 7 and 8 show in considerable detail the road patterns within the oil producing districts, as of July, 1954. It is significant that most of the road mileage shown on these maps is a direct result of oil discovery and development. For the most part these roads are well-access roads and feeder lines to the major routes of travel.

These roads are graded and are intended for all-weather use although some are lacking in special surfacing. Many are scoria topped and some are gravelled. The added mileage due to oil development is about 100 miles, and this added mileage is almost entirely the result of expenditures by the oil interests, particularly the Amerada Petroleum Corporation, which controls about 85% of the production.

As shown on the maps, most of the oil wells, and most of the added road mileage, are found in 8 townships. Six of those are in Williams County and two are in Mountrail.

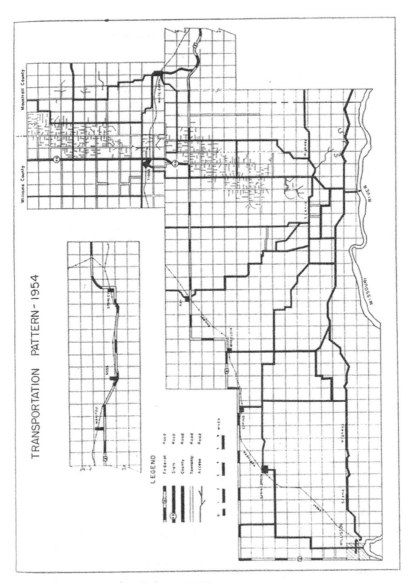

FIG. 7—Transportation Pattern, 1954

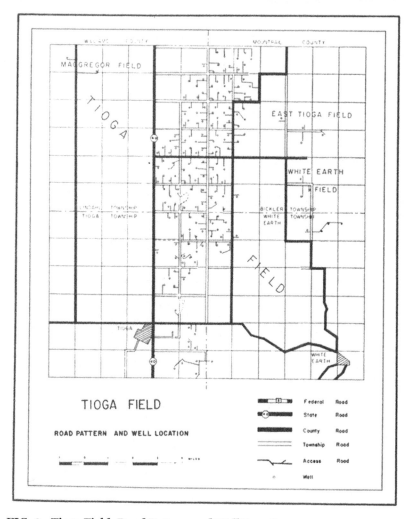

FIG. 8—Tioga Field: Road Pattern and Well Location

Traffic Flow—Traffic count data are available for 1950 through June, 1954, for U.S. Highway No. 2; but for State Highway No. 40 the data are available only for the years 1951 and 1953 (TABLE I). No traffic count data are available for roads of the county system, nevertheless certain roads of the county system do carry a considerable portion of the traffic, including the oil traffic. This is especially true of those in the Beaver Lodge Field, and on the basis of field observation it may reasonably be assumed that the traffic count on certain of the county roads, such as the Ferry Road, would approximate the figures given for State Highway No. 40.

An analysis of Table I shows a pronounced increase in vehicular traffic for each of the years following the discovery of oil. However, it is necessary to remember that this increase in traffic includes all vehicles using the roads, not merely those involved in the oil activity. Thus to a certain, but to an indeterminate, amount other factors combined with the oil activity to account for the increases.

Perhaps more important than volume of traffic and its increase, as results of oil development, was the increase in weights of vehicles used on the roads. Oil drilling rigs and associated equipment are very ponderous and weighty, and heavy loads on heavy trucks and dollies are an integral part of oil development. Thus, almost every facet of the oil program brought increased burdens and wear upon a road system which had been built to serve a relatively simple agricultural economy.

Table I

TRAFFIC COUNT—U.S. HIGHWAY NO. 2
WILLISTON TO STANLEY

Comparison of Average Daily Traffic for All Days of each month at
Automatic Traffic Counter

	1950	1951	1952	1953	1954
January	335	437	450	936	766
February	370	417	641	968	909
March	502	356	749	1060	928
April	697	814	1200	1346	1103
May	630	815	1236	1361	1185
June	929	1043	1473	1767	1688
July	1194	1265	1854	1961	
August	1176	1253	1860	2125	
September	1011	1016	1498	1732	
October	828	923	1389	1464	
November	665	800	1219	1162	
December	541	500	1084	924	
Annual Average	— —	— —	— —	— —	— —
24 Hr. Traffic	740	809	1221	1401	......

State Highway No. 40—Annual Average 24 Hr. Traffic
1951—Junction No. 2 to Tioga   610
Tioga to McGregor Junction   370
1953—Junction No. 2 to Tioga   2615
Tioga to McGregor Junction   590

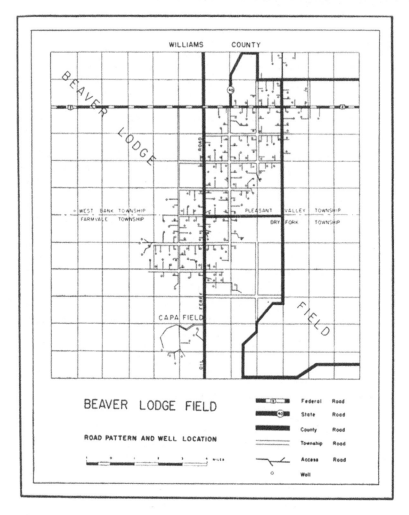

FIG. 9—Beaver Lodge Field: Road Pattern and Well Location

Roadway Construction and Maintenance

Road construction in the area under survey was renewed in 1951 following the discovery of oil. New road construction by Williams and Mountrail counties was insignificant for their highway expenditures were directed to maintenance of existing roads. However, considerable construction was done by the state of North Dakota and by the Amerada Petroleum Corporation.

Table II shows actual expenditures for road construction and for maintenance during the period 1950–June, 1954, by the state of North Dakota, by Amerada Petroleum Corporation and by Williams County. The expenditures by Williams County are almost entirely for maintenance. Table III shows the expenditures for Williams County by the state of North Dakota for each year.

An analysis of these tables shows a significant increase in expenditures during the period of oil development. Percentagewise the greatest costs are involved in routine surface operations.

As in the case of increased traffic, not all of the increase in maintenance costs can be attributed to the oil development program, but that the oil program contributed cannot be questioned.

The harshness of the cold winter season and one of its effects on road maintenance is evidenced by the percentage of maintenance costs involved in controlling snow and ice. For the four-year period 1950–1954 approximately 15 per cent of all maintenance expenditures were so utilized.

TABLE II
N.D. HIGHWAY CONSTRUCTION COSTS, JANUARY, 1950 TO JUNE, 1954 BY AGENCY AND BY TYPE OF EXPENDITURE

State of North Dakota
Highway No. 40
Tioga to Jct. ½ mile south of McGregor (1952) - 14 miles...............$18,002.30
Tioga Jct. to Tioga (1953) - 3½ miles 36,772.63

Highway No. 2
Ross to Stanley (1953) - 8 miles..81,151.82
Tioga Jct. to Ross (1953) - 18 miles..241,304.27
Ray east to Tioga Jct. (1954) - 10½ miles 145,428.25

$522,661.27

MAINTENANCE AND CONSTRUCTION

Amerada Petroleum Corporation
Period from April, 1950 to June, 1954
Construction of Roads.. $475,285.43
Maintenance of Roads 121,604.06
Removal of Snow 42,986.00

$639,875.49

ROAD AND BRIDGE EXPENDITURES

Williams County

	Federal Aid	Other Road Expenditures—County
1954–55	$62,535.36	$380,281.70
1953–54	105,633.36	291,491.25
1952–53	55,970.86	257,596.78
1951–52		236,312.97
1950–51		259,231.16
	$224,140.18	$1,424,913.86
		224,140.18
		$1,649,154.04

Pipelines

The preceding discussion has dealt solely with surface transportation, and in the early days of the oil development program that was the only means of transportation, even for the crude oil. By 1955, however, virtually all of the crude produced in the study area was being transported by buried pipe lines.

The system is as follows: In the oil fields there is a collection system wherein pipe lines three or four inches in diameter, lead from the wells to larger (six and eight inch) main lines which carry the oil to Tioga. At Tioga there is a pumping station which starts the oil on its way to Mandan, North Dakota, approximately 175 miles distant. From Tioga the oil moves southward through a ten inch line to the Ramberg pumping station in the Beaver Lodge field. From there the line extends southward as a 12 inch line approximately 70 miles to the Keene pumping station south of the Missouri River. From Keene the oil is pumped southeastward approximately 95 miles through a 16 inch line to Mandan where it is refined in the 30,000 barrels-per-day capacity Standard Oil Refinery.

TABLE III

MAINTENANCE EXPENDITURES FOR WILLIAMS COUNTY
BY THE NORTH DAKOTA STATE HIGHWAY DEPARTMENT,
1950–1954

	1950	1951	1952	1953
Routine Roadway Surface Operations	$16,822.00	$15,598.00	$37,045.00	$49,737.00
Shoulders and Side Approaches	76.00	19.00	77.00	216.00
Roadside and Drainage	3,068.00	2,848.00	3,869.00	2,469.00
Removal of Weeds and Brush	1,651.00	2,324.00	2,692.00	4,386.00
Traffic Services	1,005.00	3,113.00	1,673.00	5,728.00
Sand, Ice and Snow Control	1,332.00	1,662.00	1,691.00	2,115.00
Sand, Ice and Snow Removal	5,379.00	6,263.00	5,742.00	4,291.00
Prorated Accounts	1,098.00	915.00	2,861.00	2,344.00
Special Roadway Surface Operations	......	......	26,205.00	......
	$30,432.00	$32,742.00	$81,856.00	$71,286.00

January through June, 1954

Routine Roadway Surface Operations	$15,674.00
Roadside and Drainage	566.00
Removal of Weeds and Brush	134.00
Traffic Services	2,465.00
Sand, Ice and Snow Control	547.00
Sand, Ice and Snow Removal	1,919.00
	$21,305.00

Similarly the natural gas from the oil fields, formerly "flared" into the atmosphere, is now brought by a pipe line collection system to the Signal Oil and Gas Company's Tioga-Beaver Lodge Gasoline plant at Tioga where propane, butane, natural gasoline and sulphur are extracted from the gas. The remaining "sweetened" natural gas is sent by pipe line for domestic and industrial uses to points east as far as Minot, west to Williston.

Surplus gas not used when produced is piped into Montana where it is returned underground into natural storage.

Population Characteristics of Williams and Mountrail Counties[3]

In recent decades, North Dakota has been one of those few states experiencing a decline in population. This fact has in large measure resulted from the prevailing character of the American agricultural scene, in a state where a relatively narrow agricultural economy is dominant. Fewer and larger farms with an increase in the numbers of non-resident farm operators has resulted in a steady decline in rural settlement with an accompanying increase in the urban areas, and an exodus of youth from the state due to limited opportunities. The development of any newly found resources is bound to stimulate hope in such an area. This trait has been notable in the enthusiastic manner with which the opening of the Williston Oil Basin was greeted. The population features associated with this event provide an indication of how such developments may or may not assist in easing the state's problems.

General Characteristics

Williams and Mountrail Counties, the principal counties affected by the oil industry to 1954, have traditionally been noted for their wheat and cattle industries. Reflecting the extensive system of land use essential in this subhumid zone, the settlement pattern consisted of dispersed farmsteads, occasional hamlets, and a single small urban center. Then, as now, the populations of both counties were classified as rural farm or rural non-farm with the lone exception of Williston. Since 1930, the general trend in population has seen a steady decline in rural farm residents, a fairly constant population level being maintained in the rural-nonfarm hamlets, and a constant rise occurring in Williston.

It is against this distribution of people that the recent alterations in terms of arrangement and numbers developed. The effects of the oil industry have brought numerous changes to this general area; however, significant developments have been limited to a rather small portion of the two counties. This area where the bulk of activity has taken place includes Williston, functioning as the supply and service center; Tioga, Tioga Environs, and Ray, the small villages located in the heart of the oil area, all in Williams County; the Impact Townships of both counties; and the county seat of Mountrail County, Stanley (FIGURE 2). These centers will on occasion be referred to as the oil affected areas.

---

[3] This section was written by Richard V. Smith. It is based upon the data collected by the University of North Dakota field research team in the summer of 1954.

The Number of Inhabitants

Between 1950 and 1954, the population of Williams County increased by 26.8% while that of Mountrail County decreased by 5.5% (TABLE IV).[4] However, a basic pattern of change existed in both counties. The statewide trend of declining rural numbers persisted here, both within the oil impact townships and throughout the remainder of the rural area. In marked contrast to this rural reduction is the sharp increase noted in each of those nonfarm centers affected by the oil development.

TABLE IV
WILLISTON BASIN AREA: NUMBER OF INHABITANTS
1950-1954

| | POPULATION | | | PER CENT CHANGE | |
	1940	1950	1954	1940–50	1950–54
WILLIAMS					
Williston	5,790	7,378	9,717	+27.4	+31.7
Ray	579	721	1,479	+24.5	+105.1
Tioga	385	456	1,608	+18.4	+252.6
Tioga Environs	......	......	931	......	......
Impact Townships[1]	1,915	1,392	1,236	–27.3	–11.2
Other Rural[2]	6,018	4,923	4,372	–18.2	–11.2
Hamlets	1,628	1,572	1,500	–3.4	–4.6
Total Williams Co.	16,315	16,442	20,843	+0.8	+26.8
Total Oil Areas[3]	8,669	9,947	14,971	+14.7	+50.5
MOUNTRAIL					
Stanley	1,058	1,486	1,645	+40.5	+10.7
Impact Townships[1]	720	562	528	–21.9	–6.0
Other Rural[2]	6,362	4,675	4,224	–26.5	–9.6
Hamlets	2,342	2,695	2,500	+15.1	–7.2
Total Mountrail Co.	10,482	9,418	8,897	+10.1	–5.5
Total Oil Areas[3]	1,778	2,048	2,173	+15.2	+6.1

1. Depicted in Fig. 2
2. Rural farm areas other than impact townships.
3. Williston, Ray, Tioga, Tioga Environs, Impact Townships in Williams County. Stanley and Impact Townships in Mountrail County.

SOURCE: 1940—United States Bureau of the Census.
1950—United States Bureau of the Census
1954—Projections from sample census.

---

[4] Appendix A is devoted to a discussion of the methods used in obtaining 1954 figures.

Rates of increase in these centers reflect their location with respect to the principal areas of interest and the functions which each center performed in this development. Tioga, Tioga Environs, and Ray benefited enormously as logical sites for settling migrants involved in the establishment and operation of the fields. Williston became the central supply and focal point for the oil industry, while Stanley absorbed the overflow resulting from crowded facilities in the other, more ideally located, towns.

In general it would seem that Williams County has, at least for the present, benefited considerably in terms of population change. Mountrail County, on the other hand, exhibits a pattern typical at the moment of most rural North Dakota counties, with the steady rural decline and the relatively slight but steady growth of the county seat. This general picture of alterations in population directly reflects the advantages possessed by Williams County as the area of principal interest and the logical site for location of installations and personnel.

Age and Sex Composition

While all of those areas affected by the oil industry possessed a net population increase, with the exception of the rural impact townships, the relative importance of that increase varied from area to area as noted above. This same pattern exists with reference to the proportions of people in the several age groups. In general, those areas most affected, the rural non-farm villages, showed significant relative increases in the younger age groups. Two age groups are particularly notable: first, that from 20–29 years with 19.6% of the total population in 1954 against 12.9% in 1950, and secondly, that from 0–4 with 18.1% in 1954 compared with 11.1% in 1950. (TABLES V, VI, VII). This pattern would seem to reflect the oil industries' need for a considerable youthful element in the labor force, composed in this instance of young married men whose children were within the youngest age category.

Complementing these changes was the relative decline in the other age groups. Most significant of these was the sharp decline in the oldest group, those over 65 years of age. The trend in these rural non-farm centers was towards a much more youthful population level.

Urban Williston possessed a stabler pattern, though relative increases enhanced the importance of the 0–4 and 5–19 groups. Again the complementing factor was a decline in the 30–64 and 65 age groups.

In contrast to these non-farm centers, the rural impact townships retained expected rural characteristics. Reflecting the continuing agricultural occupation of the people, a generally older age pattern existed. No marked changes occurred in the age groups between 1950 and 1954.

The age composition of these oil affected areas indicates the extent to which individual areas were altered by these developments. As the impact of the new industry increased in terms of areas, more pronounced effects on the age groupings were felt, with a trend to a younger age level.

Significant changes in the ratio of men to women are not apparent. Both the total and relative importance of each group remained relatively constant in population totals, age group totals, and between the several areas concerned. The one notable exception to this characteristic occurs in Williston where in the 20–29 age group, the number of males increased whereas the relative number of females declined markedly.

Marital Status and Relation to Head of Household

Marital status characteristics varied considerably from area to area, depending in large measure upon the type of activities carried on and upon the intensity of the oil industry's impact. In general, there is a higher percentage of married males in the more urbanized areas while the reverse is true for females, though on a much reduced scale (TABLE VIII). In the former case, about 40% of the rural-farm male population was single compared with only 17–20% of the women in such areas. In the urban area the figure for both sexes is similar, about 20%. In the rural non-farm areas, these figures vary considerably depending upon the stability of the area; for example, in Tioga 28.9% of the men were single whereas in Ray 21.5% were single. Similar variations might be noted, but the pattern remains essentially that of the generalization stated above.

Relation to the head of the family presents a relatively constant picture throughout the counties. Certain variations from the standard are notable, however, as for instance the higher percentages of sons than daughters in the rural farm areas; no doubt this is an adjustment to the labor requirements inherent in agriculture (TABLE IX). Lodgers and hired workers as members of households are found in the area of maximum migratory labor, the rural non-farm centers.

TABLE V
WILLISTON: NUMBER OF INHABITANTS BY AGE AND SEX, 1950 AND 1954

Age	MALE				FEMALE				TOTAL			
	1950		1954		1950		1954		1950		1954	
	No.	%	No.	%	No.	%	No.	%	No.	%	No.	%
0–4	485	13.1	785	15.9	420	11.4	713	14.9	905	12.3	1498	15.4
5–19	861	23.3	1191	24.1	878	23.8	1359	28.4	1739	23.6	2550	26.2
20–29	543	14.7	805	16.3	629	17.1	665	13.9	1172	15.9	1470	15.1
30–64	1405	38.1	1720	34.8	1411	38.3	1651	34.5	2816	38.2	3371	34.7
65 and over	400	10.8	346	7.0	346	9.4	297	6.2	746	10.0	643	6.6
No data	......	......	89	1.9	....	.....	96	2.1	....	.....	185	2.0
TOTAL	3694	100	4936	100	3684	100	4781	100	7378	100	9717	100

SOURCE:1950 United States Bureau of the Census. 1954 Projections from sample census.

TABLE VI
RURAL NONFARM:* NUMBER OF INHABITANTS BY AGE AND SEX, 1950 AND 1954

Age	MALE				FEMALE				TOTAL			
	1950		1954		1950		1954		1950		1954	
	No.	%	No.	%	No.	%	No.	%	No.	%	No.	%
0–4	150	10.8	507	16.7	145	11.4	518	19.8	295	11.1	1025	18.1
5–19	351	25.2	703	23.1	362	28.5	645	24.6	713	26.8	1348	23.8
20–29	174	12.5	556	18.3	169	13.3	555	21.2	343	12.9	1111	19.6
30–64	510	36.6	962	31.6	460	36.2	682	26.0	970	36.4	1644	29.0
65 and over	208	14.9	134	4.4	134	10.6	147	5.6	342	12.8	281	4.9
No Data	....		179	5.9	....		75	2.8	....		254	4.6
TOTAL	1393	100	3041	100	1270	100	2622	100	2663	100	5663	100

* Ray, Tioga, Tioga Environs, Stanley.

SOURCE: 1950 United States Bureau of the Census. 1954 Projections from sample census.

TABLE VII
RURAL FARM:* NUMBER OF INHABITANTS BY AGE AND SEX,
1950 AND 1954

Age	MALE				FEMALE				TOTAL			
	1950		1954		1950		1954		1950		1954	
	No.	%	No.	%	No.	%	No.	%	No.	%	No.	%
0–4												
	131	11.8	104	10.4	124	14.6	100	13.2	255	13.0	204	11.6
5–19												
	272	24.6	268	26.8	240	28.3	224	29.3	512	26.2	492	27.8
20–29												
	139	12.6	124	12.4	105	12.4	108	14.2	244	12.5	232	13.1
30–64												
	444	40.1	412	41.3	315	37.1	264	34.6	759	38.8	676	38.3
65 and over												
	120	10.9	84	8.3	64	7.6	64	8.3	184	9.5	148	8.5
No Data												
	....		8	0.8	....		4	0.4	....		12	0.7
TOTAL												
	1106	100	992	100	848	100	760	100	1954	100	1764	100

*Impact Townships of Williams and Mountrail County

SOURCE: 1950 United States Department of Commerce. 1954 Projections
from sample census.

TABLE VIII
PERCENT DISTRIBUTION OF MARITAL STATUS FOR THOSE
14 YEARS YEARS OF AGE AND OVER, 1954

	Williston	Ray	Tioga	Tioga Environs	Stanley	Williams County	Montrail County
MALE (number)							
	3262	503	641	354	569	496	204
Marital Status (percent)							
Married	73.6	73.0	56.0	64.6	70.6	54.8	54.9
Single	20.6	21.5	28.9	21.5	25.4	40.3	39.2
Divorced or							
separated	0.4	0.6	1.5	......	......	......	......
Widowed	4.3	1.8	3.0	......	4.0	3.2	5.9
No Data	0.1	3.1	10.5	13.9	......	1.6	......
TOTAL	100.0	100.0	100.0	100.0	100.0	100.0	100.0
FEMALE (number)							
	3140	429	446	241	557	352	160
Marital Status (percent)							
Married	71.2	80.0	78.9	96.1	64.9	75.0	67.5
Single	18.3	11.4	13.5	3.9	18.0	17.0	20.0
Divorced or							
separated	1.4	2.1	......	......	0.5	......	2.5
Widowed	8.5	5.7	7.0	......	9.5	6.8	10.0
No Data	0.6	0.7	0.5	......	7.1	1.1	......
TOTAL	100.0	100.0	100.0	100.0	100.0	100.0	100.0
MALE &							
FEMALE (number)							
	6402	932	1087	595	1126	848	364
Marital status (percent)							
Married	72.4	76.2	65.4	76.9	67.7	63.2	60.4
Single	19.4	16.8	22.6	14.6	21.6	30.7	30.8
Divorced or							
separated	0.9	1.3	0.9	......	0.2	......	1.1
Widowed	6.4	3.6	4.7	......	6.8	4.7	7.7
No Data	0.4	2.0	6.4	8.5	3.6	1.4	......
TOTAL	100.0	100.0	100.0	100.0	100.0	100.0	100.0

SOURCE: Projections from sample census.

TABLE IX
PERCENT DISTRIBUTION OF RELATION TO HEAD OF
FAMILY, 1954

	Williston	Ray	Tioga	Tioga Environs	Stanley	Impact Areas William & Mountrail
Head	27.5	26.6	25.1	28.7	28.3	26.1
Wife	22.5	23.9	21.7	23.8	23.1	20.0
Son	21.8	26.2	21.1	18.8	21.7	28.6
Daughter	20.8	18.5	20.2	20.8	21.0	18.6
Lodger-Hired Worker	2.1	3.5	8.8	6.4	3.7	0.7
Relatives	2.1	1.2	2.2	0.5	1.9	5.4
No Data	3.2	......	0.7	1.0	0.3	0.7
TOTAL	100.0	100.0	100.0	100.0	100.0	100.0
(Number)	9717	1479	1608	931	1645	1764

SOURCE: Projections from sample census.

Persons and Families by Dwelling Types

The relative stability of population numbers is in part indicated by the type of dwelling occupied (TABLE X). In basically more stable areas such as Williston and the rural farm impact townships, dwelling types were almost exclusively of a permanent single or multiple nature.

TABLE X
NUMBER AND PERCENT OF PERSONS BY RESIDENCE TYPE,
1954

		Total Persons	Single Persons	Trailer Persons	Multiple Persons	Other Persons
Williston	Number	9717	7025	408	2274	10
	Percent	100.0	72.3	4.2	23.4	0.1
Ray	Number	1479	686	558	229	6
	Percent	100.0	46.4	37.7	15.5	0.4
Tioga	Number	1608	1093	343	172	......
	Percent	100.0	68.0	21.3	10.7	......
Tioga	Number	931	253	465	100	113
Environs	Percent	100.0	27.2	50.0	10.7	12.1
Stanley	Number	1645	1073	321	239	12
	Percent	100.0	65.2	19.5	14.5	0.8
Impact	Number	1236	1205	17	14	......
Willians	Percent	100.0	97.5	1.4	1.1	......
Impact	Number	528	528	......	......	......
Mountrail	Percent	100.0	100.0	......	......	......

SOURCE: Projections from sample census.

However, in those areas of maximum relative recent population increase, the rural non-farm centers, this pattern is in large measure reversed. Here, the recent importation of labor for development and operation of the oil fields has resulted in severe taxing of available permanent dwellings. Here also have settled those workers whose jobs are in large part related to the development of a single aspect of the installations and whose tenure in a given area is likely to be of a rather short duration. As a consequence the number of trailers was of great significance in those areas. In 1954 in Ray 37.7% of the population occupied trailers, in Tioga 21.3%, and in the Tioga Environs 50%. Multiple dwellings are of recent origin in all of these areas except Williston, where this type of dwelling is more common. The numbers living in multiple dwellings become progressively less as less urbanized conditions are encountered.

The average household size throughout the area of study was relatively constant (SEE TABLE XI). Larger household units (3.8) were found in rural farm areas, the smaller in the more urbanized areas (3.65). This pattern is roughly similar to the general range of household sizes normally found.

Migration Characteristics

The bulk of the population increase in Williams and Mountrail Counties has resulted from in-migration stimulated by the development of the oil industry. The general pattern throughout the area of study reflects the degree to which the industry has affected each of these areas. As would be expected, the rural farm impact townships have been the stablest areas, with slightly over 80% of their population having been resident in 1950 (TABLE XII). Williston, the largest and most diverse center, had 66.7% of its 1954 population having been resident in 1950. Stanley, the least affected of the rural non-farm areas, had 61.4% of its population then resident. Ray and Tioga, both basically altered in character by the proximity of the fields, had 39.7% and 34.6% respectively having been resident in 1950. Tioga Environs has the distinction of having been nonexistent in 1950, hence owing its new settlement exclusively to the oil industry.

TABLE XI

NUMBER AND PERCENT OF FAMILIES, BY RESIDENCE, TYPE,
AND AVERAGE HOUSEHOLD SIZE, 1954

	Total Families	Single Families	Trailer Families	Multiple Families	Other Families	Average Household Families
Williston						
Number	2662	1858	112	689	3	3.65
Percent	100.0	69.8	4.2	25.9	0.1	
Ray						
Number	390	192	145	50	3	3.79
Percent	100.0	49.2	37.1	12.9	0.8	
Tioga						
Number	433	297	102	34	......	3.71
Percent	100.0	68.7	23.5	7.8	......	
Tioga Environs						
Number	248	68	135	9	36	3.75
Percent	100.0	27.3	54.5	3.6	14.6	
Stanley						
Number	467	305	82	71	9	3.52
Percent	100.0	65.4	17.6	15.1	1.9	
Impact Williams						
Number	325	312	8	5	......	3.80
Percent	100.0	96.0	2.6	1.3	......	
Impact Mountrail						
Number	136	136	......	......	......	3.87
Percent	100.0	100.0	......	......	......	

SOURCE: Projections from sample census.

Each of these areas drew a part of its population increase from nearby tributary areas; however, the bulk of the increase was attracted from some distance. A portion of these in-migrants came from the remainder of North Dakota and from contiguous states. However, very considerable proportions have come from more remote states, mainly the principal oil states of the southern Great Plains. In this latter category, 10.2% of Williston's 1954 population, 44% of Ray's, 21.4% of Tioga's, and 55.6% of Tioga Environs were attracted from these more distant points. By and large, these individuals were permanently connected with the larger oil companies engaged in the development of the Williston Oil Basin, and in some considerable part might be considered a floating element of the population; that is, being continually on call for transfer to some new site of development. The importance of this group and the nature of their functions will probably be reflected in the persistent shifts and fluctuations of the population totals of the centers where they are now resident.

TABLE XII
PERCENT DISTRIBUTION OF INHABITANTS BY 1950 RESIDENCE

	Williston	Ray	Tioga	Tioga Environs	Stanley	Williams County	Mountrail County
MALE:							
Same	66.7	36.8	35.2	.....	59.1	83.8	85.7
Within Area Other	4.9	4.7	9.8	10.3	10.1	4.8	3.2
North Dakota Contiguous	11.4	8.5	25.4	24.4	16.0	0.6	7.9
States	5.6	2.3	8.5	6.4	3.4	3.0	1.6
All Other	11.2	47.7	21.1	58.9	11.3	7.8	1.6
Total	100.0	100.0	100.0	100.0	100.0	100.0	100.0
(Number)	4151	650	805	382	697	648	248
FEMALE:							
Same	66.8	43.2	33.9	......	63.6	76.0	77.8
Within Area Other	5.9	5.7	12.9	7.8	12.8	9.1	13.0
North Dakota Contiguous	13.0	9.7	23.4	35.9	12.8	0.8	7.4
States	5.1	1.7	8.1	4.7	3.1	4.1	1.8
All Other	9.3	39.7	21.7	51.6	9.1	8.0	......
Total	100.0	100.0	100.0	100.0	100.0	100.0	100.0
(Number)	4068	525	578	296	705	460	204
MALE AND FEMALE:							
Same	66.7	39.7	34.6	......	61.4	80.1	82.1
Within Area Other	5.4	5.2	11.2	9.2	11.4	6.6	7.7
North Dakota Contiguous	12.2	9.0	24.5	29.6	14.3	0.7	7.7
States	5.4	2.1	8.3	5.6	2.7	3.5	1.7
All Other	10.2	44.0	21.4	55.6	10.0	8.7	.8
Total	100.0	100.0	100.0	100.0	100.0	100.0	100.0
(Number)	8219	1175	1383	678	1402	1108	452

SOURCE: Projections from sample census.

The bulk of the in-migrants to this area were in the age groups from 5–9, 20–29, and 30–39 years, again reflecting the relatively youthful manpower needs of the industry and the composition of these workers' families (TABLE XIII). In terms of the male-female ratio, the total in-migrants were about 55% male and 45% female.

Employment and Labor Force Characteristics

The current characteristics of the population's economic activities are dealt with in a later section of this report. The concern here is with the changes in industry group status of workers as indicated by their activities in 1950 and 1954.

In the urban area, Williston, the industrial group categories showing the greatest increase were mining and construction, trade and services. The increases in these categories reflect initially the development of the oil fields and secondly the increases in those activities which directly serve the industry and the individuals employed by the industry. In general, recruits into these activities were drawn rather equally from original residents of the area and from migrants. (TABLES XIV, XV).

TABLE XIII

PERCENT DISTRIBUTION OF INHABITANTS BY AGE BY 1950 RESIDENCE

	5-9	10-13	14	15-19	20-29	30-39	40-49	50-64	65+	No Data	TOT.
WILLISTON:											
Resident	13.1	9.3	1.7	8.7	12.6	15.8	13.1	14.3	9.9	1.5	100.0
Migrant	18.5	5.8	0.8	4.1	31.6	22.5	9.2	4.7	2.4	0.4	100.0
No Data	2.3	2.3	......	13.7	38.6	31.8	9.1	2.2	......	......	100.0
RAY:											
Resident	9.3	7.6	2.3	8.1	19.7	9.9	13.4	11.2	17.4	1.1	100.0
Migrant	18.0	7.0	1.5	6.5	34.5	25.5	4.0	3.0	......	......	100.0
No Data	......	....	......	.....	33.3	50.0	......	16.7	......	......	100.0
TIOGA AND TIOGA ENVIRONS:											
Resident	12.7	6.9	2.3	11.2	15.0	15.4	15.8	8.5	10.8	0.8	100.0
Migrant	15.5	6.7	1.5	5.7	26.8	23.2	12.8	3.7	0.2	3.9	100.0
No Data	......	......	7.4	11.1	29.7	11.1	22.2	18.5	......	......	100.0
STANLEY:											
Resident	9.6	8.1	3.8	10.2	15.0	9.3	12.3	13.8	12.6	5.3	100.0
Migrant	19.7	4.9	......	4.9	37.7	23.8	6.5	1.6	......	0.9	100.0
No Data	4.8	14.3	4.8	4.8	19.1	43.0	......	9.2	......	......	100.0
WILLIAMS AND MOUNTRAIL COUNTY:											
Resident	13.6	8.3	1.2	8.0	12.4	13.6	14.2	16.9	10.9	0.9	100.0
Migrant	24.4	4.9	2.4	4.9	30.0	19.6	2.4	9.8	2.4	......	100.0
No Data	......	8.3	......	16.7	33.3	16.7	8.3	16.7	......	......	100.0

TABLE XIV

WILLISTON: RESIDENCE AND INDUSTRY GROUP FOR EM-PLOYED PERSONS, 1950 AND 1954

	Residents		Migrants		No Data		Total	
Industry	1950	1954	1950	1954	1950	1954	1950	1954
Agriculture	247	214	94	25	......	......	341	239
Mining & Construction	176	305	204	292	......	16	380	613
Manufacturing, Durable	13	9	4	12	......	......	17	21
Manufacturing, Non-Durable	36	66	24	21	......	4	60	91
Transportation, Communications, & Public Utilities	357	401	69	107	......	4	426	512
Trade	421	603	78	263	......	65	499	931
Finance, Insurance & Real Estate	57	89	25	32	......	8	82	129
Service	386	458	66	107	......	21	452	586
Public Administration	439	98	262	48	......	16	701	162
No Data	200	83	131	49	......	......	331	132
TOTAL	2332	2326	957	956	......	134	3289	3416

SOURCE: Projections from sample census.

Industrial group classifications for those workers residing within the oil field itself (rural non-farm and rural farm) indicated a simpler pattern. The major change occurred in the mining and construction category, which accounted for 16.2% of the workers in 1950 and 37.4% in 1954. Much more moderate changes were characteristic of the other categories.

TABLE XV
IMPACT AREAS OTHER THAN WILLISON: RESIDENCE AND INDUSTRY GROUP FOR EMPLOYED PERSONS, 1950 AND 1954

Ray, Tioga and Tioga Environs, Stanley, Williams & Mountrail Impact Townships:

	Residents		Migrants		No Data		Total	
	1950	1954	1950	1954	1950	1954	1950	1954
Industry								
Agriculture	639	641	99	31	......	12	738	684
Mining & Construction	81	199	314	658	......	123	395	980
Manufacturing, Durable	.....	......	6	......	......	......	6	......
Manufacturing, Non-Durable	3	5	11	......	....	......	14	5
Transportation, Communications, & Public Utilities	79	112	41	79	......	6	120	197
Trade	168	243	88	131	......	6	256	380
Finance, Insurance & Real Estate	9	20	6	12	....	......	15	32
Service	72	133	45	60	......	3	117	196
Public Administration	228	43	188	11	......	5	416	59
No Data	147	32	213	46	......	6	360	84
TOTAL	1426	1428	1011	1028	......	161	2437	2617

SOURCE: Projections from sample census.

Indicated Changes 1954–1955

During the summer of 1955, a field survey was made to observe changes occurring since the exhaustive field study of 1954, from which the foregoing statistics were derived. The impression left by this check survey and reinforced by the statements of numerous residents of the area was that a contraction in activities had developed.

Available evidence indicates that the peak of the oil boom was experienced during the summer of 1954, followed by a decline initiated by the exit of refinery and pipe line construction workers, and rig crews as drilling moved south of the Missouri River. In a more positive sense, the attitude was simply that the area was reaching a level of stability adjusted to the present apparent potentials of the area and the likely exploitation of the oil resource in the near future.

The significance of this would seem to lie in the characteristic labor demands of the oil industry. During the exploration and development stages a very sizable labor force is required. However, this long term phase following that initial development, that is, the production stage, is marked by much reduced labor requirements in a rather highly mechanized industry. This character of the industry remains valid as long as subsidiary industries based on the resource do not locate in the area. As of this writing such developments have not taken place.

Population trends during the year following the field study and census are distinctly downward. The extent of this decline varies markedly from area to area with the most notable changes having occurred in Ray and Tioga Environs. In the former, a local official estimated that the decline had reached something over 300 people. This estimate was supported by a count of the temporary housing units in Ray which revealed the following: of the four trailer courts within the town limits, one remained full; a second had 23 units, compared to a 1954 peak of 59; and the fourth had 13 units; a third had 33 units, compared to a 1954 peak of 102 units; a third had 33 units, compared to a peak of 59; and the fourth had 13 units and a capacity of 18. Ray's decline is further supported by such events as the mid-year cancelling of one of the two original first grade sections in the local school, the considerable number (17 of 34) of empty units in a modern housing development of duplexes, and the fact that just five new permanent residences were built during the period from September, 1954 to July, 1955.

Similar patterns are evident on a lesser scale in the other centers. It would seem that the centers in question are reaching a lower but more stable population level which is likely to persist for some time.

Chapter 4
The Geographic Setting of the
Bakken Oil Shale Play

2018

Bradley C. Rundquist and Gregory S. Vandeberg

Introduction

Oil development in northwestern North Dakota has expanded greatly since the 1958 *Williston Report*, with oil fields covering most areas of the counties including the towns of Williston and Stanley. Petroleum development on a regional scale has also changed from the Williston Basin in 1958 to the Bakken Formation at present, with much overlap between the two. This chapter focuses on the changing physical and human geography of the region, including oil production and population dynamics of the top four oil-producing counties in North Dakota: McKenzie, Mountrail, Dunn, and Williams (Figure 4.1). Because the cost of oil extraction from the Bakken Formation is higher than most other shale oil plays where horizontal drilling and hydraulic fracturing (or "fracking") are used, the region is particularly prone to boom-to-bust cycles. Longtime North Dakota geographer Bernt Wills's contribution to the *Williston Report* on the "Physical Attributes of the Area" (chapter 3) was published when the 1950s boom was on the wane. Just as Wills reflects back upon the effect of the 1950s oil boom on northwestern North Dakota, the authors of this chapter, also North Dakota geographers, analyze the impact of the 2008–14 boom post peak.

Geographic Setting

Bernt Wills's 1958 chapter described petroleum production in the region as centered along the east-west boundary between Williams and Mountrail counties in a region approximately five miles wide and thirty-five miles long (Figures 4.1 and 4.2; see also Figure 3 in chapter 3). The Williston Basin was the main geologic formation of interest, with oil wells extending between

8,000 and 11,000 feet below the surface along the Nesson Anticline (p. 36). Agriculture was the main economic driver for the area before the successful production of oil (300 barrels in seventeen hours) from the Clarence Iverson No. 1 well on April 4, 1951. The report detailed an average temperature of 69.4°F for July in Williston, and 7.9°F in January (p. 40). The average annual precipitation was 14.66 inches at Williston, with winter being the dry season.

The 1958 *Williston Report* documented changes in the cultural landscape with the construction of roads, oil drilling derricks, tanks and pump jacks associated with petroleum production. Transportation changes in the 1950s included the construction of 200 miles of new "all weather" secondary county, township, and oil company service roads, mostly in the oil producing areas. The major highways, U.S. Highway 2 and State Highway 40, were "hard surfaced," with the remaining roads being gravel (p. 41). Roads are typically oriented north-south or east-west along section lines and township boundaries. Most of the new road construction costs were expended by the state of North Dakota and the Amerada Petroleum Corporation, with Williams and Mountrail counties concentrating on maintenance and upkeep costs due to increased road traffic. Most of the oil was transported by pipelines by 1955, including a 10-inch line that was constructed to Mandan.

Population changes varied between Williams and Mountrail counties between 1950 and 1954. Williams County population increased by 26.8 percent, whereas Mountrail County lost 5.5 percent of its total population from 1950 to 1954 (p. 53). At the same time, the cities of Williston and Stanley gained population, and the rural areas saw a decrease in population. The age groups of 0–4 years and 20–29 years increased in the non-farm rural areas. The ratio of men to women stayed similar between 1950 to 1954, with 49.2 percent women in 1954 compared to 50.8 percent men of all ages. There was a notable increase of men (14.7 percent to 16.3 percent) in the 20–29 age group in Williston, compared to a decrease of the number of women (17.1 percent to 13.9 percent) (p. 56). Population increases were mostly the result of in-migration.

Topography

North Dakota's core oil producing counties are within the Northwestern Glaciated Plains and the Northwestern Great Plains ecoregions (Bryce et al. 1998). These ecoregions are part of the Great Plains physiographic province mapped by Fenneman (1931). The northern parts of the counties are covered by glacial deposits and consist of a flat-lying landscape interspersed with small hills

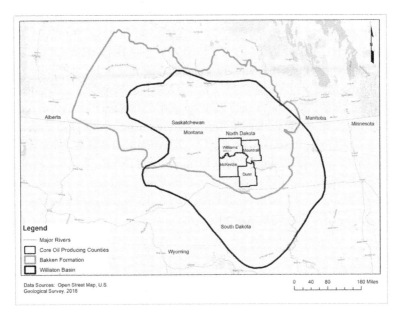

Figure 4.1. Core oil producing counties in North Dakota in the context of the Williston Basin and Bakken Formation (source: author)

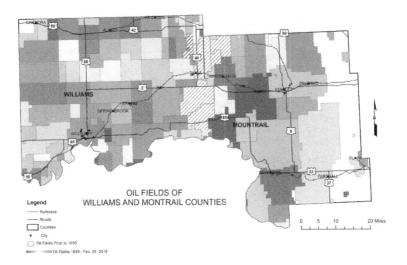

Figure 4.2. Oil fields of Williams and Mountrail Counties, North Dakota, by year opened (source: author)

and glacially-formed kettle lakes (knob and kettle topography), especially in Mountrail County (Bluemle 2000). Large glacial erratic boulders are common. The southern parts of Williams and Mountrail counties, known as the Couteau Slope, consist of a hilly and eroded landscape that forms bluffs along the northern border of the level terraces of the Missouri River Valley (Fenneman 1931; Bluemle 2000). The present location of the Missouri River in this region marks the southern boundary of the most recent continental glacier advance in the area of the Wisconsinan stage of glaciation that ended about 10,000 years before present (Bluemle 2000). McKenzie and Dunn counties are within the Missouri Plateau and Little Missouri badlands and are characterized by rolling hills and very heavily eroded hilly areas adjacent to the Little Missouri River (Bryce et al. 1998; Bluemle 2000) (Figure 4.3).

Figure 4.3. Little Missouri River Valley and badlands topography, North Unit, Theodore Roosevelt National Park, ND (source: G. Vandeberg 2005)

Geology

The Williston Basin is a subsurface geologic structure with its base in Precambrian crystalline rocks of the Canadian Shield (Gerhard et al. 1982; Gibson 1995). The basin is somewhat elongated in a northwest to southeast direction and underlies portions of Saskatchewan, Manitoba, Montana, North Dakota

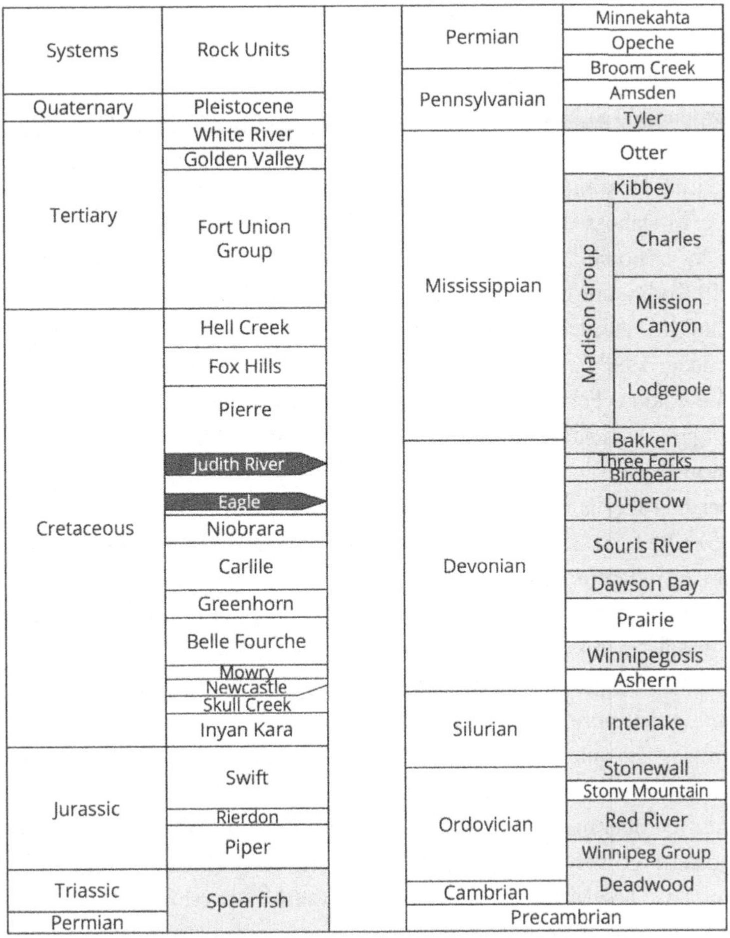

Systems	Rock Units
Quaternary	Pleistocene
Tertiary	White River
	Golden Valley
	Fort Union Group
	Hell Creek
Cretaceous	Fox Hills
	Pierre
	Judith River
	Eagle
	Niobrara
	Carlile
	Greenhorn
	Belle Fourche
	Mowry
	Newcastle
	Skull Creek
	Inyan Kara
Jurassic	Swift
	Rierdon
	Piper
Triassic	Spearfish
Permian	

Systems	Rock Units	
Permian	Minnekahta	
	Opeche	
	Broom Creek	
Pennsylvanian	Amsden	
	Tyler	
Mississippian	Otter	
	Kibbey	
	Madison Group	Charles
		Mission Canyon
		Lodgepole
	Bakken	
Devonian	Three Forks	
	Birdbear	
	Duperow	
	Souris River	
	Dawson Bay	
	Prairie	
	Winnipegosis	
	Ashern	
Silurian	Interlake	
Ordovician	Stonewall	
	Stony Mountain	
	Red River	
	Winnipeg Group	
Cambrian	Deadwood	
Precambrian		

Figure 4.4. Generalized stratigraphic structure of the Williston Basin. Rock units shaded lightly are petroleum-bearing, and those shaded darkly are gas-bearing. (source: North Dakota Geological Survey 2000)

and South Dakota (Figure 4.1). The deepest part of the basin is more than 16,000 feet below the surface and contains a thick sequence of sedimentary rocks that have been faulted or folded to create structures important for petroleum production, as well as petroleum-rich geologic formations (Figure 4.4). The basin is not visible on the land surface.

Recoverable petroleum requires specific geologic conditions: the presence of a source rock and a reservoir rock. Petroleum is typically produced from organic-rich rock such as shale (source), and accumulates in a more porous (reservoir) rock such as sandstone or limestone (carbonates). Faults and other structures within the rock formations help to trap and accumulate the petroleum in specific locations. These structures are especially important for oil production in North Dakota, where the Nesson, Antelope, Little Knife, and Cedar Creek anticlines and the Red Wing Creek geologic structure are major producing locations (Bluemle 2000). Most of the early petroleum production in North Dakota covered by the 1958 *Report* and extending into the 1990s was in carbonate rocks of the Madison Formation (Figure 4.4) (Bluemle 2000). Today, one of the most important formations for the production of oil within the Williston Basin is the Bakken Formation (Smith and Bustin 1995; Schmoker 1996; Zamiran, Rafieepour, and Ostadhassan 2018).

The Bakken Formation consists of three members: the lower member is an organic-rich shale (source rock), the middle member consists of variable siltstones and sandstones (reservoir rock) that are finely cemented, and the upper member is organic-rich shale (LeFever et al. 1991; Smith and Bustin 1995). The formation has a maximum thickness of 150 feet in the Williston Basin with depths greater than 7,000 feet below the surface in North Dakota (LeFever et al. 1991; Abarghani et al. 2018). The main reservoir thickness of the middle member is up to 87 feet (LeFever et al. 1991; Sonnenberg and Pramudito 2009). The middle member of the Bakken has a low permeability, meaning that pore spaces within the rock are poorly connected, and therefore fracturing is required to recover substantial amounts of oil from the formation (Sonnenberg and Pramudito 2009). Furthermore, the limited thickness of the middle member means that standard vertical wells have had limited success in petroleum recovery from the unit. The advance of horizontal drilling and fracturing has allowed for the increased development of oil from the Bakken, as well as other oil shale fields in the United States such as the Eagle Ford shale in Texas (Gaswirth and Marra 2015; Hao et al. 2018). The first horizontal well in the Bakken was drilled in North Dakota in 1987, and most of the wells drilled in the Williston Basin since that time have been horizontal (Bluemle 2001). Multiple wells are currently being drilled from the same drilling pad, limiting the footprint of drilling in the basin (Shrestha et al. 2017).

Climate

The Köppen-Geiger Climate Classification System (Köppen 1918; Geiger 1954, 1961) is the most commonly used method to classify climates at continental and global scales. Researchers have applied the system to a wide range of climate and climate change studies and have updated world maps to account for new data. Under a widely cited Köppen-Geiger update for 1951–2000 (Kottek et al. 2006), the Bakken region is in a transitional zone between Cold Semi-Arid Steppe (BSk) in its western portion to Warm-Summer Humid Continental (Dfb) to the east. That is, Bakken Formation climates range from cold and dry (but not as dry as a desert) in the west to continental (large seasonal variations in temperature) with precipitation distributed throughout the year (no monsoon) in the east. Nearly all of North Dakota outside of the western Bakken is classified Dfb (Kottek et al. 2006).

Weather observers have kept records for the Williston area (BSk) since 1894. Mean annual precipitation at Williston is 14.40 inches, although it has varied between a low of 6.13 inches in 1934 to a high of 22.04 inches in 1896 (NOAA 2018). By decade since 1960, precipitation has been near the long-term average except for the 1980s and the 2010s (Table 4.1). In the 1980s, the area was part of a larger region of the Midwest that experienced an extended drought that was most severe in 1983. The Williston area received below-average precipitation from 1979 to 1981 and 1983 to 1985, with only 9.52 inches falling in 1983. The 2010s so far have been wetter than average, highlighted by 21.28 inches received in both 2010 and 2013 and 19.23 inches in 2011 (NOAA 2018). Average annual rainfall in the 2010s has been more variable than in any other decade since the 1960s (Table 4.1).

TABLE 4.1. AVERAGE PRECIPITATION AND TEMPERATURE STATISTICS FOR THE WILLISTON AREA SINCE 1960 (SOURCE: U.S. DEPARTMENT OF COMMERCE, NATIONAL ATMOSPHERIC AND OCEANIC ADMINISTRATION, NATIONAL WEATHER SERVICE, NOWDATA 2018)

Decade	Mean annual precipitation (inches)	Standard deviation of mean annual precipitation (inches)	Mean Monthly Temp. January (°F)	Mean Monthly Temp. July (°F)
1960s	14.09	2.95	7.55	70.68
1970s	14.67	3.07	5.01	69.89
1980s	12.72	3.61	12.91	73.35
1990s	14.84	2.84	8.80	67.96
2000s	14.38	1.84	12.56	71.62
2010s (to 2017)	15.70	4.04	14.38	71.78

Minot (Dfb), about 110 miles to the east on the eastern edge of the Bakken Formation, generally experiences more rainfall annually and cooler temperatures than Williston (Table 4.2). The weather at Minot is also more variable in terms of mean annual rainfall and mean monthly temperature. When data from the Minot International Airport (collected since 1948) are used to fill data gaps in the Minot Experiment Station record (collected since 1905), mean annual precipitation is 16.88 inches (NOAA 2018). Precipitation by decade since 1960 shows that the 2010s have been the wettest and most variable (Table 4.2). High variability in the 2010s is, to date, attributed to extreme conditions this decade, with a record high 32.35 inches of precipitation in 2013 and a drought in 2017 when only 11.34 inches fell. The year 2017 was the driest in Minot since 1992, and the ninth driest year since 1905 (NOAA 2018).

TABLE 4.2.
AVERAGE PRECIPITATION AND TEMPERATURE STATISTICS FOR MINOT SINCE 1960 (SOURCE: U.S. DEPARTMENT OF COMMERCE, NATIONAL ATMOSPHERIC AND OCEANIC ADMINISTRATION, NATIONAL WEATHER SERVICE, NOWDATA 2018)

Decade	Mean annual precipitation (inches)	Standard deviation of mean annual precipitation (inches)	Mean Monthly Temp. January (°F)	Mean Monthly Temp. July (°F)
1960s	16.08	3.95	4.72	68.83
1970s	19.60	4.55	3.46	68.54
1980s	17.91	3.70	10.96	69.44
1990s	18.68	4.71	7.28	66.60
2000s	16.01	3.37	12.04	69.17
2010s (to 2017)	21.67	6.36	11.79	69.43

Mean annual snowfall in Williston is 38.0 inches. February is, on average, the month with the most snowfall at 7.1 inches, followed by January at 6.7 inches and April at 6.6 inches. Annual accumulation of snowfall has varied from 8.0 inches in winter 1908–9 to 107.2 inches in winter 2010–11 (NOAA 2018). Minot's mean annual snowfall is slightly higher at 39.1 inches. January tends to be the snowiest at Minot, with 7.1 inches falling on average, followed by March at 6.7 inches and 6.6 inches in December (NOAA 2018).

Because it is located near the center of a continental land mass, the Bakken region experiences extreme annual variability in temperatures. Williston's coldest month is January, with a mean monthly temperature of 9.3°F, and its warmest month is July at 70.2°F (NOAA 2018). The record daily high of 110°F occurred on July 5, 1936, and the record low of –50°F has occurred twice: on February 16, 1936, and December 23, 1983 (NOAA 2018). In 1936, then, there was a 160°F swing in temperature from the daily low on February 16 to the daily high on July 5. The 2010s have witnessed the warmest January temperatures since the 1960s (Table 4.1).

January (7.5°F) and July (68.6°F) are also the coldest and warmest months at Minot (NOAA 2018). A record daily high of 109°F was recorded twice at the Minot Experiment Station: on June 20, 1910, and July 11, 1936. The station's record low of –49°F was measured on February 15, 1936 (NOAA 2018). As in the Williston area, Minot experienced an enormous swing in seasonal temperatures in 1936. January and July mean monthly temperatures in Minot during the 2010s are among the warmest since the 1960s (Table 4.2).

Land Cover and Land Uses

The dominant land covers in the core oil-producing counties are grassland (pastureland) and cropland, and the primary land uses are livestock grazing and crop production. There is more pastureland than cropland in Dunn and McKenzie counties and more cropland than pastureland in Mountrail and Williams counties (Table 4.3). The most recent continental glaciation covered most of Mountrail and Williams counties, leaving behind topography and soils well suited for crop production. The development of the oil industry has resulted in conversion of some pasture and cropland to oil well pads, oil field roads, and other oil-related infrastructure (Preston and Kim 2016; Torgerson 2017).

TABLE 4.3.
TRENDS IN AGRICULTURE IN CORE OIL PRODUCING
COUNTIES FOR SELECTED YEARS SINCE 1925
(SOURCES: USDA CENSUS OF AGRICULTURE
1925, 1950, 1982, 2012)

	1925	1950	1982	2012
DUNN				
Number of farms	1,459	1,157	697	628
Average farm size	668 acres	1,063 acres	2,005 acres	1,642 acres
Total cropland	353,862 acres	447,947 acres	448,598 acres	374,287 acres
Total pastureland	365,146 acres	767,542 acres	978,778 acres	646,709 acres
Cattle and calves	38,851	55,629	84,773	79,898
Corn for grain	20,607 bu	39,764 bu	32,325 bu	936,778 bu
Wheat for grain	2,068,041 bu	1,298,357 bu	2,792,201 bu	5,811,485 bu
McKENZIE				
Number of farms	1,721	1,234	778	574
Average farm size	520 acres	968 acres	1,506 acres	1,854 acres
Total cropland	309,068 acres	513,200 acres	499,163 acres	425,625 acres
Total pastureland	433,083 acres	651,731 acres	669,212 acres	614,787 acres
Cattle and calves	35,181	53,883	71,151	92,383
Corn for grain	28,710 bu	7,481 bu	48,285 bu	54,510 bu
Wheat for grain	2,145,564 bu	1,839,371 bu	4,391,154 bu	6,214,714 bu
MOUNTRAIL				
Number of farms	1,927	1,484	881	670
Average farm size	383 acres	770 acres	1,147 acres	1,438 acres
Total cropland	405,747 acres	673,481 acres	693,423 acres	578,761 acres
Total pastureland	202,983 acres	431,128 acres	297,917 acres	347,622 acres
Cattle and calves	28,182	26,576	36,697	28,797
Corn for grain	3,399 bu	1,630 bu	8,984 bu	332,630 bu
Wheat for grain	2,963,171 bu	3,391,231 bu	6,927,065 bu	9,951,091 bu
WILLIAMS				
Number of farms	2,195	1,157	971	758
Average farm size	414 acres	1,063 acres	1,196 acres	1,403 acres
Total cropland	482,666 acres	447,947 acres	811,330 acres	739,086 acres
Total pastureland	259,034 acres	767,542 acres	335,128 acres	279,947 acres
Cattle and calves	32,678	23,923	33,999	22,574
Corn for grain	10,297 bu	2,345 bu	(D)	301,553 bu
Wheat for grain	2,842,544 bu	3,544,688 bu	8,690,944 bu	13,521,568 bu

Indigenous Population

Several Indigenous groups lived in or made use of the region just prior to Euro-American settlement. With overlapping territories, they were the Assiniboine (Nakota), Absarokee (Crow), Lakota, and Hidatsa, among others (Robinson 1966). In the early 1800s, the Anishinabe (Chippewa) from the Turtle Mountain region of north-central North Dakota hunted seasonally in today's western Williams County and areas of northeastern and north central Montana (North Dakota State Historical Society 2018). The Mandan and Sahnish (Arikara) were found farther south along the Missouri River at the time, but moved into the region by the mid-1800s following the devastating smallpox epidemic in 1837 that killed an estimated 90 percent of the Mandan and 70 percent of the Hidatsa (Meyer 1977; Parker 2011).

Lands of the Mandan, Hidatsa, and Arikara (MHA) Nation are now within the Fort Berthold Reservation, which was established in 1870. The area of the reservation is 988,000 acres, with 457,837 acres owned either by individual tribal members or communally by the affiliated tribes. The size of MHA land holdings has been reduced significantly from the approximately 12 million acres assigned to the Three Affiliated Tribes by the 1851 Treaty of Fort Laramie. More than 152,000 acres of the reservation were taken in the 1950s during the construction of the Garrison Dam and creation of Lake Sakakawea, much of which was agriculturally productive riparian land (Meyer 1977; Parker 2011). The reservation is contained within McLean, Mountrail, Dunn, McKenzie, Mercer, and Ward counties. Tribal headquarters are now in New Town within Mountrail County. New Town was platted in 1950 as a replacement for the towns of Sanish and Van Hook, both of which were flooded by the creation of Lake Sakakawea. The population of the Fort Berthold Reservation was 5,874 in 2000, 6,341 in 2010, and 7,611 in 2015 (Taft 2017). The median age of its residents was 29.3 in 2000, 31.0 in 2010, and 29.3 in 2015 (Taft 2017).

Established in 1975, the Trenton Indian Service Area (TISA) is a semi-independent extension of the Turtle Mountain Band of Chippewa. Because there was not enough land within the Turtle Mountain Reservation to satisfy the provisions of the General Allotment (or Dawes) Act of 1887 and subsequent amendments, the U.S. government allotted parts of Divide, Williams and McKenzie counties, as well as areas in northeastern Montana, to Turtle Mountain Band members (North Dakota State Historical Society 2018). TISA, headquartered in Trenton about 14 miles west of Williston, provides a governing structure and services to the descendants of Chippewa who settled on those allotted lands, although TISA is legally bound to the Turtle Mountain Reservation centered at Belcourt, 250 miles to the east.

Pre-Oil Euro-American Population and the Arrival of Railroads

The Euro-American population of the region grew throughout the late 1800s and early 1900s because of land availability, railroad access, and weather that was favorable most years for crop and forage production. It is challenging to estimate population in the region before 1910 because contemporary county names and boundaries, which serve as census enumeration units, were not yet set. All four counties examined were created within the Dakota Territory in the 1870s and 1880s. Following statehood in 1889, however, Dunn County was annexed by Stark County, and Mountrail County by Ward County. The state legislature eliminated McKenzie County because of the lack of settlement. The first Williams County, established in 1873, was replaced by a second in 1891, encompassing an entirely different geographic area. Dunn County reappeared in 1901, its current boundaries finally set in 1908. The North Dakota legislature recreated McKenzie County in 1905 and Mountrail County in 1909. The area of today's Divide County was split from Williams County in 1910.

The populations of what are now Mountrail and Williams counties grew faster than those of Dunn and McKenzie counties for a few reasons. First, lands in Mountrail and Williams counties are more suited to crop cultivation, a factor that favored those areas for homesteading. Second, those counties had access to railroad transportation much earlier than Dunn and McKenzie. The St. Paul, Minneapolis, and Manitoba Railway (StPM&M, renamed the Great Northern Railway by 1889) extended its main line from Minot through Mountrail and Williams counties in 1887 (Hidy, Hidy, Scott, and Hofsommer 1988), two years before North Dakota statehood. StPM&M's push through Mountrail and Williams counties was part of its "Long March to Montana" in 1887, when an incredible 545 miles of track was laid from Minot to Great Falls (Hidy et al. 1988). Development companies associated with the railroad founded many towns along the new railway: Tagus, Palermo, Stanley, Ross, Manitou, and White Earth in Mountrail County, and Tioga, Temple, Ray, Wheelock, Epping, Spring Brook, Williston, Trenton, and Buford in Williams County (Rand, McNally and Co. 1911; Wick 1999). In 1911, the Great Northern built a nearly 51-mile branch from its main line in Stanley to Wildrose in Divide County (Hidy et al. 1988), which led to the founding of Lostwood and Lund's Valley (Rand, McNally and Co. 1911; Wick 1999). The town of Plaza, founded in 1906 in Mountrail County, was the terminus of a Minneapolis, St. Paul, and Sault Ste. Marie ("Soo") branch out of Max (Rand, McNally & Co. 1911; Wick 1999) until 1914, when the line was extended to Sanish through the newly formed towns of Wabek, Parshall, and Van Hook. Coulee was founded on the Great

Northern branch from Berthold in Ward County to Ambrose in Divide County (Rand, McNally and Co. 1911; Wick 1999). All of the rail lines in Mountrail and Williams are still in operation.

The first rail service in McKenzie County came from the west in 1913 when the Great Northern extended a line thirty miles from Fairview, Montana, to Arnegard, North Dakota, and an additional 7.5 miles to Watford City in 1914 (Hidy et al. 1988). Burlington Northern abandoned that entire stretch in 1992 (North Dakota Public Service Commission 2018). Dunn County received rail service in 1914 when the Northern Pacific Railway laid 34 miles of track west from Golden Valley in Mercer County to Kildeer in Dunn County, resulting in the founding of Dodge, Werner, and Dunn Center and the relocation of Halliday (Rand McNally 1942; Wick 1999). Burlington Northern abandoned 41 miles of that line, including all within Dunn County, in 1984 (North Dakota Public Service Commission 2018).

By 1920, the foreign-born in McKenzie, Mountrail, and Williams counties were predominantly Norwegian, although there were also notable populations from Canada, Denmark, Germany, Russia (primarily Black Sea Germans), and Sweden (Sherman and Thorson 1988). Williams County recorded 77 Syrians (Lebanese), with another 22 in Mountrail County (Sherman and Thorson 1988). Dunn County had more Germans from Russia than Norwegians, as well as notable representations of Austrians (Ukrainians) and Hungarians (Banat and Burgenland Germans) (Sherman and Thorson 1988).

After peaking in about 1930, the region's population declined both during and after the "Great Drought" of the mid-1930s. Although the region declined overall, migration into larger towns meant continued growth, albeit slow, of regional trade centers like Williston, Dickinson, Bismarck, and Minot. Smaller trade centers lost population because fewer farm families on the surrounding landscapes (Table 4.3) meant less demand for the goods and services they provided. For example, Williston grew by 13.4 percent between 1930 and 1940 while its county, Williams, shrank by 16.6 percent. Nearby small towns like Tioga and Ray lost 11.5 percent and 6.8 percent of their residents, respectively (U.S. Bureau of the Census 1941).

Agriculture

As the number of farms and farm families declined across North Dakota, the average size of a farm increased steadily (Table 4.3), the result of larger and more efficient agricultural machinery and improved agricultural technologies. Still, the average size of a farm in northwestern North Dakota has been large relative to the rest of the state since at least 1925. The USDA Census of Agriculture reported statewide average farm sizes of 452 acres in 1925, 630 acres in 1950, 1,104 acres in 1982, and 1,268 acres in 2012, while McKenzie County's average farm size was 520 acres in 1925, 968 acres in 1950, 1,506 acres in 1982, and 1,854 acres in 2012 (Table 4.3).

Larger-than-average farms in today's "oil patch" are attributable to the region's dry climate that generally limits crop yields per acre. For example, Cass County, in the more humid southeastern corner of the state, was North Dakota's top corn-producing county in 2012 with 44.9 million bushels (an average yield of 129 bushels per acre), while yield in similarly-sized Mountrail County was 332,630 bushels (64 bushels per acre) (USDA 2012). Cass County's wheat yield in 2012 was 5.3 million bushels, averaging 56 bushels per acre, while Mountrail County harvested about 10 million bushels at 36 bushels per acre (USDA 2012). North Dakota ranks second in the U.S. in wheat production behind only Kansas (National Agricultural Statistics Service 2017). Among the state's counties, Mountrail ranked twelfth and Dunn nineteenth in spring wheat, while Williams led the state in the production of Durum wheat (National Agricultural Statistics Service 2017).

Cattle ranching has been an important economic activity in the Bakken region since the 1880s, with cattle thriving on extensive tracts of grassland, including the Little Missouri National Grassland (LMNG) managed by the U.S. Forest Service. At more than 1 million acres, the LMNG is the largest grassland area in the United States, and a significant portion is located in McKenzie County. In 2016, Dunn County ranked fourth among the 53 counties in North Dakota in the number of cattle and calves, while McKenzie was sixth, Mountrail was eighteenth, and Williams was twenty-ninth (National Agricultural Statistics Service 2017). North Dakota ranked sixteenth among U.S. states in cattle and calves on hand as of January 1, 2017 (National Agricultural Statistics Service 2017).

Oil Development

Oil was first discovered in North Dakota with the completion of the Clarence Iverson well in Williams County on April 4, 1951, to a depth of 11,660 feet (Bluemle 2001). This well, located about 8.5 miles south of Tioga and 11 miles east of Ray (SW ¼, SW ¼, Sec. 6, T. 155 N., R. 95 W), was the start of many more oil wells drilled and developed in the 1950s and subsequent years. Based on data from the North Dakota Department of Mineral Resources, 2014 was the peak year for the maximum number of wells spudded (that is, those that companies began drilling), at 2,656 for all counties, with 2,277 of these wells in Dunn, McKenzie, Mountrail and Williams counties (Figure 4.5). Figure 4.5 clearly shows the periods of high drilling activity centered on the years 1959, 1968, 1981 and 2014. Note that the study area counties have a substantial percentage of the total wells drilled beginning in about 2008, with development of the Bakken Formation oil in full swing.

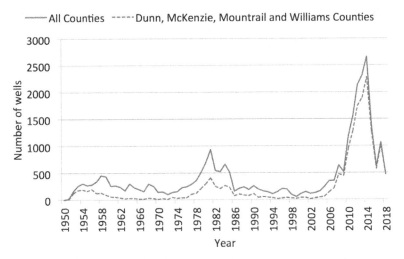

Figure 4.5. Number of oil wells spudded per year, 1951–2018 (source: North Dakota Oil and Gas Division 2018)

The years 1966, 1984, and 2015 show three peaks in North Dakota crude oil production (Figure 4.6). The yearly production in 1966 was more than 27 million barrels (42 gallons per barrel), versus more than 52 million barrels in 1984. More than 432 million barrels of oil were produced in 2015, with almost 90 percent of the production coming from the four counties of this study. Daily oil production in North Dakota first exceeded 1 million barrels in 2014. The U.S. Geological Survey (2015) has estimated that 7.38 billion barrels of oil remain in the Bakken and Three Forks formations, so oil development is expected to continue, depending upon crude prices.

Boom-to-bust Population Trends

Agricultural economics help to steer the population dynamics of northwestern North Dakota, but the boom-to-bust cycles of oil economics have been the dominant factors since the discovery of oil there in 1951. Zealous investors who rushed to develop the new oil field drove the state's first oil boom, called the "discovery boom" (Bluemle 2001). The 1950s, however, were a time of global overproduction of petroleum, which meant low market prices for oil. This eventually prompted U.S. producers to band together to limit supply, increase prices, and ensure that every producer received a fair market share (Bluemle 2001). The discovery boom ended in about 1960, but slower-paced development of the oil economy of the region continued.

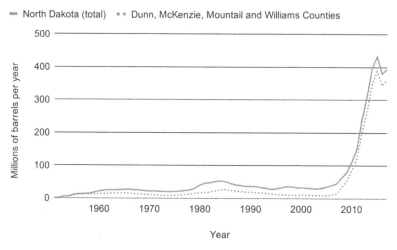

Figure 4.6. Number of barrels of oil produced per year in North Dakota and in study area counties (Dunn, McKenzie, Mountrail, and Williams), 1951–2018 (source: North Dakota Oil and Gas Division 2018)

The first boom had a significant but localized impact on population. The location of the Clarence Iverson well in Williams County was near Tioga and Ray. Between 1950 and 1954, Tioga's population grew by 253 percent and Ray's by 105 percent (Table 4.4). Williston and Stanley grew noticeably during that same time, although Mountrail County lost population overall. Wills (p. 53) concluded that Tioga and Ray "benefited enormously as logical sites for settling migrants involved in the establishment of the [oil] fields," while Williston became a central supply point for the nascent oil industry and Stanley, located about 26 miles east of the discovery well, absorbed overflow population from Tioga and Ray. With later limits on production, the population of those towns regressed significantly by 1970.

The second boom, called the "oil price boom," began in the mid-1970s with the discovery of a significant new oil field in 1972 (the Red Wing Creek

Structure in McKenzie County about 40 miles south of Williston) and the success of the Organization of Petroleum Exporting Countries (OPEC) in limiting petroleum production by its member nations. OPEC's oil embargo forced the price of a barrel of oil from about $4 in 1973 to $9 in 1974 (Bluemle 2001). The increase made Williston Basin exploration profitable, and exploration led to the opening of several additional fields in the late 1970s and early 1980s. During the second boom cycle, the state's oil production peaked in 1981 at 45 million barrels. By 1982, oil prices began to fall, accelerated by overproduction by OPEC. The second boom ended by early 1986.

The impact of the second boom on the region is most evident in the 20 percent increase in the population of Watford City between 1970 and 1980. Watford City is about twenty miles north of the Red Wing Structure (Table 4.4). McKenzie and Williams counties experienced 16 percent and 15 percent increases in population, respectively, while Williston grew by about 19 percent (Table 4.4).

The period from the mid-1980s to 2006 was one of out-migration. Census records show that every core oil-producing county lost population between 1980 and 1990 and between 1990 and 2000 (Table 4.4). From 1980 to 2000, Dunn County lost 22.2 percent of its residents, while McKenzie lost 19.6 percent, Mountrail 13.6 percent, and Williams 11.1 percent. While the larger city of Williston lost 6.2 percent between 1980 and 2000, the region's smaller cities suffered the most: Watford City declined by 32.3 percent, Ray by 30.3 percent, Tioga by 29.6 percent, and Stanley by 21.6 percent (Table 4.4).

The third boom, called the "technology boom" because of the heavy reliance on horizontal drilling and hydraulic fracturing, began in about 2006 with the discovery of the Parshall oil field (near the town of Parshall in Mountrail County). That find occurred during a period of high oil prices (more than $100 per barrel between October 2007 and August 2014). The break-even price for Parshall oil at the time was about $38, by far the lowest among Bakken fields, making extraction especially lucrative. The boom continued until oil prices crashed globally between August 2014 ($103 per barrel) and February 2016 ($27 per barrel, well below the break-even price) because of global overproduction.

TABLE 4.4.
POPULATION STATISTICS FOR CORE OIL PRODUCING COUNTIES AND SELECTED COMMUNITIES, 1940–2016 (SOURCES: U.S. CENSUS BUREAU 1940, 1950, 2000, 2010; WILLS, CURRENT VOLUME; AMERICAN COMMUNITY SURVEY 2012–16)

			Population and Percent Change (in parentheses)						
1940	1950	1954	1960	1970	1980	1990	2000	2010	2016
WILLIAMS									
16,315	16,442	20,843	22,051	19,301	22,237	21,129	19,761	22,398	31,643
	(0.8)	(26.8)	(5.8)	(-12.5)	(15.2)	(-5.0)	(-6.5)	(13.3)	(41.3)
Williston									
5,790	7,398	9,717	11,866	11,230	13,336	13,136	12,512	14,716	23,902
	(27.8)	(31.4)	(22.1)	(-5.4)	(18.8)	(-1.5)	(-4.8)	(17.6)	(62.4)
Ray									
579	721	1,479	1,049	776	766	603	534	592	483
	(24.5)	(105.1)	(-29.1)	(-26.0)	(-1.3)	(-21.3)	(-11.4)	(10.9)	(-18.4)
Tioga									
385	456	1,608	2,087	1,667	1,597	1,278	1,125	1,230	1,126
	(18.4)	(252.6)	(29.8)	(-20.1)	(-4.2)	(-20.0)	(-12.0)	(9.3)	(-8.5)
MOUNTRAIL									
10,482	9,418	8,897	10,077	8,437	7,679	7,021	6,631	7,673	9,675
	(-10.2)	(-5.5)	(13.3)	(-16.3)	(-9.0)	(-8.6)	(-5.6)	(15.7)	(26.1)
Stanley									
1,058	1,486	1,645	1,795	1,581	1,631	1,371	1,279	1,458	2,328
	(40.5)	(10.7)	(9.1)	(-11.9)	(3.2)	(-15.9)	(-6.7)	(14.0)	(59.7)
Parshall									
570	935	–	1,216	1,246	1,059	943	981	903	1,125
	(64.0)	–	(30.1)	(2.5)	(-15.0)	(-11.0)	(4.0)	(-8.0)	(24.6)
McKENZIE									
8,426	6,849	–	7,296	6,127	7,132	6,383	5,737	6,360	10,718
	(-18.7)	–	(6.5)	(-16.0)	(16.4)	(-10.5)	(-10.1)	(10.9)	(68.5)
Watford City									
1,023	1,371	–	1,865	1,768	2,119	1,784	1,435	1,744	4,596
	(34.0)	–	(36.0)	(-5.2)	(19.9)	(-15.8)	(-19.6)	(21.5)	(165.5)
DUNN									
8,376	7,212	–	6,350	4,895	4,627	4,005	3,600	3,536	4,284
	(-13.9)	–	(-12.0)	(-22.9)	(-5.5)	(-13.4)	(-10.1)	(-1.8)	(21.2)
Killdeer									
650	698	–	765	615	790	722	713	751	903
	(7.4)	–	(9.6)	(-19.6)	(28.5)	(-8.6)	(-1.2)	(5.3)	(20.2)

During the third boom, oil-producing counties all grew (Table 4.4). Williston and other towns also grew between 2000 and 2010, as well as 2010 and 2016. For example, Watford City grew by 166 percent, Williston by 62 percent, and Stanley by 60 percent (Table 4.4). Such statistics are more impressive when one considers the likelihood of population declines between late 2014 and early 2016, a period of relatively low oil prices. Ray and Tioga show decline between 2010 and 2016, suggesting that populations in those Williams County towns began to decline earlier than in other parts of the Bakken region.

Demographics

The three oil booms and subsequent busts since 1951 have affected the age and sex structures of the region. From 1950 to 1960 in Williston, the number of preschool-aged children (0–4 years old) increased by 83 percent (Table 4.5) and school-aged children and young adults (5–19 years) increased by 100 percent (some older teenagers arrived in Williston for work, not for school). The "working age" population (20–65 years of age) in Williston went from 3,988 in 1950 to 5,534 in 1960, a 39 percent increase. The male working age group increased by 36 percent while the female group rose 41 percent (Table 4.5). Williston's male-to-female ratio for 20- to 29-year-olds was 89 per 100 in 1950 and 72 per 100 in 1960, while the 30–64 age group held at 1:1 (Figure 4.7). It is curious that Williston's male-to-female ratio for the 20–29 age group decreased during the first oil boom, but the census reveals an increase of only 33 men compared to 167 women in that age cohort between 1950 and 1960. Oil production sites, dominated by male workers, were near Tioga and Ray. For census years 1950 and 1960, Williston's male-to-female ratios for all age cohorts were less than the state averages (Figure 4.7), meaning there were fewer men per women there than in the state overall. The median age in Williams County went from 29.1 years in 1950 to 25.4 years in 1960, compared to the statewide median age of 26.2 years in 1960 (Figure 4.8). The percentage of married people increased while the percentage of single people decreased in Williams County between 1950 and 1960 (Table 4.6), suggesting that those entering the county for oil-related work at the time were either married when they arrived or got married after they arrived, which contrasts sharply with later booms.

TABLE 4.5.
WILLISTON POPULATION BY AGE GROUP AND SEX, DURING THE
FIRST (1950–60) AND THIRD (2000–16) OIL BOOMS
(SOURCES: U.S. CENSUS BUREAU 1940, 1950, 2000, 2010; WILLS, CUR-
RENT VOLUME; AMERICAN COMMUNITY SURVEY 2012–16)

Age	1950 Male	1950 Female	1960 M	1960 F	2000 M	2000 F	2010 M	2010 F	2016 M	2016 F
0–4	485	420	869	814	381	383	556	547	1,086	909
5–19	861	878	1,719	1,756	1,451	1,440	1,385	1,364	2,402	1,906
20–29	543	629	576	796	686	698	1,350	1,086	2,930	2,279
30–64	1,405	1,411	2,073	2,089	2,667	2,702	3,381	2,932	5,842	4,383
65+	400	346	576	598	807	1,297	835	1,280	871	1,294
Total	3,694	3,684	5,813	6,053	5,992	6,520	7,507	7,209	13,131	10,771

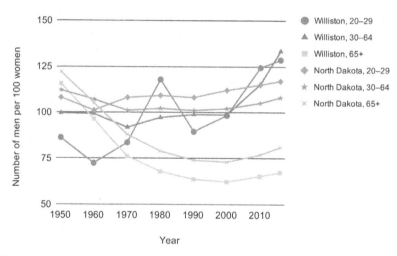

Figure 4.7. Number of men per 100 women for Williston and the state of North Dakota since 1950 (source: U.S. Census Bureau 2010; U.S. Census Bureau, American Fact Finder 2016)

TABLE 4.6.

SEX AND PERCENT DISTRIBUTION OF MARITAL STATUS FOR THOSE 14 OR 15 YEARS OF AGE AND OLDER,[1] 1950-60 AND 2000-16 (SOURCES: U.S. CENSUS BUREAU 1950, 1960, 2000; AMERICAN COMMUNITY SURVEY 2012-16)

	DUNN				McKENZIE			
	1950	1960	2000	2016	1950	1960	2000	2016
MALE	2,493	2,074	1,419	1,836	2,585	2,559	2,146	4,329
Married	60.3%	62.9%	62.0%	52.3%	59.0%	62.8%	61.7%	45.9%
Single/ Never Married[2]	36.1%	33.5%	21.6%	32.4%	36.2%	32.0%	27.3%	36.7%
Divorced	3.5%[3]	0.9%	6.9%	10.7%	4.9%[3]	2.0%	7.3%	10.5%
Widowed		2.7%	3.5%	4.5%		3.2%	3.7%	2.7%
FEMALE	2,197	1,861	1,397	1,628	2,109	2,199	2,192	3,700
Married	67.7%	70.2%	60.4%	60.4%	71.6%	72.4%	60.2%	52.9%
Single/ Never Married[2]	25.4%	21.3%	20.1%	20.5%	17.8%	17.1%	19.2%	28.8%
Divorced	7.0%[3]	0.6%	7.3%	10.6%	10.6%[3]	1.2%	7.4%	10.5%
Widowed		7.9%	12.1%	8.5%		9.4%	13.2%	7.9%

	MOUNTRAIL				WILLIAMS			
	1950	1960	2000	2016	1950	1960	2000	2016
MALE	3,741	3,427	2,515	4,191	6,275	7,167	7,656	13,686
Married	55.8%	62.9%	59.1%	45.9%	61.6%	68.6%	58.2%	49.5%
Single/ Never Married[2]	38.0%	31.3%	28.1%	42.4%	32.4%	26.1%	27.9%	36.2%
Divorced	6.2%[3]	1.7%	10.2%	9.9%	6.0%[3]	7.6%	10.4%	12.9%
Widowed		4.1%	2.6%	1.8%		3.6%	3.5%	1.5%
FEMALE	2,936	3,140	2,615	3,376	5,465	6,967	8,088	11,031
Married	70.8%	68.6%	54.9%	45.3%	69.6%	70.5%	56.3%	56.1%
Single/ Never Married[2]	18.9%	19.5%	21.5%	33.6%	19.2%	18.0%	21.1%	25.5%
Divorced	10.3%[3]	1.9%	7.5%	12.3%	11.2%[3]	1.7%	9.9%	10.3%
Widowed		10.1%	16.1%	8.6%		9.9%	12.7%	8.1%

[1] 14 years of age was the cut-off in the 1950 and 1960 U.S. censuses; 15 years of age was the cut-off in the 2000 census and the 2012–16 American Community Survey (ACS).

[2] The term "single" was used in the 1950 and 1960 censuses; the term "never married" was used in the 2000 census and the 2012–16 ACS.

[3] The "divorced" and "widowed" categories were combined in the 1950 census.

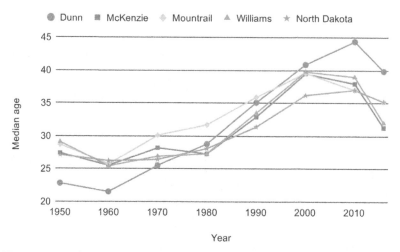

Figure 4.8. Median age for core oil-producing counties and the state of North Dakota since 1950 (source: U.S. Census Bureau 2010; U.S. Census Bureau, American Fact Finder 2016)

Census years 1970 and 1980 can be used to characterize the mid-1970s to mid-1980s boom. The male-to-female ratio for 20- to 29-year-olds living in Williston rose from 84 per 100 in 1970 to 118 per 100 in 1980 (Figure 4.7). The number of men aged between 20 and 29 years increased by 159 percent during the 1970s, while women of the same age increased by 84 percent. Clearly the second oil boom in the region brought more young men to Williston than did the first, and there was no corresponding boom in pre-school or school-aged children: 0- to 4-year-olds increased by 1.6 percent between 1970 and 1980 and 5- to 19-year-olds actually decreased by 24 percent. The median age in McKenzie County dropped from 28.2 in 1970 to 27.3 in 1980, while Mountrail and Williams counties saw reduced rates in the aging of their populations (Figure 4.8).

Regional changes in age and sex structure since 1950 are most evident during the most recent boom (2006 to 2014). For example, Williston grew by 91 percent between 2000 and 2016, driven primarily by a 276 percent increase in 20- to 29-year-olds and a 161 percent increase in 0- to 4-year-olds, likely the children of the 20- to 29-year-olds, and a 90 percent increase in 30- to 64-year-olds (Table 4.5). The core oil-producing counties all exhibited median ages greater than the state median between 1990 and 2010. According to Census Bureau estimates, McKenzie, Mountrail, and Williams counties fell to less than or equal to the state median by 2016 (Figure 4.8).

The male-to-female ratios for the period indicate that more men than women have moved to Williston in recent years in the 20- to 29-year-old and 30- to 64-year-old cohorts (Figure 4.7). For example, in the 20–29 age group there were 98 men per 100 women in 2000, increasing to 129 per 100 in 2016 (Figure 4.7). The 30–64 age group increased from 99 men per 100 women in 2000 to 133 per 100 in 2016 (Figure 4.7). Ratios are greater in Stanley, where most age groups went from less than 100 men per 100 women in 2000 to 2016 when all age cohorts were at more than 100 per 100 (Figure 4.9). The 2016 ratio for 20- to 29-year-olds in Stanley was more than 200 men per 100 women (Figure 4.9).

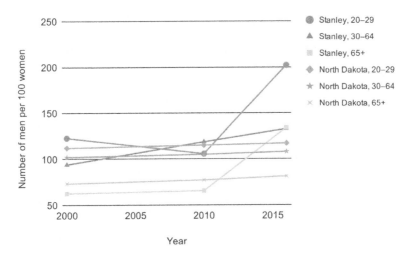

Figure 4.9. Number of men per 100 women for Stanley and the state of North Dakota since 2000 (source: U.S. Census Bureau 2010; U.S. Census Bureau, American Fact Finder 2016)

The percentage of both married men and married women declined between 2000 and 2016 in all four core oil-producing counties, with corresponding increases in the number of those who have never married (Table 4.6). For example, in McKenzie County the percentage of married men went from 61.7 percent in 2000 to 45.9 percent in 2016, suggesting that more than 70 percent of the 15+-year-old males added to the county's population between 2000 and 2016 were never married. To put that into perspective, there were 1,589 never-married men in McKenzie County in 2016 compared to 1,066 never-married-women (Table 4.6), or 149 never-married men per 100 never-married women.

In 2016, 9.5 percent of all people in North Dakota (10.0 percent of men and 9.1 percent of women) were divorced, numbers lower than those in most of the oil patch (Table 4.6). In most cases, the change in the percentage of those divorced increased by more than 2.5 percent between 2000 and 2016. Data for McKenzie County show 157 divorced men and 162 divorced women in 2000, rising to 455 divorced men and 389 divorced women in 2016. While some people arrived in the county already divorced, there has been an increase in the number of divorce filings: 136 during 2000, 155 during 2010, and 200 during 2016 (North Dakota Supreme Court 2018).

The most current statistics for the region compared to state averages (Table 4.7) indicate that people living there have higher median household incomes but also higher median home values and rent. Among residents of McKenzie and Williams counties, the proportion of people born in North Dakota is about 10 percent lower than the state average, while the proportion of those born in another U.S. state is higher (Table 4.7). The proportion of oil patch residents born outside of the United States is less than in the state as a whole (Table 4.7).

By far, most regional residents are white, but in some counties the proportion of American Indians is significant (Table 4.7). The percentage of people identifying as Hispanic or Latino of any race is higher in the four-county area than the state as a whole. The proportion of Black/African-American residents is low compared to the state as a whole, with the exception of Williams County (Table 4.7).

TABLE 4.7.
SELECTED SOCIO-ECONOMIC STATISTICS FOR CORE OIL-PRODUCING
COUNTIES, 2016 AND 2017
(SOURCES: U.S. CENSUS BUREAU 2016; AMERICAN COMMUNITY
SURVEY 2012–16; NORTH DAKOTA JOB SERVICE WORKFORCE INTEL-
LIGENCE NETWORK 2018)

	North Dakota	Dunn	McKenzie	Mountrail	Williams
Median household income[2]	$59,114	$66,964	$78,179	$68,082	$90,080
Median value of owner-occupied housing units[2]	$164,000	$162,700	$202,800	$161,400	$224,000
Median rent for occupied buildings paying rent[2]	$736	$900	$895	$723	$915

	North Dakota	Dunn	McKenzie	Mountrail	Williams
Mining, quarrying, and oil and gas extraction, 2017[3]					
Jobs	17,841	506	1,448	1,261	8,027
Percent of all jobs	4.3%	25.5%	16.0%	22.1%	30.0%
Average weekly wage for mining, quarrying, and oil and gas extraction, 2017[3]	$1,944	$1,929	$1,817	$1,914	$1,996
Average annual wage, all job types, 2017[3]	$50,313	$68,365	$70,987	$65,544	$74,287

PLACE OF BIRTH[2]

	North Dakota	Dunn	McKenzie	Mountrail	Williams
North Dakota	64.6%	61.0%	53.1%	68.8%	54.9%
Other U.S. state	32.1%	37.0%	46.1%	29.4%	42.2%
Outside of United States	3.3%	2.0%	0.9%	1.8%	2.9%

RACE[1]

	North Dakota	Dunn	McKenzie	Mountrail	Williams
White	87.9%	85.5%	83.0%	67.2%	87.3%
Black or African American	2.9%	1.0%	1.6%	1.1%	4.6%
American Indian or Alaska Native	5.5%	9.6%	11.9%	28.4%	3.8%
Asian	1.5%	1.5%	1.0%	0.3%	1.1%
Native Hawaiian or Other Pacific Islander	0.1%	0.0%	0.0%	0.0%	0.1%
Other Race or Two or More Races	2.1%	2.5%	2.6%	3.0%	3.3%
Hispanic or Latino (of any race)	3.6%	4.9%	7.8%	7.2%	6.8%

[1] U.S. Census Bureau (2016)
[2] American Community Survey (2012–16)
[3] North Dakota Job Service Workforce Intelligence Network (2018)

Environmental Impacts

The development of oil in the Bakken and other formations requires hydraulic fracturing to increase the permeability of the formations and the ability to remove oil. Water, proppant (sand or other granular material), and chemicals are pumped down a well under high pressure to fracture the formation, and to hold open the fractures to allow for oil or gas to flow more readily through the system (Haines et al. 2017). The amount of water required for fracturing in the Bakken in North Dakota has increased from 770 million gallons in 2008 to 4,274 million in 2012 (Shrestha et al. 2017), and will continue to increase with each additional well that is drilled and developed. Estimates of water requirements for hydraulic fracturing of wells show that from 2.5 million to 6.0 million gallons of water are required for each well (Table 4.8). This is no small impact for an area of limited precipitation, surface water, and ground water resources. Currently, most of the water used in well development is coming from the Missouri River or ground water (Shrestha et al. 2017).

TABLE 4.8.
VALUE ESTIMATES FOR WATER AND PROPPANT USE FOR OIL WELL
DEVELOPMENT IN THE BAKKEN
(SOURCE: HAINES ET AL. 2017)

Input Value	Minimum	Mode	Maximum	Mean
Water per well for hydraulic fracturing (million gallons)	2.5	4.0	6.0	4.17
Proppant (sand, granular material) to water ratio (lb/gal)	1.0	1.2	1.5	1.2
Water per well for drilling and cement (million gallons)	0.10	0.15	0.20	0.15

One of the byproducts of hydraulic fracturing, well development, and petroleum extraction is brine water. Brine water has high concentrations of ions such as chloride, bromide, and sodium and other toxic elements that make it unsuitable for use for agriculture or drinking water (Lauer, Harkness, and

Vengosh 2016; Shrestha et al. 2017). This water must be reinjected to keep it from contaminating local surface water and ground water sources. The brine water is often transported to the injection sites via pipelines. As drilling has increased, so has the number of brine spills within North Dakota, from about 200 in 2007 to more than 800 in 2014 (Shrestha et al. 2017). Brine spill data for the four counties of the study area indicate a maximum spill amount of 96,835 barrels in 2015 (Figure 4.10). The 2015 data includes a 70,000 barrel release of brine water into Blacktail Creek in Williams County in January (Lauer, Harkness, and Vengosh 2016).

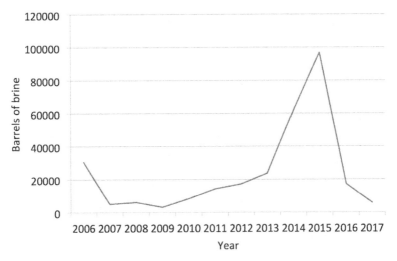

Figure 4.10. Contained and uncontained brine water spills in Dunn, McKenzie, Mountrail, and Williams counties (source: North Dakota Department of Health 2018)

Oil spill amounts have also increased as production and the number of wells have increased. The year 2013 had the highest amount of spillage within the study area at 32,602 barrels (Figure 4.11). There was an oil spill of more than 20,000 barrels in October 2013 from a pipeline rupture near Columbus in Burke County, North Dakota, just north of Mountrail County, that has been identified as the "largest oil spill on U.S. soil" (Golgowski 2013). Oil spills have also been associated with rail derailments, since up to 75 percent of all North Dakota Bakken production in 2013 was delivered by rail to Canada, the eastern United States, and the Gulf Coast (Reed 2013). At least 47 people were killed in the town of Lac-Mégantic, Quebec, when 72 tanker cars of Bakken crude derailed and ignited (Reed 2013). Numerous other explosive derailments of

Bakken crude have resulted in inquiries regarding the volatility of the oil and the safety of tanker cars being used in both the United States and Canada (Reed 2013; Thomas 2015).

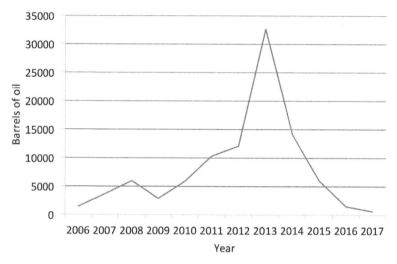

Figure 4.11. Oil spill volumes by year in Dunn, McKenzie, Mountrail, and Williams counties (contained and uncontained) (source: North Dakota Department of Health 2018)

Major Conclusions

The review of the geographic setting of petroleum production in western North Dakota shows several conclusions and differences when compared to the 1950s as documented by the 1958 *Report*. First, oil production has switched to the Bakken Formation starting in the 1980s, with much higher production rates and number of wells. Just over 1,214 petroleum wells were present as of 1958 in the western part of North Dakota, whereas in 2016, there were more than 14,000. Oil production was at almost 18 million barrels for the state in 1958, and more than 380 million barrels in 2016. Second, oil production has greatly expanded from a 5-mile by 35-mile area in Williams and Mountrail counties in 1958 to oil fields covering most of Williams, Mountrail, McKenzie and Dunn counties in 2016, including production within the major cities of Williston, Stanley, and Watford City. This in turn has greatly increased the number and length of oil service roads throughout the region compared to 1958. Third, climatic factors of precipitation and temperature have become more variable since the 1950s. The mean January temperature for Williston in the 1950s was 9.3°F and 70.2°F in July. The mean January temperature for Williston from 2010 to 2017 was 14.4°F and 71.8°F in July. Precipitation mean values for the 2010 to 2017 period in Williston were also slightly higher at 15.70 inches than the 1950s mean of 14.40 inches. Fourth, population demographics for the 2010s are different from the 1950s. Williston experienced a 62 percent increase in population from 2000 to 2010, and Stanley experienced 68 percent growth during this same period. The disparity between the number of men versus women also was greater in this period, with 129 men per 100 women in the 20–29-year-old range in 2016, and 133 men per 100 women in the age group of 30 to 64. The number of married men and women declined from 2000 to 2016. Finally, Wills's chapter in the 1958 *Report* concludes that a decline in construction and oil field activities had occurred by 1955. Current oil field and construction activities in the study area in 2019 have also constricted since the major drilling and oil field developments in 2014–15. Many infrastructure projects such as new roads, hospitals and schools have been completed, and the oil development has matured. The completion of new pipelines such as the Dakota Access Pipeline have reduced the need for transportation of crude via train or truck.

In summary, the discovery of oil in the Bakken region of North Dakota in 1951 heralded boom-to-bust cycles that were heavily influenced by global geopolitics and economics. Drivers of landscape and demographic change that are largely outside of the control of the state and region have confronted the area's longer-term residents with change so rapid and at such magnitude that carefully planned responses were often not possible, especially during the most recent boom. On top of significant demographic shifts, the landscape of the region has been altered dramatically, most notably through the losses of agricultural and range lands to land covers associated with oil production. In addition, the weather of the region has been more variable in recent years when compared to the historical record. It's fair to say that all of these phenomena have resulted in a general sense of uncertainty for the future of the region.

References

Abarghani, A., M. Ostadhassan, T. Gentzis, H. Carvajal-Ortiz, and B. Bubach. 2018. "Organofacies Study of the Bakken Source Rock in North Dakota, USA, Based on Organic Petrology And Geochemistry." *International Journal of Coal Geology* 188: 79–93.

Bluemle, J.P. 2000. *The Face of North Dakota*. Bismarck, ND: North Dakota Geological Survey.

Bluemle, J.P. 2001. *The 50th Anniversary of the Discovery of Oil in North Dakota*. Miscellaneous Series No. 89. Bismarck, ND: North Dakota Geological Survey.

Bryce, S.A., J.M. Omernik, D.E. Pater, M. Ulmer, J. Schaar, J. Freeouf, R. Johnson, P. Kuck, and S.H. Azevedo. 1998. "Ecoregions of North Dakota and South Dakota." In *U.S. Geological Survey* [database online]. Jamestown, ND: Northern Prairie Wildlife Research Center Online. https://store.usgs.gov/assets/MOD/StoreFiles/Ecoregion/21629_nd_sd_front.pdf.

Fenneman, N.M. 1931. *Physiography of Western United States*. New York: McGraw-Hill.

Gaswirth, S.B., and K.R. Marra. 2015. "U.S. Geological Survey 2013 Assessment of Undiscovered Resources in the Bakken and Three Forks Formations of the U.S. Williston Basin Province." *AAPG Bulletin* 99: 639–60.

Geiger, R. 1954. "Klassifikation der Klimate nach W. Köppen (Classification of climates after W. Köppen)." In *Zahlenwerte und Funktionen aus Physik, Chemie, Astronomie, Geophysik und Technik (alte Serie)*, edited by Landolt-Börnstein, 603–7. Berlin: Springer.

Geiger, R. 1961. *Köppen-Geiger/Klima der Erde* [map]. Gotha: Klett-Perthes.

Gerhard, L.C., S.B. Anderson, J.A. LeFever, and C.G. Carlson. 1982. "Geological Development, Origin, and Energy Mineral Resources of Williston Basin, North Dakota." *American Association of Petroleum Geologists Bulletin* 66: 989–1020.

Gibson, R.I. 1995. "Basement Techtonics and Hydrocarbon Production in the Williston Basin: An Interpretive Overview." In *1995 Guidebook: Seventh International Williston Basin Symposium*, edited by L.D.V. Hunter and R.A. Schalla, 3–9. Billings, MT: Montana Geological Society.

Golgowski, N. 2013. "North Dakota Farmer Discovers Largest Oil Spill on U.S. Soil in the Middle of His Wheat Field." *New York Daily News*, October 16. http://www.nydailynews.com/news/national/farmer-field-largest-oil-spill-u-s-soil-article-1.1487225.

Haines, S.S., B.A. Varela, S.J. Hawkins, N.J. Gianoutsos, J.N. Thamke, M.A. Engle, M.E. Tennyson, C.J. Schenk, S.B. Gaswirth, K.R. Marra, S.A. Kinney, T.J. Mercier, and C.D. Martinez. 2017. "Assessment of Water and Proppant Quantities Associated with Petroleum Production from the Bakken and Three Forks Formations, Williston Basin Province, Montana and North Dakota, 2016." *United States Geological Survey Fact Sheet* 2017-3044. https://doi.org/10.3133/fs20173044.

Hao, Q., L.I. Lintao, Y. Zuo, W. Chen, W.U. Lei, and Y.I. Junjie. 2018. "Petroleum Distribution Characteristics of the Americas and the Exploration Prospect Analysis." *Acta Geologica Sinica* 92: 378–93.

Hidy, R.W., M.E. Hidy, R.V. Scott, and D.L. Hofsommer, eds. 1988. *The Great Northern Railway: A History*. Boston: Harvard Business School Press.

Köppen, W. 1918. "Klassifikation der Klimate nach Temperatur, Niederschlag und Jahresablauf (Classification of climates according to temperature, precipitation and seasonal cycle)." *Dr. A. Petermanns Mittelungen Aus Justus Perthes' Geographischer Anstalt* 64: 193–203 and 243–8.

Kottek, M., J. Grieser, C. Beck, B. Rudolf, and F. Rubel. 2006. "World Map of the Köppen-Geiger Climate Classification Updated." *Meteoroogische Zeitschrift* 15 (3): 259–63.

Lauer, N. E., J. S. Harkness, and A. Vengosh. 2016. "Brine Spills Associated with Unconventional Oil Development in North Dakota." *Environmental Science and Technology* 50: 5389–97.

Lefever, J.A., C.D. Martiniuk, E.F.R. Dancsok, and P.A. Mahnic. 1991. "Petroleum Potential of the Middle Member, Bakken Formation, Williston Basin." *AAPG Bulletin* 76: 11–21.

Meyer, R.W. 1977. *The Village Indians of the Upper Missouri: The Mandans, Hidatsas, and Arikaras*. Lincoln: University of Nebraska Press.

National Agricultural Statistics Service. 2017. "North Dakota Agricultural Statistics." https://www.nass.usda.gov/Statistics_by_State/North_Dakota/Publications/Annual_Statistical_Bulletin/2017/ND%202017%20Annual%20Bulletin.pdf.

NOAA (National Oceanic and Atmospheric Administration). 2018. "NOWData—NOAA Online Weather Data." http://w2.weather.gov/climate/xmacis.php?wfo=bis.

North Dakota Geological Survey. 2000. "Overview of the Petroleum Geology of the North Dakota Williston Basin." In *North Dakota Geological Survey* [database]. https://www.dmr.nd.gov/ndgs/.

North Dakota Job Service. 2018. "Workforce Intelligence Network." https://www.ndworkforceintelligence.com/.

North Dakota Oil and Gas Division. 2018. "North Dakota Drilling and Production Statistics." https://www.dmr.nd.gov/oilgas/stats/statisticsvw.asp.

North Dakota Public Service Commission. 2018. "North Dakota Rail Abandonments." https://psc.nd.gov/docs/consinfo/railroad/rail-abandonments.pdf.

North Dakota State Historical Society. 2018. "Trenton Indian Service Area." https://www.ndstudies.gov/tm-trenton-indian-service-area.

North Dakota Supreme Court. 2018. "North Dakota Courts Records Inquiry." http://publicsearch.ndcourts.gov/default.aspx.

Parker, A.K. 2011. "Taken Lands: Territory and Sovereignty of the Fort Berthold Indian Reservation, 1934–1960." PhD diss., University of Michigan.

Preston, T.M., and K. Kim. 2016. "Land Cover Changes Associated with Recent Energy Development in the Williston Basin, Northern Great Plains, USA." *Science of the Total Environment* 566–7: 1511–18.

Rand, McNally and Co. 1911. North Dakota Railroads [map]. *Rand McNally Commercial Atlas of America*. Chicago: Rand, McNally and Co.

Rand, McNally and Co. 1942. Popular Map of North Dakota [map]. Chicago: Rand, McNally and Co. http://www.ghostsofnorthdakota.com/wp-content/uploads/2016/02/1942-map-2000px.jpg.

Reed, M. 2013. "Runaway Train Calamity Underscores Crude-by-rail Concerns." *Pipeline and Gas Journal* 240: 48.

Robinson, E.B. 1966. *History of North Dakota*. Lincoln: University of Nebraska Press.

Schmoker, J. W. 1996. "A Resource Evaluation of the Bakken Formation (Upper Devonian and Lower Mississippian) Continuous Oil Accumulation, Williston Basin, North Dakota and Montana." *Mountain Geologist* 33: 1–10.

Sherman, W.C., and P.V. Thorson, eds. 1988. *Plains Folk: North Dakota's Ethnic History*. Fargo: North Dakota Institute for Regional Studies.

Shrestha, N., G. Chilkoor, J. Wilder, V. Gadhamshetty, and J.J. Stone. 2017. "Potential Water Resource Impacts of Hydraulic Fracturing from

Unconventional Oil Production in the Bakken Shale." *Water Research* 108: 1–24.

Smith, M.G., and R.M. Bustin. 1995. "Sedimentology of the Late Devonian and Early Mississippian Bakken Formation, Williston Basin." In *7th Annual International Williston Basin Symposium 1995 Guidebook*, ed. L.D.V. Hunter and R.A. Schalla, 103–14. Billings: Montana Geological Society.

Sonnenberg, S. A., and A. Pramudito. 2009. "Petroleum Geology of the Giant Elm Coulee Field, Williston Basin." *AAPG Bulletin* 93: 1127–53.

Taft, S.S. 2017. "Three Affiliated Tribes 2017 Enrollment Summary." https://static1.squarespace.com/static/5a5fab0832601e33d9f68f-de/t/5a98103071c10b8e2fcb662b/1519915058846/2017+Enroll-ment+Report.pdf.

Thomas, D. 2015. "Oil Train Wrecks Spotlight Tank Car Limits—and Dilbit's Dangers. (Update)." *Railway Age* 216: 10.

Torgerson, E. 2017. "Oil Infrastructure Development and Resulting Land-Cover Change in McKenzie County, North Dakota, 2009–2014." MS thesis, University of North Dakota.

U.S. Bureau of the Census, 1927. *U.S. Census of Agriculture 1925. Volume 1, Part 18: North Dakota.* Washington, DC: U.S. Government Printing Office.

U.S. Bureau of the Census. 1941. *16th Census of the United States, 1940. Number of Inhabitants. North Dakota.* Washington, DC: U.S. Government Printing Office.

U.S. Bureau of the Census. 1951. *U.S. Census of Population, 1950. Number of Inhabitants. North Dakota: Totals for Cities, Small Areas, Counties, Urban & Rural.* Washington, DC: U.S. Government Printing Office.

U.S. Bureau of the Census, 1952. *U.S. Census of Agriculture 1950. Volume 1, Part 11: North Dakota and South Dakota.* Washington, DC: U.S. Government Printing Office.

U.S. Bureau of the Census. 1962. *U.S. Census of Population, 1960. Detailed Characteristics, North Dakota.* Washington, DC: U.S. Government Printing Office.

U.S. Bureau of the Census. 1973. *1970 Census of Population: Volume 1: Part 36: Characteristics of the Population.* Washington, DC: U.S. Government Printing Office.

U.S. Bureau of the Census. 1982a. *1980 Census of Population: Volume 1: Part 36: Characteristics of the Population*. Washington, DC: U.S. Government Printing Office.

U.S. Bureau of the Census, 1982b. *1982 Census of Agriculture. Volume 1, Part 34: North Dakota*. Washington, DC: U.S. Department of Commerce.

U.S. Bureau of the Census. 1992. *1990 Census of Population: General Population Characteristics. North Dakota*. Washington, DC: U.S. Government Printing Office.

U.S. Census Bureau. 2000. *Census 2000: Census of Population and Housing. North Dakota*. Washington, DC: U.S. Department of Commerce, Economics and Statistics Administration, Bureau of the Census.

U.S. Census Bureau. 2010. *North Dakota, 2010. Summary Population and Housing Characteristics: 2010 Census of Population and Housing*. Washington, DC: U.S. Department of Commerce, Economics and Statistics Administration, U.S. Census Bureau.

U.S. Census Bureau, American Fact Finder. 2016. *2012–2016 American Community Survey*. https://factfinder.census.gov/.

U.S. Department of Agriculture, National Agricultural Statistics Service. 2014. *2012 Census of Agriculture. Volume 1, Part 34: North Dakota*. Washington, DC: U.S. Department of Agriculture.

Wick, D.A. 1999. *North Dakota Place Names*. Bismarck, ND: Sweetgrass Publications.

Zamiran, S., S. Rafieepour, and M. Ostadhassan. 2018. "A Geomechanical Study of Bakken Formation Considering the Anisotropic Behavior of Shale Layers." *Journal of Petroleum Science and Engineering* 165: 567–74.

Chapter 5
Political Impact

1958   *Ross B. Talbot*

I. Introduction: Scope, Method, and Limitations

Just what politics are; where they begin; where do, and should they end, have been questions of endless controversy over ages of time. If we can believe Lucy Stark—the courageous but bewildered wife of Willie Stark in Robert Penn Warren's *All the King's Men*[1]—politics eventually entwines itself in every phase of human affairs, even the most private. But this study of the politics of oil in the Williston Basin is vastly more limited in scope than that. Essentially it will attempt to do four things— show how oil has caused the formation of new political associations and modified existing ones; describe the impact of oil upon existing units of government; explain the formation and execution of oil policy; and analyze the effects of oil upon the existing political power structure. In all instances the description and analysis is necessarily somewhat general.

This is not the place to enter into a controversy about empiricism versus values, but basically this study is empirical. It may proceed somewhat contrary to accepted scientific method as no hypotheses will be advanced except during the last two sections of this chapter. Consequently much of the study is descriptive. This is admittedly a somewhat "safer" method for the social scientist but it has advantages. In a relatively unexplored field, description is necessary in order to provide an adequate frame of reference. Subsequently, it is then possible to be analytical in a more meaningful manner.

Lastly, it must be understood that the writer is not a physical scientist and not a student in the technology of oil. Many of the issues to be discussed in this chapter—well spacing, compulsory unitization, and other geological and geophysical issues—are well beyond the technical competence of the social scientist. Where such matters remain in the

---

[1] Robert Penn Warren, *All the King's Men* (New York: Harcourt, Brace, and Co., 1946), p. 355.

physical realm an attempt will be made to describe, in general terms, the conflicting attitudes, coupled with some information on the actions of other states in comparable matters. However, where these issues enter into the governmental process the discussion will be more analytical. This dichotomy between the areas of the responsibility of the physical and social scientists is difficult to define, and just as difficult to abide by, but a careful attempt will be made not to make judgments where no empirical evidence is advanced, and not to tread in technical fields of knowledge where the author has no competence.

II. A Brief Survey of North Dakota Politics and Government

The North Dakota political scene has some unique features of its own, so a brief, general statement seems necessary at this point.

Since joining the Union, North Dakota has been a one-party state. That one political party—in this instance the Republican party—has practically dominated the politics of the state. In only two instances since the turn of the century have Democrats been elected to the office of governor[2] and both times that was with the considerable aid of dissident Republican elements. In the 1955 session of the State Legislature the Democrats had four of its party candidates elected to the Senate and that was such an extraordinary event that the members actually caucussed once.

As almost invariably true in one-party states, the primary election is the "real" election. Candidates in the Republican column who are nominated in the June primary are almost always elected in the November general election. Furthermore, and as usually is the case, the dominant party is divided into factions. In North Dakota the two principal factions of the Republican party have been the Non-Partisan League (NPL) and the Republican Organizing Committee (ROC). In one form or another, this division has existed in North Dakota politics since the formation of the NPL in 1915. Some names of organizations have changed; leadership dominates, then wanes; but the basic division seems to continue. However, and this is where oil politics presently plays a role and may play a more important one, there are many and varied forms of political discontent in North Dakota at the present time. The NPL split into what might conventionally be termed liberal and conservative factions;[3] the ROC is divided into those who want to

---

[2] John Burke, 1907–1912 and John Moses, 1939–1944.

[3] The terms "radical," "liberal," and "conservative" are used herein to denote the degree of social, economic, and political changes that are desired. That is, the conservatives favor the status quo, or very cautious change, etc. In no instance

dissolve the factions and amalgamate into a single Republican party and those who are quite satisfied with the status quo; the Democratic party is largely controlled by conservatives who are not very dynamic in their party activities, but a younger, energetic, liberal group is actively attempting to gain control; there is a small, but powerful, group in the State Senate who consider themselves to be "genuine" Republicans and these individuals are seeking to erase the factionalism within the Republican party if it will enhance their interests.

To further complicate the political scene, the North Dakota Farmers Union has, since 1947, played a forceful, albeit somewhat erratic, role in state politics. Political associations—more commonly termed "pressure groups" or "interest groups"—are exceedingly common and often immensely powerful in the American political scene, but the Farmers Union is somewhat unique.[4] North Dakota is the most predominantly agrarian state in the United States and, in 1954, the Farmers Union had 42,233 dues-paying members out of a total population—21 years and over (1950)—of 366,590. Numerically, the Farmers Union is the largest pressure group in North Dakota and generally conceded to be by far the most effectively organized. As will be discussed later, this organization is definitely involved in the oil politics of the state. Its position is sometimes rather ambiguous and unpredictable but this is probably due to an ironic sequence of events. The strength of the Farmers Union is west of the Red River Valley and it is very powerful in the Williston Basin area. However, its left to left-of-center ideology has been somewhat rebuked, where oil legislation is involved, by farmers who have oil on their land or, more importantly, are certain that they will have.

Another feature of the North Dakota political scene which impressed this author during his research was the amount of intra-state sectionalism in North Dakota politics. This phenomenon seems more apparent in western North Dakota than elsewhere. There seems to prevail an attitude, notably among the political leaders, that political strategy must be based to an important degree upon their own sectional interests. Political alignments and re-alignments are often discussed in just those terms. Here, again, we shall see the impact of oil politics.

The governmental system of North Dakota—state, city, county, and special districts—is not particularly different from the national

---

are the terms used in the sense of being anti-democratic. See Clinton Rossiter, *Conservatism in America* (New York: Alfred A. Knopf, Inc., 1955), passim, but especially his introduction wherein these terms are more strictly defined.

[4] The North Dakota Farm Bureau is a new and growing organization in the state—10,196 members in 1954—but its strength in the Williston Basin area is negligible.

political pattern. However, a brief description of one feature of the state government is necessary due to its impact upon oil politics. The theory of separation of powers, coupled with a system of checks and balances, has been carried to such lengths in North Dakota that many of the state executive officers constitute what has been termed, in another instance, "the headless fourth branch of government." That is, many heads of departments and commissions are elected and thereby not constitutionally responsible to the governor, or are selected in such manner that executive responsibility becomes most difficult. This diffusion of political authority and responsibility has, as will be explained later, been an important factor in the development of oil policy, and its subsequent administration.

III. Oil and the Legislative Process

Oil was discovered in North Dakota not long after the adjournment of the 1951 Session. This meant that no action would be taken on the development of new oil policies until early 1953, unless the governor decided to call a special session. The issue was not terribly and immediately pressing. There was already in the North Dakota statutes a 1941 law providing for the regulation of the production and conservation of oil but it was apparent that 1953 would be a crucial year. Important questions had to be acted on—taxes, well-spacing, administrative authority, conservation practices, etc. The political factions began to sound about as political observers predicted, with the latter basing their judgments on historical observations. The ROC desired a low tax in order to foster, from their viewpoint, an "infant" industry and thereby attract more capital into North Dakota. The NPL was in a dilemma. The oil companies were, to some NPL legislators, predatory interlopers, but to those who represented the areas where oil was flowing, or likely to be, the issue was not so simple. An economic basis of politics quickly manifested itself in the form of a "pork chopper" attitude and the radicalism of some of the NPL'ers subsided rather considerably, particularly in regards to oil taxes.

The Formation of New Pressure Groups

As would be expected, oil brought into formation new pressure groups. Of these, the most powerful are the North Dakota Oil and Gas Association (hereafter NDOGA) and the Williams County Land Owners and Royalty Owners Association (WCLOA). Newer, and of less influence thus far, are the Tioga Land Owners Association, the North Dakota

Independent Producers and Royalty Owners Association, and the McKenzie County Mineral Owners Association.

The NDOGA was formally organized in Bismarck, North Dakota, on August 21, 1952.[5] It is an unincorporated, non-profit association and designed to assist in the discovery, production, development, and conservation of oil and gas in the state. Membership is restricted to corporations, partnerships, or associations who are engaged in any phase of the oil industry. Membership is $25.00 per year and each represented enterprise is restricted to one vote, although it may purchase any number of memberships for its officers and employees. At an annual convention, a Board of Directors composed of 40 members is elected. After receiving the nominations of a Nominating Committee, the Board selects the executive officers, including the President; the President then appoints a ten-person Executive Committee with the advice and consent of the Board. The office staff is a full-time Executive Secretary and a clerk-typist, although, during the legislative sessions, lobbyists are employed to represent the organization.[6] By the summer of 1955 the NDOGA had 400 members and this included practically all the major oil producers in the United States, as well as representatives of other phases of the oil industry, and officers from most of the major banks in Williston, Bismarck, Minot, and Jamestown. Besides attempting to influence the formation and administration of oil policy the organization conducts a public relations campaign aimed at the general public and its own members. A monthly *News Letter* is rather extensively distributed; the *Proration Schedules and Oil Production Reports* of the State Industrial Commission are disseminated to the NDOGA members, as are other pertinent and important publications. Oil displays are organized and displayed at fairs, conventions, and other such gatherings throughout the state.

The Williams County Land Owners and Royalty Owners Association was formed as a counteracting influence to the NDOGA and creates what David Truman has termed a "competing claim" relative to the latter organization.[7] In the opinion of the WCLOA the other interest group represents the "majors" (the large oil companies) and thereby, in some instances, the NDOGA overlooks, or disregards, the interests of the owner of the land on which oil is, or may be, produced.

---

[5] North Dakota Oil and Gas Association, *Articles Association and By-Laws,* dated August 21, 1952.

[6] Five persons registered with the Secretary of State during the 1955 legislative session as lobbyists for the NDOGA.

[7] David Truman, *The Government Process* (New York: Alfred A. Knopf, Inc., 1951), p. 150 and passim.

From all appearances the WCLOA is not nearly as well organized or administered as the NDOGA. Membership is $5.00 year and apparently there have been as many as 400–500 members. However, the records were not available to the writer. Annual meetings are held; a seven-person board is elected; and, since the origin of the WCLOA, Mr. Iver Solberg, State Senator from Williams County and a farmer-landowner near Ray, has been its President. To some extent the seemingly rather inefficient operation of the WCLOA is due to its limited objectives. Apparently the principal, if not the sole, purpose of the organization is to fight the major oil companies on the spacing issue. This controversy will be elaborated on later in this chapter.

Oil and the North Dakota Legislative Research Center

The North Dakota Senate had in 1951, by the passage of Senate Resolution 6, instructed the Legislative Research Committee to study and make recommendations to the next legislature relative to the issue of the development, taxation, and conservation of oil, along with other resources.[8] This Committee is comprised of six members of the House, five from the Senate. Since its inception in 1945 it has been used extensively and effectively for the study of problems which are usually important but contentious. The full Committee generally appoints a sub-committee to make the actual study. In this instance two Senators—Mr. Clyde Duffy and Mr. Iver Solberg, along with one Representative—Mr. R.H. Lynch—constituted the sub-committee. Three public hearings were held—two in Bismarck and the other in Williston; advice and material were secured from the Interstate Oil Compact Commission; Dr. Wilson Laird, State Geologist, made an on-the-spot study of oil regulations and administration in some of the major oil producing states; and the Research Director, Mr. C. Emerson Murry, along with members of the sub-committee, drafted 13 legislative measures concerned with oil. Several of the proposed bills need not concern us here but it is necessary to note the principal features of the proposed bill for the taxation of gas and oil:

1. A gross production tax was recommended rather than an ad valorem tax. The latter would have been very difficult to administer as accurate assessment of unproduced oil is hazardous, if not impossible.

---

[8] State of North Dakota, *Report the North Dakota Legislative Research Committee, 33rd Legislative Assembly*, 1953, pp. 39, 43.

2. The tax rate was set at 4¼%—4% on the value of the oil when produced and the ¼% for costs of administering the regulatory program, although this latter amount was not to be ear-marked but to go into the State's General Fund.

3. The oil tax revenues, excluding the one-quarter per cent, were to be allocated as follows:

   a. of the first $200,000 in tax revenues, 75% to the county where the oil was produced and 25% into the state's general fund.

   b. for the next $200,000 the recommended allocation was 50-50.

   c. thereafter the state was to be allocated 75% and the county 25%.

The full committee reported out this tax bill with unanimous agreement. It had drafted a bill which, in the opinion of the Committee, protected the interests of the state and local governmental units but at the same time did not discourage the oil producers from a rapid and efficient development of oil resources. A gross production tax rate of 5% was proposed but it was finally lowered one notch to encourage the oil producers to drill with full speed.[9] Also, the bill provided for no exemptions from property taxes except for the permanent equipment of the well-site and the oil itself.

The allocation of tax revenues was also debated. The system of redistribution seemed to favor the oil producing counties more than was true in other states (for example, in Oklahoma the ratio is 80-20 in favor of the state). However, Senator Solberg, who represented Williams County in the Senate, believed that the real property tax base would not increase rapidly enough to provide the increased revenue that would be needed for roads, schools, etc. His position prevailed.

The Committee adopted, essentially, the "model" oil and gas conservation bill that had been drafted by the Interstate Oil Compact Commission.[10] This proposed regulatory act grants considerable authority to the state agency that is responsible for its administration. However, the Committee did not include the compulsory, field-wide unitization feature of the model act—in substance, this permits, under certain circumstances, an oil field to be operated as a single unit under

---

[9] North Dakota's gross production tax is, at 4¼%, higher than most other states. See *Interstate Oil Compact Commission, Gross Production and Severance Taxes Imposed by Various States* (Oklahoma City, Oklahoma, no date).

[10] Interstate Oil Compact Commission, *A Form For an Oil and Gas Conservation Statute* (Oklahoma City, 1950), 33 pages.

a single operator—but it did provide for voluntary unitization and also included provisions for the determination of market demand and the regulation of oil production.

The Alignment of Political Forces of the 1953 Session

A brief account of the confusion and delay in organizing both houses of the State Legislature needs to be included herein as the outcome had a considerable impact on the subsequent oil legislation.

In the Senate, no faction had a clear majority. There were 49 senators. The ROC controlled 24 votes; the NPL had 21. There were three dissident Republicans—Carroll Day, Franklin Page, and Kenneth Pyle—and there was a solitary Democrat, Mrs. Harry O'Brien. The ROC could have organized the Senate with one more vote, but, for reasons that need not be advanced in this study, the ROC chose not to invite any of the four to its caucus. After some consternation and delay it was agreed between the NPL and the four that they would form a coalition, with R.M. Streibel as majority floor leader, and organize the Senate. This was done and the coalition never split its vote, that is, not on issues that had been previously decided upon in caucus, except on the gross oil production tax bill.

Organizing the House was hardly less confusing. Briefly, the NPL had a clear majority but its intra-factional split was becoming more and more obvious. When the House NPL members caucussed for Speaker of the House, Mr. Halvor Rolfsrud was nominated. However, Rolfsrud represented the insurgent element of the NPL. The "Old Guard" group was determined not to be thwarted so its leaders entered into an agreement with the House ROC members to support Walter Bubel, an "Old Guard" Leaguer, as Speaker. This idea prevailed and when the vote was counted in the House it was 69 for Bubel, 40 for Rolfsrud, three passed and one did not vote.[11] Thus, the coalition of ROC—Old Guard Leaguers controlled the House during the 1953 session.

The "ifs" of history are usually interesting, albeit perhaps useless, but a different legislative organization would almost certainly have produced different oil legislation.

---

[11] State of North Dakota, *Journal the House*, Thirty Third Session of the Legislative Assembly (Bismarck, Bismarck Tribune, 1953), pp. 6–10.

The Enactment of Oil Legislation at the 1953 Session

There was very little doubt in any politician's mind that oil was to be a, if not the, major political issue at the 1953 legislature session. It also seemed reasonably clear that the usual political compromises would have to be made. The ROC was rather definitely committed to a low oil tax in order, from its point of view, to aid the growth and development of an oil industry in North Dakota.[12] The insurgent NPL'ers believed that large capital investors, nearly all of them from out-of-state, were moving into North Dakota to exploit a natural resource which actually, according to their "picture"—to use Lippmann's term—belonged to all the people of the state. There were other conceptions of course, and of those two just stated, some legislators probably used them as rationalizations in order to disguise their own self-interest. Also, an oil tax makes an excellent political issue in the sense of personal popularity and prestige and this factor can never be overlooked in understanding the political process in a democracy.

The Legislative Research Committee's gross oil production tax bill was introduced on January 16, 1953, became Senate Bill Number 41, and was sent to the Committee on Finance and Taxation.[13] Forty-four days later (February 8, 1953) the bill emerged "without recommendation"

---

[12] The word "low" is somewhat of a value term as used in this sentence. The ROC considered the tax to be "moderate."

[13] It is not considered necessary to document very extensively this account of legislative action on oil measures. The printed sources are the *Grand Forks Herald* and, to lesser extent, the Fargo *Forum*, Bismarck *Tribune*, Williston *Herald*, Non Partisan League *Leader*, North Dakota *Union Farmer*, and the official House and Senate *Journals*. Also, the author would like to acknowledge some of the persons whom he interviewed on this subject of oil legislation. Their assistance was cordially granted and most helpful. They were: W. Davidson, Sr., President of the American State Bank in Williston; Carroll Day, State Senator from the 6th District in Grand Forks County and leader in the Senate Coalitions in 1953 and 1955; C. Emerson Murry, Director of the Legislative Research Committee; Iver Solberg, State Senator from Williams County; Harry Polk, publisher of the Williston *Herald*; Arley Bjella, attorney in Williston and member of the State ROC Executive Board; Arthur Link, former chairman of the McKenzie County Farmers Union and presently State Representative from the 41st District; James Key, chairman of the Democratic party in Williams County; Clair Amsberry, prominent Farmers Union member and Vice-Chairman of the Williams County Democratic party; and Walter Burk, Williston attorney who is acting Secretary for the Williams County Land Owner's and Royalty Owner's Association and President of the Upper Missouri Development Association. Many other persons were very cooperative and generous with their time and information but in the field of oil politics the above named interviewees were of the most assistance.

for passage after the adoption of about two pages of amendments. The most vital change was the proposal of a 5¾% gross production tax with ½ of 1% for administration of the tax. While the bill was in Committee the lobbyists had been laboring diligently. Mr. C.E. Boone, a vice-president of Amerada Oil Corporation and a skilled lobbyist, maintained an office at Bismarck during all of the session. In his testimony before the Senate Finance Committee on January 27, he recommended a 3¼% gross oil production tax. Mr. William Pearce, a Bismarck attorney representing the NDOGA, declared any such tax to be unconstitutional as it taxed owners instead of property. Mr. Harold Pollman, lobbyist for the WCLOA, testified, on February 8, in favor of a 4¼% tax if the oil producers, including the landowners, were permitted a 27½% depletion allowance.[14] The position of the Farmers Union was somewhat ambiguous. At its 1951 State Convention, the Union had advocated a "moderate" severance tax on oil.[15] After Mr. Quentin Burdick, counsel for the North Dakota Farmers Union, had completed his trip through the oil states he wrote a series of articles for the *North Dakota Union Farmer* in the last of which he stated that "it is the writer's opinion, that in no event should the initial tax be less than 5%."[16] At the Senate hearings on S.B. 14, Burdick testified in favor of a 6, 7, or 8% gross production tax if there was to be a depletion allowance, but, apparently, not claiming then to represent the Farmers Union.[17] Mr. Alex Lind, a longtime North Dakota politician, principal lobbyist for the Farmers Union, a resident of Williston, and a landowner in Williams County, was a persistent advocate of a tax no higher than 4¼%. During this period, according to the late Senator Day, the Senate coalition group had caucussed and decided to push for a 6¼% tax reasoning that, in the opinion of the caucus, "The Standard Oil Company of Indiana could stand more tax."[18] In any respect the proposed amendments were voted

[14] In essence, depletion allowance permits the oil companies and other owners of mineral rights to deduct a certain percentage from their income tax, on the income received from oil, and be taxed only on the remainder. Federal law has such a provision but North Dakota, prior to 1953, did not. The theoretical justification for the depletion allowance is that the oil that is produced depletes the capital investment and consequently such a provision is necessary in order to attract more and adequate risk capital.

[15] North Dakota Farmers Union, *Policy and Action Program—1952* (Jamestown, 1952), p. 24.

[16] Burdick, op. cit. p. 16.

[17] Grand Forks *Herald*, February 13, 1955.

[18] Interview with Senator Day, July 1955. He also stated that there was some dissension within the Senate Coalition regarding the allocation of revenues

on the next day and adopted but not before Senator J.A. Bridston (5th District—Grand Forks County) had moved for a 4¼% tax.[19] However, Senator Gilman Klefstad (ROC) made a substitute motion for 5% and Bridston then withdrew his motion. The vote on the substitute motion was 24-25. The Coalition had not lost a vote. After the clincher motion was applied by Senator R.M. Streibel, S.B. 41 went to the House.[20] Political pressure continued to be applied. The Williston Junior Chamber of Commerce conducted a statewide newspaper advertising campaign favoring a 4¼% tax and a 27½% depletion allowance.

Then, on February 28, 250 western North Dakota farmers and businessmen "snake danced" through the Senate and House Chambers demonstrating in favor of a 4¼% tax.[21] Prior to that energetic procedure, this group had held a meeting with Mr. Harry Polk as chairman, in the Bismarck City Auditorium. Of the approximately 300 persons present, newspapermen estimated, from a show of hands, that about three-fourths of the demonstrators were farmers. There was counter-agitation on March 1st when 25 persons, primarily Farmers Union county and local officers from Burke and Divide Counties, attended a House hearing and advocated "at least 5¾%."[22] But, on March 3rd, the House Committee on Finance and Taxation voted out S.B. 41 with a recommended 4¼% tax, and the next day the vote on accepting the amendment was 70-41 in favor. Of the Representatives from Williams, Mountrail, and McKenzie Counties (at that time the "oil counties") only Mr. T.O. Rodhe of New Town voted against the lower tax, and on the vote for final passage, 81-14, Mr. Rodhe did not vote at all. Thus, if the Senate Coalition group refused to accept the lower tax, the bill would have to go to Conference Committee. At this juncture the oil lobbyists, led in this instance by W.S. Davidson, Sr., President of the American State Bank in Williston, threatened to file recall petitions against Senator Solberg unless he changed his vote. In fact, several interviewees stated that Davidson stood directly behind Solberg (the latter's Senate seat being right next to the outer rail) with recall petitions in hand while the vote was being taken. Solberg switched; the vote was 25-24

received from the tax but in order to obtain the support of Senator Solberg, and other "oil" Senators, it was decided not to disturb that feature of the bill.

[19] State of North Dakota, *Journal of the Senate*, 33rd Session (Bismarck; State Capitol, 1953), see Index, p. XIV.

[20] The purpose of the clincher motion is to make reconsideration of a bill more difficult.

[21] Grand Forks *Herald*, February 28, 1953. There is some question as to whether a "snake dance", or anything like it actually occurred.

[22] *Ibid.*, March 2, 1955.

in favor of the House Amendment; and the oil tax was to be 4¼%.[23] The ROC governor, C. Norman Brunsdale, was a leading advocate of the lower tax so a veto was not even considered a possibility. Senator Day, in an interview with the author in July, 1955, claimed that even Mr. C.E. Boone, after consulting his superiors in the Amerada Petroleum Corporation, had agreed to accept 5¼%. (He also made this statement at a talk given in the Spring of 1953 at the University of North Dakota.) Further, he claimed that at no time during the Senate hearings was there a single pressure group that was willing to support the 6¼% tax advocated by the Senate Coalition.

S.B. 41 was the "showdown" bill, so to speak, for all oil legislation and it proved to be the only instance in which the Coalition refused to abide by a decision made in its caucus.[24] On the issue of depletion allowances, Senators Clyde Duffy and Milton Rue introduced S.B. 89 and S.B. 203, respectively. Rue's bill was indefinitely postponed. The legislative process concerning S.B. 89 was rather comparable with S.B. 41. The bill was reported out of the Senate Committee on Finance and Taxation with a "do pass" recommendation for a 27½% depletion allowance. Senator Streibel moved to change it to 25% and his motion passed. After Senator Rue attempted to rescind the change, and failed, S.B. 89 passed the Senate by 49-0. Then the House changed the bill back to 27½%. On March 3rd, the Senate concurred again by a vote of 25-24 as Senator Solberg switched his vote although Senators Hagen and Olson continued to vote with the Coalition. However, Senator Day insisted that the Coalition group decided not to make a concerted fight for the lower depletion allowance.

S.B. 32 was the "model" oil and gas conservation bill. Although an extremely important and potent piece of legislation it did not encounter any considerable difficulties in either House. As stated earlier in this chapter, the compulsory unitization feature was deleted but oil lobbyists appearing before the Legislative Research Committee were agreeable to voluntary unitization. The Committee on Natural Resources in both Houses made only minor changes. In the Senate hearings on the bill, Mr. Harold Pollman and Mr. Milton Higgins testified in favor of including a 40 acre spacing provision in the law. Dr. Wilson Laird, State Geologist, testified to the contrary, that is, he advocated that the

---

[23] Senator Orville Hagen of McKenzie County and Senator Axel Olson of Mountrail County stayed with the Coalition on the 25-24 vote, but on the vote for final passage of the amended bill, 28-21, Hagen voted "aye."

[24] Senate Journal, *op. cit.* pp. 720–724, has the remarks of Senators Schrock, Day, Duffy, Bridston, Streibel, and Nordhaugen after the final passage of S.B. 41. Also, Senator Nordhaugen's statement is on pp. 463–465.

Industrial Commission be authorized to make administrative rulings as to proper spacing—such was then, and still is, the procedure. Mr. Boone stated that the issue should be decided between landowners and operators.[25] Charges and denials between Mr. Higgins and Dr. Laird apparently became rather heated but the Committee made no changes in regard to spacing procedure.

S.B. 35 was introduced by the Legislative Research Committee and was designed to regulate oil brokers. A few of the brokers had proven to be unethical and financially irresponsible so the use of the state's police power seemed necessary to the Committee. There was some discussion of licensing the oil brokers, but this seemed to pose several administrative difficulties and it would not have necessarily enabled the injured parties to have received any compensation. The bill was passed after considerable opposition and a substantial number of amendments. The NDOGA opposed the bill and Harold Pollman, representing the WCLOA, recommended licensing of oil brokers rather than bonding. The former organization apparently testified against S.B. 35 in order to get the support of the small oil producers for S.B. 32. When the Senate Judiciary Committee completed its hearing it recommended that the $10,000 bonding provision be changed to $3,000. The Senate and House approved this change, along with several others, and the bill received little other opposition.

There were other "oil" bills of some importance that were introduced and passed at the 1953 Legislative Session but the process outlined above accounts for the most important and controversial items of oil legislation.

The Relative Inactivity of the 1955 Session

The "built-in" confusion of the North Dakota political system continued in the 1955 legislative session. The 1954 elections brought rather moderate successes for the ROC. Its majority in the House was substantial—the ROC nominee for Speaker being elected 64-45, four members not voting. But in the Senate, the Coalition of 1953 was again successfully formed. The NPL had maintained its strong minority group; the "independent" Republicans had lost one cohort—Senator Pyle, but there were now three Democrats in the Senate and toward the end of the session that figure was increased by the special election of another Democrat. Senator Day was elected the leader of the Coalition group.

---

[25] Grand Forks *Herald*, February 8, 1953.

The 1955 Session encountered a substantial number of serious problems but the issues concerning oil were very few. This situation was probably created by two main factors. With the two Houses controlled, in essence, by opposite factions it was rather evident that no major policy changes would be made in the field of oil. Also, public opinion—in the sense of interested and articulate groups—on the oil issue was sort of at the fulcrum point. The initial lust and enthusiasm for oil had rather died away as drilling was greatly diminished and "dry holes" became more frequent. The politician was not too certain how to move on the oil issue. This was a year of watching and waiting. But a few interesting pieces of oil legislation were introduced, although none by the Legislative Research Committee.

Senators Solberg, Dewing, Hagen and Olson dropped in a bill on January 27, 1955, to prohibit the flaring of gas. This became S.B. 148 and it had a short but lively career. Many persons in the state, and in the State Legislature, were increasingly concerned about the flaring of natural gas in the oil fields. For some considerable time the gas had been flared at the well-site but by the late summer of 1954 the Signal Oil and Gas Company had completed its plant at Tioga. After that development the gas was piped into the Signal plant whereupon the butane, propane, and sulphur were removed but the natural gas that remained was still burned. Only a few days before Senator Solberg's bill was introduced, he, and several other Senators, had offered concurrent Senate Resolution "H" which urged the effective utilization of natural gas and stated that approximately 30 million cubic feet of gas was being flared each day in North Dakota oil fields, including the Signal plant.[26] Just what Senator Solberg and the other Senators had in mind when they introduced S.B. 148 is not known positively by the writer but it seems fairly clear that it was an attempt to bring pressure upon Amerada and the Montana-Dakota Utilities Company, or some other utility, to negotiate a contract for the sale of the gas. The bill prevented the flaring of refined or dry natural gas and imposed a fine of $500 a day on each violator. Mr. Pearce (NDOGA), Mr. Richard Cook (Superintendent, Signal Oil and Gas Company), and Mr. C.E. Boone (Amerada) testified before the Senate Committee on Industry and Business that passage of the bill would force the cessation of production of both crude oil and natural gas; that no other state had such a law; and that there were not any adequate storage facilities for natural gas in North Dakota. Then on February 8, the Montana-Dakota Utilities Company announced that it had consummated a contract with Amerada, subject to the approval of

---

[26] Fargo *Forum*, January 27, 1955.

the North Dakota Public Service Commission, for the purchase of all the gas produced at the Signal plant. The following day S.B. 148 was reported out of the Committee with a recommendation for indefinite postponement and such a report, in the North Dakota legislature, is tantamount to killing a bill.

Then, on January 28, Senators Schoeder, Berube, and Tuft—all of them influential in the Farmers Union—introduced a bill to increase the gross oil production tax by 2% and this additional revenue was all to go into the state's general fund. At its 1954 State Convention, the Farmers Union had proposed a "higher rate" for the oil production tax with the revenues to be used for "schools and social services."[27] At the January, 1955, meeting of the Farmers Union Board of Directors that group recommended to the legislature that the tax be increased to 6¼%. This recommendation was, in substance, the content of S.B. 181. However, in his biennial message to the state legislature in early January, 1955, Governor Brunsdale had opposed any increase in the gross oil production tax. Also, the Senate Coalition, in caucus, had decided not to make the oil tax an issue at the session ostensibly because the House was ROC and no increase in the tax had even a slim chance of passage. Furthermore, the Farmers Union seemed to be again working at cross purposes. Mr. Stanley Moore, the assistant lobbyist for the Farmers Union, was working hard to garner votes for S.B. 181 but Mr. Alex Lind seemed convinced that the existing tax was equitable, and conducted himself accordingly. Mr. Boone stated before the Senate Committee on Finance and Taxation that Amerada had a gross investment of $71,000,000 in North Dakota on which it had earned a profit of only $18,500,000 and claimed therefore that a tax increase was not justifiable. Mr. Ernest Fleck, an attorney for the NDOGA, was of like opinion and said that the oil industry had an investment of $450,000,000 in North Dakota but that the oil production rate in the state was less than one-half of one percent of United States production. Thus he agreed that the higher tax would only impede the growth of the oil industry in the state. The bill came out of committee "without recommendation" and, when the bill came before the Senate for action, Senator Hagen moved for indefinite postponement contending that a higher tax was "poor psychology, when we're trying to attract industry to our state."[28]

On January 31, Senator Day introduced a bill (S.B. 214) which would have authorized the Public Service Commission to regulate natural gas rates at the wellhead. As was the case with S.B. 148, the bill

[27] North Dakota Farmers Union, *Policy and Action Program*—1955, p. 36.

[28] Grand Forks *Herald*, February 19, 1955.

seemed designed to act as a further lever against the oil companies in an attempt to make them negotiate more rapidly for the utilization of the wasted natural gas. Also, as Senator Day remarked in a personal interview, "the bill might have been introduced to get natural gas for Grand Forks." In any respect the oil lobbyists acted quickly and sharply. Hearings were held in the evening in the famous Room 200 at the Patterson Hotel. Mr. William H. Hunt, the Texas oil multi-millionaire, flew in for the hearings. Mr. Pearce, representing the NDOGA, and several independent producers spoke against the bill by using the following arguments—no state has such a regulation; it would be difficult to administer; such a law would impede wildcatting, etc. Mr. Boone claimed that there was no monopoly in the production of natural gas.[29] The bill emerged from the Committee on February 16 with a recommendation for "indefinite postponement." Senator Dewing, a close friend and coalition supporter of Senator Day, moved that the Committee report be adopted and this was done without a roll call vote.

The 1955 Session of the State Legislature adjourned without acting on any other major oil bills, and of those that were considered none were passed.

IV. The Administration of Oil Policy

Before the beginning of this century, Woodrow Wilson theorized on the future role of public administration in modern government. He predicted correctly the increasing emphasis on bureaucracy and observed the hazards of attempting to separate politics from administration.[30] For, as some sage has remarked, "policy is often made in the interstices of administration." Thus it has been with the oil policy in North Dakota, to a certain extent. A legislature cannot foresee all of the facets and ramifications of the policies it enacts; so, wisely, the law in most instances is given sufficient flexibility to meet changing conditions. This means that when a legislature has adjourned the political process moves over to the administrative agencies and the struggle for control and influence continues.

In North Dakota there are principally four state administrative agencies concerned with the execution of oil policies—the Industrial Commission, State Geologist, Public Service Commission, and the Tax Commissioner.

---

[29] Grand Forks *Herald*, February 10, 1955.

[30] Woodrow Wilson, "The Study of Administration," *Political Science Quarterly* (1877), Vol. II, pp. 197–222.

A. The Industrial Commission

Both the 1941 and 1953 state laws for the control of oil and gas resources gave the Industrial Commission the primary authority for the formulation of oil conservation regulations. The Commission was created in 1919 for the primary purpose of supervising the state-owned industries. It is an ex-officio organization composed of the Governor, Attorney General, and Commissioner of Agriculture and Labor. Because of its powers, and its control over some patronage, the Commission has always been kept closely in mind by the politicians when it comes to "slate-making time" at the pre-primary conventions. Since 1950, with the exception of the brief period that Mr. Paul Benson was Attorney General after the resignation of Mr. E.T. Christiansen, the NPL has controlled the Industrial Commission, although not the office of Governor.[31] But in no instance, unless one includes the 1954 election of Mr. Leslie Burgum to the office of Attorney General, has the insurgent group in the NPL had much authority in the Industrial Commission. For better or worse, this situation has strongly affected policy. That is, the conservative Leaguers and the ROC have determined the Commission's actions. In the field of oil conservation the authority of the Commission is largely due to its powers of issuing drilling permits, determining market demand and regulating production, and deciding upon spacing issues. The Commission's procedure follows the rather set pattern that has been established in order to comply with the due process clause of the Fourteenth Amendment of the United States Constitution—due notice, hearing, appeals to the regular courts, etc. The principal problems of the Commission have been concerned with well spacing and market demand rulings, particularly the former.[32]

The oil spacing issue has been a lively one in North Dakota and still is. When a "pool" is determined for particular area, the Commission makes a temporary spacing ruling, which is in effect for not more than 18 months. After the expiration of that time period, it must make a "permanent," or proper, spacing rule. The Commission is guided in its actions, officially at least, by the testimony of interested parties at the hearings and the advice of the State Geologist. The controversy has arisen over the demands of the mineral rights owners for the drilling

[31] It should be noted that the Governor has veto power over the decisions of the Commission.

[32] An interesting, although rather confusing, analysis of the well-spacing issue is found in a volume which contains the transcripts of hearings held by the North Dakota State Industrial Commission in Bismarck from January 16–18, 1952, *Hearing on Eighty Acre Spacing for Beaver Lodge Pool* (Bismarck: State of North Dakota, 1952), 256 pages.

of more wells. This demand has often been echoed, if not originally advanced, by the businessmen in areas where drilling rigs are becoming scarce and, consequently, so are the customers. An interviewee in Tioga claimed, to the writer, that $8,000 had been collected from the local businessmen and the small independent producers to fight the temporary 80 acre spacing in the Tioga and Beaver Lodge fields from being changed at the October, 1955, meeting of the Industrial Commission to a "permanent" 80 acre spacing rule. This group would certainly prefer a permanent 40 acre spacing rule. However, by the time the October meeting had come and gone it was apparent that the $8,000 had not been collected by the Tioga Field Mineral Association. That organization did not offer any testimony by technical witnesses at the hearing and the Industrial Commission thereupon issued a "permanent" 80 acre spacing order.

The persons in the Williston area who are most aroused over the situation are primarily concerned with having more wells in order, in their opinion, to have more income.[33] Spacing, of course, is not an end in itself. It is ostensibly a conservation measure designed to maintain the highest possible "maximum efficient rate of production," and, thereby, to drain the field as thoroughly as possible. The usual spacing order of the Commission reads—"one well to 80 acres in order to drain efficiently, all of the recoverable oil from the sand pool, assure orderly and uniform development and avoid the drilling of unnecessary wells, and prevent waste in a manner that will protect correlative rights."[34]

But the Commission has not been able to reconcile the differing conflicts of interest. The WCLOA has vociferously charged that the larger spacing ruling (primarily 80 acres)[35] is solely for the benefit of the major oil producers as the latter presently do not need the oil and want to avoid the expense of extra drillings. The findings of the State Geologist seem to concur generally with the major oil producers, but he—the State Geologist—believes that the allocation formula is equitable to all parties concerned as the amount of oil allocated to a given

[33] But there does seem to be a serious question of ethics involved here. In any respect, a few of the landowners who were interviewed claimed that verbal promises were made that the drilling on their land would be based on 40 acre spacing. There seems to be adequate evidence to state that these and other such types of practices occurred but by whom, and to what extent, is much more difficult to ascertain.

[34] State of North Dakota, Minutes of the Industrial Commission, May 10, 1954. Case No. 60, Order No. 67 (Fryburg-Madison Pool).

[35] The rulings vary with geological condition, etc. The Newburg field in Bottineau County has 40 acre spacing; most other fields have an 80 acre ruling; the Sanish field has 160 acre spacing.

well is based on acreage and an increase in the size of the spacing unit increases, in proportion, the allowable quota for each well. His critics seem to have an unquenchable belief that an "independent" geologist should be hired to make a "scientific" ruling rather than an economic one. The WCLOA claims that other states have 10, 20, 40 acre spacing, which in some instances is true,[36] but comparisons are rather futile unless many geophysical factors are closely correlated. Factional politics also play an important role as the NPL has become an advocate, for the most part, of 40 acre spacing while the ROC adheres more closely to the findings of the geologists for the state and the oil producers.

The market demand features of the oil conservation law are also a source of conflict. The avowed purpose of a market demand provision is to prevent waste of a natural resource by permitting only enough oil to be produced as will "clear" the market. The Interstate Oil Compact Commission (IOCC) believes that this is not an involved decision to make—"it is not difficult to determine the current demand for crude oil and the increasing or decreasing trend in that demand."[37] Probably that is correct in North Dakota as the Standard Oil Purchasing Company at Mandan is, by all odds, the largest single purchaser of the oil; in fact, almost the sole purchaser.

A market demand law may well be necessary for proper conservation, an orderly market, and adequate risk capital,[38] but in the short run it means that an oil well may be able to produce its quota for the month in a few days.[39] Also, as long as the monthly quota remains lower than the capacity of the wells to produce, and the formula remains unchanged, the discussion over spacing seems rather academic. But that judgment is not concurred in by many landowners, businessmen, etc., in the Williston area. When the question of proper spacing for the Tioga and Beaver Lodge fields was discussed before, and decided by, the Industrial Commission in the fall of 1955 a considerable amount of political conflict was expected, but failed to develop. The landowners were apparently divided as to the strategy which should be followed.

---

[36] Letter, from Mr. Lawrence R. Alley, Assistant Executive Secretary, Interstate Oil Compact Commission, to the author, August 25, 1955.

[37] Interstate Oil Compact Commission, *Oil for Today—And For Tomorrow* (IOCC, Oklahoma City, 1953), p. 66.

[38] *Ibid.*, p. 69.

[39] These quotas are based on a calculation which takes into account the acreage of the field and the depth of the well, among other factors. That is, the larger the spacing rule in that field, and the deeper the depth of the individual well, the greater the production quota. See the Industrial Commission of North Dakota, *General Rules and Regulations for the Conservation of Crude Oil and Natural Gas*, adopted December 1, 1953, Rule 505, p. 53–54.

B. The State Geologist and State Geological Survey

The professor of geology at the University of North Dakota is also, ex-officio, the state geologist. As pertains to oil, he directs the activities of the State Geological Survey and "as supervisor, is charged with the enforcement of regulations and orders of the Industrial Commission governing North Dakota oil and gas resources."[40] In the administration of the duties and responsibilities of his office, the State Geologist, Dr. Wilson M. Laird, has organized the survey into three divisions—geology, administration, and conservation.[41] It is in the conservation activities of the last named division that Dr. Laird has encountered political difficulties. In his role as what might be termed the "principal advisor" to the Industrial Commission on geological matters, politics and science have become somewhat intertwined. Some individuals and organizations in the Williston Basin area have, and do, charge Dr. Laird with too close cooperation with the major oil producers and with failing, as one politician phrased it, "to assist the landowners of North Dakota whom he supposed to represent." This matter of representation raises vital administrative questions. Who is Dr. Laird supposed to represent? From his point of view, his responsibilities are to administer the provisions of chapter 38-08 (Control of Gas and Oil Resources of the 1953 Supplement to the North Dakota Revised Code of 1943) in as scientific and objective a manner as possible. But his findings, notably in the field of well-spacing and conservation, have led him to reach in many instances the same conclusions as the major oil producers. To those who consider their interests and conclusions to be contrary to those of the producers, Dr. Laird is not performing in a manner that is most beneficial for the citizens of the state. This is a serious and delicate matter and the author has only the competence to state the issues, not decide them. The concept of "state interest," like its larger counterpart—the "national interest"—has always been vague and confusing. The following questions are some of the important ones asked by influential persons in the Williston area and they indicate that a consensus of opinion has not been reached on several matters regarding oil production and conservation. Is Amerada, for example, not really concerned with conservation in the spacing issue but rather wants to keep North Dakota oil off the market and thereby protect her investments and production in foreign nations and other states? Does

---

[40] State of North Dakota, *North Dakota Blue Book* (Bismarck: Bismarck Tribune, 1954), p. 90 and Chapter 38-0804 of the 1953 *Supplement to the North Dakota Revised Code* 1943.

[41] Grand Forks *Herald*, June 20, 1954.

80 acre space most efficiently and completely drain the oil fields where such an order is in effect, or is much oil left that will never be recovered and thereby jeopardize the interests of mineral owners, the state, and the nation? Is justice here not decided in the interests of the stronger, that is, stronger in terms of political pressures, public relations, financial resources, etc.?

C. Public Service Commission

The Public Service Commission in North Dakota has the responsibility for the regulation of public utilities in the state. Its powers of issuing licenses, permits, certificates of convenience and necessity, setting rates, and the like, make it a potent force in the economic life of North Dakota. The three members of the commission are elected for overlapping six year terms—assuming that it is not a special election. Because of the authority of the office and the patronage that is to be dispensed, control of this commission is avidly sought for by the political factions.

The commission has not played a particularly important role in oil politics in the state but recently there have been attempts to secure the Commission's approval for the construction of natural gas pipelines to certain cities and villages in North Dakota. The political and legal maneuvers that followed have somewhat shifted the conflicts centering around oil politics from the Industrial Commission to the Public Service Commission.

On November 27, 1953, the North Dakota Natural Gas Transmission Company (hereafter NDNGT) applied to the Commission for a certificate of convenience and necessity in order to build a pipeline from the Signal Plant at Tioga which would serve many of the major cities and towns in the northern section of the state east of Tioga and, also, in the Red River Valley area. This project was estimated in cost at $10,700,000. The Commission issued its findings of fact, conclusions, and order on May 24, 1954.[42] In essence, the plan was approved if the NDNGT would meet nine conditions. These need not be reiterated here but they imposed substantial demands upon NDNGT in such matters as underground storage facilities, standby wells, and some financial features which were not satisfactory with the Commission. NDNGT claimed that it could not comply with six of the 16 stipulations set forth by the Commission and applied for an extension of time, which was granted. Then on June 21, 1954, the Northern Natural Gas Company of Omaha proposed to the Commission the construction of a

---

[42] See North Dakota Public Service Commission, *Sixty-third and Sixty-fourth Annual Report*, for the biennial period ending June 30, 1954, pp. 93–112.

somewhat similar line at a cost of $18,280,700. These companies were apparently unable to meet the standards established by the Commission and all the while a presumably vital natural resource was being flared away. It was not until June 23, 1955, that the issue began to jell.[43] On that date, Montana-Dakota Utilities Company announced an agreement with Amerada on the use of the natural gas being flared at the signal gas plant. This was to be, if approved, a five million dollar pipeline extending east to Minot and west to Williston. Hearings before the Commission were held during parts of August. There seemed to be general approval of the proposal as far as it went but the eastern cities in the state were, in some instances, rather ardently opposed to the idea.

There were some interesting developments in this Montana-Dakota arrangement which indicate a "politics of business." W.S. Davidson Sr., President of the American State Bank in Williston and a definite power in state politics, is reported to be the largest stock-holder in Montana-Dakota Utilities Company. The former owners of the Minot Gas Company were the sponsors for the NDNGT. Also, Mr. Ralph F. Davis, a natural gas consultant, studied the availability of gas situation for the Montana-Dakota Utilities Company and claimed there was only enough gas to satisfy Williston, Minot, and the cities and towns in-between. Two days after this was announced by Montana-Dakota Utilities, the president of Amerada denied, by telegram, the lack of availability of gas.

In considering oil politics within the state, the most important development was the division that occurred within the Public Service Commission over the proposed pipelines of Montana-Dakota Utilities Company from Tioga to Williston and from Tioga to Minot. The former pipeline involves interstate commerce and is thereby a matter to be decided by the Federal Power Commission but the latter line is a matter of intrastate commerce. To summarize a lengthy and complicated dispute, the North Dakota Public Service Commission authorized, in late November, 1955, the Tioga-Minot pipeline, but subject to several restrictions regarding price and future commitments which Montana-Dakota Utilities and Amerada would not accept. To further confuse the situation, that pipeline was already being constructed; the Public Service Commission was trying to bring contempt proceedings against the public utility as no construction certificate had been issued; and many users of gas in the Minot area were protesting the ostensible shortage of gas. The day before Christmas, 1955, District Judge A.J.

---

[43] Williston *Herald*, June 23, 1955; Minneapolis *Tribune*, June 25, 1955.

Gronna authorized Montana-Dakota Utilities Company to begin immediately the distribution of natural gas in Minot.

Whatever the final outcome, this matter was becoming more and more embroiled in North Dakota politics. One member of the Public Service Commission, an interim appointee of the Governor following the death of an elected member, was to run for election in 1956 to a full six year term on the Public Service Commission, and, on this aforementioned issue, his vote had been favorable to the position of Amerada and Montana-Dakota Utilities Company. In the 1956 election the issue of pipelines, rates, etc., was almost certain to be an influential campaign issue.[44]

D. The Tax Commission

The general provisions of the North Dakota Oil and Gas Gross Production Tax Law (chapter 57-51, North Dakota Revised Code, 1953 Supplement) were outlined in Section III, Part B, of this chapter. The State Tax Commissioner, an elected officer, is responsible for the administration of the act.[45] Table Number XVI provides statistical data concerning the collection and distribution of revenue received under the provisions of the law. In comparative terms the tax has not been much of an income producer as yet. That is, the state sales tax brought in $12,696,000 for the fiscal year 1954 compared to the $335,831 that oil tax accounted for in almost a two year period. Also the ¼ of 1% for administration has not been equal to the actual increase of administrative costs. For 1952–54, the State Geological Survey's budget was $310,000. Actually the Survey had no full-time employees prior to 1951, other than the State Geologist, and his activities were principally those of a teacher. By 1954 the staff had increased to 18 full-time and eight temporary employees.[46]

Although the administration of the oil tax law is basically a ministerial function there are a couple of features which need to be mentioned. It is clear from information received at the Tax Commissioner's office that there are instances where the discretionary powers of the Tax Commissioner in the interpretation of the law are of considerable

---

[44] For more detailed information regarding this dispute, reference is made to Case No. 5351 and Case No. 5353, Public Service Commission, State of North Dakota.

[45] Table No. XVI.

[46] Grand Forks *Herald*, June 20, 1954.

importance.[47] In addition, the tax is somewhat novel in that it appears to be collected 100%. The reason for this apparently perfect collection is due to the source of collection, that is, the tax is collected at the refineries.

E. Other State Agencies

Two other state agencies that have been directly affected by oil discoveries in North Dakota are the Board of University and School Lands and the Bank of North Dakota. The Land Department had 723,000 acres under lease by the end of 1954. Income from leases and royalties since 1936 has totaled $4,332,448. The revenue from leases is apportioned to state schools and institutions while the income from royalties goes into a permanent fund for reinvestment. The Bank of North Dakota has collected $1,421,634 since it first leased mineral acreage in 1948. A million dollars of these receipts was used to cover a transfer payment to the motor vehicle fund directed by the state legislature in 1953.[48]

Both of the above organizations are ex-officio and politics, in the sense of struggle for control, are moderately evident, but oil has, thus far, played a minor role.

TABLE XVI

NORTH DAKOTA OIL AND GAS GROSS PRODUCTION TAX
COLLECTIONS AND ALLOCATIONS, 1954–1955, BY COUNTIES

TAXES COLLECTED ALLOCATED AS
FOLLOWS TO STATE GENERAL FUND

County	Total taxes collected from each county	To each county per 57-5115 (2)	¼% tax per 57-5115 (1)	Per 57-5115 (2)	Total to State General Fund
Billings	$18,450.92	$13,024.16	$1,085.35	$4,341.41	$5,426.76
Bottineau	6,073.87	4,287.44	357.29	1,429.14	1,786.42
Bowman	1,332.25	933.35	77.77	311.13	388.90
Burke	6,427.35	4,536.95	378.07	1,512.33	1,890.40
McKenzie	54,588.67	38,533.19	3,211.11	12,844.38	16,055.48
Mountrail	225,955.72	159,498.16	13,291.51	53,166.05	66,457.57
Stark	.63	.44	.04	.15	.19
Williams	750,956.99	449,651.15	44,173.95	257,130.89	243,826.06
TOTAL	$1,063,786.40	$670,464.84	$62,575.09	$330,735.48	$335,831.79

SOURCE: Office of the North Dakota Tax Commissioner, July, 1955.

---

[47] Letter, Office of the Tax Commissioner, to the Carter Oil Company, April 20, 1955; and Letter, Office of Tax Commissioner, to the Hunt Oil Company, August 14, 1953.

[48] Grand Forks *Herald*, December 28, 1954.

V. The Impact of Oil Upon City Government

The discovery of oil in the Williston Basin area in April, 1951, enabled almost any student of government to forecast the need for expansion of municipal facilities and services in that area. This growth was certain to be accompanied by increasing financial problems. The unanswerable question seemed to be—how much? Hindsight is invariably simpler and more accurate than foresight but even now it is difficult, and perhaps too soon, to state whether the expansion of municipal activities in Williston, Ray, and Tioga was overly optimistic or unduly pessimistic. This section of the study is not intended to provide an economic analysis of the public finance problems that were, and are, involved. Rather it is to trace the growth of municipal services in the three cities and to relate and account for the serious conflicts that arose over municipal issues and institutions. Included within this discussion of municipal government are the operations of the independent school districts. Although separate units of government from the municipalities, the problems of the school districts are comparable in cause and scope to those of the cities.

Williston

(1) Expansion of Services and Facilities and the Problem of Finances

The United States Bureau of the Census declared Williston had a population in 1950 of 7,378. In a prior section this study indicated that by 1954 the population was approximately 9,717. This meant, in terms of municipal services, that the city needed more and improved streets, sewer and water main extensions, additional storm sewers, and improved waterworks, and more street lights—the new sewer system, alone, cost $350,000.[49] In addition to these rather obvious necessities, Williston had drawn the plans and secured city approval for a new Armory building with probable construction in 1956, had funds to build a city garage, and had remodeled the city hall.[50] These capital improvements do not include new buildings and additions to the educational system, or other non-governmental civic enterprises. Some of this activity would certainly have occurred if oil had never been discovered but the tempo of change was much greater because of that event.

---

[49] League of North Dakota Municipalities, *Bulletin*, February, 1954, Vol. XXII, *Bulletin II*, p. 39. Apparently some of the residents complained about the imposition of a sewage charge because Mr. Willard Webster stated that the charge was "unavoidable" as $150,000 of the costs of the new sewer here were to come from special assessments and $200,000 from revenue. The Williston *Herald* opposed the bond issue (April 1954) in a front page editorial.

[50] Williston *Herald*, June 28, 1955 and June 29, 1955.

This building and improvement program meant that by May 31, 1955, the city owed $2,237,500 in general obligation and revenue bonds, refunding special assessment warrants, and special assessment warrants other than those of the refunding type.[51] (SEE TABLE XVII)

TABLE XVII

WILLISTON BONDED INDEBTEDNESS, MAY 31, 1955

	Amount of Issue	Funds on Hand
General obligation bonds	$153,000.00	$118,347.87
Revenue bonds	226,000.00	77,896.09
Refunding special assessment warrants	1,578,000.00	481,103.21
Other special assessment warrants	280,500.00	72,857.03
TOTAL	$2,237,500.00	$750,204.20

Even considering this substantial expansion of city facilities and consequent debt, Mr. H.L. Grimstvedt considered the city to be on a sound financial basis in May, 1955.[52] No events seem to have transpired since that time to cause a revision of opinion.

Property valuations—real and personal—have experienced a substantial steady increase; mill levies have remained relatively stable since 1952; and revenues have consequently moved upward. (SEE TABLE XVIII)

TABLE XVIII

WILLISTON PROPERTY MILL LEVIES, VALUATION AND EXPECTED TAX REVENUES, 1950–1955

Fiscal Year	Combined* Mill Levies	Taxable Valuation	Expected Revenue
1950	96.86	$4,837,541.00	$468,564.00
1951	98.93	5,185,454.00	512,996.00
1952	120.07	5,801,790.00	......
1953	125.08	6,845,675.00	......
1954	123.36	7,511,671.00	926,634.00
1955	......	13,423,649.00 (Est.)	......

* State, County, City, Park, School, Special

Table XIX shows how tax revenues, appropriations, and actual expenditures (including special projects) increased; how the demands for

[51] *Ibid.*, June 25, 1955.

[52] *Ibid.*

more services advanced the costs of strictly governmental services, and how they moved upward. The figures are self-explanatory and comparative percentage estimates would not be particularly meaningful.

TABLE XIX
WILLISTON TAX REVENUES, APPROPRIATIONS AND EXPENDITURES, FISCAL YEARS 1950–1951 TO 1954–1955

Fiscal Year Year	Total Tax Revenues	Total Appropriations	Total Expenditures
50–51	$105,112.67	$163,828.00	$124,058.60
51–52	122,688.77	196,769.00	175,982.12
52–53	200,466.03	269,270.00	243,241.66
53–54	219,118.26	337,392.61	955,957.00*
54–55	252,695.96	426,815.19	......

* This includes $489,554.23 for the construction fund plus $126,320.00 for bonds.

The problems of the Williston school district are different in type, but not magnitude, from those of the city. Two elementary schools had to be built; another school was enlarged; a new parochial school was completed; a $300,000 high school gymnasium was constructed by early 1954 and two classrooms were used there during the 1954–55 school year. In July, 1952, there were $275,000 in outstanding school bonds; $325,000 more were added in 1952–53 and another $118,000 in 1953–54. By mid-year in 1955 the school district had a bonded indebtedness of $687,000 due to its construction and improvements program. (SEE TABLE XX)

TABLE XX
WILLISTON SCHOOL DISTRICT ENROLLMENTS AND TAX RATES, FISCAL YEARS 1950–1951 TO 1954–1955

Year	Number of Students	General Fund Mill Levy
1950–51	....	21.57
1951–52	1,664 + 76 parochial students	23.54
1952–53	1,972 + 93 parochial students	25.04
1953–54	2,239 + 100 parochial students	25.7
1954–55	2,315 + 194 parochial students	25.99

From the year 1952–53 school year to the 1954–55 school year, the school system in Williston—public and private—experienced a little over a 44% increase. This was a serious enough problem in itself but the migratory nature of oil-drilling meant that the students were coming and going at a rate which made student integration and administrative efficiency even more complicated.

By the summer of 1955 the population cycle was at a sort of plateau stage but there seemed to be what might be termed a careful optimism among the public leaders in Williston about the financial condition of the city and the schools. The indebtedness was substantial and the oil boom was definitely tapering off but they looked for a period of stability which would enable them to meet their financial responsibilities, and continue to move forward, but at a slower pace.

(2) Internal Political Controversies and City Elections

As far as the author could ascertain, there was little evidence of oil politics, of a direct type, in the organization or operation of city government in Williston. But there were two rather bitterly fought municipal elections in 1954—one special, the other regular—which were precipitated by the sudden and rapid growth of the city due to the oil boom. So, indirectly oil was certainly involved in local politics but it seems doubtful if the officers and employees of the different types of oil companies played a very significant role.

The expansion of municipal services and the concomitant increase in taxes and assessments were the seeds of some discontent.[53] A number of the persons in the outlying areas of the city were dissatisfied with the services and the cost of those services. The charge was also made that organized labor had no representation on the Commission. Others claimed the Police Department was operated in an inefficient, even crude, fashion; and one interviewee stated that the rate of arrest had been five times that of any other city in North Dakota.[54] All five of the Commissioners were, inadvertently it seems, living on the east side

---

[53] Since April, 1913, Williston has had a Commission form of government. Four Commissioners and president of the Commission are elected at large for five years, overlapping terms. The president has no veto power. The salary for each of the five officers is $780 per year.

[54] One of the leaders for retaining the Commission form contended, in an interview, that the police chief was a "news-hound" and thus created an over-emphasis on the activities of the Police Department. Also, he believed that some of the new personnel lacked judgment and maturity.

of the city and this created charges of favoritism.[55] One of the former members of the City Commission had been, while a commissioner, an employee of the engineering firm which was consulted about a new sewer project. But he did not vote when the contract was decided on by the City Commission. Nevertheless, some claimed this was a serious "conflict of interest." The City Attorney—Mr. Everett Palmer—contended that the Commission had discussed the ethics and legality of his action and was advised by the Attorney-General of North Dakota that his (Mr. Webster's) actions were legal. Also, an opposition leader stated, in a personal interview, that the former Commissioner's participation in the sewer contract matter was not made an election issue as there were no indications at all of illegal actions.

In any respect, 1801 citizens of Williston signed petitions favoring the aldermanic form of government and on February 23, 1954 the citizens voted on the issue—"Shall the city of Williston change from its organization under the Commission system of government and become a city under the Council form of government?" The leaders of the opposition apparently desired to have a Council-Manager form but disagreement within their own ranks dictated the expedient strategy of making a Mayor-Council form the first objective.

Pressure groups were formed on both sides. There were the "Women's Vote for the Commission Form of Government," and the "Committee for Progress"—all favoring the existing form. The opposition formed an organization called the "Civic Improvement League." Mr. Palmer, the City Attorney, came to be the "...principal spokesman for the Commission Form of Government."[56] Mr. Walter Burk switched sides, at least the reformers declared so, and delivered a radio address just prior to the election in favor of the Commission form. The League of Women Voters worked diligently, seemingly in an impartial manner, gathering and publishing facts about the issues. A prominent doctor was, according to a leader for the aldermanic form, to provide the campaign eve "punch blow" through a radio address favoring the change, but almost an hour before the broadcast he withdrew due to pressure from his associates and the bank he was connected with. Apparently the American State Bank "rode the fence" by contributing $50.00 to each side.

---

[55] It should be pointed out that, at the time of their election, two of the Commissioners lived on the west side of the city and the third Commissioner lived on the far north side, north of Harmon Park. Afterward, however, the three of them bought or built new homes on the east side of the city.

[56] Williston *Herald*, February 22, 1954. One of the city officials doubted if Mr. Palmer had taken a leading role in this particular issue at all.

The reform group seemed to have a scarcity of funds for campaigning while the status quo group had considerable financial resources. By studying the advertising of the *Williston Herald* for five days (excluding Sunday as there is no edition that day) it was determined that the "for Commission" forces spent $1,031.40 on political advertising as compared to $28.80 for the "aldermanic" forces.[57] After the ballots were counted on February 23, 1954, it was announced that the vote was 1041 "yes" (in favor of aldermanic form) to 1195 "no" votes.

However, the conflict was not yet resolved as the regular election was now due on the 13th of April. A group of interested and prominent citizens caucussed regarding a slate and decided not to support the existing President of the City Commission and two other Commissioners whose terms were to expire. As its slate, this group selected Dr. L.M. Carlson, a Williston dentist, to run for the office of president, and Mr. A.J. Thomas and Mr. T.S. Bosh for the other two openings on the Commission. "Tony" Bosh was considered to be a representative of the organized labor. A few days before the election, Mr. W.N. Dittsworth, then president of the Commission, withdrew from the race; Mr. Oscar N. Lee, a Commissioner, declared himself not to be a candidate; and Mr. Harris Anderson, the other Commissioner and who was then in charge of the police and fire departments, did run but was defeated. Table XXI shows the results of the election.

TABLE XXI
WILLISTON COMMISSION ELECTION RETURNS, BY CANDIDATES AND BY WARDS, FOR THE ELECTION OF APRIL 13, 1955

Pres. of B/C	1st	2nd	3rd	4th	5th	6th	7th	Totals
G.M. Carlson*	137	154	272	291	282	196	238	1570
Harry England	86	62	146	202	165	155	189	1005
W.N. Dittsworth	......	1	2	......	......	......	......	3
Comm.								
A.J. Thomas*	145	154	257	326	274	210	270	1636
Gust Stokke	64	59	103	170	108	105	105	714
Harris Anderson	48	50	144	96	179	91	139	747
C.A. Scott	46	38	49	91	93	70	108	495
T.S. Bosh*	124	126	230	294	206	198	189	1367

* Elected

[57] *Ibid.*, February 17-18-19-20-22, 1954.

Doctor Carlson died unexpectedly on June 27, 1955 so the Commission had to call a special election. The "interested and prominent" leaders again caucussed and the contest was between Mr. Burk, Mr. H.M. Zahl—a former newspaper publisher—and Mr. Russ Nelson. The election was held on September 19, 1955 and Burk received 1393 votes to 455 for Zahl and 399 for Nelson.

Tioga

(1) Municipal Services and Finances

Tioga calls itself the "Oil Capital of North Dakota." The oil boom began practically in the city's front yard. This study has already noted what this discovery meant to Tioga in demographic, economic, and social terms. From a population in 1950 of 456 the city has leaped forward in a somewhat convulsive fashion to a point, by the summer of 1955, where a city official estimated the population to be 1200.[58]

There seems to have been, among the Tioga residents, a rather severe ambivalence about this oil boom. Some were ardently attracted to the powerful dynamism of an oil economy while others were much more concerned about the destruction of a way of life which they had found quite satisfactory. This conflict will be elaborated on to a greater degree in the next section but this situation delayed the construction and operation of new municipal facilities.[59]

But the rate of progress had still been considerable. Special improvement bonds of $743,000 value have been issued from 1951 to about mid-1955 for water, sewers, curbs and gutters, sidewalks, etc. Paving projects were not carried forth in a particularly speedy fashion but the change was persistent. A sizeable program was carried out in 1954 and in the late summer of 1955 bids were opened on paving, gutter, and storm sewer projects with the apparent low bids being $120,626 for 34 blocks of paving curb and gutter and $13,505 for storm sewers.[60] A new city hall, including a new jail, was constructed and, for the most part, in operation by January, 1954.

---

[58] Our own research indicated that the population of Tioga in the summer of 1954 was 1,608.

[59] North Dakota League of Municipalities, *Bulletin* Vol. XXI, No. 11, November, 1953, pp. 25–26. This article is a report of an earlier editorial from the Bismarck *Tribune*.

[60] *Ibid.*, September 1955, p. 41

The general budget of the city went from $9,149.58 in 1952–53 to $39,946.61 in 1954–55. There was no park district in 1952–53 but by 1954–55 one had been organized and its budget for that year was $1,976.

Construction and extension of school buildings advanced at a comparable pace. School bonds for the amount of $158,000 were issued in 1954 and in May, 1955, the voters approved a $70,000 bond issue for new school buildings by a vote of 119-24. An election was to be held in the fall of 1955 as to whether or not the community desired a $400,000 bond issue for a new high school.

All this building meant, almost surely, more taxes. But the mill levy, although high, was on the decline after 1953 as Table XXII indicates. Assessed valuations for the city increased from about $405,000 in 1951 to $740,548 for 1955. The increase in valuation was even more substantial for the Tioga School District, which includes farming areas outside Tioga, but the, perhaps, more realistic valuations have permitted a decrease in mill levies. Table XXIII also indicates that the pupil population has increased over 300% since the discovery of oil.

TABLE XXII
TIOGA PROPERTY VALUATIONS AND TAX RATES, 1950–1955

Year	Property Valuations	Mill Levies
1950	$153,430.00	112.44
1951	155,551.00	109.21
1952	196,095.00	124.11
1953	614,864.00	113.79
1954	740,548.00	110.75
1955	......	100.00 (Est.)

TABLE XXIII
TIOGA SCHOOL DISTRICT ENROLLMENTS, PROPERTY VALUATIONS AND TAX RATES, 1950–1954

Year	School Population	Property Valuation	General Fund Mill Levy
1950	......	$412,466.00	54
1951	187	475,631.00	51
1952	350	1,102,418.00	51
1953	515	2,625,221.00	32
1954	601	......	30.47

(2) Internal Controversies and Elections

The conflicts have probably been more considerable in Tioga than in Ray but of a somewhat different variety. Tioga had been a village until 1953 but, by an almost unanimous popular referendum held that year, it incorporated and became a municipality with a commission form of government. The city limits have not been extended to include the Signal gas plant because the property that is used by that plant belongs to the Great Northern Railroad Company and the strategy seems to be to build city improvements first and, perhaps later, annex more property.

An early, and apparently rather bitter, conflict concerned what was called the "wets and drys" issue. The "wets" wanted city water and sewage and the "drys" favored the status quo. Even after referenda were conducted and bond issues thereby authorized, a series of lawsuits were begun which sought writs of injunctions against these new improvements. There was a substantial amount of community animosity and neighbors were, even in the summer of 1954, sometimes quite irate toward each other over this issue, although the water system was installed in 1952.

Newcomers to the community were gradually being elected to the Tioga City Commission and the school board. In the summer of 1955 there were two on each of the five-member boards. The elections have been relatively peaceful although a Catholic-Protestant conflict did arise in the 1955 election to the school board. Thirteen teachers voluntarily resigned from the school system and, because a Catholic was chairman of the school board, there were charges made that the vacancies would be filled from teachers of that faith. In the election, two Protestant candidates entered the race, one later withdrew, and the Protestant candidate received 25 more votes than the incumbent chairman. However, both were elected as there were two vacancies. Apparently many of the citizens of Tioga, including the editor of the *Tioga Tribune* who did some editorializing on the matter, looked upon this ruckus as sort of an unfortunate affair and it now seems to have substantially subsided.

The time of troubles is certainly not over for the governmental organizations in Tioga but the peak period seems to have passed.[61] There has been a water shortage but the city installed a new pump in the south well to alleviate that problem. An influx of trailers had created

---

[61] Grand Forks *Herald*, February 17, 1953. The financial plight of the schools was apparently so serious in the winter of 1952–53 that some of the Tioga teachers received IOU's rather than paychecks.

a difficult sort of problem for the City Commission but an ordinance regulating trailer parking has mitigated that situation. There was a noticeable reluctance to provide the city with natural gas after the Signal plant was in operation so in July, 1954, the City Commission let it be known that it was considering the construction of a municipal gas plant. During the following month the Montana-Dakota Utilities Company announced that natural gas service would be available in Tioga by October 15, 1954. This statement became a reality and, by the summer of 1955, 239 permits had been issued for the use of natural gas.

Ray

(1) Municipal Services and Finances

The city of Ray is several miles west of the original oil discovery areas but the boom soon pervaded the life of the whole community. The natural topography of the city favored additional development and there was available already a municipal water and sewage system to attract the oilmen and their families.

Accurate statistical information was more difficult to secure in Ray but the general impressions were that the financial situation was less satisfactory than in Tioga. Leaders in the community stated, in personal interviews, that the bonded indebtedness for schools in Ray was up to the legal limit; that the mill levy was up to 141 (71–72 mills for school district,[62] 26 for City, and the rest State/County and minor levies); and that the City budget for 1954–55 was $22,000–$23,000. But the city of Ray had no bonded indebtedness in 1954, although it did incur one in 1955 of $13,800 in order to install new storm sewers. One of the residents provided the author with a statement of the property taxes for his own home and these figures indicated a gradual increase in property taxes from $82.09 in 1951 to $102.24 in 1955.

The activities of the Farmers Union Credit Union in Ray indicated the economic trend to some extent. In 1955, it had assets of $488,950 and 771 members while in 1952 the assets were $390,000 and the membership was 625. However, if these statistics indicate pessimism as to the future it should be quickly stated that such did not seem to be the prevalent attitude in the summer of 1955, although there was a much more cautious optimism than a year previously. Table XXIV points out the increases in property valuations and mill levies.

---

[62] He was including the mill levies for sinking, reserve, and building funds.

TABLE XXIV
RAY PROPERTY VALUATIONS AND TAX RATES, 1950–1954

Year	Property Valuation	Total Mill Levy
1950	$221,374.00	113.76
1951	234,786.00	130.45
1952	246,336.00	140.83
1953	333,693.00	140.69
1954	381,134.00	141.69

The schools had to meet a new and pressing situation. Three bond issues totalling about $225,000 had to be floated. One school burned; another started but could not be completed until another bond issue had been sold. However, again, the community leaders believed that the burden could be handled. The following table (TABLE XXV) outlines the general picture of school population increases and the financial situation.

TABLE XXV
RAY SCHOOL DISTRICT ENROLLMENTS, PROPERTY VALUATIONS AND TAX RATES, 1950–1954

Year	School Population	Property Valuation	General Fund Mill Levy
1950	......	$505,673.00	45.00 mills
1951	246	528,920.00	42.50 mills
1952	393	620,274.00	40.65 mills
1953	413	679,808.00	40.00 mills
1954	413	......	40.00 mills

There was, in 1955, criticism of high taxes. One community leader estimated that taxes had been doubled since the coming of oil; another thought the increase was 65–70%. This writer, at least, gained the general impression that more skepticism toward the future was prevalent in Ray than in either Williston or Tioga.

(2) Internal Controversies and Elections

The political schisms in Ray rather compared with those already noted in Tioga. The issue was largely between the "Old Guard" and the "Progressives," or in other words, the "status quo" group versus the "reformers." Prior to the April, 1954, election there was considerable criticism of the existing city commission. The then President of the Commission had occupied that position for 12 years but decided not to run for reelection, perhaps because of considerable criticism of his actions by some of the residents. A slate of "Progressives," including a member of the Commission to run for the office of President, was put forward in the April election and all were voted into office. It seemed to be a rather prevalent opinion that the new Commission came about primarily because a majority of the citizens thought that community development was preceding too slowly. But in the referenda on community projects the storm sewer proposal was defeated 56-165 while the curbs and gutters proposal was approved by 142-81. The new President of the City Commission, Mr. Arnold Anderson, seemed confident that the schisms were not overly serious; rather they were largely those, he believed, of a small town nature in which everyone knows everyone else's business and resulting frictions are the consequence.

Public Attitudes on Local Government Services and Educational Facilities

The Questionnaire Survey team spent most of the summer of 1954 in the Williston area. The different methodological aspects of this survey have been discussed in Appendix A. Two of the questions that were directed to the respondents provided some worthwhile data as to the opinions of the citizenry of Williston, Tioga, Ray, and the Impact Area relative to the condition of local government services, including education.

In regards to local governmental services, the question was—"Since the beginning of the oil boom have local government services improved?" This question was varied slightly in Tioga and Ray in order to interject the possibility of a decline in the quality of the services but the changing of the question resulted in approximately the same type of answers so no distinction is included in Table XXVI following.

TABLE XXVI
TYPES OF ANSWERS, BY WILLISTON BASIN LOCALITY RESIDENCE, TO THE QUESTION: "SINCE THE BEGINNING OF THE OIL BOOM HAVE LOCAL GOVERNMENT SERVICES IMPROVED?"[1]

Types of Answers	Williston						Impact	
	Old[2]	New	Either	Total	Tioga	Ray	Areas	Totals
Improved	209	45	4	258	27	36	13	334
No Change or Declined	84	26	156	266	9	36	81	392
Both	4	1	......	5	1	......	......	6
Don't Know	53	49	2	104	10	27	4	145
TOTALS	350	121	162	633	47	99	98	877

1. This question was re-worded in Tioga and Ray but obtained the same kinds of answers.
2. The word "old" means that the interviewees lived in that particular city, or area, prior to 1951.

The results of the survey seemed to point to no particular change in attitudes about local governmental services because of the oil boom. But a substantial number—334 out of 877—believed that the services had improved and that was rather remarkable in itself considering the large expansion in population over a brief period of time. The status quo category (a minority indicated a decline in the quality of services) was preponderant but such an attitude might well be considered a commendation during such a period of development.

The question concerning educational institutions was phrased as follows—"Has the rapid increase in population affected educational facilities in your area? If 'yes'—How?" For Tioga, the question was re-stated—"How have educational facilities been affected?" The alteration, in the case of Tioga, was made because the wording of the original question was somewhat leading. That is, stressing the fact that there had been rapid increase in population rather led the respondent to believe that the educational institutions might have been drastically affected. Table XXVII outlines the results on these particular questions.

TABLE XXVII
TYPES OF ANSWERS, BY WILLISTON BASIN LOCALITY RESIDENCE, TO QUESTIONS CONCERNING THE PRESENCE AND NATURE OF CHANGES IN EDUCATIONAL FACILITIES

Types of answers	Old	Williston New	Either	Total	Ray	Impact Areas	Total
No—no data	......	1	......	1	3	39	43
No—data not available	7	8	......	15	......	......	15
Yes, better—improved teaching	1	1	......	2	3	1	6
Yes, better—improved facilities	59	20	......	79	......	12	91
Yes, better—improved administration	......	......	......	......	23	......	23
Yes, better—data not available	2	......	......	2	2	......	4
Yes, worse—poorer teaching	3	3	......	6	2	2	10
Yes, worse—poorer facilities	146	38	4	188	50	32	270
Yes, worse—data not available	1	1	......	2	......	2	4
Both—some facilities better, others worse	43	9	......	52	2	......	54
Both—some teaching is better—others worse	......	2	......	2	......	......	2
Both—no data	1	......	......	1	......	......	2
Indefinite—teaching may be worse	1	......	......	1	......	......	1
Indefinite—facilities may be worse	13	5	......	18	......	3	21
Indefinite—data not available	27	16	......	43	......	......	43
Indefinite—no data	4	1	......	5	18	6	29
No opinion—data not available	17	30	......	47	......	......	47
TOTALS	325	135	4	464	103	98	665

It points to a dislike of the way that educational facilities have fared since oil discovery. Almost 43% believed that the schools were in worse condition and nearly all of the criticism was directed at what the respondents considered to be poorer facilities. But a rather sizeable proportion—nearly 18%—were of the opinion that education institutions had improved in various ways. It would seem that, in the long run, oil discovery would improve the quality of educational institutions, at least in terms of plant and equipment, due to the extensive building programs that have occurred. The key issue will probably be one of finances. That is, can the payments on the bond issues be met without lowering the quality of educational services?

VI. The Impact of Oil Upon the Government of Williams County

A new courthouse building was slowly coming to be an absolute necessity in Williams county but the discovery of oil and the aura of wealth and power that followed hurried along its construction. Somehow this courthouse seems to symbolize the coming of a different era for this county. Probably the economic revolution will not be as rapid or thorough as was originally contemplated, at least by a few, but it has been substantial.

A. Increased Governmental Activities

One needs to do very little research in order to arrive at an accurate generalization about Williams County government—oil discovery meant that all county governmental offices had more work to do and needed a larger budget. Presumably even the coroner was more active than before but this section will only deal with those offices which felt the impact quite severely.

The administrative personnel of the County Public Welfare Board seemed convinced that "oil" added greatly to their problems. It was one interviewee's opinion that, in terms of public welfare costs, oil had been harmful. But the situation was apparently about what they had expected. The influx of oil workers, particularly from 1951 to 1954, meant more transients, more marital desertions, more stranded persons, and the like. However, it does not appear from statistics that the burden was as much as one might conjecture. For example, the "General Assistance"[63]

---

[63] Part of the Federal grant-in-aid program initiated by the Social Security Act of 1937.

load was 40 families in 1953–54 as compared to 80 families in 1954–55. But the increase was probably due to lower farm income that year as much as a decline in oil development in the area. The oil workers were mostly from warmer climates and had lived in a somewhat different culture. Child welfare work became more of a problem due to a considerable increase in child neglect, etc. Also, the "white collar" oilmen and their families were "accepted" but the laborers were much more isolated. Perhaps it was just a misleading stereotype but several of the interviewees made a definite distinction between the oil executives, etc., who were "educated and cultured," and the oil workers, who were often characterized as "bums," "drunks," etc.[64] This "black and white" distinction appears to be vastly overdrawn; in fact, there were a few interviewees who believed that the moral standards of the oil workers were superior to those of the "native" population, and these persons were not "outsiders." But this aforementioned dichotomy was rather a commonplace finding. Where increased public welfare needs did arise—and that occurred primarily in Williston, Tioga, and Ray—many voluntary non-governmental associations were very helpful in assisting the needy and, thereby, in aiding the public welfare officials. Church organizations were, in some instances, quite effective in helping the oil workers; business organizations also contributed to the mitigation of their problems. The Public Welfare office constantly needed more staff personnel but it was most difficult to secure them, and that situation still existed in the summer of 1955.

Since 1947, Williams County has been a part of the Upper Missouri District Health Unit, as have the counties of Divide, McKenzie, and Mountrail. The headquarters for the District are in Williston. Oil has meant a noticeable increase in the activities of this public health organization but by the summer of 1955 the peak period seemed to have passed. Along with a District health officer, the authorized staff consists of a sanitary engineer, two sanitarians, five public health nurses, and a clerk, but it has been difficult to recruit a full staff, particularly so in regards to the public health nurses. The District is financed by a ¾ mill levy and the income from the mill levy has increased due to the rise in property valuations. There was a considerable amount of work to be done in Tioga and Ray as the District had to approve plans for water and sewer systems, inspect plumbing, approve semi-private water supplies and sewage disposal systems for trailer camps, and certify restaurants and taverns as to health standards. Also, there was a substantial increase in the medical examinations (vision, hearing,

---

[64] This is a general statement and does not necessarily reflect the attitudes of the public welfare staff.

general physical condition and immunizations) that had to be given in the rural and city schools. All of these functions would, of course, have been carried out even without the discovery of oil and the rapid influx of new workers, facilities, etc., but the burden and responsibilities were much greater because of this expansion.

Oil created a new type of responsibility for the County Agent. He advises, rather than dictates to, the farmer, but now his advice concerned such matters as mineral rights, royalty rights, compensation claims for damage to land and crops, and other such situations that arise between lessor and lessee in an oil development area.[65] Oil was a unique and often exciting experience for the farmer. On occasion, his enthusiasm, coupled with a lack of legal knowledge, led to consequences that were not in his best interests. In order to assist the farmer to arrive at a more judicious decision the County Agent decided to provide him with some general but accurate instruction in the science and economics of oil development. To meet this situation, Mr. Don Hotchkiss, the County Agent, conducted 14-15 meetings throughout Williams County to familiarize farmers with mineral rights. The meetings were well-received and well-attended. Apparently the County Agent was so successful in this educational venture that a group of oilmen offered him a lucrative job—contacting farmers about selling, leasing, etc., their mineral rights. He declined. According to the County Agent, the farmer in the oil area has, in general, not altered his attitudes or his techniques to any appreciable degree because of oil. There was an original burst of enthusiasm and a period of great expectations but as drillings slowed down and the oil fields proved to be restricted to rather limited areas the farmer began to develop a considerably more cautious "wait-and-see" attitude.

The County Superintendent of Schools has been an important participant in a rapidly moving educational system. Her responsibilities have not increased proportionately due to the fact that the main changes occurred in city schools—Williston, Tioga, and Ray—which are largely beyond her jurisdiction, but the ministerial duties of her office have increased. There was a rapid upsurge in school population in the Pleasant Valley School District near Tioga, as indicated by Table XXVIII, but this situation was apparently well under control by 1955.

---

[65] See S.N. Voelker and L.A. Parcher, *Land Ownership Problems and Oil Development*, North Dakota Agricultural College and U.S. Department of Agriculture, Agriculture Economics Report No. 6 (Fargo: N.D. Agricultural College, December 1952) and Stanley Voelker, *Mineral Rights and Oil Development in Williams County, North Dakota*, North Dakota Agricultural College and the U.S. Department of Agriculture, Bulletin 395 (Fargo: North Dakota Agricultural College, September, 1954.)

TABLE XXVIII
PLEASANT VALLEY SCHOOL DISTRICT (RURAL TIOGA)
ENROLLMENTS, PROPERTY VALUATIONS AND TAX RATES,
FISCAL YEARS 1950–1951 TO 1954–1955

Year	Students	Property Valuation	General Fund Mill Levy
1950–51	......	$138,804.00	33
1951–52	13	160,200.00	33
1952–53	75	453,902.00	22
1953–54	44	561,048.00	20.03
1954–55	47	......	......

In general, the Superintendent of Schools considered the children of the oil workers to be reasonably well-behaved and usually rather apt pupils but the migratory sort of life that many of them had to lead meant some retardation. These pupils usually assimilated well and the "ins-outs" relationships were not considered to be at all a serious problem.

Oil has not caused any vast changes in School District No. 8 which is, in itself, larger than the State of Rhode Island.[66] For the year 1954–55 the gross oil production tax had brought in over $6,000 in revenue for the school district but increased tuition costs in the Williston school— where some children outside of the Williston area must attend, and that includes a trailer camp west of Williston which is in the District No. 8 area—have been an additional burden on the District's budget.

The District Court of the Fifth Judicial District in North Dakota, which has original jurisdiction over nearly all important civil and criminal cases, had a somewhat busier calendar due to the discovery of oil, but, as Table XXIX indicates, perhaps not as much so as one might conjecture.

Lastly, the County Highway Department was faced with constructing and reconstructing many county roads, or at least assisting in the process. This interviewer heard quite variegated opinions about the conditions of secondary roads before and after the discovery of oil. Comments such as "we never had any roads to begin with," to denunciations of the destruction of these roads by heavy oil drilling equipment, to opinions that the roads were much better in 1955 than in 1950, were all garnered. Just in terms of finances it would seem that the

[66] There is an article on School District No. 8 in the *Farm Journal*, October 1953, pp. 50–51, 183–85.

oil production tax was not sufficient to meet the additional expenses incurred although there are many factors to be considered. However, in about a two year period (July 1, 1953–June 2, 1955), the amount of the fund allocated to counties which had been directed to roads totalled $179,860.40 while the highway appropriations increased from $307,610 in fiscal year 1952 to $490,860 in fiscal 1953. Still, this increase might have been primarily due to an improved revenue situation.

TABLE XXIX
FIFTH JUDICIAL DISTRICT COURT CRIMINAL AND CIVIL
CASES, 1951–1955

Time Period	Number of Criminal Cases[1]	Time Period	Number of Civil Cases[2]
Jan.–Dec., 1951	46	Aug. 19–Dec. 31, 1952	122
Jan.–Dec., 1952	50	Jan. 9–Dec. 31, 1953	236
Jan.–Dec., 1953	66	Jan. 4–Dec. 31, 1954	204
Jan.–Dec., 1954	54	Jan. 5–June 15, 1955	115
Jan.–June, 1955	29		

1. Most of these persons were charged with "driving under the influence of intoxicating liquor."
2. Most of the civil cases were "actions to quiet title" although this type of case is becoming less frequent, for example:

Month	Total Cases	Actions to Quiet Title
October, 1952	34	17
October, 1953	23	6
October 1954	27	5

B. Financing Government

From what has been discussed thus far it becomes obvious that Williams County had to have more income in order to meet the increased governmental costs (SEE TABLE XXX). The tables are so self-explanatory that few comments need be made in the way of description or analysis.

Tax collections stayed remarkably high—100% in some areas—although the percentage seemed to decrease as the anticipation of oil discovery lessened. For example, in the city of Tioga the collections were 99.84% in 1951, 98.09% in 1952, and 87.14% in 1953.

Table XXXI shows the funds that were actually appropriated for administering the various activities of government in Williams County. When one considers that in a four year period appropriations had increased somewhat over 45% the impact of oil discovery becomes more apparent.

TABLE XXX

WILLIAMS COUNTY PROPERTY VALUATIONS, BY TYPE, AND
TAX RATES, 1950-1954

Year	Real Estate Valuations	Personal Property Valuations	Public Utility Valuations	Total Property Valuations	County Mill Levy
1950	$9,406,404	$2,781,318	$3,365,187	$15,552,909	31.75
1951	9,709,184	3,168,281	3,448,721	16,336,186	34.16
1952	10,005,710	3,974,908	3,485,301	17,465,919	35.84
1953	11,249,553	4,972,631	3,718,131	19,940,315	36.33
1954	13,040,654	5,301,063	4,151,832	22,572,583	31.63

This study has practically excluded the impact of oil in other counties in the Williston Basin area, notably Mountrail and McKenzie counties, but a cursory investigation indicated that the effects were less in those counties than in Williams. It is impossible to predict at present whether this will continue to be true but the recent discoveries of oil in Bottineau, Burke, and Renville counties strongly indicate that oil development in North Dakota is still in a period of flux.

TABLE XXXI

WILLIAMS COUNTY APPROPRIATIONS, BY TYPE OF PURPOSE,
FISCAL YEARS 1951-1952 TO 1954-1955

General Gov't	Protection to persons & propt.	Health and Sanitation	Ag. and Econ. Develop.	Relief Charities	Education	Recreation	Highway	TOTAL
51-52								
$116,700	$38,140	$7,778	$6,408	$97,890	$9,596	$......	$307,610	$584,122
52-53								
121,780	56,485	8,139	6,408	94,323	9,770	400	448,400	745,705
53-54								
134,186	57,473	13,049	6,702	93,839	10,414	......	485,075	800,038
54-55								
161,728	61,353	14,979	10,324	101,245	11,134	......	490,960	851,722
Totals by Purpose								
$534,394	$213,451	$43,944	$29,842	$387,297	$40,914	$400	$1,732,045	$2,981,587

C. Federal Agencies and Oil Development

It was deemed to be somewhat outside the scope of, or at best periph-
eral to, this study to relate the changes made by oil discovery to the
operation of Federal agencies. However, a general inquiry brought to
the surface enough facts to state that the functioning of the Farmers
Home Administration, the Agricultural Stabilization and Conservation
Committee (formerly the PMA), and the Soil Conservation Service was
influenced by the discovery of oil. For example, the Williams County
official for the Farmers Home Administration—Mr. John Freeman—
estimated that at least four farmers received sufficient income from
the sale of mineral rights to pay off all their FHA loans; another ten
farmers had made, and were making, enough from their oil leases to
pay off their farm ownership loans. It is true that the emergency, sub-
sistence, and production loans increased from approximately $150,000
in 1953–54 to $163,508 in 1954–55, but this was due primarily to the
hail and drought that had struck in the northern and southwestern
parts of Williams County. How much, if any, oil had changed the attitudes of farmers toward soil conservation who are in the Little Muddy
Soil Conservation District and the Eastern Williams Soil Conservation
District, a soil scientist assigned to the Soil Conservation Service office would not, when interviewed, predict, but the logic of the situation
was that more income would mean more conservation. An indication
that farmers in the oil county had not radically revised their attitudes
toward national farm policy was discovered in a perusal of the wheat
referendum that was held on June 24, 1955, in the Tioga area. Those
in favor of marketing quotas and acreage allotments totalled 153; only
two farmers were opposed. The total vote for Williams County was
2,150 for and 62 against.[67]

VII. Oil and the Political Power Structure in the Williston Basin Area

A. The Locus of Political Power and the Decision-Making Process

The general hypothesis of this section is that the political power structure in the Williston Basin area remains essentially the same today
as it was prior to the discovery of oil.[68] The one exception pertains to

---

[67] Tioga *Tribune*, June 30, 1955.

[68] Power, herein, is defined as the ability of certain men to control and/or influence the actions of other men in obtaining the deference, goods, and services
which the former desires. There are many definitions of power. See Floyd

oil policy where the interests of the oilmen have added what might be termed a new dimension to the power structure.

The specific hypothesis of this section is—businessmen[69] and some professional men, primarily lawyers, are the community leaders and largely determine oil policy, and attitudes toward oil policy, in the communities of Williston, Tioga, and Ray.[70] Such a supposition does not mean that these individuals and their associations are always in agreement—there are conflicts—but the ideas that become formalized in laws and administrative decisions are mainly formulated and espoused by these individuals and groups.[71] This hypothesis does not adequately account for the power of the Farmers Union in rural areas but, as has already been noted, the deviation here in terms of oil policy is not as drastic as one might expect.

In order to test this tentative theory regarding the locus of power and to determine those who are the decision-makers, the researcher must offer adequate and effective empirical data. The sources of that type of factual information, in this instance, are primarily two—the questionnaire type of survey which has already been referred to many times in this chapter, and personal interviews with those who were considered, by others as well as the writer, to be leaders in various phases of community political activities. The following brief analyses of certain power situations are presented as a substantiation of the above-stated hypotheses.

Hunter, *Community Power Structure* (Chapel Hill: University of North Carolina Press, 1953), pp. 2-3-4-139; John Hallowell, *Main Currents in Modern Political Thought* (New York: Henry Holt and Co., 1950), Chapter I; V.O. Key, Jr., *Politics, Parties, and Pressure Groups* (New York: Thomas Y. Crowell Co., 1952), Chapter I.

[69] The term "businessmen" includes the top officials of the different types of oil concerns.

[70] See Hunter's observations relative to "Regional City," *Ibid.*, pp. 81 and 102.

[71] A prominent state official questioned seriously the validity of this hypothesis. He believes the evidence reveals that the Legislative Research Committee was "the" prime formulator of oil policy in North Dakota, notably the Committee's role in the 1953 legislative session. But it is interesting to speculate as to what might have occurred if the proposals of the Legislative Research Committee and those of the business interests in the Williston area had been in substantial opposition.

(1) Oil and Gas Legislation

The principal oil and gas legislation for North Dakota has already been discussed earlier in this chapter. What is to be considered at this juncture is policy formation and public attitudes concerning the gross oil production tax. When one considers the pressures that were exerted upon the 1953 legislature, and especially upon Senator Solberg, the logical assumption would be that a low tax had the support of the constituents, in the Williston Basin area. But, as Mr. Justice Holmes once wrote: "Logic is not the life of the law, but experience," and such seems to be the situation in this instance. Parenthetically, it is not contended here that the results of the survey are by any means infallible, rather the contention is that the data is generally indicative as to whether or not the interviewee understands the issue. The following question was asked those who were interviewed in Williston, Ray, and the rural impact areas: Question 10: Do you know what the main features of the state oil tax are? If "YES"—a. Do you believe that the gross production tax is too high or too low? Why? b. Are you in favor of the 27½% depletion allowance? If "YES" or "NO"—why?

The results of the survey are disclosed by Table XXXII and it should be noted that those questionnaires on which no data on this question was contained have been excluded from the tabulation.

In analyzing these results one has to exclude the results received in Ray as the great preponderance of interviewees did not participate in answering this question, but for Williston, in particular, the results are noteworthy. Out of a grand total of 475 (143+332) respondents to this question 431 did not have any factual understanding of the issue. In other words, only slightly over 10% had any comprehension of the oil production tax at all and even they were undecided or showed no particular grasp of the issue. Perhaps a closer questioning of the interviewees might have produced more enlightened answers but there is little reason to believe so. However, of those community political leaders who were interviewed, all could discuss this oil tax issue although there were a few instances where they were not certain as to how the refunds to the county were allocated. A rather certain conclusion seems to be that oil policy is understood by a very few, that is, those who—to use a phrase of John Dewey's—have a "perception of the consequences."[72] In fact, it seems to be confined to the community leaders—businessmen, lawyers, politicians, newspapermen, officials of oil concerns, and the like. With them, the issue was created, articulated, and meaningful.

---

[72] John Dewey, *The Public and Its Problems* (Chicago: Gateway Books, 1956), p. 59.

TABLE XXXII
TYPES OF ANSWERS, BY WILLISTON BASIN LOCALITY RES-
IDENCE (AND LENGTH OF RESIDENCE IN WILLISTON),
TO THE QUESTIONS: "DO YOU KNOW WHAT THE MAIN
FEATURES OF THE STATE OIL TAX ARE? IF 'YES': A. DO YOU
BELIEVE THAT THE GROSS PRODUCTION TAX IS TOO HIGH
OR TOO LOW? WHY? B. ARE YOU IN FAVOR OF THE 27½% DE-
PLETION ALLOWANCE? IF 'YES' OR 'NO': WHY?

| | Williston | | | |
Answers to the Question	New Residents	Old Residents[1]	Ray	Impact Areas (Old)
No—				
Did not understand the issue	130	301	7	16
Yes, O.K.—no reason	4	10		2
No—not necessary				
Undecided—no reason		3		1
Others	9	18	6	10
Totals	143	332	13	29

1. Where the respondent did not signify whether he was "new" or "old" he has
been included as "old." There were few such instances.

The future of this oil tax issue will be interesting to observe. In the
summer of 1955, opinion on this matter among the leaders was in a
process of re-thinking. Roughly half of those interviewed still believed
that the present tax was proper; none desired a lower tax—or at least
would not openly advocate such; the other half was moving toward
higher tax but almost invariably no more than "1–2% more." Whether
this gradually changing opinion will create "higher oil tax atmosphere"
in the 1957 legislative session remained to be seen.

(2) The Question of Factionalism

In *The Federalist* (No. 10), James Madison stated that "liberty is to faction what air is to fire, an aliment without which it instantly expires."
Then he proceeds to explain that although factions do, even must, exist
in a republic it is still mandatory to control their effects.

The results of the survey seem to indicate that factions are actually
considered to be non-existent by a very large majority of the respondents in Williston, although this is much less true in Tioga. Further, the
discussion in the earlier sections of this chapter point to the active and

effective operations of factions in different phases of policy-making. Here, again, the evidence points to apathy and indifference to public affairs on the part of the many. The results of the survey on this particular issue are presented in Table XXXIII.

TABLE XXXIII
TYPES OF ANSWERS, BY WILLISTON AND TIOGA RESIDENCE
AND LENGTH OF RESIDENCE TO THE QUESTION AS TO
WHETHER OR NOT THERE WERE LOCAL FACTIONS AND
WHO CONSTITUTED THE FACTIONS

	Williston		Tioga	
Types of Answers	Old	New	Old	New
No	205	63	27	40
No opinion	108	57	8	10
Labor	1			3
Farm Organizations	1			
Religious Groups	7	1		1
Business Groups	1			3
Banking Groups	3	4		
Other (including combinations)	15	8	9	12
Total	341	133	44	69
GRAND TOTAL	474		113	

Less than 9.5% of those interviewed in Williston stated they believed there were factions but almost 33% acknowledged their existence in Tioga. This might indicate a more satisfied and static community atmosphere in Williston but incidents that have already been recounted in this chapter tend to a contrary opinion. One seems rather directed to the conclusion that the "interests" Madison refers to are definitely minorities and that the majority did not realize that the minorities were organized into factions and that these factions formulate public policies. His comment that "...measures are too often decided, not according to the rules of justice and the rights of the minor party, but by the superior force of an interested and overbearing majority party" should perhaps be revised by interchanging the words "minor" and "majority" and then changing "minor" to read "minority."

The results of this survey are not offered, by any means, as conclusive evidence but are rather just another example of a growing body of data concerning this political reality.[73]

---

[73] Hunter, *op. cit.* pp. 81, 102, 109, 148. Also David Riesman's *The Lonely Crowd* (New York: Doubleday Anchor Books, 1953), particularly Chapter X, contains

(3) The Issue of Leadership

On the issue of oil policy, the leadership has come predominantly from the business community in the Williston Basin area, primarily bankers, the Williston Chamber of Commerce, and lawyers.[74] Again, the "public" has been very limited but it is growing and the story of the techniques used in forming the public into a mold which is favorable to the oil companies needs to be related.

In 1946, all the oil companies in the United States which were members of the American Petroleum Institute formed, within the API, an Oil Industry Information Committee. After considerable research and assistance from some educators, there was begun a "Petroleum Industry School Program" that was designed to provide a reciprocal exchange of information and understanding between the oil industry and the schools.[75] In the words of the OIIC, the objectives of its "school program" are:[76]

---

several useful insights and hypotheses bearing on this matter of political power in present-day America. But "veto groups" were not at all apparent in oil politics in North Dakota, except in regards to the spacing issue. However, to use Riesman's term, the public was the "unorganized."

[74] At the state government level, a few of the politicians and government officials have provided a moderate amount of leadership.

[75] It should be clearly stated here that the author believes there is considerable merit in the educational program of the American Petroleum Institute. The knowledge of most laymen will be substantially broadened by studying the material. However, it is questionable if this is education. Are there no alternatives to the courses of action presently followed by the major oil companies? Have no controversies arisen over the organization and actions of the oil industry? What different arguments were advanced by those engaged in the conflict? The questionable nature of this kind of an educational approach seems to be indicated by the text that the Committee issued on the economics of petroleum. (American Petroleum Institute, *What Makes This Nation Go*. New York: American Petroleum Institute, 1955.) A fine example of Spencerian philosophy is noted in the statement that "...every month last year, many hundreds of businesses were forced out of the race. Many have failed to offer the right product at the right price, and have seen their customers drift away..." "In time, the profit motive weeds out the inefficient and encourages the best." Ibid., p. 11. This may be true, or at least partially so, but are there not alternative philosophies as well as alternative analysis of what has actually occurred, that would need to be offered in a truly educational process?

[76] American Petroleum Institute (OIIC), *Conducting the Petroleum Industry School Program* (New York: American Petroleum Institute, 1954), pp. 2–3.

1. To provide information about the oil industry to the schools in various acceptable ways, with the expectation that teachers, students and parents may thereby better understand the industry's contribution to the well-being, security and improved standards of living of the American people.
2. To inform oil men about the schools and acquaint them with the people and problems of education, with the expectation that they will be stimulated to take greater personal interest in education and more effectively lend their support and cooperation to the schools at local, state, and national levels.

The program has three basic and important characteristics:

FIRST: It has been developed from the outset in accordance with principles recommended by educators as a result of a study concerning business-sponsored educational materials. It has been designed to furnish teachers and students with accurate and objective information about the oil industry. It has been prepared to fit appropriately into regular courses of study.

SECOND: It is now being conducted on a basis planned to provide experience and guidance for sound expansion of the program during succeeding years. The ultimate goal is a nation-wide school program.

THIRD: Responsibility for contact with the schools, for distribution of the materials, and for providing the program services is placed with the local oil men.

Apparently the American Petroleum Institute had a survey conducted of public attitudes toward the oil industry and discovered that many people knew about the Teapot Dome, the exploits of John D. Rockefeller Sr., and the like, but little about the vast dynamic developments in the oil industry.

Mr. Gregg Kildow, II, a sales officer of the Northern Mud Company in Williston, spearheaded the activities of the Oil Industry Information Committee in the North Dakota oil areas. The Committee had (1955), approximately 80 members and each membership was $5.00, although that appears to be only a minimum charge. Members of this local OIIC organization have visited many of the high schools in Williams, McKenzie, Mountrail, Divide, Burke, Bottineau, and McHenry counties, talked to school assemblies, and informed the school superintendents and teachers of the study program which was offered, free of charge, for their use.[77] The printed materials have been prepared for junior and senior high school students, are attractively presented, and are comprehensive in coverage. The many phases of the oil industry from chemistry to the social sciences are discussed in individual booklets; film strips are included; movies on the oil industry may be borrowed at no cost; and teacher's aids and a handbook are a part of the total package.

During the 1954–55 school year the Committee became particularly active. First, a panel of experts on all phases of the oil industry was organized. Then, during the school year, the panel visited high schools—10 in 1954—and at scheduled assemblies they answered any questions regarding oil production, etc., which the students were interested in asking.[78] Second, an essay contest was held with the theme being, "What Has Oil Done for Me?" Every school that participated received a $25 Savings Bond and an engraved plaque for the two winners—one junior and one senior high school student. Six hundred students participated, and an area prize of a $50 bond for the best essay was awarded. A banquet was then held in Williston for the winners and their high school teachers. Third, a radio program—30 minutes every Monday night—called the "Oil Forum" was initiated. It was a mixed panel composed of oil experts and local citizens. The local citizens would pose questions concerning the various phases of the oil industry and radio listeners would call in questions for the panel of experts to answer. The local OHC group paid for the radio time. From all appearances the activities of this Committee have been well received. It cannot be foreseen at this time whether this Committee will take the lead when, and if, the issue of compulsory unitization of oil fields arises,[79] but it appears that the issue will become important in the not too distant future. However, it does seem worth noting that the North Dakota OIIC was considered the best in the nation in 1954 by the American Petroleum Institute.

The Williston Chamber of Commerce has also been very active in taking the lead in advancing the interests of the oil industry and thereby, in the opinion of the Chamber, the interests of the region and the state.

---

[77] The committee, or its representatives, visited 24 high schools in 1954 and all placed orders with the committee for the free materials.

[78] Mr. Kildow insists that "political" questions—such as a "proper" oil production tax—were the only kind that received no answers. The line between political and non-political questions would be difficult to draw but he believes that it has been strictly adhered to.

[79] See the booklet published by the American Petroleum Institute, *The Conservation of Petroleum*, 1954, p. 10, and the Interstate Oil Compact Commission, *Oil For Today—And For Tomorrow, op. cit.*, pp. 23, 30, 43, 57.

Since 1953, one Director on the 15 member board of the Chamber of Commerce has been an oilman. The Chamber has lobbied for a low oil production tax, 27½% depletion allowance, and a market demand law; but opposed the anti-flaring bill. The activities of the Upper Missouri Development Association—this organization has been almost solely concerned with attempting to defeat an 1850 foot level for the Garrison dam—have been largely financed by the Chamber and this issue is presumed to be of significant interest to the oil companies as the additional flooding of land will increase drilling costs. The Chamber has assisted in the radio programs of the OIIC, pushed for a commercial airline stop at Williston which the oilmen desired, and sponsored an annual Oil and Farm Festival Day in Williston. It has been avowedly neutral in the oil spacing issue because, as has been previously discussed, there has been definite conflict here between the oil industry and the Williams County Landowner's and Royalty Owner's Association. With this last possible exception, the Williston Chamber of Commerce has energetically sponsored and promoted activities which were presumably in the interests of oil development in the Williston area.

The results of a survey question concerning leadership are interesting and somewhat indicative. The question posed was—"What about town leaders? Who in your opinion are the town leaders?" Only the interviewees in Williston and Tioga were quizzed. The results are presented in Table XXXIV.

TABLE XXXIV
TYPES OF ANSWERS, BY WILLISTON AND TIOGA RESIDENCE
(AND LENGTH OF RESIDENCE IN WILLISTON), TO THE
QUESTION AS TO WHO WERE LOCAL LEADERS

	Williston[1]		
Types of Answers	Old	New	Tioga
There are none	4	2	5
Don't know	109	64	39
Business Groups	73	21	5
Professional Groups	13	2	8
Politicians and government officials	35	8	31
Other	5	1	4
Older Group	17	3	4
New Group	4	3	10
TOTAL	260	104	106

1. The "either" category are included in the "old" column.

Thus, approximately 47% of those polled in Williston did not know if there were any town leaders to provide the community with leadership but the percentage was lowered to about 38% in Tioga. However, nearly 26% of those questioned in Williston considered business groups to be the source of leadership; in Tioga, that percentage had decreased to less than five. To this writer, it seemed rather remarkable that almost 30% of the respondents in Tioga selected politicians and government officials as the town leaders but that the percentage was less than twelve in Williston. But the results seem generally to support, either directly or indirectly, the original hypothesis—most people are not interested enough in community affairs to be concerned about leadership or else they look mainly to business groups to supply the necessary leadership.[80]

(4) The Farmer Versus the Corporation

In a hearing before the House Finance and Taxation Committee of the North Dakota state legislature in late February, 1953, Mr. C.E. Boone, a vice president of the Amerada Oil Company, was queried as to how the Northern Pacific Railroad Company was able to get a 30% royalty agreement with Amerada for any oil that might be discovered under the extensive tracts of land which the Northern Pacific owned in western North Dakota. Mr. Boone's comment was: "there will always be exceptional deals."[81] Thus the farmer's usual ⅛ or 12½% becomes 30% for the railroad, or, in other words this railroad receives about 2½ times the customary amount of oil income.

Again, Professors Voelker and Parcher write that "the most common primary term for leases granted by private owners in North Dakota is 10 years, although many leases for 5 and 7 year terms have also been recorded. Where a state or a political subdivision holds the mineral rights, the leases are generally for 5 year terms."[82]

Both of these situations have been related in order to exemplify the concept of power in the formation of oil policy. One might conjecture as to what would have happened if the farmers had organized themselves effectively into a "land bloc" which could then have presented itself to the oil companies as a genuine "countervailing power."[83]

---

[80] Riesman believes that "the only followers left in the United States today are those unorganized and sometimes disorganized unfortunates who have not yet invented their veto group." Riesman, *op. cit.*, p. 247.

[81] Grand Forks *Herald*, March 2, 1953.

[82] Voelker and Parcher, *op. cit.*, p. 5.

[83] The term is explained in some detail in John Kenneth Galbraith's *American Capitalism* (Boston: Houghton Mifflin Company, 1952).

VIII. The Future of Oil Politics in North Dakota

In the early years of oil discovery in North Dakota there was an abundant amount of speculation as to how oil would affect the political scene. The major postulate of this section is that oil has, thus far, meant more of the same. The northwestern area of North Dakota is strong Non-Partisan League country. The election returns point up the following general voting patterns in this area for the years 1950, 1952, and 1954. The NPL'ers vote for their candidates who have thus far filed in the Republican column in the primary and the Democrats are not much in evidence. In fact, many of the latter, as well as some independents, vote for the NPL candidates. Then in the fall the Democratic candidates receive a vote four to ten times more than was true in the primary. Apparently that vote comes from NPL'ers who switch to the Democratic column, from some "stay-at-home-in-the-primary" Democrats, and from those inscrutable, but prevalent, independents.

A. An Influx of Democrats

The political soothsayers in North Dakota have been conjecturing upon the voting habits of the new population that oil has brought into the state. The simple syllogism was—Southerners are Democrats; Southerners have moved into North Dakota. North Dakota will receive an influx of Democrats. The election returns seem to indicate that the oil workers have not stayed in North Dakota long enough to meet residence requirements or that most have simply failed to exercise the franchise. The questionnaire was used again in an attempt to gain some further insight into this matter. In Williston, Ray, and the Impact Areas, this question was posed—"Would you please state your political party or factional affiliation, if any, in 1952? Today?" and the resulting answers were compiled and organized into Table XXXV.

The results of this survey appear to substantiate partially the hypothesis although the years used were 1952 and 1954 and a pre-oil discovery year, such as 1950, was not a part of the question. The Democrats, according to the survey, increased their strength in Williston by over 6% from 1952 to 1954, but the Republican, ROC, and Republican-NPL vote for 1954 (196 votes) is still substantially more than the Democrat and Democrat-NPL combination (146). The key vote then is in the "independent" and "undecided" categories (121 votes). Some political unrest and uncertainties are clearly evident from a percentage increase in the "undecided" vote from 5 in 1952 to 38 in 1954.

The data obtained in the Impact Area are indecisive. There was a noticeable loss in the Republican and Republican-NPL vote but the respondents seemed to be rather negative in terms of present intentions.

The statistics from Ray may be rather deceptive. It appears that slightly over 50% of the respondents were Democrats in 1952, although the percentage had decreased by 1954. However, the Democrats never carried Ray in any election from 1950 through 1954 for federal offices, or the office of governor. It is always possible that the Democrat vote stayed at home, but not likely.

All in all, there is only slight evidence of any influx of Democrats into North Dakota because of the discovery of oil. The potential Democratic vote was of a migratory type and the more or less permanent oil personnel is not of sufficient numerical size to alter the existing patterns to any appreciable degree. Nevertheless, the "independent" and "undecided" vote is significant and offers the potential for a considerable shift in the political intentions of the electorate.

TABLE XXXV
POLITICAL AFFILIATIONS, BY WILLISTON BASIN LOCALITY
RESIDENCE AND LENGTH OF RESIDENCE,
FOR 1952 AND 1954

Types of Answers

	Williston Old		Williston New		Williston Totals		Impact Areas Old		Impact Areas New		Impact Areas Totals		Ray	
	1952	1954	'52	'54	'52	'54	'52	'54	'52	'54	'52	'54	'52	'54
Democrat	90	97	44	44	134	143	14	15	1	1	15	16	54	46
Democrat-NPL	2	3			2	3	1	1			1	1	1	2
Republican	100	84	31	33	144	117	13	9	1		14	9	19	19
Republican-ROC	38	37	19	18	58	55	15	15			15	15	6	5
Republican-NPL	21	18	6	6	27	24	20	13			20	13	2	2
Independ.	67	57	31	25	97	83	17	17	5	5	22	22	21	21
Other		2		1		1		8				8		3
Undecided	4	23	1	15	5	39	3	4	...	...	3	4	5	2
No Data		1				1			1	1		2	1	9
TOTALS	322	322	142	142	464	464	83	83	7	7	90	90	109	109

B. Oil and Possible Political Realignments

Without exception, those political leaders in Williston and surrounding areas who were interviewed stated that the oil companies
and their interests were being supported by the ROC. Some believed
that the coming of oil had definitely been instrumental in the increased
strength of the ROC in the Williston area. But others thought a reaction was setting in, especially among the farmers, due to increased farm
labor costs, poorer farm roads, higher legal fees, the arbitrary attitude
and procedure of a few of the oil companies, and decreased drilling.
Heretofore, however, the ROC had supported the oil companies on
every major oil policy issue and has not especially suffered at the polls
for doing so.

There is considerable diversity of opinion as to the role the oil companies have played thus far in direct support of the ROC. A prominent
leader in the NPL said that the oil companies had remained aloof from
any factional affiliation and would continue to do so on his advice. An
important official in the ROC said that the oil companies, as such, had
made no contributions to the ROC and he believed that individual
oilmen, in 1954, had furnished not more than $500 of the Williams
County ROC budget of around $3,500. But a well-known Williston
lawyer "knew" that the Williams County ROC organization had contributed $25,000 to beat Senator Carroll Day in the 1954 primary
and that most of this money was from oil interests. However, Senator
Day, in a personal interview, estimated the sum to have been around
$15,000 and he was not certain as to its source, but "probably some of
it came from oil interests."[84]

This information is obviously somewhat contradictory and, just as
obviously, someone is in error. What this means for the future one can
only conjecture. If the NPL stays in the Republican column it appears
more and more likely that the organization will favor a slightly higher
oil tax. In such a case the oil interests may become more than lobbyists
and actually participate, at least financially, in the factional fights. If
the Democratic and NPL organizations merge, the issue of oil politics
remains in doubt. One political leader who might be influential in this
merger, or in preventing it, thought that the gross oil production tax
should be increased up to even 50%, "such as is done in Saudi Arabia."
If this were openly advocated in the campaign, oil politics in North Dakota would really be at the explosive stage.

---

[84] Senator Carroll Day was killed in an airplane crash on March 4, 1956.

C. The Key—The Future of Oil in North Dakota

The future role of oil politics in North Dakota appears to be governed primarily by the future of oil development in this state. If a relatively static condition, such as was evident in the latter part of 1954 and during most of 1955, continues then oil interests are going to be a powerful lobby but not "king oil" as some have claimed. But an expansion of the oil fields—such as might occur in Burke, Renville and Bottineau counties where wildcat wells have proved to be producers—might well change the political scene. It must be remembered that usually 12½% of the gross income from oil goes to the landowner, or the owner of mineral rights. If oil production becomes very widespread—and it is also worthy of note that, in statewide terms, "discovered" oil fields account for a very small percentage of total land area—the oil "public" will be expanded somewhat proportionately. Discovery of many new fields, or substantial enlargement of those already discovered, would also increase the political base of the oil interests. The reason for the increase in power is rather well summarized by recent story—"the last time you reported on him [a cousin] they had struck oil on his land and his liberalism was going down just as fast as the oil was coming up."[85]

Thus we return to the ancient dialogue between Socrates and Thrasymachus—"Listen, then, Thrasymachus began. What I say is that 'just' or 'right' means nothing but what is to the interest of the stronger party. Well, where is your applause?"[86] Whether one applauds or not is question of values.

---

[85] *The Leader*, September 1, 1955.

[86] Francis M. Cornford (ed.), *The Republic of Plato* (New York: The Oxford University Press, 1945), p. 18.

2018

Chapter 6
Political Impacts of Oil in an Era of Sustainability

Andrea Olive

The impacts of the recent (2008–14) oil boom in the Williston Basin are far-reaching. They include increases in population and state revenue, and they have made transportation and infrastructure more complex and produced numerous environmental externalities (see, for example, Caraher and Conway 2016; McGranahan, Allen, Fernando, and Kirkwood 2017; Ruddell, Jayasundara, Mayzer, and Heitkamp 2014). The political impacts cannot be overstated, as the government of North Dakota is mainly responsible for regulating oil development in balance with social, economic, and environmental issues. The main concern is no longer developing an oil industry and economy in the state, as it was the 1950s, but instead balancing this booming industry with society's best long-term interests—including economic (see Chapter 8) and social (see Chapters 10, 11 and 13) interests.

This chapter will provide a brief overview of North Dakota politics and the government administration of oil. Similar to Ross Talbot's 1958 "Political Impact" chapter, this one is also authored by a social scientist as opposed to a physical scientist or a scholar of oil technology, and the focus is still on government processes and regulation. This chapter tries to follow the structure and format of the original 1958 piece, but has had to include new actors (like Native Americans and their governance systems), new regulations, and an entirely new emphasis on the environmental impacts of oil, given the realities of science, climate change, and sustainability.

In the 1950s and 1960s, the regulation of oil was centralized in a few government agencies, especially the North Dakota Industrial Commission. Today, regulation has moved from a narrow government model to a governance model whereby actors outside of state government are also involved in oil administration. These new actors include not just other agencies inside the state, but also Native American tribal councils and interest groups. In 2018, there are hundreds of laws associated with oil production in the state, as compiled into the state *RuleBook* (North Dakota Department of Mineral Resources 2017). The focus of this chapter will be four areas of policy where the government is trying to balance oil development with environmental protection: severance taxes, flaring regulations, water permits, and transportation policy. In each area the government and other actors have created new, and sometimes innovative, regulations and rules to govern oil.

Brief Survey of North Dakota Politics and Government

While North Dakota has long been associated with Republican Party rule, between 1958 and 2018, Democratic-NPL politicians held the governorship for twenty-seven years. Historically, the Nonpartisan League (NPL) was a third party in North Dakota, but in the early 1950s that party split into two—one side merged into the state Republican Party and the other side merged with the Democratic Party of North Dakota to formally create the Democratic-NPL party in 1956. Thus, today North Dakota is a two-party state with the Republicans and the Democratic-NPL. The latter held the governorship of the state with a continuous twenty year stretch between 1961 and 1981 and a seven-year stretch from 1985 to 1992. The governorship has since been dominated by Republicans. The current governor is Doug Burgum, who was elected December 15, 2016, with 75 percent of the popular vote. The remainder of the executive branch's main office holders, from the lieutenant governor to the agriculture commissioner, are all members of the Republican party. See Table 6.1 for a list of main executive offices. Some of these offices have longtime incumbents, such as Al Jaeger, who has been the secretary of state since 1993, and Kelly Schmidt, who has served as state treasurer since 2001. These individuals have served North Dakota through the entirety of the recent oil boom.

TABLE 6.1.
OFFICE, PARTY, NAME, AND YEAR ELECTED FOR MAIN EXECUTIVE
BRANCH POSITIONS

Office	Party	Name	Year Elected
Governor	Republican	Doug Burgum	2016
Lieutenant governor	Republican	Brent Sanford	2016
Secretary of state	Republican	Al Jaeger	1993
Attorney general	Republican	Wayne Stenehjem	2017
State auditor	Republican	Josh Gallion	2017
State treasurer	Republican	Kelly Schmidt	2001
Agriculture commissioner	Republican	Doug Goehring	2009
Public Service commissioners	Republican	Julie Fedorchak	2012
		Randy Christman	2013
		Brian Kroshus	2017
Insurance commissioner	Republican	Adam Hamm	2007
Tax commissioner	Republican	Ryan Rauschenberger	2013

The state House and Senate are also both dominated by Republicans. At the outset of 2018, the House had eighty-one elected Republican and thirteen Democratic-NPL members, while the Senate had thirty-eight Republican and nine Democratic-NPL members. The congressional districts that comprised the Williston Basin have long been dominated by Republican officials. For example, during the sixty-third, sixty-fourth, and sixty-fifth legislative assemblies, District 1 in Williams Country had a Republican senator and two Republican representatives (North Dakota Legislative Branch 2018). However, at the federal level North Dakota has elected at least one U.S. senator from the Democratic-NPL party since 1959. And both U.S. senators from North Dakota were Democratic-NPL from 1989 to 2011, when Republican John Hoeven was elected.

North Dakota is a predominantly rural state. There are fifty-three counties, and the U.S. Census Bureau classifies thirty-nine of them as completely rural, meaning there are fewer than 50,000 people (North Dakota Census Office 2017). However, North Dakota's population has experienced a significant increase in the past ten years. The U.S. Census Bureau estimates the state population to be 755,393 as of July 1, 2017. That is a 12 percent increase over the 2010 census population, and a significant gain since the twentieth century low of 617,000 in 1970 (Census Bureau n.d.a). Most of the recent newcomers have moved into the Williston Basin to work in the oil industry. When oil was discovered in the Williston Basin in 1951, the city of Williston had only

7,000 people, while North Dakota had only 617,000 people. By 2010, the city of Williston had a population of 14,716, and by 2015 the population grew to 26,426 (Census Bureau n.d.b). The demographics of North Dakota reveal that the population is mainly white (88 percent) with a median household income of $59,000 in 2016, which is above the U.S. average of $57,000 (Census Bureau n.d.a).

While migration to North Dakota has occurred in step with oil production, the state maintains a vibrant Plains Indian heritage. In 2018, Native Americans comprise about 5 percent of the population, or 31,000 individuals. There are five federally recognized tribes: the MHA Nation (Mandan, Hidatsa, and Arikara Nation), the Spirit Lake Nation, the Standing Rock Sioux Tribe, the Turtle Mountain Band of Chippewa Indians, the Sisseton-Wahpeton Oyate Nation, and the Trenton Indian Service Area (North Dakota Indian Affairs Commission n.d.). These tribes each have a reservation and govern themselves according to their own constitutions. However, in recent years Native Americans have started to run electoral campaigns for seats in North Dakota's legislature (Fragoso 2016). Notably, in the 2016 election, Ruth Buffalo became the first Native American Democratic woman elected to the North Dakota Legislature. She beat the incumbent, Republican Randy Boehing, who had previously sponsored a bill to limit the Native vote in the state (see Figure 6.1).

Administration and Governance of Oil Policy

The administration of oil policy is highly decentralized in the United States. The federal government has a minimal role to play in the exploration, production, or refining of oil across the fifty states. Issues pertaining to interstate commerce and transportation as well as the protection of some environmental resources (such as air quality or water quality) involve federal agencies and regulations. However, oil is predominantly a state issue. As evidenced in the original "Political Impact" chapter, in 1958 North Dakota had four state administration agencies largely responsible for oil policy and administration—the Industrial Commission, the state geologist, the Public Service Commission, and the Tax Commission. In 2018 these offices are still central to the regulation of oil, but governance has expanded to include other government agencies as well as Native Americans, non-governmental agencies, and federal agencies. While not all actors involved in the administration of oil can be reviewed here, it is worth highlighting the main actors in North Dakota.

State Agencies

The Industrial Commission, which was created in 1919 to manage certain utilities and industries, consists of the governor, attorney general, and agriculture commissioner. This commission includes the Oil and Gas Division, the Oil and Gas Research Program, the Pipeline Authority, and the Geological Survey division. In this sense, it remains the key agency for oil and gas regulation in North Dakota. However, the Public Service Commission also oversees issues related to oil and gas production, including energy plant sitings, railroads, and pipeline safety. This commission comprises three elected officials who serve a six-year term. Finally, the Tax Commission is also important to oil and gas production as it oversees the different state taxes, such as production and extraction taxes, related to the oil industry in North Dakota.

Outside of these main commissions, there is a plethora of other actors relevant to the administration of oil and gas in 2018. This is largely because oil production, especially hydraulic fracturing, is associated with numerous environmental risks. These include impacts on water quality and quantity, methane emissions (climate change), soil quality, air pollution, wildlife habitat destruction, and earthquakes. There is a small but growing literature on the

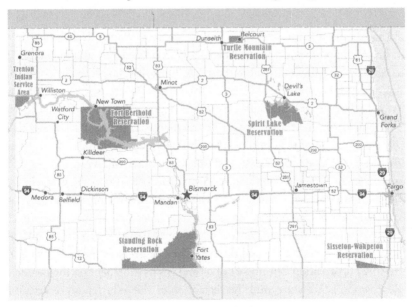

Figure 6.1. Location of Native American reservations in North Dakota (source: ND Indian Affairs Commission n.d.; image source: David Veller)

environmental impacts in the Bakken Formation (see for example, Hill and Olson 2013; Horner et al. 2016; Olive 2018; Scanlon, Reedy, Male, and Hove 2016; Shrestha et al. 2017; Thompson, Johnson, Niemuth, and Ribic 2015).

In order to govern the areas that oil production impacts, other government agencies are now involved in oil regulation and policy. These include agencies such as the Water Commission, the Department of Health, the Department of Labor, the Game and Fish Department, and the Parks and Recreation Department. For example, the Air Quality division of the North Dakota Department of Environment is responsible for granting construction permits to new projects that will impact air quality in the state. Likewise, the Water Commission is responsible for granting permits to withdraw surface and groundwater in the state for all recreational and industrial uses. This means that oil firms need a water permit before they can begin oil production. In the 1950s, the environmental externalities of oil production were both smaller and less studied, so regulation was either nonexistent or appeared unnecessary. Today oil production is known to have substantial impact on the environment and, therefore, requires a larger governance structure to oversee policy.

Native Americans

Although missing from the 1958 "Political Impact" chapter, Native American tribes are important actors in North Dakota oil and gas administration in 2018. As noted, there are more than 30,000 Native Americans living in the state as members of several Plains Indians tribes. There are five reservations, two of which cross into South Dakota (see Figure 6.1 for a map). Inside the Williston Basin, the Fort Berthold Reservation is 1,319 square miles with a 2015 population of 6,840 people (North Dakota Census Office 2015). These peoples—the Mandan, Hidatsa, and Arikara Nations (MHA Nation)—are divided into six segments on the reservation. The Tribal Council has an elected representative of each segment, as well as a chair. These members then serve on the council's five committees: natural resources, health and human resources, judicial, economic development, and education (MHA Nation n.d.b). The MHA Nation has a constitution, and the tribal council oversees policy on the Fort Berthold Reservation. The impact of oil and gas development on the Berthold Reservation is immense, and the regulation of the industry on reservation lands is notoriously complex (see Raymond 2011).

The Indian Affairs Commission is the liaison between the executive branch of the North Dakota state government and the tribal councils. Part of the commission's mandate is also to "increase the economic self-sufficiency" of American Indians in the state (North Dakota Indian Affairs Commission n.d.). This would include encouraging management of oil and gas development on the reservations. Given the location of the Fort Berthold Reservation, it is not surprising that there are significant oil reserves beneath it. Crude oil production on the reservation has been steadily increasing over the past ten years. Today there are more than 1,300 oil wells, which account for almost 20 percent of North Dakota's oil production (Energy Information Administration 2018). However, the vast majority of these wells have been drilled and produced by non-Native American oil companies.

In 2012, the MHA Nation received approval from the federal Department of the Interior to take control of part of its reservation land (which is held in trust by the federal government) to build an oil refinery (Smith 2012). This is known as the MHA Nation Clean Fuels Refinery, and it is operated by a tribal-owned entity called Thunder Butte Petroleum Services. Construction of phase one of the project was started in 2014 (see MHA Nation n.d.a). The MHA Nation also owns an oil company, the Missouri River Resources, and in 2015, it drilled its first tribe-owned well (Sisk 2016). As oil production continues in the state, Native American involvement will likely increase. An on-reservation oil refinery will be an important source of revenue for the MHA Nation, but also a much-needed refinery for the Bakken Formation and the state, which presently has only two oil refineries.

Interest Groups

Environmental groups, which have evolved over the twentieth century, are now significant actors in North American oil and gas politics (Dodge 2015; Dokshin 2016; Gullion 2015). In the context of North Dakota, they are probably associated mainly with opposition to the Dakota Access Pipeline and the Keystone XL pipeline (see Sisk 2016). However, at a smaller and more local level, environmental non-governmental groups act as pressure points and collaborators in the governance of land, water, air, and other environmental resources in the state. For example, the Sierra Club Dacotah Chapter has led campaigns to advocate for and support flaring regulations in the state (see Sierra Club Dacotah Chapter n.d.). Similarly, the Dakota Resource Council has focused on oil and gas issues since the group's founding in 1978. Their campaigns have included advocacy for flaring regulations, pipelines, and public land conservation (see Dakota Resource Council n.d.). As the environmental risks of oil production are becoming better known, participation by environmental groups is increasing. In fact, in some states, like New York, environmental groups have led campaigns to ban hydraulic fracturing because of the associated environmental externalities (Dodge 2015; Dokshin 2016).

The oil industry has also formed its own interest groups to lobby the state government for pro-oil policy and regulations. The oil sector was the top contributor to former-Governor Jack Dalrymple's political campaigns. In 2012, Dalrymple raised $3.6 million total, with about 10 percent or $370,000 coming from oil interests (Kusnetz 2017). The North Dakota Petroleum Council is one of the largest and most prominent oil interest groups in the state. It represents about five hundred oil and gas companies and is overseen by a Board of Directors, chosen every four years at the group's annual meeting. Their main goal is "promoting and enhancing the discovery, development, production, transportation, refining, conservation, and marketing of oil and gas in North Dakota" (North Dakota Petroleum Council n.d.). Whether the oil industry has become too rich and politically influential in the state is contested (Kusnetz 2017). But suffice it to say, the oil interest groups do wield substantial power.

Federal Government

The federal government can also be an important actor in state administration of oil and gas by creating national regulations and standards for issues in federal jurisdiction. One example is the transportation of oil and gas through North Dakota. Pipelines and railways are an area of shared governance in the U.S. federal system. Railway and pipelines that cross state and international borders are always part of the federal domain. The U.S. Secretary of Transportation has general regulatory and enforcement authority regarding protection against risks to life and property posed by pipeline transportation and pipeline facilities (Murrill 2016). Similarly, the Pipeline and Hazardous Materials Safety Administration (PHMSA), inside the Department of Transportation, is responsible for developing and enforcing regulations for the safe, reliable, and environmentally sound operation of pipeline transportation (Murrill 2016). This is a top-down system in which the federal government sets regulations that states are required to follow for all interstate railways and pipelines. However, for intrastate issues, the North Dakota Public Service Commission can "establish and enforce minimum safety standards for the design, construction, and operation" of pipelines and railways that distribute or move oil and gas (North Dakota Public Services Commission 2018).

The federal government is also responsible for interstate waters and safe drinking water in the country. The Clean Water Act and the Safe Drinking Water Act (SDWA) set federal regulations in these domains. In the context of the Williston Basin this is important because the Missouri River system crosses state lines and, therefore, permits to withdraw water are granted by the U.S. Army Corps of Engineers. Under the SDWA, North Dakota is required to meet drinking water quality standards as set out by the federal Environmental Protection Agency (see Environmental Protection Agency n.d., 2016). These regulations are discussed further below. But similar to transportation, water is an issue that draws the federal government into oil administration in the fifty states.

Oil Legislation

Ever since oil was discovered in North Dakota in 1951, it has been a major issue on the government docket. Oil governance is decentralized, and states oversee much of the production and some of the transportation. As noted in other chapters (Rundquist and Vandeberg, current volume), one of the biggest differences between 1958 and 2018 is the size of the oil patch and the consequential environmental externalities that require government oversight. Essentially, states "must weigh fundamental trade-offs between aggressive pursuit of resource development and aggressive pursuit of environmental protections" (Rabe 2014, 8371). While there have been hundreds of oil regulations created in North Dakota since 1958, this section will focus on four areas of oil policy that speak to the challenge of balancing oil production with environmental protection.

Severance Taxes

Severance taxes put a cost on the extraction of natural resources, such as oil, as they are being removed or "severed" from the earth. The impetus behind these taxes is generally to capture revenue from a nonrenewable resource that is being permanently withdrawn and consumed (Rabe and Hampton 2014). In the U.S., states have a long history of applying such taxes to coal and other minerals. In the twentieth century, severance taxes were attached to oil and gas development in many U.S. states. Texas was the first to pass a severance tax in 1905, while Michigan and Louisiana followed in the 1920s. In the twenty-first century, especially with the oil boom of the last decade, these taxes have garnered significantly more attention. Questions of how much states tax extraction and how they choose to allocate those funds (that is, general revenue versus environmental or heritage funds) are now scrutinized more carefully by policymakers and academics (Rabe and Hampton 2014).

North Dakota has overlapping severance taxes—an oil and gas production tax and an oil and gas extraction tax. These are imposed on the industry in lieu of property taxes. The state enacted its first production tax in 1953, when it set a 4.25 percent tax rate on the gross value of a well. And it enacted its first oil and gas extraction tax in 1980 through a ballot measure passed by voters in the general election. The oil extraction tax was set at 6.5 percent, which was to be distributed to the state general fund (45 percent), schools (45 percent), and a trust fund (10 percent) (see North Dakota State Tax Commission 1998).

As of 2018, the oil and gas *production* tax is a 5 percent rate applied to the gross value of all oil produced at a well (with exemptions for Native American holdings within the boundaries of a reservation). The oil *extraction* rate fluctuates between 5 percent and 6 percent depending on whether the average price of oil is above or below $90 a barrel for three consecutive months (see State of North Dakota State Tax Commission 2016). See Table 6.2 for recent changes to North Dakota's severance tax scheme.

TABLE 6.2.
LEGISLATIVE CHANGES TO NORTH DAKOTA'S SEVERANCE TAX
(2010–PRESENT)

Year	Legislation	Summary
2010	HCR3054 and ballot measure	Development of a Legacy Fund and ballot measure that allocates 30 percent of oil and gas revenues to the fund
2013	SB2014	Allocates oil extraction development funds to newly created energy conservation grant fund
2013	HB1358	Changes revenue allocation to counties and some cities
2013	HB1278	Changes portion of production tax revenue to newly created Heritage Fund
2015	HB1476	Beginning January 1, 2016, the oil extraction tax rate is reduced from 6.5 percent to 5 percent and a new "high price" trigger method is created that raises the oil extraction tax rate to 6 percent in a triggered-on environment.

North Dakota has seen so many recent changes to these taxes where "the combination of growing social strains and abundant revenue intake has made Bismark a place for near-constant debate over revenue use" (Rabe and Hampton 2015, 404). The share of state severance tax revenue in total tax revenue has increased from almost 17 percent in 2005 to 46 percent in 2013 (Rabe and Hampton 2014). This represents a significant amount of increasing government revenue—in dollars this is a jump from roughly $262,000 in 2005 to $2.5 million in 2013 (Rabe and Hampton 2015). What this money can and should be used for is a contentious political debate.

In 2010, the state's referendum process led to a constitutional amendment (Section 26, Article X) to create the North Dakota Legacy Fund. The state puts 30 percent of annual severance tax revenues into a designated fund, overseen by the elected state treasurer, that has no specific purpose or plan for expenditure. Instead, the fund reflects "a broad political desire to set aside substantial portions of revenue for longer term needs, including those that might be tied to the impacts of share development or consequences of any future decline in production" (Rabe and Hampton 2015, 405; see also Gold 2012). The Legacy Fund was created in such a way that accumulating revenue was invested in stocks and bonds. No interest from the fund could be allocated or spent until 2017. See Figure 6.2 for a depiction of how the fund is designed.

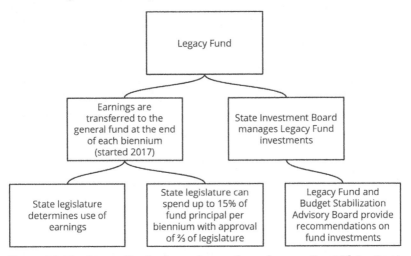

Figure 6.2. The Legacy Fund rules and procedures (source: Great Plains Institute 2015)

Outside of the 30 percent designated to the Legacy Fund, the separate statutes of 2013 concern reallocation of some other portion of the severance tax funds. House Bill 1278 allocates money to a new "outdoor heritage fund" that protects water quality and nature resources. The fund will collect up to $40 million per biennium to provide grants to state agencies, tribal governments, and interest groups that want to support wildlife and outdoor activities (North Dakota Industrial Commission n.d.). There is a hierarchy for funding projects that prioritizes projects that (1) create fish and wildlife habitat and provide access to hunters, (2) improve or restore water quality, soil quality, plant diversity, and other wildlife stewardship activities, (3) develop or enhance conservation of wildlife and fish habitat, and (4) develop parks or other recreation areas (North Dakota Industrial Commission n.d.). The money is overseen by the Outdoor Heritage Fund Advisory Board as part of the North Dakota Industrial Commission. By the end of December 2016, the board had distributed over 28 million dollars in seven grant cycles. The projects can be found on the Industrial Commission's website.

In 2013, another bill addressed reallocation of severance revenue. Senate Bill 2014 allocated money to "hub cities" where oil and gas development was having the biggest social or infrastructure impact. Specifically, the bill provided money for schools, fire departments, nursing homes, emergency medical services, policy services, and hospitals. There was also money for roads and highways in oil counties (Andrist 2013). However, this funding was still inadequate, leading Governor Jack Dalrymple, in 2014, to sign into law $1.1 billion in "surge funding"—as a "one time infusion of funding for infrastructure repair and development in oil-producing areas" (Rabe and Hampton 2015, 404). How much revenue from severance taxes is allocated to counties that produce oil is an ongoing discussion in the state and a likely topic for each biennial legislature. Counties that produce oil, such as those in the Williston Basin, argue that they require the most funding since they need more and better roads and have increased costs associated with water quality and other environmental issues (Dalrymple 2017).

Flaring Regulations

When oil is extracted from the Williston Basin, the wells also produce significant—and potentially valuable—natural gas. The Bakken also contains 6.7 trillion cubic feet of natural gas and 530 million barrels of natural gas liquids (NGLs) (Energy Information Administration 2018). However, this produced gas is often considered just a byproduct of the oil producing process. Moreover, natural gas production exceeds pipeline capacity in the state (Energy Information Administration 2018). Thus, the gas is typically flared (burned) rather than collected for storage and transport. For environmental and safety reasons, North Dakota prohibits venting, or releasing the gas into the air, without flaring or collecting it. Natural gas contains dangerous and toxic hydrocarbons such as propane and butane. It also contains methane, which is a very potent greenhouse gas (Energy Information Administration 2016). While flaring natural gas does create carbon dioxide, another greenhouse gas, it is less potent that methane, so it is considered better to flare gas than to release it.

Over the past decade, North Dakota has carefully examined natural gas policy in light of oil production. From the state's perspective, flaring gas is problematic not just because of the lost revenue and royalties, but because it is associated with environmental and public health externalities. Ideally, oil firms should be capturing the natural gas for energy. However, the low price of natural gas makes it unprofitable for the oil industry or the state to invest in the necessary infrastructure to capture, store, and use natural gas for energy.

In 2014, the state did something to dramatically shift how gas is treated in the Williston Basin. The North Dakota Industrial Commission passed one of the country's most aggressive laws to reduce gas flaring—Commission Order 24665. Under this law, all operators must capture a minimum percentage of gas produced at their wellsites—starting at 77 percent of gas produced in 2016 and climbing to 91 percent by 2020. These percentages must be met monthly by each firm. However, there is some flexibility in how firms can meet standards. Firms can allocate these captured percentages across all their wells in the region and they can bank excess gas captured for up to three months (Lade and Rudik 2017).

As a result of this new regulation, both the production side and the processing side of the industry are responding. Oil firms are now busy installing connecting wells to pipeline infrastructure in the Williston Basin. Essentially, they install small pipelines, or "gathering lines," that connect the oil well site to larger pipelines that transport the captured gas to a processing plant (Lade and Rudik 2017). On the industry side there are two projects in the development stages that could significantly add to North Dakota's gas gathering and processing capacity. The first is the construction of a new plant in McKenzie County near Watford City capable of processing 200 million standard cubic feet of gas per day. The region has been void of processing capacity and, consequently, is one of the worst areas for excess flaring (Jean 2018). The second project is a gas gathering system in McKenzie County, near Fort Berthold (Jean 2018).

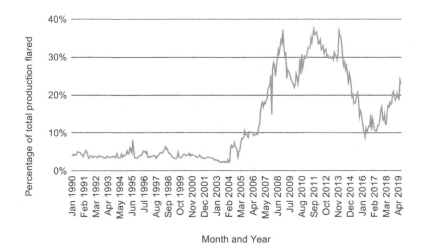

Figure 6.4. Flared natural gas in North Dakota, as total percent of natural gas produced, 2002–19 (source: North Dakota Department of Mineral Resources 2019)

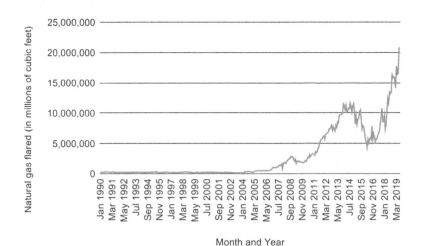

Figure 6.3. Flared natural gas in North Dakota, 2002–19 (source: North Dakota Department of Mineral Resources 2019)

Since the new regulations went into effect, flaring has fallen sharply in North Dakota. In March 2016, 10 percent of total natural gas production was flared, even as total natural gas production grew (Energy Information Agency 2016) (see Figures 6.3 and 6.4). However, in 2018, the state appears to still be struggling with flaring, as gas capture peaked and then plateaued around 88 percent (Nemec 2018). In December 2017, twelve companies failed to make their three-month target but have not faced any restrictions for two reasons. First, under the 2014 law, wells are allowed to produce unrestricted amounts of gas for the first ninety days, and second, regulators exempt wells that produce less than one hundred barrels daily from the main regulations (Associated Press 2017). With so many firms missing targets, the North Dakota Petroleum Council has reconvened its industry task force to deal with the issue, and the North Dakota Department of Mineral Resources is also studying flaring regulation (Nemec 2018). Natural gas flaring is a good example of a negative environmental externality in the oil patch, and so far, North Dakota has struggled to find the balance between growing the industry and regulating emissions.

Water Regulations

Oil production is deeply tied to water quantity and quality issues. This is particularly true of hydraulic fracturing, where the fracking of a single well can use 2–8 million gallons of water and create wastewater that contains high levels of total dissolved solids (TDS) and must be treated, disposed of, or recycled (Konkel 2016). In places like the Williston Basin, where a shale boom has occurred, "local water resources are impacted by this rapid development, through both an increased demand for water, which is used for oil extraction and to support the burgeoning population of workers, and an increased production of saline wastewater from the oil-bearing formation" (Horner et al. 2016, 3275). Indeed, the amount of water consumed annually for hydraulic fracturing activities in the Bakken play has increased more than five-fold, from 770 million gallons to 4.27 billion gallons, over the five years from 2008 to 2012 (Horner et al. 2016). North Dakota has no choice but to confront the water quality and water quantity issues created by oil production in the state.

Quality

For water quality, the Industrial Commission is responsible for regulations for wastewater storage and requirements for the protection of underground and surface water during the oil production process. Similar to other states, North Dakota requires oil firms to submit a list of chemicals using in the fracking process to FracFocus.org. It is important that regulators know what chemicals the industry is pumping into the ground because 10 to 90 percent of fracking fluid is returned to the surface during production (Colborn, Kwiatkowski, Schultz, and Bachran 2011). In general, produced water (water that flows out of the shale during fracking) and extraction liquids that return to the surface have been stored in "open evaporation pits" until the well is shut down, potentially years later. Toxic chemicals are found in these pits and can pose a threat to wildlife, soil, and public health (Ramirez 2010; Trail 2006). Even where chemicals are re-injected underground—a growing practice in the Bakken, and common in the eastern United States—they can create a "potential sources of extremely toxic chemical contamination" (Colborn et al. 2011, 1054). The U.S. Safe Drinking Water Act is the main federal law protecting water quality across the country. However, the 2005 U.S. Energy Policy Act exempts from the Safe Drinking Water Act the phase during which water mixed with chemicals is injected into the ground as part of the hydraulic fracturing process. This means that North Dakota has enforcement authority for underground water injections in the state.

The production of wastewater during oil production cannot be understated. In North Dakota, wastewater produced per well is rising (about five times between 2005 and 2012) and is higher than that of other shale plays: produced water amounts are about 440,000 gallons per year for wells completed during 2005–7, but 2.2 million gallons per year for wells completed in 2011 and 2012 (Horner et al. 2016). Wastewater from the Bakken is among the most saline of all shale formations, and most of it is disposed through "deep-well injection," meaning it is "pumped back underground into depleted oil formations or deep saline water reservoirs" (Horner et al. 2016, 3280). There are now over 400 saltwater disposal wells operating in the state (Horner et al. 2016). Another disposal option is the reuse of wastewater for fracturing other wells, which is a practice common in some other shale plays such as the Marcellus in the eastern United States. However, in the Bakken no wastewater is recycled because of the high salinity of the formation's water. Recent developments in water recycling designed specifically for the Bakken have been piloted with technical success but are not yet "economically competitive" (Horner et al. 2016, 3280). Instead, there are now 479 saltwater disposal wells in the Bakken (Scanlon et al. 2016, 10273).

Wastewater spills are also an area of growing concern in the Williston Basin. In 2015 alone, there were "12 spills greater than 21,000 gallons (79,500 liters), five spills greater than 42,000 gallons (160,000 liters), and one spill of 2.9 million gallons (11 million liters)" in North Dakota (Environmental Protection Agency 2016, 31). These spills were a result of either human or equipment failure, or leaks from hoses or storage equipment. In the Bakken, wastewater spills are reported to occur mainly during wastewater transportation by pipeline and during the filling or emptying of holding tanks (Lauer, Harkness, Vengosh 2016). These spills have been reported to impact both groundwater and surface water in the state. Studies of air and water quality surrounding Williston during the time of a large (11.4 million liter) wastewater spill in January 2015 described elevated levels of chemicals used in fracking, such as boron and strontium, with effects including fish deaths and estrogen inhibition in downstream fish (Cozzarelli et al. 2017). Other studies of wastewater spills in the Bakken have also detected naturally occurring radioactive materials, high salinity, and toxic trace elements (Lauer et al. 2016).

North Dakota presents an ideal case to test for wastewater effects because there was virtually no twentieth century conventional oil production that led to soil and water contamination before the past ten years of unconventional development (Lauer et al. 2016). In 2017, the North Dakota House of Representatives passed Bill 1409 to require that water quality tests be conducted prior to oil production (on a surface owner's property) and reported to the North Dakota Department of Health, which then analyzes the test and adds the results to a database maintained by the department. This helps state regulators understand the impact of oil production on water quality with "before and after" data.

Quantity

When it comes to water quantity, administration depends on the water source. Most of the water used for oil production in the Williston Basin is from public or private water distribution sites and trucked to the oil wellsite (Horner et al. 2016). These distribution sites, or water depots, can source water from surface or groundwater. The State Water Commission administers and enforces water law, including permitting for different water uses throughout the state. The permitting process includes assessing the availability of ground and surface water, the impacts on prior water users, the impacts on water quality and quantity, and the "probable long-term effects of climatic variation" on water supplies (see North Dakota State Water Commission n.d.). A water permit is required for all industrial uses of water in the state, but temporary permits (those that do not go through the entire impact process) can be granted for up to twelve months.

North Dakota recognizes a hierarchy of appropriated water uses, with domestic and municipal at the top, agricultural/irrigational second, industrial third, and recreational (related to fish and wildlife) lowest (Scanlon et al. 2016). While in theory this means water transfers from higher to lower priority uses are not allowed, a policy was developed in 2011 to "accommodate a change in purpose from irrigation to industrial water uses through temporary water permits (1 year maximum) termed 'Industrial Use In Lieu Of Irrigation Policy' (ILOP)," which generated thirty-three permits and supplied almost 30 percent of water used in fracturing—also reducing water truck traffic and wait times at depots (Scanlon et al. 2016). The program was phased out in most places by the end of 2015 due to expansion in pipelines and water depots (Scanlon et al. 2016).

The federal Army Corps of Engineers controls permits for interstate waters, such as the upper Missouri River system, which includes Lake Sakakawea. This river system is the largest and most reliable source of water in the Williston Basin. Since the Bakken Formation is so large, transportation of water from the river system can be costly. Thus, there are numerous oil firms that source their water from the nearest water depot, managed by the state (Horner et al. 2016).

As of 2018, there is enough water in the state for oil production, but no single source alone is adequate. Up to 3.7 billion gallons of groundwater can be withdrawn annually in North Dakota, but in 2012, 4.3 billion gallons were needed just for hydraulic fracturing in the Bakken (Horner et al. 2016). Thus, surface water withdrawals are necessary. Up to 10.3 billion gallons annually are permitted for withdrawal from surface waters in the state. Lake Sakakawea has at least 32.5 billion gallons of annual surplus water that are being made available by the Army Corps of Engineers (Horner et al. 2016).

In 2017, the North Dakota House of Representatives passed HB1020, which makes changes to the operation and composition of the state water commission. The bill also mandates a legislative management study of industry water use in the oil and gas industry.

Transportation Regulations

There are thousands of oil and gas pipelines that cross through North Dakota—some small gathering lines and some very large and internationally significant pipelines. However, despite all of these pipelines, oil producers were, and still are, sometimes forced to ship crude oil by rail or truck simply because production has outpaced pipeline capacity. In 2013, roughly 75 percent of crude oil produced in the state was shipped by rail. This number has fallen, and in 2016 only about 30 percent of oil was shipped on the railroad (Energy Information Administration 2018). Rail and pipeline transport were roughly the same in 2012, before rail transport increased as pipeline transport decreased.

The safety of oil transportation is a controversial and political issue in the United States and Canada. In 2013, a train carrying crude oil from North Dakota to a refining plant in New Brunswick, Canada, crashed and exploded in Lac-Mégantic, Quebec. The result was not just the destruction of thirty buildings in the downtown core, but more tragically the death of forty-seven people. This was the deadliest non-passenger train railway accident in Canada's history. The incident immediately put railway safety—and the Bakken Formation—on the front page of every newspaper in Canada and the United States. And the federal governments of both countries acted quickly to issue emergency orders.

Nevertheless, in 2014 a train carrying 3.5 million gallons of oil crashed into a grain train and forced the evacuation of more than 1,000 residents in the town of Casselton, North Dakota. This event again led to more media coverage that focused attention on the Bakken Formation. A *New York Times* exposé appeared on Page A1 on January 26, 2014, about oil transportation in North Dakota. At the time, about 65 percent of oil produced in North Dakota's Bakken was shipped on railway, often because of a shortage of pipelines. According to the *Times*, "Safety officials have warned for more than two decades that these cars were unsuited to carry flammable cargo: their shell can puncture and tears up too easily in a crash" (Krauss and Mouawad 2014). However, the problem was more than just tank cars, as the *Times* also brought to light the fact that "crude oil produced in the Bakken appears to be a lot more volatile than other grades of oil, something that could explain why the oil trains have had huge explosions" (Krauss and Mouawad 2014).

As a result of these crashes and the U.S. federal government's emergency orders, the North Dakota Industrial Commission created new standards for oil being transported from the state. Order 25417 set new operating standards in

2014 for the equipment that separates production fluids into gas and liquid. These standards include "new parameters for temperatures and pressures under which the equipment must operate to ensure that light hydrocarbons are removed before oil is shipped to market." The oil's temperature must be raised to at least 110°F to boil off the most volatile fractions which become highly flammable or even explosive if they become separated in transit. North Dakota standards are now more stringent that federal regulations. Bakken crude oil must be at a vapor pressure of no more than 13.7 pounds per square inch (psi) whereas the federal standard is 14.7 psi. Order 25417 applies without exception to all Bakken crude oil produced in North Dakota (North Dakota Industrial Commission 2014).

To confront transportation problems, the state also opened a new oil refinery in 2015, with plans to open more in the future. In 2018 the state has two oil refineries, the Mandan Refinery in Mandan and the Dakota Prairie Refinery in Dickinson. But to keep pace with production and prevent transportation delays and risks, more refineries are necessary. Meridian Energy Group has proposed a facility, the Davis Refinery, in western North Dakota, just outside the Theodore Roosevelt National Park. In December of 2017, the North Dakota Department of Health Air Quality Division granted a draft permit to construct the refinery. The Billings county board already approved the project and necessary zoning for the facility in 2016. The process for a finalized permit to construct is ongoing (Meridian Energy Group 2018).

Future of Oil Politics in North Dakota

Oil production in the United States is experiencing a historic resurgence. This is due largely to the discovery of new deposits and the development of new technologies that enable oil recovery at cheaper rates. In November of 1970, the U.S. produced 10.04 million barrels of oil per day (see Figure 6.5). Between 1970 and 2010, oil production steadily declined with few interruptions (a brief period in the 1980s, for example). However, since 2010, production—largely due to fracking technology—has been rising. In January 2018, the United States produced 10.2 million barrels of oil per day. North Dakota is producing about 1.2 million barrels per day—almost 10 percent of total production in the United States. Oil production in the Williston Basin is prospering.

While the future of oil looks stable, the pressures of climate change are creating real political and social pressure across the country and throughout the world. In 2015, by executive order, President Obama created the Clean Power Plan—a policy aimed at reducing greenhouse emissions from electrical power generators and coal-fired power plants in each U.S. state. This signaled a new era of climate change policy in the United States. In 2015, President Obama also signed the United Nation's Paris Agreement, which further committed the United States to reducing its greenhouses gas emissions over the next thirty years (the Agreement goes into force in 2020). The election of Donald Trump in 2016 signaled yet another era in American climate change policy. Trump campaigned on a pro-energy (anti-environmental regulation) campaign and after sweeping into the White House, he quickly asked the Environmental Protection Agency to repeal the Clean Power Plan, which was under review by the U.S. Supreme Court. President Trump has spoken against the Paris Accord, and in June 2017 he announced that the United States would withdraw from the international agreement. (However, the earliest possible withdrawal date by a signatory to the 2015 agreement is November 4, 2020—so the United States technically remains a party to the convention.) Trump remains very skeptical of climate change and is against environmental regulations that slow U.S. energy production (Parker and Davenport 2016). During a 2016 campaign stop in Bismarck, Trump told a packed arena of thousands that he wants to see "more fossil fuel drilling and fewer environmental regulations" (Parker and Davenport 2016). Not surprisingly, in the 2016 election, Trump won North Dakota's three electoral college votes with 63 percent of the popular vote in the state. In Williams County, Trump won 10,069 votes compared to Hillary Clinton's 1,735 votes (New York Times 2017).

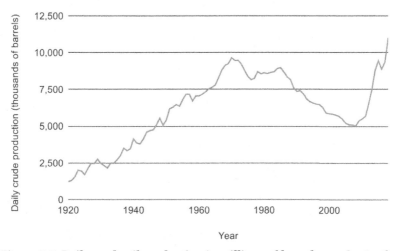

Figure 6.5. Daily crude oil production in millions of barrels per day in the United States, 1920–2018 (source: Energy Information Administration 2019)

However, even in light of the Republican administration and Trump's support in the Williston Basin, it seems clear that North Dakota oil production will be accompanied by increasing alternative energy production in the state. Like oil and gas, North Dakota also has abundant renewable energy resources, especially wind energy. In 2016, the state ranked fifth in the United States for electricity generation produced by wind energy (Energy Information Administration 2018). And North Dakota still has significant undeveloped wind energy resources. In 2017, the Industrial Commission approved $1.1 million in research and development grants for three renewable energy projects—two involving portable solar development and one developing geothermal energy for residential use (North Dakota Industrial Commission 2017a). North Dakota is already one of the top ten ethanol-producing states with five ethanol plants, and among the top ten in biodiesel production capacity (Energy Information Administration 2018). It also generates hydroelectricity through the Garrison Dam outside of Bismarck. The dam produces about 5–7 percent of the state's net electricity (Energy Information Administration 2018). Although the state is committed to oil production, it is not forgoing other energy production opportunities.

North Dakota is also pursuing carbon-and-capture storage (CCS) technology. It is a process whereby carbon dioxide emitted from large projects, such as coal-fired power plants, is captured, transported, and deposited underground. The purpose is to prevent the carbon dioxide from entering the atmosphere. However, it can also be used for "enhanced oil recovery" where that carbon dioxide is injected into the ground to help recover more oil. This is a process used in Saskatchewan to increase oil production in its portion of the Bakken while decreasing emissions from the province's coal-fired power plants. In May 2017 the state became the first to receive EPA approval for CCS. Essentially, North Dakota now has primary regulatory authority over the geologic storage of carbon dioxide (North Dakota Industrial Commission 2017b). Saskatchewan already as a CCS facility in its Bakken region, just outside Estevan. In December 2017, the province signed a memorandum of understanding with Montana, North Dakota, and Wyoming related to CCS technology. The four subnational jurisdictions will "collaborate on carbon capture, utilization and storage (CCUS) related to sharing of capacity, as well as regulatory expertise in the fields of carbon dioxide capture, transportation, storage and enhanced oil recovery" (Fraser 2017).

The balance between oil production and environmental protection will be an ongoing political pursuit in the Williston Basin. Responsible oil production requires a plethora of actors and a complex governance system. The North Dakota administrative system has increased capacity and opened up avenues for non-government actors. While the main emphasis still appears to be increasing oil production, there is now greater attention to the environment. The state has set aside severance funds specifically earmarked for outdoor heritage projects and has a legacy fund that could potentially be used to offset landscape changes or other environmental externalities of the oil patch. Water quality and quantity as well as flaring and transportation are now regulated by North Dakota's government. The past ten years has shown that North Dakota is taking more seriously the environmental responsibility of oil production. And there is certainly more state regulation of the industry and the environment in 2018 than in 1958, at the time of the first *Williston Report*. However, the balance still tips toward fossil fuel production. North Dakota, like many U.S. states, has been unable to balance the industry's booms with society's long-term interests in an era of sustainability.

References

American Enterprise Institute (AEI). 2018. "Historic Energy Milestone: U.S. Oil Output Surges to New Record Highs Reflecting America's Deep Pools of Ingenuity, Risk Taking, and Entrepreneurship." http://www.aei.org/ publication/historic-energy-milestone-us-oil-output-surges-to-new-record-highs-reflecting-americas-deep-pools-of-ingenuity-risk-taking-and-entrepreneurship/.

Andrist, Steve. 2013. "N.D. House Approves Funds for Oil Patch." *Bismarck Tribune*, May 1. http://bismarcktribune.com/ bakken/n-d-house-approves-funds-for-oil-patch/article_7f60d980-b2ca-11e2-8bf9-0019bb2963f4.html.

Associated Press. 2017. "Natural Gas Flaring Increases in North Dakota's Oil Fields." *U.S. News*, December 11. https://www.usnews. com/news/best-states/north-dakota/articles/2017-12-11/ natural-gas-flaring-in-oil-fields-flares-up-in-september.

Caraher, William, and Kyle Conway, eds. 2016. *The Bakken Goes Boom: Oil and the Changing Geographies of Western North Dakota*. Grand Forks: Digital Press at the University of North Dakota.

Census Bureau. n.d.a. "Quick Facts: North Dakota." Accessed October 22, 2018. https://www.census.gov/quickfacts/ND.

Census Bureau. n.d.b. "Quick Facts: Williston City, North Dakota." Accessed October 22, 2018. https://www.census.gov/quickfacts/fact/table/ willistoncitynorthdakota/RHI125216#viewtop.

Colborn, Theo, Carol Kwiatkowski, Kim Schultz, and Mary Bachran. 2011. "Natural Gas Operations from a Public Health Perspective." *Human and Ecological Risk Assessment* 17 (5): 1039–56.

Cozzarelli, Isabelle M., K.J. Skalak, D.B. Kent, Mark A. Engle, A. Benthem, A.C. Mumford, K. Haase, A. Farag, D. Harper, S.C. Nagel, L.R. Iwanowicz, W.H. Orem, D.M. Akob, J.B. Jaeschke, J. Galloway, M. Kohler, D.L. Stoliker, and G.D. Jolly. 2017. "Environmental Signatures and Effects of an Oil and Gas Wastewater Spill in the Williston Basin, North Dakota." *Science of the Total Environment* 579: 1781–93.

Cross, Raymond. 2001. "Development's Victim or Its Beneficiary?: The Impact of Oil and Gas Development on the Fort Berthold Indian Reservation." *North Dakota Law Review* 87 (4): 535–69. https://law.und.edu/_files/ docs/ndlr/pdf/issues/87/4/87ndlr535.pdf.

Dakota Resource Council. n.d. "Responsible Energy Development." Accessed October 23, 2018. http://drcinfo.org/oil-gas/.

Dalrymple, Amy. 2017. "Western N.D. Opposes 'Taking' of Oil Tax Revenue." *Bismarck Tribune*, April 18. https://bismarcktribune.com/news/state-and-regional/western-n-d-opposes-takings-of-oil-tax-revenue/article_2fe37125-237e-52ba-86e7-8df5777eb7e1.html.

Department of Energy. 2009. Office of Fossil Energy and National Energy Technology Laboratory. "State Oil and Natural Gas Regulations Designed to Protect Water Resources." https://hero.epa.gov/hero/index.cfm/reference/details/reference_id/2079158.

Dodge, Jennifer. 2015. "The Deliberative Potential of Civil Society Organizations: Framing Hydraulic Fracturing in New York." *Policy Studies* 36 (3): 249–66.

Dokshin, Fedor A. 2016. "Whose Backyard and What's at Issue? Spatial and Ideological Dynamics of Local Opposition to Fracking in New York State, 2010 to 2013." *American Sociological Review* 81 (5): 921–48.

Energy Information Administration (EIA). 2016. "Natural Gas Flaring in North Dakota Has Declined Sharply Since 2014." https://www.eia.gov/todayinenergy/detail.php?id=26632.

Energy Information Administration (EIA). 2018. "North Dakota: State Profile and Energy Estimates." https://www.eia.gov/state/analysis.php?sid=ND.

Energy Information Administration (EIA). 2019. "U.S. Field Production of Crude Oil." https://www.eia.gov/dnav/pet/hist/LeafHandler.ashx?n=-pet&s=mcrfpus1&f=a.

Energy Policy Act of 2005, Public Law 109-58. 119 Stat. 594. https://www.ferc.gov/enforcement/enforce-res/EPAct2005.pdf.

Environmental Protection Agency (EPA). n.d. "Drinking Water Contaminants—Standards and Regulations." Last modified April 22, 2017. https://www.epa.gov/dwstandardsregulations.

Environmental Protection Agency (EPA). 2011. "Draft Investigation of Groundwater Contamination Near Pavillion, Wyoming." https://www.epa.gov/region8/draft-investigation-ground-water-contamination-near-pavillion-wyoming.

Environmental Protection Agency (EPA). 2016. "Hydraulic Fracturing and Drinking Water Assessment—Executive Summary." https://www.epa.gov/sites/production/files/2016-12/documents/hfdwa_executive_summary.pdf.

Fragoso, Alegandro Davila. 2016. "Meet the Native American Candidate the Oil Industry Doesn't Want in Congress." Think Progress, November 4. https://thinkprogress.org/north-dakota-native-american-candidates-make-history-a1682dbe8e30/.

Fraser, D.C. 2017. "Wall Signs Carbon Capture Agreement in U.S." Regina Leader-Post, December 1. http://leaderpost.com/news/saskatchewan/wall-signs-carbon-capture-agreement-in-u-s.

Great Plains Institute. 2015. "North Dakota's Legacy Fund: Building a Bridge to the Future." https://www.betterenergy.org/wp-content/uploads/2018/03/North_Dakota_Legacy_Fund_Recommendations.pdf.

Gullion, Jessica Smartt. 2015. Fracking the Neighborhood: Reluctant Activists and Natural Gas Drilling. Cambridge, MA: MIT Press.

Hill, M.J., and R. Olson 2013. "Possible Future Trade-offs Between Agriculture, Energy Production, and Biodiversity Conservation in North Dakota." Regional Environmental Change 13: 311–28. https://doi.org/10.1007/s10113-012-0339-9.

Horner, R.M, C.B. Harto, R.B. Jackson, E.R. Lowry, A.R. Brandt, T.W. Yeskoo, D.J. Murphy, and C. E. Clark. 2016. "Water Use and Management in the Bakken Shale Oil Play in North Dakota." Environmental Science & Technology 50: 3275–82.

Jean, Renee. 2018. "Hess-Targa, Rimrock Project Could Help Solve Flaring Issues in North Dakota." Williston Herald, January 26. http://www.willistonherald.com/news/hess-targa-rimrock-projects-could-help-solve-flaring-issues-in/article_353a7352-023e-11e8-ad98-bb28ba79c1c2.html.

Konkel, Lindsey. 2016. "Salting the Earth: The Environmental Impact of Oil and Gas Wastewater Spills." Environmental Health Perspectives 124 (12): A230–5.

Krauss, Clifford, and Jad Mouawad. 2014. "Accidents Surge as Oil Industry Takes the Train." New York Times, January 25. https://www.nytimes.com/2014/01/26/business/energy-environment/accidents-surge-as-oil-industry-takes-the-train.html.

Kusnetz, Nicholas. 2017. "North Dakota's Oil and Gas Boom Has Brought Prosperity, But Critics Wonder About the Costs." Huffington Post, December 6. https://www.huffingtonpost.com/2014/07/21/north-dakota-oil-and-gas-boom-costs_n_5600691.html.

Lade, Gabriel E., and Ivan Rudik. 2017. "Costs of Inefficient Regulation: Evidence from the Bakken." NBER Working Papers 24139, National Bureau of Economic Research. https://www.nber.org/papers/w24139.pdf.

Lauer, Nancy E., Jennifer S. Harkness, and Avner Vengosh. 2016. "Brine Spills Associated With Unconventional Oil Development in North Dakota." *Environmental Science & Technology* 50 (10): 5389–97.

McGranahan, Devan Allen, Felix N. Fernando, and Meghan L.E. Kirkwood. 2017. "Reflections on a Boom: Perceptions of Energy Development Impacts in the Bakken Oil Patch Inform Environmental Science & Policy Priorities." *Science of the Total Environment* 599–600 (1): 1993–2018.

Meridian Energy Group. 2018. "Permit to Construct Public Comment Meeting for Davis Refinery Held By North Dakota Department of Health—Air Quality Division." Nasdaq Globe Newswire, January 22. https://globenewswire.com/news-release/2018/01/22/1298711/0/en/Permit-to-Construct-Public-Comment-Meeting-for-Davis-Refinery-Held-by-North-Dakota-Department-of-Health-Air-Quality-Division.html.

MHA Nation. n.d.a. "MHA Nation Clean Fuels Refinery. About Us." Accessed October 23, 2018. http://www.mharefinery.net/.

MHA Nation. n.d.b. "Tribal Council." Accessed October 23, 2018. http://www.mhanation.com/main2/elected_officials.html.

Murrill, Brandon J. 2016. "Pipeline Transportation for Natural Gas and Crude Oil: Federal and State Regulatory Authority." Congressional Research Services. https://fas.org/sgp/crs/misc/R44432.pdf.

National Oceanic and Atmospheric Administration (NOAA). 2016. "North Dakota's Bakken oil and gas field leaking 275,000 tons of methane per year." Accessed October 23, 2018. http://www.noaa.gov/news/north-dakota-s-bakken-oil-and-gas-field-leaking-275000-tons-of-methane-year

Nemec, Richard. 2018. "Natural Gas Flaring Still North Dakota's Problem Child." *NGI's Shale Daily*, February 18. http://www.naturalgasintel.com/articles/113407-natural-gas-flaring-still-north-dakotas-problem-child.

New York Times. 2017. "North Dakota Presidential Race Results: Donald J. Trump Wins." *New York Times*. https://www.nytimes.com/elections/results/north-dakota-president-clinton-trump.

North Dakota Census Office. 2015. "Native American Population in North Dakota." *Census Newsletter*, December. https://www.commerce.nd.gov/uploads/8/CensusNewsletterDec2015.pdf.

North Dakota Census Office. 2017. "Defining Rural Population." *Census Newsletter*, December. https://www.commerce.nd.gov/uploads/26/CensusNewsletterDec2017.pdf.

North Dakota Department of Mineral Resources. 2017. *Rulebook*. August 2017. https://www.dmr.nd.gov/oilgas/rules/rulebook.pdf.

North Dakota Department of Mineral Resources. 2018. "ND Monthly Oil Production Statistics." https://www.dmr.nd.gov/oilgas/stats/historical-oilprodstats.pdf.

North Dakota Department of Mineral Resources. 2019. "Historical Month Gas Production and Sales Statistics." https://www.dmr.nd.gov/oilgas/stats/Gas1990ToPresent.xls.

North Dakota Indian Affairs Commission. n.d. "Tribal Nations." Accessed October 23, 2018. http://indianaffairs.nd.gov/tribal-nations/.

North Dakota Industrial Commision. n.d. "Outdoor Heritage Fund." https://www.nd.gov/ndic/outdoor-infopage.htm.

North Dakota Industrial Commission. 2014. "Industrial Commission Adopts New Standards to Improve Oil Transportation Safety." http://www.nd.gov/ndic/ic-press/dmr-order25417.pdf.

North Dakota Industrial Commission. 2017a. "North Dakota Industrial Commission Supports New Renewable Energy Projects." http://www.nd.gov/ndic/ic-press/renew-17-5.pdf.

North Dakota Industrial Commission. 2017b. "North Dakota Class VI Primacy Application for Carbon Capture Storage Approved." http://www.nd.gov/ndic/ic-press/dmr-primacy5-17.pdf.

North Dakota Legislative Branch. 2018. "District 1." http://www.legis.nd.gov/districts/2013-2022/district-1.

North Dakota Petroleum Council. n.d. "Advocacy & Policy." Accessed October 23, 2018. https://www.ndoil.org/menu-pages/advocacy-policy/.

North Dakota Pipeline Authority. 2015. "July 2015 Monthly Update." https://ndpipelines.files.wordpress.com/2012/04/ndpa-july-10-2015-update.pdf.

North Dakota Public Service Commission. 2018. "Jurisdiction: Pipelines." https://www.psc.nd.gov/jurisdiction/pipelines/index.php.

North Dakota State Tax Commission. 1998. "State and Local Taxes: An Overview and Comparative Guide." http://www.nd.gov/tax/data/upfiles/media/98redbook.pdf?20180208072553.

North Dakota State Tax Commission. 2016. "Report." October 23. https://www.nd.gov/tax/data/upfiles/media/Reporting%20Procedures%20for%20Legislative%20Changes%20Letter_final.pdf?20180208074023.

North Dakota State Water Commission. n.d. "Appropriation: Water Permits." Accessed November 24, 2018. http://www.swc.nd.gov/reg_approp/waterpermits/.

Olive, Andrea. 2018. "Oil Development in the Grasslands: Saskatchewan's Bakken Formation and Species at Risk Protection." *Cogent Environmental Sciences* 4 (1). https://doi.org/10.1080/23311843.2018.1443666.

Parker, Ashley, and Coral Davenport. 2016. "Donald Trump's Energy Plan: More Fossil Fuels and Fewer Rules." *New York Times*, May 26. https://www.nytimes.com/2016/05/27/us/politics/donald-trump-global-warming-energy-policy.html.

Rabe, Barry G. 2014. "Shale Play Politics: The Intergovernmental Odyssey of American Shale Governance." *Environmental Science and Technology* 48: 8369–75.

Rabe, Barry G., and Rachel L. Hampton. 2015. "Taxing Fracking: The Politics of State Severance Taxes in the Shale Era." *Review of Policy Research* 32 (4): 389–412.

Ramirez, P. 2010. "Bird Mortality in Oil Field Wastewater Disposal Facilities." *Environmental Management* 46 (5): 820–6.

Ruddell, Rick, Dheeshana S. Jayasundara, Roni Mayzer, Thomasine Heitkamp. 2014. "Drilling Down: An Examination of the Boom-Crime Relationship in Resource Based Boom Counties." *Western Criminology Review* 15 (1): 3–17.

Scanlon, Bridget R., Robert C. Reedy, Frank Male, and Michael Hove. 2016. "Managing the Increasing Water Footprint of Hydraulic Fracturing in the Bakken Play, United States." *Environmental Science & Technology* 50 (18): 10273–81.

Shrestha, N., G. Chilkoor, H. Wilder, V. Gadhamshetty, and J.J. Stone. 2017. "Potential Water Resource Impacts of Hydraulic Fracturing from Unconventional Oil Production in the Bakken Shale." *Water Research* 108: 1–24. https://doi.org/10.1016/j.watres.2016.11.006.

Sierra Club Dacotah Chapter. n.d. "About." Accessed October 23, 2018. https://www.sierraclub.org/north-dakota/about-sierra-club-dacotah-chapter.

Sisk, Amy. 2016. "While One Tribe Fights Oil, Another Cautiously Embraces It." *Inside Energy*, November 26. http://insideenergy.org/2016/11/22/while-one-tribe-fights-oil-another-cautiously-embraces-it/.

Smith, Nick. 2012. "Three Affiliated Tribes to Get Control of Land for Oil Refinery." *Bismarck Tribune*, October 10. http://bismarcktribune.com/

bakken/three-affiliated-tribes-to-get-control-of-land-for-oil/article_42150bf4-1307-11e2-b7ec-001a4bcf887a.html.

Thompson, S.J., D.H. Johnson, N.D. Niemuth, and C.A. Ribic. 2015. "Avoidance of Unconventional Oil Wells and Roads Exacerbates Habitat Loss for Grassland Birds in the North American Great Plains." *Biological Conservation* 192: 82–90. https://doi.org/10.1016/j.biocon.2015.08.040.

Trail, P.W. 2006. "Avian Mortality at Oil Pits in the United States: A Review of the Problem and Efforts for its Solution." *Environmental management* 38 (4): 532–44.

1958

Chapter 7
The Economic Impact of Oil Development

Samuel C. Kelley, Jr.

An area that is committed to an economic function specialized in agriculture and in particular to a specialized commodity structure is invariably characterized by a level of income that is significantly lower and far more unstable than that of an economy founded on manufacturing activity. Extreme fluctuation and chronic depression in the commodity market accompanied by rapid technological change in methods of agricultural production have produced, in areas such as North Dakota, a low wage structure, persistent underemployment and standards of living that are not in accord with the dynamic growth present in other areas of the national economy.

Much of the current argument which treats the agricultural problem as one of improper allocation of resources to be corrected by the market mechanism is appropriate only to areas where alternative uses of resources are technically possible. In those areas where the alternatives are limited, as in North Dakota and much of the Great Plains area, the alternative to continued employment in agriculture is migration to other geographic areas. The many forces which act to restrain population movements assure that the short term will be characterized by a labor force excessive relative to demand. For the long term the residual population of the declining area must continue to bear an unreasonably high and increasing overhead cost of the public and private services essential to the community welfare.

The impact of economic decline upon the population of the agricultural areas of the nation is evident in the fervor with which they have sought protective legislation and in the intense competition through which they are now attempting to broaden the economic base of their communities. Throughout the South and increasingly in the Great Plains area, private and public agencies are engaged in gigantic promotional efforts to attract nonagricultural industries. Offers of financial assistance, tax offsets, land grants, low wage rates and "favorable" labor laws are the bait being used to attract new industries to areas in desperate need of additional employment opportunities and a bigger tax base.

Many of these areas are at a distinct disadvantage in the competitive struggle. Their small populations offer no concentrated market; they are remote from the urban concentrations that consume a large part of the nation's product; the labor force possesses few of the skills required in the complex of industrial production, and the physical resources possessed by the area are usually exploited most economically by shipping them in unprocessed form to established manufacturing areas. Their primary asset is an abundant labor supply continuously supplemented by the technological displacement of farm workers.

A taxonomic description of the impact of oil discovery on a local economy is in itself of little value to anyone other than the local historians and those eager members of the Chamber of Commerce who search for microscopic evidence of the utopian characteristics of their communities.

It may well be that the results of this study will serve no other purpose. It is, however, our premise that the Williston Basin Area possesses some relatively unique characteristics and that these characteristics provide an analytical basis for inference that may be applied appropriately in other situations and in other times.

The economic process which may be described here in terms of a real situation is the process of the induced response of an economy to a major autonomous change within it. In the majority of real situations the complexity of interrelationships between economic components and a wide variety of institutional restraints serves to confuse the analyst and to obscure the causal relationships between autonomous and induced changes.

From an economic viewpoint the characteristics that lend value to data derived from this area are the internal simplicity of the local economy and the simplicity of its relationship with other portions of the larger economy of which it is part.

It is in this type of economic environment that the Williston Basin oil development occurred. To interpret many of the economic phenomena within this development some general description of the environment is required. The Williston area is typical of the state in nearly every respect. The differences between it and other regions of the state are differences of magnitude rather than kind.

The two counties selected for analysis were selected primarily because at the time of the study they contained nearly all activity directly related to oil development in North Dakota. Fortunately, they also comprise the most important components of the economy of the area and inferences can be drawn for the residual areas with a relatively high level of confidence as to their validity.

The Economic Area

The basic economy of these two counties and the counties contiguous to them is agricultural. Until the oil discovery in 1951, land was the only natural resource in use, and all labor resources were used in direct or indirect relation to its cultivation.

Even the structure of the area's agriculture is simple. Limited rainfall, severe northern climate, conditions of topography, and isolation from major consumer markets have limited land use to the production of two basic commodities, small grains and livestock. The same conditions have required an extensive use of land, and the area is characterized by a relatively small number of very large farm units. Since the dry-farming techniques appropriate to the area permit extensive use of mechanical farm equipment, the labor requirements per farm unit are very small, normally being met by family labor.

This type of agriculture has limited the development of local manufactures in two ways. First, the farm products are those which may be shipped to areas closer to primary consumer markets in unprocessed form more economically than in processed form. There is no processing of agricultural products in this area other than that required for immediate domestic consumption. In fact, only a relatively small part of the local consumption of milled grains and livestock is satisfied by local production. Even the farmers of the region produce little for their own use, depending on the sale and export of their products in raw form and the import of finished goods.

A second way in which the development of local manufacture has been inhibited by the type of agriculture dominant in the region is that its limited and declining need for labor has produced a very low population density. In 1950, McKenzie County had fewer than three persons per square mile; Mountrail five persons, and Williams fewer than eight. Further, the population of the area has declined continuously since 1930. The net number of persons leaving Mountrail County in the period 1940–1950 was equal to 24 percent of its 1940 population. The Williams County loss was nearly 14 percent, although the city of Williston had a population increase of over 27 percent in the period.

A sparse and declining population offers little opportunity for the development of domestic manufactures intended to serve local markets, such as are found in most areas of the United States. In the Williston Basin, this industry group has been limited to a few dairies, bakeries, job printers and newspapers. Virtually all other commodities used in the area are produced elsewhere and nearly all that is produced in the area is exported from the area in a raw state.

In essence, the area is a raw materials producing economy which trades its raw commodities for finished goods imported from "abroad." Like most areas of the world's economy which produce raw materials for export, the local welfare is directly dependent upon economic conditions in other areas. Further, the dependence of the manufacturing economy on the welfare of this "basic" component is tenuous and remote. The demand for the commodity materials which it supplies is relatively inelastic under ordinary conditions of economic activity. In contrast, the conditions of supply are extremely competitive. This kind of an economic relationship has tended to promote and to preserve a rather primitive economy with the type of economic institution characteristic of the national scene at the turn of the century.

The primary employment is farming. The major secondary employment is in trade and transportation. Although farm establishments are very large in terms of land use relative to the national pattern, business establishments are very small. The proprietorship, partnership and cooperatives are far more characteristic than the corporate form of business organization. No firm in the area other than major utilities employed more than 200 persons prior to oil discovery.

The communities of the area are also small. Williston, the only urban area in the two counties, had a 1950 population of less than 8000, and there is no larger community within a radius of one hundred miles. Williston is the trade center of the area and a very large percentage of the goods consumed in the area pass through it in much the same way that imports arrive at and are distributed from a port city in the more primitive economic areas of the world. To a lesser degree, much of the area's product is collected for export through the facilities of this trade center.

The smaller communities of the area serve two basic functions. They are secondary areas of distribution for those consumer products which meet day-to-day needs such as groceries or farm materials and building supplies. They are also residential communities for retired farmers and for many of the numerous farmers and ranchers who do not live on their farms in the winter months.

The Trade Area Structure

Some evidence of the relative importance of Williston as a center for trade and service to the Williams County area is contained in the results of a sample of farm families and residents of the major secondary communities. It should be noted that these data were collected in 1954 and reflect a part of the developed changes induced by the oil activity.

Although Williston is approximately 50 miles from the oil field area (impact area), 73 percent of all families interviewed in this area bought their dress apparel from Williston merchants. Nearly all bought household furnishings in the same place, and more than a third did their banking in Williston banks. One development resulting directly from oil activity was the establishment of a medical clinic in Tioga, which is contained in this area, yet half of all residents in the area went to Williston for medical care.

Of all farm families in areas of Williams County, other than the eastern townships defined as the impact area, slightly more than half generally bought their groceries in Williston. Nearly 95 percent bought clothing there and went there for more medical care. About 90 percent thought of Williston as their center for bank transactions. Even more pertinent is the fact that in Tioga and Ray, the largest secondary trade centers in the area, two-thirds of all resident families purchased dress apparel and other consumer goods of the same class in Williston rather than in their own community.

The eastern edge of Williston's trade area is a topographical feature, a long coulee running north and south through Mountrail County passing through the community of White Earth just east of the major producing oil fields. This barrier has interrupted the county and township roads which would normally permit a westward movement. Westward traffic must move on U.S. No. 2 or to the north of the county line.

Much of the area to the east of this feature is served by Stanley, the county seat of Mountrail County, or by Powers Lake to the north. The trade distribution in this area is not so sharply defined as in Williams County. Stanley is a much smaller community than Williston and is without the variety of business establishments found there. The smaller communities of the county, Parshall and Newtown, are able to compete in the types of consumer demand usually satisfied in nonurban places. More important, Minot in Ward County is the State's third largest community and attracts many of the area's consumers of durable consumer goods and higher quality non-durables. For the western range of townships, Powers Lake is the dominant trade center. In all other areas of the county, using clothing and medical care as illustrative of consumption items, Stanley serves about a third of all farm families, while Newtown and Parshall together serve about 15 percent and Minot 40 percent.

The concentration of the area's trade and service activity is Williston; Stanley's and Minot's has been reduced in some ways and increased in others by the development of the oil extracting industry in the area. In a few cases, notably Tioga and Powers Lake and to a lesser extent Ray, the influx of population and the daily presence of large numbers of oil field workers has resulted in the establishment of new trade and service establishments and in the modernization and expansion of others. However, the majority of these establishments are bars, restaurants and grocery stores or service establishments of the business repair type. In several of the relatively few cases of additions to merchandising establishments, the new establishment has been a branch outlet for an existing firm in Williston.

In contrast to this slight diversification of trade in the area, Williston has experienced a greater increase in new establishments and in new lines of service than has the remainder of the area. This is primarily a result of the fact that although Williston is nearly 50 miles from the major oil discoveries, it occupies the center of the apparent geological area for oil prospects. By 1954, only the fringes of the area had been developed, in the Tioga area on the east and in the Montana fields on the west. In appraising both the existing situation and future possibilities, the major producers and the firms supplying materials for drilling activity selected Williston as their base of operations as a result of its location as well as its size.

In this sense, the trade structure of the area has not been modified by oil activity. Although growth in a few areas such as Tioga has been great relative to the past, Williston continues to dominate business activity in the area. The major economic impact of the development, changes in employment, income, sales and receipts, can be measured in terms of the changes in the economy of Williston. These changes are described and related to the causal development in a following section.

The Oil Industry

The autonomous factor inducing change in the area was the abrupt development of an industry completely new to the region. There had been interest and activity related to oil in the region for many years. The early activity was largely speculative, involving the sale of mineral leases based upon limited, intermittent and unsuccessful drilling activity. At the time of the present discovery, there was little or no interest among the general population in the oil potential of the area. The discovery well unleashed a psychological force which was intensified by the great need of the area for supplemental income and employment and by the fact that earlier failures had eliminated many expectations for this line of development.

In this type of situation, the petroleum extracting industry is particularly well suited to induce a wave of secondary development based upon the psychological and economic impacts of direct oil activity. As an industry, it is somewhat unique in the present American economic scene. It is a heterogenous mixture of speculative finance, production and service. It is a hard, driving, competitive business with the overtones of a circus and is encompassed in the speculative manipulation of a legislative session. In its totality it is as much a movement as an enterprise.

It is doubtful whether any other act of industrial development with equivalent economic potential can generate the psychological impact that is induced by an oil discovery. The search for oil involves several major acts of chance and provides an area of speculation for those who participate on the fringe. The speculative nature of oil development originates in two facts. First is the fact that in spite of the great improvement in the techniques for the study of the subsurface geological structure, there is no way to prove the presence of an oil reserve except to drill for it. Well drilling is an expensive operation, in particular when drilling depths are great. The cost of an exploratory well may range from 50,000 dollars to twice or three times that amount. The probability of success for a wildcat well is probably about 10 percent for the nation as a whole. On the other hand, the potential rewards are sufficient to induce many gamblers, large and small, to join the game.

A second condition adding greatly to the psychological impact is that the oil producer seldom owns the right to the oil which he hopes to discover and produce. He must obtain these rights by lease or in rare instances by purchase of the mineral rights. The rental that he must pay for the right to explore and produce oil on another's land will depend largely on the amount of interest by others and thus on the competition for lease rights. Delay rentals may vary from ten cents a mineral acre when there is little prevailing interest to more than one dollar when there is an actual oil show in the area. Further, it is customary for the lessee to pay a bonus at the time of leasing. Bonus payments may range from ten cents or even nothing to ten dollars or more.

To maximize his potential gain and to assure an unrestricted right to exploration, the producer must acquire mineral leases without initiating competition by his own acts of acquisition. Yet, the earlier he moves, the less information at his disposal with which to improve his estimate of the probabilities of success. As in stud poker, every turn of a card adds to one's knowledge of the probable value of the hand. At the same time, it increases the cost of staying in the game.

The oil game is played by amateurs and professionals. The fervor with which it is played is due in part to the fact that nearly everyone can get into the game. The sharp trading in leases adds to the cross current of rumor and confusion. The competitive pressures on rental price induce an optimism and excitement in the community that may easily lead to a rate of investment in other areas of local economy which are not warranted by the realities of the situation.

The pattern of lease buying in the Williston Basin has been described in an excellent pamphlet by Stanley Voelker of the North Dakota Agricultural College. He notes that Amerada Petroleum Corporation and Hunt Oil Company were assembling lease blocks early in 1948. By September 1949, several companies and brokers were competing for leases and slightly more than 120,000 mineral acres had been leased. In this early period, delay rentals averaged 13 cents a mineral acre, as did bonus payments. In the next six months, ending with the completion of the discovery, well acreage leased increased 189 percent and average delay rentals and bonus payments increased to 20 cents and 21 cents respectively. The most intense leasing activity began at the time of discovery in April, 1951. By the end of October of the same year, more than 568,000 additional acres were brought under lease. Average delay rentals had increased to 85 cents and bonus payments to 1.52 dollars per mineral acre. In terms of monthly rates, leasing activity in the seven months following discovery was 215 percent of the rate in the six months preceding activity. At the beginning of leasing activity, 82 percent of all leases were at 10 cents an acre. In the period after discovery, 99 percent were at one dollar or more. Dr. Voelker estimates that bonus payments varied from less than 10 cents (in some cases, nothing) to an extreme of 135 dollars in a few cases in the oil field area.

Data comparable to Dr. Voelker's data for Williams County are not available for other areas. However, the location of the proven oil fields indicates that the leasing pattern for Mountrail County was very similar to that of Williams County. As wildcat drilling extended through the Williston Basin, in attempts to define the area, lease activity occurred in nearly every area of the state. The extent and rapidity of the action is evident in the fact that by January 1954, 67 percent of the land area of North Dakota was under oil or gas leases. The boom characteristics of this phase of the oil development are indicated in a comparison of North Dakota and Oklahoma, a state with a much older oil extraction industry. These two states are of nearly equal size, yet only 39 percent of Oklahoma's land area was under lease.

In contrast to these indications of extremely rapid development in the Williston area, nearly all of those persons who came into the area with oil producing or contract and service companies felt that the Williston Basin development was restrained. At least, its development was slow relative to their experience in the Texas, Oklahoma and Wyoming areas.

This restraint is explained in several ways. Physical factors such as the greater than average drilling depth, the extreme cold of prolonged winters and the geographical isolation of the area all add to drilling costs and discourage marginal independent producers.

Institutional factors, in particular such political issues as depletion allowances, production tax rates, well spacing and production allowances appear to have encouraged major producers to move slowly in an effort to improve their position of power. These issues are discussed elsewhere in this study. From the standpoint of economic impact, it should be noted here that the domination of the Williston Basin Development by the Amerada Petroleum Company was generally believed by those interviewed to be a paramount factor in the relatively slow development of the area. The position taken by the corporation on oil issues was almost universally echoed by the local business people where the success of their business ventures was contingent on oil related expansion.

In the development of an oil reserve, charges are often levied against the producers concerning intentional restraint of the development, usually by the owners of mineral rights. Some land owners insisted that supposed dry wells were potential producers. They believe that the producing company is exercising a means of market control in a glutted domestic market. This type of attitude may be more prevalent in the Williston area than in many other oil producing regions of the United States, first, because the isolation of the area, the supply problem in the national market, the lack of refining facilities and the limited means of transport of crude combined to create serious market problems. This situation was not relieved until the completion of the Standard Oil Refinery in Mandan and the pipelines from it to the east.

Second, the Williston development has been dominated by one major producing company, Amerada. It is more logical to attribute monopolistic activities to a dominant firm than to assume conspiracy among many otherwise competitive firms. The records of the State Geologist indicate that by mid-year 1954, drilling permits had been issued to more than 150 producing companies. Many of these are large and established firms. Many others were "one-shot" combinations of individuals or business firms joined for the single purpose of producing one well.

Although the large number of "wildcat" operations provide an illusion of feverish competitive activity and support the psychological pitch of the community, a very large proportion of exploration and production has been conducted by Amerada. By mid-year 1956, there were 699 wells producing oil in the state. Nearly 76 percent of these (533) were drilled on leases owned by this company. Eight of every ten barrels of oil produced in the state prior to 1956 were produced through Amerada wells. Eighty-five percent of the state's oil output was produced in one of two fields, the Beaver Lodge and Tioga fields. Amerada produced 84 percent of this output.

It appears quite probable that Amerada did follow a very conservative development policy, as many employees of the company and its drilling contractors have stated. Such a policy may have been intended to serve the industry in the power struggle on regulatory issues. It seems also to have served the community by permitting a more orderly development with fewer stresses and unwarranted actions than might have been experienced under other conditions.

Economic Impacts

Oil field exploration and development has affected the local economy in quantitative and qualitative ways. It has increased the population, income and employment of the area. It has also changed the structure of the labor force and of business. The measurement of these changes is complicated by the fact the area of development is extensive and transitory. As was noted above, leasing activity has extended throughout the state, geological survey has also moved over a large area, and drilling activity in a particular location varies from week to week. The employees of a producing company and those who provide contract services are scattered in varying patterns among the many fields under production or areas under exploration.

Consequently, the measurements of income and employment, related to the industry, described below, have for the most part been derived by allocation of aggregate amounts on the basis of measures of activity such as the number of wells drilled or the volume of production. The basic data from which the allocations were derived were obtained from the individual well records of the State Geologist. In some cases, the results of allocation may differ slightly from later summary figures due to two major causes. One is the fact that the disposition of a well may change, the other, that the completion date of a well does not indicate accurately the period in which drilling activity occurred, in particular if completed early in the year.

In the structure of the petroleum industry, the producing company is the prime mover and the primary source of direct income. It initiates exploration, assembles lease blocks, sells and distributes the recovered oil. Most of the drilling activity is accomplished by a hierarchy of specialized subcontractors. Nationally, about 90 percent of all drilling is done on subcontract. In turn, drilling contractors contract for such specialized services as logging and cementing wells, rig moving and acidizing. The extent of sub-contracting complicates income accounting when income is accounted for on a cost basis. To avoid these complications, estimates of total cost have been based on average cost per well in North Dakota in 1954. These costs were then allocated by aggregating the major expenses of firms engaged in crude petroleum extraction and those in oil and gas field contract services. Major expenses include contract expenses only if they cannot be allocated within the major industry group.

Apart from leasing activity and geophysical exploration, the beginning of the present oil development was in 1950 and the initial production year was 1951. Tables XXXVI and XXXVII indicate the rapidity of development and the concentration of activity in Williams and Mountrail Counties. By the end of the study period, the preponderance of drilling activity had moved out of the two county area although the area continued to produce nearly 90 percent of the state output of petroleum.

TABLE XXXVI
WELLS COMPLETED IN NORTH DAKOTA—BY AREA AND BY
PRODUCING STATUS, 1951–1954

| | 1951 | | 1952 | | 1953 | | 1954 | |
	P*	NP**	P	NP	P	NP	P	NP
Williams County	1	0	80	17	119	10	107	13
Mountrail County	0	0	10	2	42	2	42	6
Other	0	9	2	58	19	85	39	136
State	1	9	92	77	180	97	188	155
Total Wells (Yearly)	10		169		277		343	
Total Wells (Cumulative)	10		179		456		799	

* Producing Wells.
** Non-Producing Wells.

TABLE XXXVII
PRODUCTION OF CRUDE PETROLEUM, NORTH DAKOTA AND
SELECTED AREAS, 1951–1954 (THOUSANDS OF BARRELS)

	1951	1952	1953	1954
Williams County	25	1,481	4,248	4,135
Mountrail County	0	91	900	1,253
Other	0	26	218	637
North Dakota	25	1,598	5,466	6,025

It should be noted in the drilling record that in the wildcat area only two of eight wells drilled have produced oil. Within the area nearly nine of every ten wells drilled have produced oil, although not always continuously in commercial quantities. This fact adds to the concentration of oil related income in the two county area in view of the additional cost of completing and equipping a producing well.

These data indicate the concentration of oil production in Williams and Mountrail counties in the years prior to 1955. Further, nearly two-thirds of all production in other areas of the state occurred in McKenzie County; most of it in the Charlson (Madison) field. McKenzie County adjoins Williams County on the south and is relatively isolated from areas to the east by the Missouri River. It is a part of the Williston trade area, and a very large part of oil related income originating in this county is spent in Williston.

On the basis of this record of drilling activity and oil production it is estimated that the total income derived from oil field expenditures in North Dakota amounted to approximately $700,000 in 1951. By 1954, annual expenditures had increased to nearly $33,000,000. These estimates do not include income derived from mineral leases, bonuses, oil royalties, the sale of mineral deeds or expenditures for the improvement of oil lands. The latter estimates are discussed below. Table XXXVIII contains estimates of expenditures by county and state for the years 1951–54. It is probable that they understate actual expenditures in 1951 due to the reliance on well drilling activity as the basis of estimate. Developmental activities such as geophysical exploration tend to be underestimated by this technique.

TABLE XXXVIII
EXPENDITURES BY THE CRUDE PETROLEUM INDUSTRY IN
NORTH DAKOTA, 1951–1954 (THOUSANDS OF DOLLARS)

	1951	1952	1953	1954
Williams County	120	10,890	15,220	13,940
Mountrail County		1,350	5,270	5,530
Other	580	3,960	7,780	13,500
North Dakota	700	16,200	28,270	32,970

The potential effects of these expenditures on the economy of the area is limited by two factors. First, in oil field exploration and petroleum production, labor costs are small relative to the costs of supplies and machinery. Second, few of the materials and none of the equipment used is produced in the area or in the state. Of the amount spent for such goods, only that portion that is attributed to transport and distribution accrues to the benefit of the local economy. Further, the supply of drilling materials and equipment is a specialized area of business. The major suppliers follow the field establishing branch distribution outlets in competition for the market. Although these units may provide additional income to the area through consumption expenditure by staff and in the construction of service facilities, the major portion of their revenue is used to pay for a product produced elsewhere. For example, a major cost of completing a well is the cost of casing. Several major steel companies have established distribution centers in Williston and Tioga. These distribution points are relatively small establishments with few employees. The wage and salary income originating in their activity is a very small portion of the total expenditure for their product.

The distribution of expenditures by type and by area may be noted in Table XXXIX.

TABLE XXXIX
EXPENDITURES BY OIL PRODUCERS AND OIL AND GAS FIELD CONTRACTORS BY TYPE OF EXPENDITURE BY AREA, 1951–1954 (THOUSANDS OF DOLLARS)

	Wages & Salaries	Supplies, Minerals, Fuel & Energy	Machinery & Equipment	Not Allocated	Total
Williams County					
1951	18	24	64	17	123
1952	1,714	2,318	5,225	1,632	10,890
1953	2,285	3,091	7,665	2,176	15,218
1954	2,123	2,873	6,910	2,023	13,930
Period	6,140	8,306	19,854	5,848	40,160
Mountrail County					
1952	213	286	652	201	1,353
1953	780	1,054	2,695	742	5,273
1954	850	1,149	2,723	809	5,530
Period	1,844	2,489	6,070	1,752	12,156
North Dakota					
1951	174	235	127	165	701
1952	2,963	4,006	6,411	2,822	16,202
1953	4,871	6,589	12,167	4,639	28,266
1954	6,015	8,136	13,084	5,729	32,964
Period	14,023	18,966	31,789	13,355	78,133

In the four years after 1950, oil activity, exclusive of the acquisition of mineral rights, cost more than 40 million dollars in Williams County and over 12 million in Mountrail. Of these amounts, approximately 8 million was spent for wages and salaries by oil producers and contractors. They spent nearly 11 million on supplies, minerals and fuel, and more than twice that amount (26 million) on machinery and oil well equipment. The total expenditure includes nearly 14 million dollars that has not been allocated by type of expenditure. These unallocated expenditures contain two major accounts; the entrepreneurial profits of contractors and expenditures for contract services outside of the industry group.

Of major importance in estimating the direct impact of the oil development on the local economy is the fact that less than 16 percent of the total expenditure was for wages and salaries. It has been noted above that a very small proportion of expenditures of other types benefit local establishments and payrolls.

In contrast to oil field expenditures, income from mineral leases and royalty payments are received in large part by the landowners of the area and are a source of additional consumption expenditure. The magnitude of income of this type has been estimated for the years 1948–53 on the basis of the Voelker study for Williams County. The pattern of leasing activity has been described above where it was noted that the leasing of mineral rights began in 1948. In the first two years of activity, total payments for leases and bonuses in Williams County are estimated at less than $50,000. By 1951, lease activity in the area reached a peak and bonus payments above exceeded one million dollars. By the end of 1953, royalty payments had reached the same level and offset the decline in bonus payments. Total income from mineral rights approximated $2,000,000. Due to the sale of mineral acres by mineral deed it is impossible to estimate the proportion of lease and royalty income accruing to original owners in the area. In 1951, the value of mineral acres sold was slightly more than three million dollars. Approximately one-third of the acreage sold was sold by owners, the remaining two-thirds by brokers. Income derived from sales are a type of transfer payment and duplicate in part the income received from lease payments and oil royalties. In one sense, the owner is receiving a prepayment of lease and royalty income with the sale of mineral acreage. The speculative gains of brokers are primarily transfers of income from other persons or corporations and are not usually net addition to income.

Data on the pattern of leasing activity in Mountrail County are not available. In view of the location of the major proven fields, it is probable that the pattern approximates very closely that of Williams County and that income from leases and bonuses is only slightly less than the amounts indicated in Table XL.

TABLE XL
DELAY RENTALS, BONUS PAYMENTS AND OIL ROYALTIES TO
INDIVIDUALS, PRIVATE CORPORATIONS AND GOVERNMENT
AGENCIES, WILLIAMS COUNTY, 1948–1953.
(THOUSANDS OF DOLLARS)

	Delay Rentals	Bonus Payment	Royalties	Total
1948–49	19	25		44
1950	50	36		86
1951	332	1,139	6	1,447
1952	644	224	374	1,242
1953	650	60	1,074	1,784

A. The Business Structure

In view of the volatility of the business expansion during the period of oil development and the high mortality of small business ventures during the period, it is extremely difficult to describe the pattern of change that occurred. Data from the 1948 and 1954 Census of Business indicate that the number of establishments in the trade and service industries increased by 32 percent in Williams County and declined by 11 percent in Mountrail County. The net increase in Williston included 82 of the total net increase of 133 establishments in Williams County. Yet a comparison of the Williston telephone directories for 1950 and 1953 indicates that the number of new establishments operating in the area during the period was much greater than census data suggest.

The 1953 directory listed 132 trade and service establishments that were not listed in 1950, exclusive of 33 firms supplying the oil industry and 24 firms in oil field contract services. Further, the 1950 directory listed 40 such establishments not listed in 1953. This difference in the number of establishments reported results in part from definitions of business establishments, in part from the inadequacy of directory information, and in part from changes in ownership and in the name of the establishment. Together, these factors account, however, for a relatively small part of the difference. Direct investigation verified the extremely large turn-over in establishments in the early period of oil development.

Table XLI below offers some comparison of the number of establishments for selected years.

TABLE XLI

NUMBER OF ACTIVE BUSINESS ESTABLISHMENTS BY TYPE
OF ESTABLISHMENT, TRADE AND SERVICE INDUSTRIES,
1948–1954, WILLISTON, NORTH DAKOTA

	1948[1]	1950[2]	1953[2]	1954[1]
Wholesale Trade:	21	19	50	46
Retail Trade:	127	142	169	153
Food Stores	16	16	26	22
Eating & Drinking	25	28	29	28
General Merchandise & Apparel	16	16	16	15
Furniture & Appliances	9	9	14	9
Automobiles & Gasoline	23	33	36	32
Lumber & Hardware	16	17	19	15
All other	22	23	29	32
Service	63	59	79	91

1. U.S. Department of Commerce, Census of Business.
2. Derived from local census and telephone directories.

The estimates derived for 1950 and 1953 are the number of establishments active in that year. As was noted above, these point data obscure the number of establishments entering and leaving the area during the period and estimates of payrolls, income and employment for the area are understated by such data.

Within this limitation, the major changes in the business structure of the study area appear to have been in the number of new establishments in wholesale trade and in the service industry. In absolute terms, Williston experienced a very large proportion of the total increase and Tioga and environs much of the residual gain. Mountrail County gained only in the number of service establishments and had a net loss in the number of firms in wholesale and retail trade. Williston contained 73 percent of the total increase in Williams County. It had 86 percent of new firms in wholesale trade, nearly 60 percent of new retail establishments and a little more than half of the net addition to the service industry. In relative terms, the greatest change in the trade and service structure was in wholesale trade, an increase of 119 percent. The greatest change in the Tioga area was in service, a gain of 104 percent. These two measures describe the pattern of development in the area, the concentration of oil field suppliers in Williston and of subsidiary services in the oil field area.

Changes in the sales, receipts and payrolls of the three industry groups are shown in Table XLII. Sales and receipts in Williams County in 1954 exceeded the 1948 level by 24,319,000 dollars or 51 percent. The gain in Williston was 19.3 million dollars, an increase of 71 per cent over 1948 and nearly 80 percent of the county gain. Williston also received 94 percent of the increase in wholesale sales and nearly 80 percent of the gain in service receipts.

TABLE XLII

SALES, RECEIPTS AND PAYROLLS IN TRADE AND SERVICE IN-
DUSTRIES, 1948 AND 1954—WILLISTON, WILLIAMS COUNTY
AND MOUNTRAIL COUNTY (THOUSANDS OF DOLLARS)

| | Sales & Receipts | | Payrolls | |
	1948	1954	1948	1954
Wholesale Trade:				
Williams County	$25,628	$39,000	$551	$1,541
Williston	10,763	23,377	338	1,073
Mountrail	(D)	(D)	(D)	(D)
Retail Trade:				
Williams County	$21,207	$30,357	$1,653	$3,030
Williston	15,601	20,914	1,277	2,294
Mountrail County	8,112	10,839	454	763
Service:				
Williams County	$972	$2,769	$166	$523
Williston	781	2,168	153	476
Mountrail County	178	426	16	52

U.S. Department of Commerce: 1954 Census of Business.

Business expansion added nearly three million dollars to payrolls
in Williams County, with the greatest absolute gain in retail trade and
the greatest relative gain in the service industry. Three-fourths of the
increase in payrolls occurred in establishments located in Williston.
Mountrail County had modest gains in payrolls in retail sales and services, however, the gain in this county as a whole was less than a third
of the increase in the same industry groups in Williston.

One general indication of the effect of oil activity on the trade structure of the area and the state may be inferred from state data on sales
tax collections for the period 1950–1953. (TABLES XLIII AND XLIV.)

TABLE XLIII

SALES TAX COLLECTIONS FOR SELECTED COUNTIES AND
THEIR SUB-DIVISIONS, 1950–1954
(THOUSANDS OF DOLLARS)

	1950	1951	1952	1953
Williams County	$375.7	$407.7	$578.6	$788.9
Williston	288.6	318.4	460.1	614.8
Ray	22.2	23.1	34.6	45.5
Tioga	11.6	12.8	30.4	70.9
Mountrail County	148.6	155.5	158.9	173.9
Stanley	62.7	62.6	65.2	74.0

TABLE XLIV
PERCENT OF STATE SALES TAX COLLECTION BY SELECTED
COUNTIES AND THEIR SUBDIVISIONS, 1950–1954

	1950	1951	1952	1953
Williams County	3.32%	3.37%	4.70%	6.30%
Williston	2.55	2.63	3.74	4.91
Ray	.20	.19	.28	.36
Tioga	.10	.11	.25	.57
Mountrail County	1.31	1.29	1.29	1.39
Stanley	.55	.52	.53	.59

SOURCE: North Dakota Tax Department, Sales Tax Division.

Both counties and their major subdivisions gained relative to the state in sales activity as reflected by tax collections. The gain in Mountrail County and in Stanley was slight and occurred late in the period as exploration spread away from the site of discovery. In Williston and Tioga, the gains were immediate and large. It is descriptive of the pattern of development that in 1950, tax collections in Ray were nearly double those in Tioga. By 1953, collections in Tioga were almost 50 percent greater than in Ray.

A second general indicator of changes in business activity is found in bank deposit data for the area.[1] These data indicate that the banks in Williams County experienced virtually no net increase. The following data for banks in the ten northwestern counties indicate the relative rates of increase.

---

[1] The analysis of bank deposit changes was made by W.E. Koenker, Professor of Economics, The University of North Dakota.

County	Percentage Change in Total Deposits Dec. 31, 1950 to Dec. 31, 1954
Burke	+15
Divide	+9
McLean	–4
Mountrail	+2
Williams	+48
Renville	–24
Bottineau	0
McHenry	0
Ward	+1
McKenzie	0
Nine counties other than Williams	+.18

The increase in deposits in Burke County is attributable almost entirely to the deposits placed in the new bank at Powers Lake, only about ten miles from the production area.

Despite the fact that a considerable portion of the oil production area lay in Mountrail County, there seems to have been little effect on deposits in banks in that area. The bank at Stanley, which was only about 20 miles away, experienced a ten percent decline in total deposits during the four year period.[2] The banks at Newtown and Parshall were too remote, too far off of Highway Two, to experience much effect from the oil business.

Except in accounting for the new bank at Powers Lake, the major impact of the oil development seems to have been in the two banks at Williston and the banks at Tioga and Ray. These banks had the following percentage increase in demand and time deposits between December 31, 1950, and the end of 1954.

Williams County Banks	Percentage Demand	Increase in Time	Deposits Total
Ray—Citizens State Bank	57	41	54
Williston—American State Bank	36	62	42
Williston—First National Bank	31	50	37
Tioga—(New bank in 1951)			
Total for all banks in the County			48

---

[2] During the last portion of this period; however, most of the oil companies operating in the area were beginning to maintain accounts at this bank as well as at the banks in Williams County. These accounts were drawn upon to make lease rental and royalty payments in the area.

In contrast with the banks at Williston and Ray having increases ranging from 37 to 54 percent in total deposits, none of the other banks in the ten county area had increases in excess of 16 percent. This included the three banks in Minot which had increases of only about 2 percent during the period.

Since the banks in the other nine counties located in the same general area of the state experienced virtually no net gain in total deposits, it seems logical to assume that the increases experienced by the banks in Williams County are attributable directly or indirectly to oil. In absolute amounts, this increase amounted to about six and one-half million dollars, an increase from $13.4 million to $19.9 million.

The increase in demand deposits was somewhat less than that for time deposits. This increase in demand deposits is significant since only one other bank in the ten state area had an increase in excess of ten percent. Two thirds of these banks experienced decreases in deposits. This increase in demand deposits in Williams County banks reflected the increased number of households and business firms serviced by these banks.

Percentage data on time deposits are somewhat more unreliable for comparison purposes since some of the smaller banks began making real efforts to attract time deposits during this period. Total time deposits, however, for all banks in the nine counties other than Williams County increased by only 13 percent. This was in contrast to the 60 percent increase in time deposits in the Williams County banks.

A concomitant of an increase in deposits is usually a comparable increase in loans and investments. In Williams County loans increased by 189 percent or an increase from about 3 million to 8.6 million dollars. This increase was very much in excess of the 45 percent increase for the other nine counties. In only one other county was the increase in excess of 80 percent.

This was a period of rather substantial expansion in loans throughout the state and some decline in assets held in the form of U.S. government bonds and other securities. The expanding communities served by the banks in Williams County, however, provided substantial outlets especially for housing and installment loans.

Data for two of the banks in the county indicate the following percentage increases in major loan categories.

	Percentage Increase Dec. 1950 to Dec. 1954	
	Bank A Medium Size	Bank B Large
Commercial and Industrial Loans	83	130
CCC Loans	390	26
Other Loans to Farmers	242	286
Real Estate Loans	1430	86
Installment Loans		
Auto	1350	217
Other	1700	267

The phenomenal increase in real estate and installment loans in the medium sized bank was a reflection of a marked change in the pattern of lending. Many North Dakota banks in this size category were just beginning to make loans of this type. Obviously, however, in this case the oil boom provided a much enhanced opportunity for loans in these categories. This is confirmed by the very marked increase in install-ment lending by the large bank which even in 1950 had a substantial amount of this kind of paper.

Another indication of the financial impact of the oil industry is to be found in sales of savings bonds. Since these are limited as to type of purchaser and to the amount which may be held, they provide some indication of liquid savings held by individuals. The growth in savings bond sales in Williams County and the decline in most of the other counties in the northwestern portion of the state is shown in the fol-lowing tabulation. Sales for the two year period of 1954 and 1955 are compared with the two year period of 1949 and 1950, because indi-vidual year comparisons are apt to be erratic.

Only two of the ten counties had significant increases. The increase in Divide County is attributable to exceptionally good crops in both 1954 and 1955. There has been a declining amount of income from lease rentals in this county, so this factor would not account for any of the difference. Some of the increase in bond sales may be due to a rather aggressive "pushing" of bonds on the part of the Crosby bank. The increase in Williams County is largely attributable to the oil devel-opment. Part of it, however, oa also due to the better than average crop in these two years. The data seem, therefore, to indicate that, while some of the increase in savings bond sales may be due to oil, that factor may be no more significant in this respect than a better than average crop.

County	Percentage Increase or Decrease 1949 and 1950 to 1954 and 1955
Burke	−21
Divide	+34
McLean	−17
Mountrail	−29
Williams	+25
Renville	−37
Bottineau	−10
McHenry	+4
Ward	−18
McKenzie	−48
Total (nine counties other than Williams County)	−13
Total for North Dakota	−17

B. Construction

The major part of contract construction stemming directly from oil development and nearly all construction induced by it have occurred in two areas, Williston and Tioga and its environs. Apart from these two localities, only Ray with two trailer camps and an unwarranted residential development and Stanley with modest residential expansion show any evidence of oil related influence on construction activity.

The pattern of construction activity in Williston is evident in an analysis of building permit valuations from 1950 to 1954. The value of construction covered by permits was $1,620,000 in 1950 and $1,380,000 in the following year. It increased abruptly in 1952 to $5,371,000 and reached peak at $7,241,000 in 1953. (SEE TABLE XLV)

TABLE XLV
VALUE OF BUILDING PERMITS, BY TYPE OF CONSTRUC-
TION—WILLISTON, NORTH DAKOTA, 1950–1954
(THOUSANDS OF DOLLARS)

Type of Construction	1950	1951	1952	1953	1954
Residential	$719	$761	$3,622	$3,707	$1,186
New	634	657	3,311	3,472	1,053
Remodel	95	105	311	235	133
Public and Other:	154	315	538	1,474	641
Commercial	737	303	1,211	2,060	1,217
All Types	1,620	1,380	5,371	7,241	3,044

Residential construction provided the major part of building activity in the four years after 1950. Approximately 54 percent of the total value of permits issued was in residential construction. In 1951, only 61 new dwelling units were authorized. In 1953, permits were issued for 273 units and for 324 units in the following year. By 1954, a surplus of housing was apparent in the community, in particular in rental apartments. The number of units declined to 84 and the value of construction authorized was less than half of the number in the preceding year.

This abrupt increase in 1952 over 1951 was without question a response to the very strong pressures exerted by the influx of population with the discovery of oil. Although there had been a significant expansion in residential building after 1948 following a peak farm income, there was little vacant housing for the addition of several hundred migrant families. The "boom" characteristic of residential building activity in Williston is obvious when compared to new residential construction authorized in all urban areas of the state.

TABLE XLVI

PERCENTAGE CHANGE FROM PRECEDING YEAR IN URBAN RESIDENTIAL CONSTRUCTION AUTHORIZED, NORTH DAKOTA AND WILLISTON, 1950–1954

Area:	1951/1950	1952/1951	1953/1952	1954/1953
Williston	+4%	+376%	+5%	–70%
North Dakota	–20%	+20%	+15%	+20%

SOURCE: Derived from original data in office of Williston City Engineer.

The impact of preliminary oil activity was more than adequate to offset a general decline in 1951. Activity moved dramatically to a high plateau where it remained relatively constant through 1953. It fell sharply in 1954 and continued to decline through the first half of 1955.

Non-residential building responded to the new development in a similar way although with less force. It, too, is largely induced in a secondary manner rather than by the immediate needs of the oil industry. Further, the lag in activity was greater in this area of construction, since a greater proportion of expenditure appears to have been induced by secondary demand. The major construction items by or for the oil industry were an office building for Amerada, a small refinery and a number of warehouses or combination office-warehouses for major suppliers and contract service firms. Both office and refinery were authorized in 1952 and more than 50 percent of the value of warehouse permits issued, were issued in the same year.

In the five years extending through 1954, the permit valuation of the offices and warehouses noted above were less than 11 percent of the total value of private non-residential building authorized. In contrast, the valuation of utility construction (primarily telephone communication) was 26 percent of the total, hotels and motels nearly 21 percent and stores and service stations, 20 percent.

The secondary effects of oil development acting through wage and salary payments, delay rentals, royalty payments and taxes, combined with the pressures exerted by a rapid increase in population, are evident in public expenditures. Within five years, Williston spent 740,000 dollars on school construction, 675,000 dollars on church buildings and 790,000 dollars for additions to hospital and clinic facilities. Another half million was spent by the county for a new courthouse in 1953.

Comparing Williston to all urban places in the state, an index of building permit valuations based on the 1947–49 average indicates that activity in Williston greatly exceeded the state pattern (SEE TABLE XLVII).

TABLE XLVII
INDEX OF BUILDING PERMIT VALUATIONS, ALL URBAN
PLACES OF NORTH DAKOTA AND WILLISTON, 1950–1954
1947 to 1949 = 100

	1950	1951	1952	1953	1954
North Dakota	201	115	133	201	167
Williston	188	160	625	842	354

SOURCE: Williston public records and U.S. Dept. of Labor, Bureau of Labor Statistics.

Since building permit valuations are not available for Mountrail County or other areas of Williams County, a precise description of building activity in these areas is not possible. Inspection of the areas suggests that there was very little primary or secondary construction in Mountrail County and that the pattern of activity in the Tioga area was similar to that of Williston in every respect save one. In Tioga, the major proportion of construction originated in the oil industry. Major expenditures by the industry included several million dollars by the Signal Oil and Gas Company for a gas refining plant just east of the community. Amerada constructed a multi-unit "village" for its field personnel south of Tioga and several suppliers and contract service firms erected office and storage facilities within and adjacent to it.

Although commercial development was far less impressive in Tioga than in Williston, it occurred in a community that at the beginning of oil activity was rapidly becoming a "ghost town." Hotel, restaurant and entertainment and recreation facilities were virtually non-existent, and the community had no paved streets, sewage system, or municipal water supply. The oil industry literally created a new and living community from the old.

In addition to the large number of oil field workers moving into the area, the construction of the gas refining plant employed more than 300 people at peak activity. Many oil field workers, in particular drilling crews, own and live in trailers. Although large trailer camps were established in Tioga and vicinity, many migrants were forced to move into intolerable housing conditions. In several cases, abandoned grain storage sheds were moved into crowded rows and, after some slight renovation, rented at exorbitant prices as family dwellings. By 1954, two relatively large housing projects were nearing completion, reducing the demand pressure and eliminating much of the market for sub-standard housing.

The completion of the gas refinery and other major construction projects had restricted the boom activity in construction in 1954. By June of that year, unemployment was a more pressing problem for construction workers than were housing accommodations.

C. Labor Force and Employment

Changes in population in the area between 1950 and 1954 have been discussed in another section of this study. It is only necessary to repeat here that the attraction of employment opportunities created by the oil industry and the employment pattern of that industry brought many migrants into the area, expanding the size of the labor force. Over the period, Williston gained nearly 32 percent in number of inhabitants, Ray over 100 percent and Tioga and its environs more than 450 percent.

In contrast Stanley experienced an increase of less than 11 percent and Mountrail County and all other areas of Williams county had population losses.

The extent to which these population gains resulted from in-migration is evident in the statistics derived from the population sample census in 1954. (SEE TABLE XII.) One of every three persons living in Williston in that year did not live there in 1950. Nearly 28 in 100 persons came to Williston from beyond the borders of the two study counties. The proportions of migrants into the smaller communities of Ray and Tioga are much larger. In both communities, approximately 65 percent of the 1954 population entered the area after 1950. Less than 5 percent of the migrants into Ray and 10 percent of those into Tioga were former residents of Williams or Mountrail county. In the Tioga environs, only 10 percent of all inhabitants were 1950 residents in the two-county area.

The impact of this migration in the local labor force was much greater than population changes indicate. This fact is a result of the age structure of in-migrants, the majority of whom are relatively young and within the normal limits of work life. In Williston, more than 63 percent of all in-migrants were between the ages of 19 and 50. Of those resident in Williston in 1950 and residing there in 1954, only 41 per cent were in this age category. These differences in age between "natives" and migrants also hold in every "oil" location in the study area. One aspect of this situation affecting the local economy, other than in terms of the labor force, is that these young migrant families had a large number of children in the younger school ages. The great increase in the school age population required new schools in Tioga and Ray, as well as Williston. The school at Ray was completed about the time that migrant population, primarily families of drilling crews, began to move on to other locations.

The impact of oil development on primary and secondary employment has been relatively great. The effect was not as great as the business leadership of the area assumed. One indication of the difference between the illusion of growth commonly held and the reality of the situation is in local population estimates. In 1954, the Williston Chamber of Commerce estimated the population of Williston to be 12,000, compared with the estimate of 9,717 derived from the sample.

Of these two estimates, the study figure must be credited with the highest validity on the basis of the employment estimates explicit in it. Two estimates of employment are available for Williston for July 1954. One is the sample estimate. The other is the estimate of the State Employment Service based on their sample of business establishments. Allowing for differences in the structure of these two samples, they compare very favorably. (SEE TABLE XLVIII.)

TABLE XLVIII

EMPLOYMENT BY INDUSTRY AND OCCUPATION, 1950 AND
JULY 1954, WILLISTON, NORTH DAKOTA

	Williston 1950 (census)	1954 (sample)	1954 (NDES)	% Change 1950–54 (sample)	% Change 1950–54 (NDES)
Agriculture	150	180		+20	
Mining & Construction	235	494	477	+110	+103
Manufacturing	120	181	190	+50	+58
Transportation, Construction and Public Utilities	535	461	387	–14	–28
Trade	880	1054	1199	+20	+36
Finance, Insurance & Real Estate	72	98	87	+36	+21
Source	679	727	774	+7	+14
Public Administration	126	221	248	+75	+97
No Data	76				
All Occupation	2863	3416	3362[1]	+19	+24
[1]Excludes Agriculture					
Professional	256	330		+17	
Farmer	113	153		+35	
Manager, Proprietor, Official	338	586		+73	
Clerical	351	411		+17	
Sales	343	384		+12	
Craft, Foreman, Kindred	448	489		+9	
Operatives	333	359		+8	
Service	363	366		+1	
Farm Laborer	27	27		0	
Other Laborer	200	311		+56	
NEC.	71				

SOURCE: U.S. Department of Commerce. 1950 Census of Population.

The survey sample shows a total non-agricultural employment of 3,236, a gain of 19 percent over 1950. The ES figure is 3,362, a gain of 24 percent over the census estimate of 1950. The similarity of the two figures suggests that unless there has been a significant decline in labor force participation rates, the local estimate of population change must be excessive.

Nothing in the characteristics of the local population suggests that the proportion of the population in the labor-force has changed in significant degree. While the number of children and young persons under age 20 has increased since 1950, the proportion of the population over 65 years of age has declined. The off-setting effects of these changes and the migration of relatively large numbers of unmarried males into the area limit the possibility of a major decline in labor force participation rates.

It will be noted in Table XLVIII that although the two estimates of employment by industry do not agree in magnitude, they do agree in the direction of change in every industry sector. In each case, the greatest gain was in mining and construction, followed by public administration and manufactures. In both samples, the service industry demonstrated the least positive gain and both agree that transportation, communication and public utilities had a decline in employment. In absolute terms much of the new employment was in mining, construction and trade. The study sample shows an increase of 433, and the ES sample 561 in these industry groups, compared to total gains of 523 and 649 respectively.

The small differences in the two samples can be explained in the fact that the study sample measures the employment of persons living in Williston without regard to their place of employment. Thus it tends to overstate employment in mining and construction in Williston since many persons dwell there who perform their employment in the oil fields. On the other hand, it is probable that a relatively large percentage of persons living outside of Williston, but employed there, are employed in trade and service and that employment in these industries is under-stated in the sample. Since the two samples measure employment in different terms, it is expected that the ES estimate should exceed the sample estimate. It should be noted that the survey sample is structured in the same manner as the decennial census and is the only one of the two measures that is comparable to it. Conversely, the ES sample is structured like the Census of Business.

Occupational changes in Williston suggest the pattern of business change. A detailed business census indicated that the intensive change in employment was slight and that most new employment was in firms new to the area. Further, most of these new establishments were small. Other than the largest oil producing companies, and major drilling companies, only one oil-related firm employed a large number of persons. In all other industry components, the small firm pattern was characteristic. As a result, the greatest change in occupation was that of managers, proprietors, and officials: a gain of 73 percent over 1950.

Detailed employment data for Ray, Tioga, Stanley and the rural impact areas are contained in tables XLIX, L, and LI. The impact of drilling activity and related construction on Tioga and Ray is obvious.

Nearly half of all employment in Ray and more than half of that in Tioga and its environs was in mining and construction. Stanley also suggests this employment effect with nearly a third in these industries. The importance of the location of a large drilling company in Ray is reflected by the large proportion of the labor force classified as operatives, nearly 41 percent. Similarly, nearly 35 percent of all employees in Tioga were in this category with another 14 percent in the category of craftsman and foreman. The latter category reflects the construction of Signal Oil and Gas Company's oil refinery. The project was the major employment in the area.

TABLE XLIX
LABOR FORCE AND EMPLOYMENT, PERSONS 14 YEARS AND OLDER, SELECTED AREAS, 1954

	Williston			Ray			Impact Counties			Stanley			Tioga & Environs		
	Male	Female	Total	M	F	T	M	F	T	M	F	T	M	F	T
Employed	2548	868	3416	424	59	483	612	20	632	462	123	585	824	86	906
Unemployed	57	25	82	3	6	9	4	.....	4	6	5	11	17	8	29
TOTAL LABOR FORCE	2605	893	3498	427	65	492	616	20	636	468	128	596	841	94	935
Keeping House	8	2025	2033	.....	326	326	0	423	423	.....	338	338	4	534	538
In School	147	216	363	21	28	49	33	56	89	28	50	78	41	61	102
Unable to Work	155	98	253	21	7	28	20	4	24	43	35	78	27	12	39
Retired	145	.....	145	29	.....	29	4	8	12	15	.....	15	31	.....	31
Other	21	17	38	4	.....	4	20	.....	20	3	.....	3	3	.....	3
No Data	44	28	72	1	3	4	4	4	8	13	5	18	31	3	34
TOTAL NOT IN LABOR FORCE	520	2384	2904	76	364	440	81	495	576	102	428	530	137	610	747
TOTAL IN AGE GROUP	3125	3277	6402	503	429	932	697	515	1212	570	556	1126	978	704	1682

SOURCE: Projections from sample census.

TABLE XLIX-A
PERCENT DISTRIBUTION

	Williston			Ray			Impact Counties			Stanley			Tioga & Environs		
	Male	Female	Total	M	F	T	M	F	T	M	F	T	M	F	T
Employed	97.8	97.3	97.7	99.3	90.8	98.2	99.4	100.0	99.4	98.8	95.7	98.2	98.0	90.9	97.0
Unemployed	2.2	2.7	2.3	0.7	9.2	1.8	0.6	......	0.6	1.2	4.3	1.8	2.0	9.1	3.0
Total Labor Force	100.0	100.0	100.0	100.0	100.0	100.0	100.0	100.0	100.0	100.0	100.0	100.0	100.0	100.0	100.0
Keeping House	1.6	84.9	70.7	......	89.6	74.0	......	85.5	73.4	......	78.9	63.7	2.2	87.6	72.0
In School	28.2	9.1	12.5	27.6	7.6	11.1	40.8	11.3	15.4	30.9	11.6	14.8	31.1	10.0	13.8
Unable to Work	29.8	4.0	8.7	27.6	1.9	6.3	24.7	0.8	4.2	42.4	8.2	14.8	20.0	2.0	5.3
Retired	28.2	......	5.0	38.2	......	6.6	4.9	1.6	2.1	12.1	......	2.8	22.2	......	4.1
Other	4.0	0.4	1.3	5.3	......	1.0	24.7	......	3.5	3.0	......	0.6	2.2	......	0.4
No Data	8.1	1.2	2.5	1.3	0.9	1.0	4.9	0.8	1.4	12.1	1.3	3.3	22.2	0.4	4.5
Total Not In Labor Force	100.0	100.0	100.0	100.0	100.0	100.0	100.0	100.0	100.0	100.0	100.0	100.0	100.0	100.0	100.0

SOURCE: Projections from sample census.

TABLE L
EMPLOYMENT BY INDUSTRY, SELECTED AREAS, 1954

	Ray	Impact Counties Williams Mountrail	Stanley	Tioga and Environs
Agriculture	58	524	30	72
Mining and Construction	237	60	186	498
Manufacturing, Durable	......	......	......	......
Manufacturing, Non-Durable	......	......	5	......
Transportation, Communications and Public Utilities	46	16	57	66
Trade	83	20	147	130
Finance, Insurance & Real Estate	5	......	16	9
Service	31	4	88	72
Public Administration	5	......	36	17
No Data	18	8	20	42
TOTAL	483	632	585	906

SOURCE: Projections from sample census.

TABLE L-A
PERCENTAGE DISTRIBUTION

	Ray	Impact Counties Williams Mountrail	Stanley	Tioga and Environs
Agriculture	12.1	82.9	5.1	8.0
Mining and Construction	49.0	9.5	31.8	55.0
Manufacturing, Durable	......	......	......	......
Manufacturing, Non-Durable	......	......	0.9	......
Transportation, Communications and Public Utilities	9.6	2.5	9.8	7.3
Trade	17.2	3.2	25.2	14.4
Finance, Insurance & Real Estate	1.3	......	2.8	1.0
Service	6.4	0.6	15.0	8.0
Public Administration	1.3	......	6.1	1.9
No Data	3.1	1.3	3.3	4.5
TOTAL	100.0	100.0	100.0	100.0

SOURCE: Projections from sample census.

TABLE LI
EMPLOYMENT BY TYPE OF OCCUPATION,
SELECTED AREAS 1954

	Ray	Impact Counties	Stanley	Tioga and Environs
Professional	6	12	46	17
Farm	37	479	28	55
Managers	31	4	74	81
Clerical	25	8	44	87
Sales	31	4	71	24
Crafts	49	12	52	130
Operatives	197	52	97	315
Services	25	8	52	46
Farm Laborers	22	40	3	17
Other Laborers	34	4	96	101
No Data	26	9	22	33
TOTAL	483	632	585	906

SOURCE: Projections from sample census.

TABLE LI-A
PERCENTAGE DISTRIBUTION

	Ray	Impact Counties	Stanley	Tioga and Environs
Professional	1.3	1.9	7.9	1.9
Farm	7.6	75.8	4.7	6.1
Managers	6.4	0.6	12.6	8.9
Clerical	5.1	1.3	7.5	9.6
Sales	6.4	0.6	12.1	2.6
Crafts	10.2	1.9	8.9	14.4
Operatives	40.8	8.3	16.8	34.8
Services	5.1	1.3	8.9	5.1
Farm Laborers	4.5	6.4	0.5	1.9
Other Laborers	7.0	0.6	16.4	11.2
No Data	5.7	1.3	3.7	3.8
TOTAL	100.0	100.0	100.0	100.0

SOURCE: Projections from sample census.

The employment distribution of residents compared with migrants is shown in Table LII below.

TABLE LII
PERCENT BY INDUSTRY OF ALL PERSONS EMPLOYED IN 1954 WHO LIVED IN THE SAME AREA IN 1950, WILLISTON AND OTHER IMPACT AREA

1954 Employment:	1950 Residence Williston	Other Impact Area
Agriculture	90%	95%
Mining and Construction	51	23
Manufacturing	69	100
Transportation, Communication and Public Utilities	79	59
Trade	70	65
Finance, Insurance & Real Estate	74	63
Service	81	69
Public Administration	67	80
All Industries	71%	58%

SOURCE: Projected from sample census.

While 7 out of 10 persons employed in Williston in 1954 lived in that community in 1950, only 4 of every 10 employed in other study areas were 1950 residents of the area. In both areas, the greatest penetration of migrants was into the mining and construction industry. Less than a quarter of those employed in this industry outside of Williston were native to the area of employment. In Williston, the numbers of natives and migrants in the industry were nearly equal. In the smaller communities and in the rural impact areas, there was no other industry group in which migrants were employed in greater proportion than they bear to the total labor force. Natives of the area while being interviewed often complained of the fact that the oil industry favored migrants in employment. In the long term, it may be that this factor is favorable to the community. When oil activity moves out of this area, those who will first suffer employment loss are those who came to the area in search of employment. The sustaining effects of oil derived income supplements may be adequate to maintain employment in the secondary industries in which the majority of "residents" are employed.

Chapter 8
The Economic Consequences of Oil Development

2018

David Flynn

Introduction

That oil changed the economic trajectory for Williston and Williams County in North Dakota is made clear by the data contained in the 1958 *Williston Report*. The consequences of oil industry growth are ongoing. In many ways the growth and development of Williston and the surrounding areas is a familiar story of technological progress combined with fortuitous circumstances and appropriate resource endowments. While not identical to the situation in Silicon Valley, the application of hydraulic fracturing to "tight" shale oil formations, such as those found in the Bakken Formation of North Dakota and Montana, represented a new opportunity for oil in North Dakota and the Williston area. Comparison of the current boom with the descriptions and data provided by the 1958 *Report* show that the region has gone through a third "boom" (the second having happened in the 1980s; see Rundquist and Vandeberg, current volume), a rarity in economic history, and is making even larger changes in economic growth and development than the first time.

Growth and economic development are common goals for communities of all shapes and sizes, though success in these areas is rarely absolute and often involves ambiguities or mixed signals. There are all sorts of ways to measure economic consequences, such as growth rates, economic impacts, or unemployment rates. Media reports during the 2008–14 boom focused on factors like the unemployment rate, oil output, income, and tax revenues. To accurately convey the story of the economic consequences it is important that the selected measures show the rare story of overnight success in Williston over the last decade, but set against the backdrop of the last fifty years.

The data also need to reflect the challenges in telling this story and avoid overselling both the struggles and the successes. Striking this balance requires a broader view of the economic data punctuated by key outcomes and occurrences. Some direct comparisons to the 1958 *Report* are possible, but in other cases, certain measures are more relevant to the most recent boom (and unavailable with respect to the first). The press attention focused on the oil industry, and rightly so. However, a focus on the economic consequences for Williston based solely on the performance of the oil industry is too narrow, as the 1958 *Report* showed. While oil is clearly the impetus for change, we need to understand the broader changes that occurred. At the time of this writing, Williston, the Bakken shale formation, and the state of North Dakota have been through one complete oil cycle, and that is the proper geographic scale for the analysis, unlike in 1958. And while commodity cycles are not foreign to these areas, the experience is more commonly felt in the agriculture sector. Kelley recognized the same situation with underemployment, migration being motivated as one of the "alternatives to continued employment in agriculture" (p. 189). With one iteration complete, government, companies, and workers now enter a learning phase where adjustments to the supply chain, employment circumstances, technology, and other factors occur. (For a journalistic account, see Brooks 2015; Yardley and Killelea 2016; "Bakken Seems to Be in a Steady Growth Cycle" 2018.)

What this means is that some of the euphoric praise for the industry has now settled to a low roar. There was a stark realization that oil prices can and do decline, and consequently so do other measures of economic activity in the Bakken region, such as level of employment. Oil is not gone and is not likely to disappear anytime soon, and it still represents an important economic engine and opportunity for Williston, the surrounding communities, and the state of North Dakota as a whole (Smith 2018). However, the path of decline from peak prices, including job losses and tax revenue shortfalls, represents an important part of a revised attitude towards oil and the related economic activity. While an economy is made up of more than numbers reflected in gross income or employment, the statistics are—or can be—the unbiased part of the discussion around the story of growth and development.

During the most recent boom, the story of the Williston economy in many ways became the story of the entire Bakken oil region and the state of North Dakota as a whole. This identification was more than symbolic; in many ways the singular focus of North Dakota business and industry became integration within the supply chain for the oil industry, expanded beyond the regional nature the last time. For a micropolitan area like Williston, or the larger Bakken area, to become the vital cog in the economy of the state (and so important as a source of growth) is an amazing story. In that regard, then, the consequences of oil also offer a perspective and a frame of reference with respect to the oil economy. Economic history, like most history, reflects the circumstances of the time during which the writing occurred. Perspectives change over time, and thus the important constraint on this assessment is that it comes at the end of the first fracking-induced up-and-down cycle, while the industry continues on the way up for a second time.

To measure and discuss the consequences of oil, there first needs to be a discussion of what happened with oil. The oil price and quantity data are relevant as a starting point and are interesting in their own right. The dramatic changes due to the oil industry can then first be seen through changes in taxable sales and purchases. The sales data provide a sense of the enormous change that occurred as a result of changes in business and consumer practices. The consequences for labor markets are the next topic of discussion. Labor was in short supply as oil prices took off and the voracious appetite for workers created large changes in labor force and compensation, a situation described in 1958 as "persistent underemployment" (Kelley, p. 189). There is a problem with labor market information, however. There is a very real prospect that the oil industry never sated its appetite for workers and as such the data, as impressive as they are, did not complete their upward adjustments (Milijkovic and Ripplinger 2016). To broaden the perspective, the examination turns to other income and employment data, looking at both general numbers and sector-specific information. The last industry identified for special attention is construction. The stories about inadequate housing and "man camps" make a look at the data for this industry necessary. As mentioned before, indicators of the consequences of oil abound and in fact depend on one's definition of the term "economic." I do not discuss crime data here, though that could be thought an economic consequence of oil (see, for instance, Peterson 2012; Eligon 2013; Jayasundara, Heitkamp, and Ruddell 2016; Heitkamp and Mayzer 2018). Nor is there a discussion of government budgeting or social service provision. Choices need to be made in any undertaking of this sort and these very important topics are left to other authors or other volumes for investigation and discussion.

Oil Price and Output

The attention given to oil in North Dakota might lead one to believe discoveries of oil and development of fields are recent activities when in fact the North Dakota Department of Mineral Resources data on oil go back to the 1950s, and the first *Williston Report* came out in 1958. The long presence of oil does not imply a lack of volatility. As we will see in this section, there has been significant volatility in the oil industry and Williams County in particular.

The geographic area comprising the Bakken varies somewhat (see Wills, current volume, and Rundquist and Vandeberg, current volume). There are many other counties included in the overall Bakken region, from both North Dakota and Montana, although Dunn, Mountrail, McKenzie, and Williams counties in North Dakota were some of the most productive. The focus on Williston directs us towards these counties and Williams County in particular, as Williston is the seat for Williams County.

Potential profits drive expansion and contraction in the oil industry as they do in all business sectors. The confluence of price and technological development in the form of hydraulic fracturing created a profitable opportunity for oil in the area around Williston. As we will see, the technical ability to recover oil and the profitability of actually recovering the oil are not identical, although they both represent an important part of the recent changes in Williston.

The monthly North Dakota first purchase price for oil from mid-1977 to mid-2019 in North Dakota is shown in Figure 8.1. From mid-1977 to the end of the twentieth century, the price moved within a relatively small band, a low of $8.41 per barrel and a high of $41.77. When adjusting for inflation, with January 2000 as the base period, the spread widens from $8.88 at the low end to $79.82 at the high end. At that time, it started a prolonged, though not straight-line, increase for much of the first decade of the twenty-first century. After January 2000 the low price per barrel was $16.80 while the high was $126.88. Adjusting for inflation again the spread is reduced where the low is $16.04 and the high is $98.62. Even when we control for inflation the price increase was sizable and impressive and the response of oil activity to the elevation in prices was predictable, though possibly not to the extent eventually seen.

Annual oil production in the state of North Dakota increased dramatically (Figure 8.2). Prior to the onset of the price increases in 2000, there was only a three-year period from 1983 to 1985 when state production exceeded 50 million barrels per year. In fact, after declining as low as 27.6 million barrels, production did not exceed 50 million barrels again until 2008. The eventual peak in production occurred in 2015 at more than 400 million barrels of oil per year. From the start of the series in 1951 to the peak in 2015, annual oil output increased at an annual growth rate of 16.38 percent, with most of the growth clearly coming late in the period as a response to the increase in the prices. The Bakken region was a significant driver of the eventual growth as Figure 8.3 illustrates.

Figure 8.2 also displays the distinction between this report and the 1958 *Report*. The production levels are not even remotely similar. There were increases in both time periods under analysis, but the scale of the increase in the current episode is amazing by comparison.

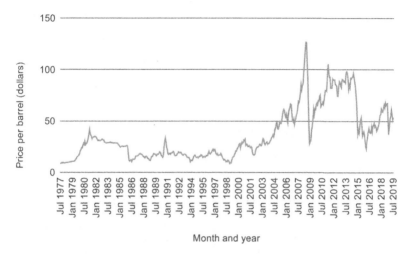

Figure 8.1. North Dakota first purchase oil price, 1977–2019 (source: Energy Information Administration 2019)

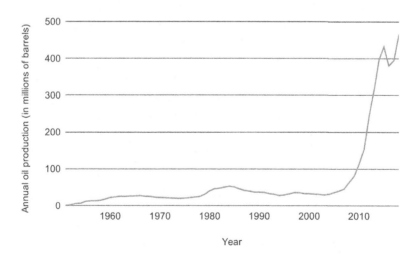

Figure 8.2. North Dakota annual oil production, 1951–2018 (source: North Dakota Department of Mineral Resources 2018)

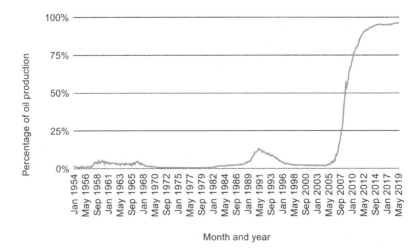

Figure 8.3. Bakken oil production as a percentage of total North Dakota oil production, 1954–2019 (source: North Dakota Department of Mineral Resources 2019a, 2019b)

The Bakken region was not always an important part of oil production in North Dakota. Prior to 1981 the highest percentage of North Dakota oil production coming from the region was only 5.28 percent. This is consistent with the perception that it was expensive to extract oil from the tight oil formations like the Bakken and therefore prices needed to rise significantly above their long-run average. In the early 1990s there was a brief increase in the share of state production coming from the Bakken, though it quickly dropped back to the normal, lower contribution. After 2000 there was a significant change.

In fact, at the end of 2004, Bakken oil production was still only 2.04 percent of total state output. By December 2005 the amount increased to 3.74 percent, with a further increase to 8.81 percent by December 2006. By the end of 2007 Bakken oil production was just shy of 25 percent of the state total at 24.38 percent, and its share continued to grow. By June 2012 the Bakken region represented over 90 percent of the state's oil production and remained above that level since crossing the threshold.[1]

Earlier production graphs may give the perception that there was no volatility in oil production for the Bakken region. This is not the case, as the monthly percentage changes in Bakken oil production show (Figure 8.4). The

[1] The highest percentage is also the last available observation at the time of writing, May 2018, at 95.61 percent.

period from the 1950s to 1970 experienced high monthly percentage changes in production, both positive and negative. This would not be surprising during the start-up phase of oil exploration and production in the industry. To remove those early effects Figure 8.5 starts with 1974, removing about the first twenty years of exploration but allowing for the oil embargo price shock of the 1970s to show in the data.

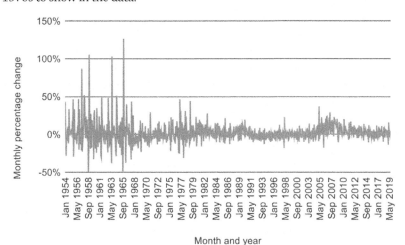

Figure 8.4. Monthly percentage change in Bakken oil production, 1954–2019 (source: North Dakota Department of Mineral Resources 2019a)

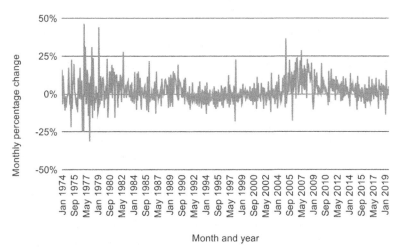

Figure 8.5. Monthly percentage change in Bakken oil production, 1974–2019 (source: North Dakota Department of Mineral Resources 2019a)

There were no moves up or down in excess of 100 percent as happened in the earlier graph. The volatility of the 1970s is quite noticeable at the early end of this figure. What is more notable and important for the growth story of Williston, the Bakken region, and the state as a whole is the period surrounding 2010. This was a time of significant expansion of the oil sector. During the eighty-four months from January 2006 to January 2013, there were only sixteen months where the monthly percentage change in oil production was negative. The average percentage change in production for positive months in this time was 9.2 percent while the average percentage decline was 4.6 percent. Oil became a more secure sector in the regional economy at this time, as these production data demonstrate. The transition into permanence can be seen in the data related to spending, such as taxable sales and purchases.

Taxable Sales and Purchases

Clearly oil price and production experienced significant changes over this time period. Evaluation and assessment of the consequences are made all the more difficult and, at some level, chaotic in that the bulk of the changes occurred in a condensed time frame. One way to proceed is to consider the larger consequences of business and consumer spending decisions. There were discussions of similar factors in the first report (for example, Table XLII, p. 206).

The micropolitan area of Williston has always been important to Williams County and the Bakken area in general as the most accessible urban location within the oil producing region (see Table 8.1). From 1998 to 2017 the city of Williston accounted for 82 percent of taxable sales and purchases in Williams County. During that time the percentage never dropped below 75 percent and was as high as 95.4 percent in 2015. Of note is the fact, however, that as the oil activity in the Bakken increased, Williston accounted for less of Williams County taxable sales and purchases because economic activity spread beyond the Williston borders into the county and the entire Bakken region.

However, as the oil industry developed and expanded within the Bakken region and the state, the city of Williston became more significant for the state as a whole, a contrast with the earlier growth story. While important for the region, the discussion did not, and likely could not, attach similar importance to oil and the region within the state's economy. Williston taxable sales and purchases in 1999 accounted for slightly more than 2 percent of the total taxable purchases for the state. For some sense of scale, in the same year, Fargo (the state's largest city) accounted for 22.4 percent of the taxable sales and purchases in the entire state. Oil activity increased taxable sales and purchases in the city of Williston and Williams County as a whole such that at its peak the city of Williston accounted for 12.8 percent of state taxable sales and purchases in 2011, which was more than the 12.3 percent accounted for by Fargo. Williston remained in this position for the next three years before falling back down below 10 percent of the state taxable sales and purchases in 2015. For contrast, Table XLIV (p. 207) in the 1958 *Report* listed a peak value for Williams County of 6.3 percent.

TABLE 8.1.
TAXABLE SALES AND PURCHASES FOR SELECT REGIONS, 1998–2017
(SOURCE: NORTH DAKOTA OFFICE OF THE STATE TAX
COMMISSIONER 1998–2017)

Year	Williston	Williams Co.	Fargo	Cass Co.	North Dakota
1998	150,295,787	165,470,498	1,442,140,395	1,610,533,335	6,476,111,865
1999	140,483,646	156,152,168	1,539,637,392	1,728,696,608	6,863,857,581
2000	169,947,181	189,571,906	1,531,075,477	1,730,867,919	6,826,387,672
2001	187,935,122	210,858,980	1,576,834,106	1,784,909,487	7,147,128,090
2002	172,187,821	190,365,110	1,621,210,606	1,837,923,479	7,044,743,275
2003	183,836,462	204,255,883	1,716,327,256	1,942,797,279	7,347,458,242
2004	210,877,027	236,898,107	1,828,816,117	2,100,762,530	8,000,269,656
2005	270,115,186	300,664,981	1,868,107,039	2,140,351,698	8,566,950,882
2006	357,546,219	398,381,346	1,981,270,180	2,262,165,598	9,284,289,973
2007	439,619,535	504,284,708	2,086,245,604	2,377,531,817	10,251,031,277
2008	773,170,192	903,807,261	2,195,210,182	2,500,612,201	12,397,074,757
2009	675,040,776	799,497,870	2,129,797,379	2,417,009,645	11,743,211,404
2010	1,336,306,479	1,611,720,192	2,221,235,368	2,526,120,822	14,137,315,824
2011	2,521,286,467	3,226,767,967	2,422,391,342	2,775,649,629	19,690,371,061
2012	3,518,532,535	4,688,118,804	2,640,098,193	3,055,069,906	25,290,676,807
2013	3,378,607,395	4,400,324,668	2,690,898,800	3,125,583,081	25,464,563,890
2014	3,682,778,083	4,732,830,190	2,797,822,914	3,256,646,158	28,222,431,451
2015	2,264,499,283	2,373,326,151	2,738,758,575	3,199,609,785	22,881,848,847
2016	1,085,477,900	1,142,355,580	2,578,604,632	3,001,106,671	17,328,567,822
2017	1,378,456,764	1,449,029,110	2,439,546,655	2,874,488,805	17,900,699,259

Spending decisions by businesses clearly changed as a result of oil. These data represent only consumption- and investment-type spending by individuals and businesses. Absent from these data is spending on labor resources. The labor market in the region experienced significant changes as a result of the oil boom as well.

Labor Market Consequences

As mentioned earlier, one of the most important economic consequences from growth in any one sector relates to the labor market changes and the permanence seen in those markets. Oil activity was the impetus for other changes in economic structure and performance in the Williston area. The sinking of new wells requires a significant amount of labor that was clearly unavailable in Williston at the time of the first price increases. Figure 8.6 demonstrates that the Bakken area did not have spare capacity with people waiting for oil prices to rise enough to generate interest in local production. It also documents the success of importing more labor resources into the region, as neither Williston nor the state of North Dakota had labor supply sufficient to accommodate the scale of the increase in oil production, let alone any other industries seeing growth at the time.

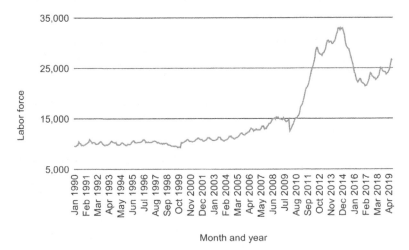

Figure 8.6. Williston labor force, 1990–2019 (source: Bureau of Labor Statistics 2019a)

The increase in labor force was nothing short of amazing, rising from a level of around 10,000 at the beginning of 2000 and increasing to around 33,000 by 2015. As oil prices cooled and economic activity related to oil decreased, the labor force retreated to a level still more than double what it had been in 2000. The pace of increase and the ever-present volatility in the economy make breakdowns of the data into industry segments questionable, seen in the first report as well (for example Table XLVIII, p. 216). We can use other data to provide some evidence of impacts on other sectors.

While there is little dispute that oil was the sector driving economic growth and expansion, the key question is whether the gains in that sector transferred to others. Figure 8.7 displays the average wage in natural resource jobs in Williams County, which increased by substantial amounts from 2001 to 2018. In that time frame, wages more than doubled, while employment in the same sector increased more than twenty times (Figure 8.8). It is important to note that the natural resource sector jobs were always, on average, higher paying than the overall average job in Williams County. Even though the employment level declined in the last few years because of reduced oil prices, the wage level did not follow suit. This fact demonstrates the importance of the sector and the beginning of the preeminence of the sector in the regional economy. Another significant outcome of the economic transformation in the Bakken region is that the average weekly wage for all private employment in Williams County more than tripled during the growth in oil prices, and remained near peak levels through 2018.

The rest of the county economy enjoyed similar change, driven by the success of the oil industry and its supply chain. This pattern included the increase as well as the decline in employment seen as oil prices declined. The connections between the various data indicate the importance of oil activity as a keystone of the local economy and the source of much of its growth and economic development.

One added value of looking at employment is the ability to discern better the additional employment effects from the oil sector. The comparison of natural resource and all occupations, along with the share of overall employment represented by natural resource employment, offers a better look at the labor market impacts beyond the gross measure of labor force. What we see is that the natural resource sector introduces significant employment impacts beyond its own industry.

Natural resource employment and overall employment moved on the same general, shallow upward trend from 2001 to 2010. There were some minor added ups and downs in overall employment that seem not to come from the natural resource sector over this time, although they do not move employment away from the overall trend. Both lines increase after 2010, but the increase in overall employment appears higher for the overall employment series. As an example, the increase in natural resource employment from January 2010 to June of 2012 was 9,850 people. The overall increase in employment for the same period was 21,887 people. This difference is significant because it means there was job growth beyond the oil sector alone, some 12,037 to be precise. However, it means that the oil sector jobs accounted for 45 percent of the total

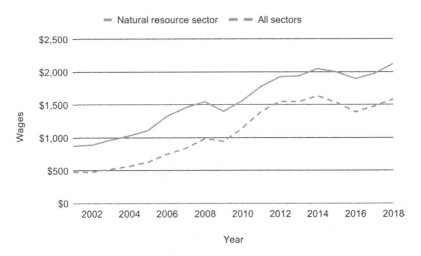

Figure 8.7. Williams County average weekly wage, 2001–18 (source: Bureau of Labor Statistics 2019b, 2019c)

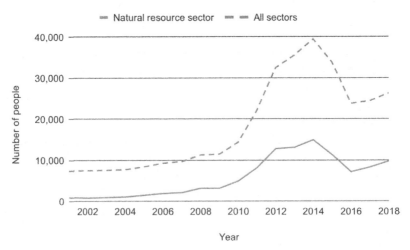

Figure 8.8. Williams County employment, 2001–18 (source: Bureau of Labor Statistics 2019b, 2019c)

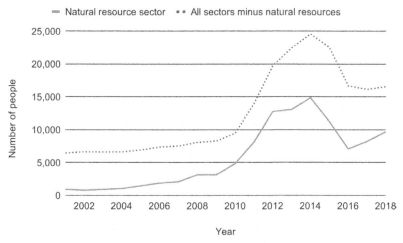

Figure 8.9. Williams County employment, 2001–18, all occupations excluding natural resources (source: Bureau of Labor Statistics 2019b, 2019c)

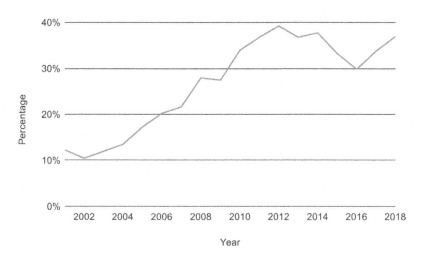

Figure 8.10. Williams County natural resources employment as a share of all occupations, 2001–18 (source: Bureau of Labor Statistics 2019b, 2019c)

increase in employment over that time period. It is difficult to imagine the ability to handle the influx of more workers, though it appears there was a need for more. This gap implies a failure to fully capitalize on the significant opportunity presented by oil development due to a binding labor constraint. To facilitate this discussion Figure 8.9 presents the natural resources employment as before, and then deducts that series from the overall employment.

It is not surprising that the gap between the two series narrows, further evidence of the importance of the oil sector. It is easier to identify when the oil impacts transferred to other sectors in this graph. After mid-year 2012, the adjusted overall series rises more sharply than the natural resources employment data. That pattern continues until the end of 2014, at which time both series start to take a significant and sharp drop. Another way to think about this is through the percentage of overall employment represented by the natural resources sector (Figure 8.10).

Despite the increases in both types of employment, the oil sector increased its share of overall employment with only a few periods of retreat from 2001 to early 2012, at which time it accounted for over 40 percent of employment in Williams County. This was a significant concentration of employment in the one sector paying higher wages, and therefore the jobs there filled first.

Labor markets are vital to the story in North Dakota. However, during much of the current oil expansion North Dakota experienced persistent shortages of labor, which is to say, job openings in excess of the number of people available and able to work.[2] These circumstances suggest labor market variables, while important to consider, are potentially biased, or at least less informative than usual, as economic indicators. Curtailed growth due to a lack of population growth or willingness on the part of people to migrate in numbers sufficient to fill positions can bias downward the relative contribution or importance of sectors. Such a bias may influence the relative importance of a sector in the economy.

Income and Earnings

In an attempt to overcome this problem, I report income and earning measures in addition to employment and wage measures. The income and earning measures counteract some of the potential bias in labor market measures. A sector facing a labor shortage and an inability to readily hire sufficient workers locally

[2] Such information can be gleaned from the North Dakota Workforce Intelligence Job Openings Reports prepared by Job Service North Dakota for various time periods.

will likely increase wages in an effort to attract more workers. Greater wages should increase total earnings and compensation in the sector. As a result, even if employment is not increasing, the compensation to that sector should rise and indicate increasing vitality and importance in the region.

There was a major change in the classification of industries in this time with the switch from the Standard Industry Classification (SIC) system to the North American Industry Classification System (NAICS) for the 2001 data and later. These changes in classification represent important changes in economic and industrial structure occurring in the United States and the world, but they also make comparisons of data difficult. The SIC system includes data from 1969 to 2000, while only NAICS data are available for 2001 and beyond.

The per capita personal income in the Williston micropolitan area saw a significant increase over this time as well. In nominal terms it was $3,406 in 1969. Peak per-capita income occurred in 2014 at $128,586, again in nominal terms. This is per capita, not per worker, so it includes the entire official population, even those not working. The implied annual growth in per-capita personal income over that time period was 8.4 percent. When adjusted for inflation the growth rate remains 4 percent per year.

The Williston micropolitan area earning structure was closely tied to commodity prices, whether viewed through the lens of agriculture or energy extraction. There is a certain volatility that comes from these sectors, and the importance of the sectors does not always show up directly in numbers. Farm earnings, for example, ranged from a low of –5 percent of total earnings to a high of 39.6 percent. The average of farm earnings as a share of total earnings from 1969 to 2000 was right around 8 percent. The next two highest averages over this time period were mining (almost exclusively oil and gas extraction) and services. The highest subcategory within services over this period was health services, at 11 percent. Manufacturing in the Williston micropolitan area ranged from a low of 2 percent to a high of 8.88 percent.

A similar story plays out from 2001 to 2016 with the NAICS data. Manufacturing earnings range from a low of 1.09 percent to a high of 3.39 percent. Even though there is significant economic growth in income and other metrics, this growth does not transfer to or transform the manufacturing sector in Williston. Some may view this as a lost opportunity for economic diversification, but as the price of oil demonstrates, the returns on energy activity are high and investment in that specific activity could be viewed as nothing less than rational.

Oil and gas extraction changes significantly between the two classification schemes. From 1969 to 2000, under the SIC scheme, oil and gas extraction ranged from 9.6 to 36.9 percent, averaging 20.6 percent per year. Oil and gas extraction after 2001 averaged 4.6 percent only with a range from 2.7 to 8.4 percent. The incredible increase in the volume of activity would seem to contradict these percentages, though it becomes easier to understand when we look at the category of support activities for mining, broken out under mining in the NAICS scheme. Support activities ranged from 11.6 to 41.3 percent, averaging 27.8 percent per year. The two combined show an increase in activity after the price increases commenced at the beginning of the twenty-first century.

The breakout into services and extraction is also important, although it does not represent diversification with respect to the industrial base of the area. Extraction was the important basic activity that created and allowed for extensive add-on activities in the form of service provision. The amount of 41.3 percent represents a significant addition to the activity. At its peak in Williston, the general category of mining was almost 44.2 percent of the nonfarm private earnings (Figure 8.11).

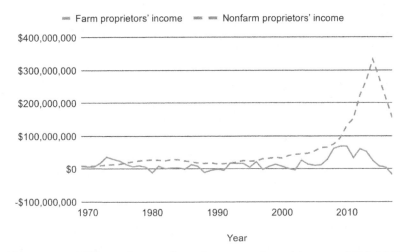

Figure 8.11. Williston farm and nonfarm proprietors' income, 1969–2017 (source: Bureau of Economic Analysis 2019a, 2019b)

With respect to general economic sector rivalries in North Dakota, agriculture tends to be pitted against energy, a situation that has been exacerbated since the rise of shale oil in the Williston area. With respect to proprietors' income in the Bakken area, there is a noticeable divide between farm and nonfarm income. The separation between the two is not significant prior to 2000, although for the most part nonfarm proprietors' income exceeds that of farm proprietors. After 2000 there is a rapid increase in farm income as agriculture increases, but it still cannot keep pace with the nonfarm revenues. One industry sector singled out for attention here is construction. Construction, particularly of housing, was an important additional consequence of the economic changes in Williston.

Construction

Construction received special attention in the 1958 *Report* (p. 211), and it is important to provide a parallel look during this oil episode. Housing was a constant source of friction and debate in Williston during and after the recent oil expansion (Brue 2007; Dalrymple 2015; Jean 2016). An area known for lack of housing during a boom and for man camp-type residences might appear to have low shares of earnings in construction. Similar issues occurred in the 1950s too, with a discussion comparing "trailer camps and an unwarranted residential development" in some areas to permitted increases elsewhere (p. 211). The limitations on available labor would also be a significant contributor to a reduced upper bound on this sector. In the SIC data the average share of nonfarm private earnings was 7.4 percent, and although it did move higher in the post-2001 NAICS data to 10.5 percent, construction of buildings represented only 1.9 percent of earnings. However, the nonfarm private earnings increased by so much over this time that this amount is a smaller slice of a much larger pie. A better indicator of the consequences in this area comes from building permits data (Figures 8.12 and 8.13).

The permits data provide a look at both the local housing market and the change in construction activity outside the direct benefits to the oil industry. The number of permits for buildings demonstrates a sizable increase occurring contemporaneously with increased oil prices and activity in the oil sector. Simultaneously the average number of units with permits increased, although it lagged a bit until economic prosperity was more entrenched. Consistent with the labor constraint in the sector, there were some booms and busts in the building activity level as well, seen in the decline in permits and the transition into larger numbers of units with lower numbers of building permits. Other chapters focus on the various social and demographic aspects that led to a willingness to move into newly built units. One issue with the housing market was a desire to avoid overbuilding in case oil was a transitory economic phenomenon without sufficient staying power to develop long-term population changes.

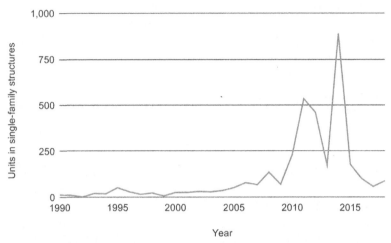

Figure 8.12. Williams County building permits for units in single-family structures, 1990–2017 (source: Housing and Urban Development 2019)

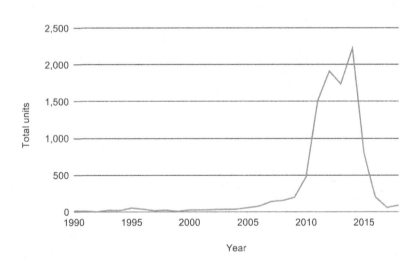

Figure 8.13. Unit counts for Williams County building permits, 1990–2018 (source: Housing and Urban Development 2019)

Conclusions

The book is not closed on the Williston economy and the oil industry in North Dakota. The fact that this is an update on an excellent report about an oil boom from the 1950s in the same area is evidence of that. The fact that this is a first fracking-induced cycle makes this an important ongoing topic for study, while the forecasts attempt to predict variations in the next cycle. Oil prices fluctuate based on policies and events far beyond the reach of individuals and companies in Williston and the state of North Dakota. As a result, company production decisions and strategies are not completely determined by events on the ground. Such a lack of control over economic direction is a difference for many communities, specifically those in western North Dakota.

What the information in this chapter demonstrates is that oil is unlikely to disappear as an economic driver in Williston and surrounding areas, even though it did before. Global politics and policy, as well as the importance of the energy sector in the economy, make such a decline unlikely. This chapter does not attempt to end discussions, but rather looks to continue them from the 1958 *Report* by pairing them with other important topics. The addition of a second commodity-based industry in the region further entrenches a potential high return, high volatility paradigm for the local economies and possibly the state as well. As the second cycle starts for Williston and the Bakken, it is clear there is still a need for planning. The first cycle caught many of the policy makers off guard, both in the region and outside of it. The primary concern is still expanding employment in oil and leveraging that growth for other sectors while improving the quality of life in the region. There should also be continued and increased focus on the impacts generated by economic growth on non-economic factors such as population growth and distribution, social infrastructure, and physical infrastructure, many of which are covered in the rest of this book.

References

"Bakken Seems to Be In a Steady Growth Cycle." 2018. *Bismarck Tribune*, March 1. https://bismarcktribune.com/opinion/editorial/bakken-seems-to-be-in-steady-growth-cycle/article_220c9440-06fa-508f-9014-209f6ead0f21.html.

Brooks, Jennifer. 2015. "In Wake Of Oil Slump, Watchful North Dakotans Adjust Expectations." [Minneapolis] *Star-Tribune*, April 18. http://www.startribune.com/in-wake-of-oil-slump-north-dakotans-adjust-expectations/300550291/.

Bureau of Economic Analysis. 2019a. "CAINC5N Personal Income by Major Component and Earnings by NAICS Industry." https://apps.bea.gov/iTable/iTable.cfm?reqid=70&step=30&isuri=1&major_area=6&area=48780&year=2000,1999,1998,1997,1996,1995,1994,1993,1992,1991,1990,1989,1988,1987,1986,1985,1984,1983,1982,1981,1980,1979,1978,1977,1976,1975,1974,1973,1972,1971,1970,1969&tableid=10&category=732&area_type=4&year_end=-1&classification=sic&state=6&statistic=71,72&yearbegin=-1&unit_of_measure=levels

Bureau of Economic Analysis. 2019b. "CAINC5S Personal Income by Major Component and Earnings by SIC Industry." https://apps.bea.gov/iTable/iTable.cfm?reqid=70&step=30&isuri=1&major_area=6&area=48780&year=2000,1999,1998,1997,1996,1995,1994,1993,1992,1991,1990,1989,1988,1987,1986,1985,1984,1983,1982,1981,1980,1979,1978,1977,1976,1975,1974,1973,1972,1971,1970,1969&tableid=10&category=732&area_type=4&year_end=-1&classification=sic&state=6&statistic=71,72&yearbegin=-1&unit_of_measure=levels.

Bureau of Labor Statistics. 2019a. "Labor Force: Williston, ND Micropolitan Statistical Area." Data for 1990–2019 downloaded October 3. https://beta.bls.gov/dataViewer/view/timeseries/LAUMC384878000000006.

Bureau of Labor Statistics. 2019b. "Quarterly Census of Employment and Wages: Average Weekly Wage in Private Natural Resources and Mining for All Establishment Sizes in Williams County, North Dakota, NSA." Series ID ENU381054051011. https://data.bls.gov/PDQWeb/en.

Bureau of Labor Statistics. 2019c. "Quarterly Census of Employment and Wages: Average Weekly Wage in Private Total, All Industries for All

Establishment sizes in Williams County, North Dakota, NSA." Series ID ENU3810540510. https://data.bls.gov/PDQWeb/en.

Dalrymple, Amy. 2015. "Group Pushes to Keep Man Camps." *Bismarck Tribune*, November 7.

Eligon, John. 2013. "An Oil Town Where Men Are Many, and Women Are Hounded." *New York Times*, January 16. https://www.nytimes.com/2013/01/16/us/16women.html.

Energy Information Administration. 2019. "North Dakota Crude Oil First Purchase Price." https://www.eia.gov/dnav/pet/hist/LeafHandler.ashx?n=pet&s=f002038__3&f=m.

Heitkamp, Thomasine, and R. Mayzer. 2018. "Implications for Practice: Risks to Youth in Boomtown." *Child Welfare* 96 (4): 47–71.

Housing and Urban Development. 2019. "State of the Cities Data Systems (SOCDS): SOCDS Building Permits Database query housing unit building permits for Williams County, ND." https://socds.huduser.gov/permits/index.html.

Jayasundara, Dheeshana S., Thomasine Heitkamp, and Rick Ruddell. 2016. "Voices from the Front Line: Human Service Workers' Perceptions of Interpersonal Violence in Resource-based Boom Communities." *Internet Journal of Criminology* Special Issue on Resource-Based Boomtowns: 72–93. https://docs.wixstatic.com/ugd/b93dd4_88d7e9607fe546d1a9b-c4c0441f9c58f.pdf.

Jean, Renee. 2016. "Williston Man Camp Court Fight to Continue." *Bismarck Tribune*, August 29. https://bismarcktribune.com/bakken/williston-man-camp-court-fight-to-continue/article_c0ec4d26-5857-5f75-95b7-28936169d693.html.

Milijkovic, Dragan, and David Ripplinger. 2016. "Labor Market Impacts of U.S. Tight Oil Development: The Case of the Bakken." *Energy Economics* 60: 306–12.

North Dakota Department of Mineral Resources. 2018. "North Dakota Annual Oil Production." https://www.dmr.nd.gov/oilgas/stats/annualprod.pdf.

North Dakota Department of Mineral Resources. 2019a. "ND Monthly Bakken Oil Production Statistics." https://www.dmr.nd.gov/oilgas/stats/historicalbakkenoilstats.pdf.

North Dakota Department of Mineral Resources. 2019b. "ND Monthly Oil Production Statistics." https://www.dmr.nd.gov/oilgas/stats/historical-oilprodstats.pdf.

North Dakota Office of State Tax Commissioner. 1998–2017. North Dakota Sales and Use Tax Statistical Reports. https://www.nd.gov/tax/search/?filter1%5B%5D=12&archive_media=1&submit=&q=%27statistical+report%27.

Peterson, Richard. 2012. "Planning for Expansion: Crime Rises as Oil Booms." *Great Falls Tribune*, 24 April.

Smith, James L. 2018. "Estimating the Future Supply of Shale Oil: A Bakken Case Study." *Energy Economics* 69: 395–403.

Yardley, William, and Eric Killelea. 2016. "Oil Boomtown in ND Eyes Act 2: Williston Thinks It Can Still Thrive Despite Price Drop." *South Florida Sun-Sentinel*, January 13.

Chapter 9
Social Change in the Basin[1]

1958 | *Robert B. Campbell*

Along with the demographic, the economic, the political and the geographic changes, specifically social change was expected—and social change there has been in the Williston Basin area since the discovery of oil. General social change occurs in three broad kinds of situations: (1) where a homogeneous society is suddenly confronted by people who differ from its members in background, and thus in attitudes and values; (2) where innovations, especially technological ones, are introduced into a static social organization system necessitating changes in that system to "absorb" the innovation; or (3) where a stable population has a sudden change in numbers. Theoretically any such situations would be marked by a conflict in values and would become "social problems," that is, conditions which are considered undesirable in terms of the previously existing values of the society. Typically those changes which result in the greatest conflict in the society are those which are brought in from outside the system, perhaps because the society is not likely to have set up techniques for handling such changes. There is likely to be no consensus as to how the situation should be dealt with; consequently the society will be characterized, however temporarily, by a conflict in attitudes. Social change proper occurs in the resolution of attitude differences and in the elimination or control of the "undesirable" conditions.[2]

The sociological research part of this project was posited on the assumptions of this theory of social change, and it was designed to discover what value conflicts and what "problems" occurred as a result of the large immigration of people from other parts of the country. It was hypothesized that: (1) local organizations which were purely social

---

[1] Conclusions drawn in this section are based exclusively upon the field work done in the summer of 1954. All supplementary information of later date is identified as to date.

[2] From the sociological point of view situations are never inherently problematic; they become problems only when they are defined as undesirable by the people involved in them.

would not attempt to attract migrants into membership while those which were primarily economic or religious would make the attempt; (2) migrants, as a category, would be the objects of negative attitudes of the local citizenry; and (3) various kinds of social problems, such as increased crime, immorality, and low-grade housing, would arise. These hypotheses were based upon the theoretical assumptions that the local social organizations already in existence would be defensive as to their unity and would tend to repel outsiders, that the migrants would be defined as "outsiders" representing different values from those of the natives, and that the presence of a large number of new people would cause the existing societal organization to fail to operate in a way that was satisfactory to its new, as well as many of its old, members. With respect to this last, it was assumed that some of the old residents would define change itself as a problem and would resist any efforts at reorganization of the community while others would seek change but would not agree as to how the change should be brought about. The former would tend to have negative attitudes toward the migrants, the latter would tend to align themselves with the migrants.

A. Local Organizations and Group Membership

Local organizations in Williston were affected only slightly by the influx of new residents. (It must be remembered that Williston—the only urban place in the research area and, thus, the only one having a relatively complete institutional organization—had only a 32% population increase as compared to 105% in Ray and 253% in Tioga, the two small trade centers.) Few of these organizations deliberately recruited new members in the migrant category, although apparently only one or two avoided, however indirectly, such membership. One group (social, educational and service) having twenty members responded to questions about the number of "oil-related" participants and the kind of effort made to get such participation as follows: "This is a small study group with a limited membership, thus your questions do not apply." Another group (social, fraternal and service) which had two of its 45 members "oil-related" and which was making no effort to get "oil-related" participation, reported that "membership is by invitation or transfer only. Invitations are primarily to local women." This latter group also answered the question as to what problems had been created for the organization by the oil development as follows: "A minor problem seemed to develop as prospective transferees moved here; however, very few are here long enough to become members of our chapter."

The most typical attitude expressed by organization officers was that the migrants who wanted to join were welcome but that the organization did not make a special effort to get them to join. For example, only two churches reported that they made a special effort to attract migrant participation and could estimate the number of such participants; and one of these expressed its limitation in the fact that "'oil people' are mainly from areas where the ——— Church is not strong." Most of the organizations polled (SEE TABLE LIII) had an increase in membership as a result of the population increase.

While the primarily social organizations showed almost no inclination to recruit members from among the migrants, neither did the religious and fraternal organizations. This generalization is indicated more markedly by the existence of two particular groups in Williston. The first of these was a new church ("H" IN TABLE LIII), the Southern Baptist Church, which was organized in 1953 apparently to minister to the unfulfilled spiritual needs of the large southern contingent of oil workers, who provided three-fourths of its membership. This group, with its 65 members, had already outgrown its building in its one full year of existence. The other group was a purely social one, the Ladies Petroleum Club, which was composed exclusively of women involved directly or indirectly with oil development and which had reached its physical limit in membership in 1954. The group was organized in the middle of 1952 and in one year's time increased its membership from 55 to 125 (the limit). That the group felt the lack of local group invitation is indicated in this voluntary comment on the questionnaire:

> Probably worth mentioning is the fact that this club was organized for the purpose of enabling oil wives to get acquainted and as a means of furnishing them with some type of social life probably not offered any other place. Frequently it is difficult for new people to step into many of the older activities of a community.

TABLE LIII
MEMBERSHIPS IN POLLED CHURCHES AND NATIONAL FRA-
TERNAL ORGANIZATIONS IN WILLISTON, 1950–1954, AND
1954 "OIL RELATED" MEMBERSHIPS

Churches			Year			Oil Related Memberships
	1950	1951	1952	1953	1954	(1954)
A	175	185	215	215	250	20
B	220	......	......	......	325	40
C	80	85	86	99	95	......
D	50	50	60	65	65	......
E	15	15	24	26	32	......
F	25	30	48	57	68	......
G	93	93	101	110	123	15
H	......	......	......	11	65	48
Fraternal Organizations						
Elks	745	831	876	973	997	175
Moose	1421	1626	1479	1445	1578	95

Some of the data above, particularly those in the "oil related" memberships column, represent the best estimate the ministers or presidents could make.

The main business group in Williston was reported by residents in informal conversations to have made a complete and deliberate change from having no migrant members to providing special positions for them. At the time of the project field work there were representatives of the petroleum industry in the business group, and there were reports that the business group had brought them into membership for the specific purpose of eliminating some of the conflict which was developing. (An interesting sidelight on the social level of this relationship is the observation of the researchers that there were two distinct informal groups which met almost daily for lunch in a popular Williston cafe. The "old" business group met for lunch, as it had for years, at a table reserved for it in one part of the cafe; the "new" group, predominantly oil men, met at another table at the same time. The humor in the situation was apparent at least to the latter in that they had adopted a name for themselves which was a "take-off" on the name of the former, like, for example, "long-snorters" and "short-snorters.")

In general, then, the hypothesis that local social organizations would not recruit migrants while religious and economic organizations would do so was only partially supported. The social groups had not attempted to bring in the new oil people, but neither had the religious organizations to any substantial degree. The business group had brought in oil people, but it did so relatively lately and, in a sense, under the duress of a potential conflict situation. These conclusions, drawn from the analysis of the organizations, are supported by responses obtained from heads of households in Ray and Williston concerning their organization memberships (TABLE LIV). Not only did "old" residents belong to organizations significantly more than did "new" residents, but the association between length of residence and organization membership was greater in Ray than in Williston.

TABLE LIV
MEMBERSHIPS IN ORGANIZATIONS FOR
OLD AND NEW RESIDENTS, BY LOCALITY
(RAY AND WILLISTON), 1954

Locality Number of Memberships	Old residents		New Residents		Total	
	Number	Percent	Number	Percent	Number	Percent
Ray (Total)	60	100	64	100	124	100
One or more	37	62	18	28	55	44
None	14	23	39	61	53	43
No data	9	15	7	11	16	13

Chi-square is 17.9 for 2X2 table, omitting "no data"; $C = .37^*$

Williston (Total)	349	100	164	100	513	100
One or more	229	66	79	48	308	60
None	116	33	79	48	195	38
No data	4	1	6	4	10	2

Chi-square is 12.1 for 2X2 table, omitting "no data"; $C = .15^*$

* C, coefficient of mean square contingency, is a measure of association whose maximum value of .707 for a 2X2 table, thus these may be considered "moderate" amounts of association.

No attempt was made to poll the organizations in the smaller communities on the assumption that they would be few and small. There were indications, on the basis of the residence sample interviews, that on a general social level organizational conflict was closer to the surface there than in Williston, reaching even to the level of political action (SEE PAGES 131–6). The ex-mayor of one of the communities cited the existence of an oil organization which had effected a considerable opposition to him in the previous election because of his refusal to make concessions to oil interests. In both localities (Ray and Tioga) at least semiformal organizations came into existence to press for change or for maintenance of the status quo. Both places were caught with a virtual lack of services for the expanded populations. The desire, particularly of newcomers, for what they considered basic and necessary services resulted in what was described by participants as a battle between the "progressives" and the "conservatives." In one of the places these organizations were the "wets" and the "drys" in the issue as to whether a water system should be installed. Paving and sewer system were other issues around which informal groups arose. In one sense these issues actually cemented relations between newcomers and some of the long-term residents much faster than might otherwise have occurred because the migrants, demanding the services, were joined by many of the regular residents. Some of the latter mentioned with obvious pride and respect that their community now had an active business group which was leading toward a general progress. (One such group was the "J-C-ettes," composed of oil workers' wives and the wives of local businessmen, which not only had a political and economic influence but which had a strong social effect in terms of developing favorable attitudes toward the oil people and toward change.)

Conflicts on the personal level in Ray and Tioga were more apparent than in Williston not only in the aforementioned political issues but also in general attitudes about people of one sort or another. One woman, whose son was a leader in the fight for the water system, reported that her neighbor had not spoken to her for a year as the consequence of the fight. Others referred to the "backwardness" of the native residents, to the "riff-raff" who came in to work the oil fields, and to the destruction of the close friendly relations between town and country since the business had begun to cater to oil workers, such statements reflecting an outspoken but numerically small group of people. (In interpreting the detailed material on personal and social attitudes, the reader should bear in mind a possible overall explanation of differences in the degree of value-conflict between Williston and the other two centers—Williston tended to draw the "white-collar" oil workers, Tioga the more nearly permanent oil field workers—the better paid, supervisory field personnel—and Ray, the transient and temporary employees.)

These differences are supported indirectly by the facts (SEE TABLE LV) that Williston's population was 66% "native" (i.e., present before April 1950) as contrasted with Tioga's 33% and Ray's 39%. Of the Williston population only 4% resided in trailers, while Tioga and Ray had 21% and 38% respectively. (The 1955 observation that Ray had lost the most population was further evidence in this regard.)

B. Intergroup Attitudes

The gross indications of conflict between "new" and "old" residents, while important in the situations in which they were found, were not sufficient to support the hypothesis that there would be generally-held negative attitudes of each grouping toward the other. One aspect of the study was an attempt to discover whether such attitudes were widespread and more nearly constant than the temporary conflicts centering around political issues. This attempt was somewhat super-ficial because of the impracticality of "depth interviewing" as far as the purposes of the general study were concerned, but it was suitable to give the broad type of answer sought.

The most important conclusion about the intergroup attitudes is that the new residents of Williston who had met many of the old ones had a good opinion of them almost without exception, 99% of them having expressed this in answer to the direct question: *Have you met many of the new residents (since 1950) of Williston?* *If "yes," what do you think of them generally?* (SEE TABLE LVI.) (The researchers missed what might have been a good chance to test the secondhand nature of stereotypes and prejudices when the 58 heads of households, 38% of the total, who replied that they had not met many of the old residents were not asked their opinion of old residents.)

*Context suggests that the author meant *old* rather than *new* in this question (Editor's note).

TABLE LV
PERCENT RESIDENCE (1954), 1950 RESIDENCE, TYPE OF
DWELLING: BY PERSONS, WITH "SAME RESIDENCE" PER-
CENT AND WITH PERCENT OF PERSONS IN TRAILERS

Persent Residence 1950 Residence	Total Number of Persons	Types of Dwelling				Percent of Persons in Trailers
		Single	Trailer	Multiple	Other	
Williston	2335	1687	98	548	2	4.2
Williston	1544	1246	12	284	2	0.8
Other N.D.	374	229	38	107	......	10.2
All other areas	417	212	48	157	......	11.5
Williston %	66.1	73.9	12.2	51.8		
Tioga	616	419	131	66	......	21.3
Tioga	202	151	8	43	......	4.0
Other N.D.	224	168	45	11	......	20.1
All other areas	190	100	78	12	......	41.1
Tioga %	32.8	36.0	6.1	65.2		
Ray	470	218	177	73	2	37.7
Ray	181	148	17	16	......	9.4
Other N.D.	62	18	16	26	2	25.8
All other areas	227	52	144	31	......	63.4
Ray %	38.5	67.9	9.6	21.9		
Stanley	560	365	109	81	5	19.5
Stanley	351	279	13	56	3	3.7
Other N.D.	131	74	40	15	2	30.5
All other areas	78	12	56	10	......	71.8
Stanley %	62.7	76.4	11.9	69.1		
Williams County	285	278	4	3	......	1.4
Williams County	236	236	......	......	......	0.0
Other N.D.	16	12	4	......	......	25.0
All other areas	33	30	......	3	......	0.0
Williams County %	82.8	84.9	0.0	0.0		
Mountrail County	116	116	......	......	......	......
Mountrail County	104	104	......	......	......	......
Other N.D.	12	12	......	......	......	......
All other areas	0	0	......	......	......	......
Mountrail Co. %	89.7	89.7	......	......	......	......

The distribution of opinions of both old and new residents of Williston as to whether or not newcomers had been accepted into the
community is, perhaps, of even more interest. As Table LVII shows,
a total of 96% of the old residents and 95% of the new residents
thought that newcomers had been accepted, 92% and 89% respectively expressing no qualifications to their opinions. Only 3% of the

old residents and 4% of the new believed that newcomers had not been generally accepted.

TABLE LVI
NEW RESIDENTS' OPINION OF OLD RESIDENTS, WILLISTON, 1954

Have Met Old Residents

Opinion	No	Yes *	Yes **	No Data	Total Number	Percent
Good		41	17		58	81
Good, qualified		8	5		13	18
Poor		1			1	1
Total of Opinions		50	22		72	100
No Opinion		2	1			
No Data		10	9		19	
Does not apply***	58			11	69	
TOTAL	58	62	32	11	163	
Percent***	38	41	21			

* (Unqualified)
** (Qualified)
*** Omitting "no data" with respect to having met old residents—The "does not apply" arose from the interviewing procedure of not asking opinions of those who had not met many of the old residents.

TABLE LVII
OPINIONS OF OLD RESIDENTS AND NEW RESIDENTS AS TO WHETHER NEWCOMERS HAD BEEN ACCEPTED INTO THE COMMUNITY, WILLISTON, 1954

Accepted?	Old Residents Number	Percent	New Residents Number	Percent	Total
TOTAL	349		164		
Yes	294	92	124	89	418
Yes, qualified	13	4	9	6	22
No, qualified	1		0		1
No	8	3	6	4	14
Indefinite	4	1	1	1	5
Total of Opinions	320	100	140	100	460
No opinion	22		14		36
No data	7		10		17

These facts certainly do not indicate the hypothesized negative attitude towards the migrants as a category or any reaction back toward the "natives"; furthermore, they appear to be out of harmony with some of the description of the conflict and lack of association in organizations in the previous section. This disharmony is "more apparent than real." Firstly, these facts were obtained from Williston residents, and Williston had a minimum of conflict about migrants for reasons described earlier. Facts from Ray, Tioga, and particularly the rural areas pointed up a greater measure of negative attitudes. Secondly, none of the failures to recruit migrants into organizations carried with them any overt negative attitude, that is, the officers of organizations did not express any antipathy toward migrants in describing their membership and recruitment policies. The failure to recruit migrants might be as indicative of the organizations' failure to identify migrants as a separate category as of the negative attitude respecting the category. Finally, the research was conducted late enough in the development that tendencies to generalize negative attitudes may have been dissipated because of the increased and increasing opportunities for association on a personal level between members of the two categories. What may have been general negative attitudes as a consequence of isolated contacts could not be expected to persist when contacts became more frequent and more personal. The conflicts may have represented issue differences rather than residence differences—at least this conclusion is more consistent with the facts than is the hypothesis that there would be generalized, negative categorical attitudes.

C. Social Problems

In order to avoid the prejudices or preconceptions of the researcher, a social problem is considered in this report as any situation which is reported by people involved in it as undesirable and, therefore, about which they express a negative opinion, possibly indicating a tendency to act to change the situation. From this point of view a situation may not be a problem to the participants despite the fact that the observer is disturbed by it. An example of a situation of this sort is one of the residences in Ray which, according to a consensual estimate of three of the researchers, was about 6 feet by 8 feet and 7 feet high. Not once did a resident of the town express a negative attitude about this particular "house," not to mention a small bus which had become someone's home. This simply was not considered a problem in Ray to the knowledge of the participants in the research project.

1. Housing

As one might easily suppose on the basis of the tremendous population changes reported earlier, housing was one of the major social (and personal) problems in the area. Even though the population peak had been passed, there was still a pressure for permanent-type housing in parts of the area. An interesting paradox is, however, that some rental housing in both Williston and Ray was "going begging" in 1955, thus creating what might be a noticeable economic problem. Realtors in all three localities were still building extensively in 1955 to meet their estimates of the market for homes, thus changing the situation which constituted a problem for many of the migrants.

According to local businessmen in Williston, the explanation of the paradox was that the demand for temporary housing had been met but that there was a backlog of demand by residents in temporary housing for permanent homes. Their theory was that many people had to take substandard housing during the boom, but in 1954 they were seeking better housing; thus there was an upward mobility toward the best housing, tending to eliminate the social problem of low-grade housing. The evidence presented in favor of the theory was that a number of homes which were being built by a Williston contractor had already been spoken for and that he planned to start an even larger number as soon as he could do so.

On the other hand, a government official reported that employment and wages had not risen sufficiently to meet the costs of better housing. As new homes became available in Williston they were filled by those families who were already living in the more expensive rental units, thus there was a gap which was not being filled from below because of the inability of the "common laboring man" to pay the high rents.[3]

The observations of the researchers tended to support this latter view. That there was a general social problem in housing was evidenced by the often-mentioned concern about the "flats" (a low-grade housing area of Williston) and the shared idea among business people that more and better housing was in continuous demand. That the general mobility upward was not taking place was indicated by the stability of the "flats" population and the availability of a number of high rental apartments (observed in both 1954 and 1955).

In Ray the "wrong side" of the problem was even more obvious. Local business interests built a large number (34 units) of high rental

---

[3] The extent of the rent pressure is indicated, perhaps, in the fact that Representative Burdick was quoted in the newspapers in February 1956 as reporting the government's approval of Williston as a low-rent government housing area.

apartments (duplex and four-plex) to relieve the pressure of trailer and basement dwelling, only to find that the demand for such residences was insufficient to make them pay. The bulk of the migrants were temporary residents who either could not afford the apartments or were satisfied to reside in their trailers. (Most of the trailer residents were employed by a drilling company which provided large, new trailers for low rent, the rent being applied toward the purchase of the trailers so that the renter would obtain ownership if he remained with the company for a certain length of time.)

However much the trailers represented a social problem for the home owners in Ray, the fact remained that they were not a problem for their inhabitants. They were, rather, the solution to the problem of high rents. The trailer camps provided ample facilities for those inhabitants, apparently.

A major housing problem arose in Tioga out of an interesting migration situation. Tioga had a considerably greater proportion of in-migration of North Dakotans than did either Williston or Ray (TABLE LVIII). Of the total population of Tioga 36% came from other parts of North Dakota while the corresponding figures for the other places were 16% for Williston and 13% for Ray. The Tioga migrants, particularly the North Dakotans among them, did not find available to them the opportunities for rental trailer residence that characterized Ray. Neither did the Tiogans have much opportunity for multiple-type dwelling units, which had only 5% of the North Dakota migrants living in them (as compared to 45% for North Dakota migrants who resided in Ray in 1954.) The result was that Tioga generally had recognizably poorer housing than the other two places, composed partly of older trailers and partly of make-shift single dwellings. The prime problem, on the basis of local comment as well as being the one the observations of the researchers indicated, was a single dwelling housing group (12 or 16 units). These were reported as being "grain bins" and "chicken sheds" which had been hauled in from a farm to be rented. One of the residents of Tioga commented on them approximately as follows:

> Did you see those grain bins down the street? People are living in those. I don't see how anyone could rent them. They can't be very substantial; they're not very heavy. I sat here one morning and watched two of them being carried on one truck.

TABLE LVIII
TYPE OF DWELLING BY PRESENT RESIDENCE (1954)
AND BY 1950 RESIDENCE,
FOR THE THREE MAIN LOCALITIES OF THE AREA

Present Residence 1950 Residence	Total 100%		Single 72%		Trailer 4%		Multiple 24%	
Williston	100%	2335	100%	1687	100%	98	100%	550
Williston	66	1544	74	1246	12	12	52	286
Other N.D.	16	374	14	229	39	38	19	107
All other states	18	417	12	212	49	48	29	157
	100%		68%		21%		11%	
Tioga	100%	616	100%	419	100%	131	100%	66
Tioga	33	202	36	151	6	8	65	43
Other N.D.	36	224	40	138	34	45	17	11
All other states	31	190	24	100	60	78	18	12
	100%		46%		38%		16%	
Ray	100%	470	100%	218	100%	177	100%	75
Ray	39	181	68	148	10	17	21	16
Other N.D.	13	62	8	18	9	16	38	28
All other states	48	227	24	52	81	144	41	31

These were actually one-room sheds with a loft which served as supplementary sleeping space and was accessible by ladder. They were made of low grade lumber which was covered, top and sides, by tar-paper roofing material.

Generally speaking, then, the increase in population created a situation of tight, "substandard" housing which was interpreted variously as a social problem—high rental apartment vacancies in Williston and Ray and grain bins in Tioga. There were other housing situations which properly were personal rather than social problems as herein conceived. Examples of these were the following:

a. One person reported that Tioga was going to require that all residences, including trailers, be connected to the sewer lines. He didn't know what to do because he couldn't comply in his trailers' present location and he didn't know where he could go.

b. A man who had just arrived in Tioga with his family met the interviewer in the yard of a small hut. He opened the conversation (after the usual introduction by the interviewer as to why he was there) by asking, "Can you do anything about this? How can they expect a man to live in something like that? I've come all the way from (a southern state) because of my job and I've never had to live in anything like this before."

RESIDENCES—TIOGA, N.D., SUMMER, 1954
The rapid increase in population created tremendous pressure on local housing resources. These sheds were hauled in by truck from a nearby farm to be used as family residences.

Additional Aspects of the Housing Situation... Despite the fact that only "problem" situations were hypothesized for the specialized research, this report would be incomplete without some description of the objective situation in housing. Referring back to Table LVIII, 72% of the Williston population, 68% of the Tioga population, and only 46% of the Ray population resided in single dwellings. In 1950, according to the U.S. Census of Housing, the figures for residences by type were 55% single dwellings for Williston and 92% single dwellings for Williams County rural nonfarm areas; these suggest that there was a great relative decrease in the supply of single dwellings in Ray and Tioga and an increase in the supply for Williston.

Trailers were ordinarily located in camps which were limited in the space they had available. As the picture indicates, the ground space allotted to each trailer household was small—an estimated 20' by 40' area being typical (inclusive of that part occupied by the trailer itself).

There was not nearly the crowding that these observations might suggest, since all three localities had space available in the immediately surrounding areas. The big trailer camps appeared at the north and south edges of Ray, the east and south edges of Tioga, the north edge of Williston, and in what has been called herein the "Tioga environs." This last was a completely new settlement area from U.S. Highway No. 2 into Tioga (a distance of about 4 miles). There were several trailer camps in this particular area and a complete village of low-rent, permanent type single dwellings (including garages) which were provided by one of the oil companies for its permanent, operating staff.

All three localities had whole areas of new rental and/or ownership single dwellings amounting, at least in Williston, to separate communities in the sociological sense. The northwestern edge of Williston had been expanded several block depths with new houses, new stores, and a new school to provide for the numerous children in the area. An exclusive, high-cost housing development occurred in the northeast corner of Williston, inhabited by both "old" and "new" residents in the city. Ray and Tioga have their new streets of new residences, too, the latter particularly having a "new community" on the south side of the railroad, inhabited primarily by migrants who are associated with the petroleum industry. As mentioned earlier (cf. Wills) one is impressed on first arriving in Ray or Tioga by the obvious combination of the new and the old in the residential as well as other building. Most buildings appear as being either pre-World War II or post-1952.

2. Crime and Immorality

As soon as one hears that a particular place is a "boom" area, he is likely to think of a general laxity of law enforcement or, at least, of a greater incidence of loose spending for illegal and barely legal pleasures. Couple that conception with the idea that there has been a considerable increase in population composed largely of unmarried men in "rough" occupations and the ingredients are complete for a common-sense prediction that criminality and immorality will be greatly increased. Such a prediction would have been only partly correct, apparently, in the Williston Basin. Assuming that there are some exceptions to a generally useful theory, the problem is to explain why some things did not occur as well as why some did.

First, the assumption that a large proportion of the increased population was composed of unmarried men was contrary to the facts. The bulk of the oil field workers not only were married but had children. (In both Ray and Tioga only about one-fourth of the men were single.)

Second, there was a general provision of increased law enforcement facilities. As the data presented in Table LIX indicate, Williston had an increase in expenditure for the purpose of expanding the police protection as well as increases in revenues from fines levied against offenders. There had been an increase in police department employees from 6 in 1949 to 13 in 1954.[4] Ray had employed a full-time policeman who was reported by the citizens as being "tough" on violators of any sort but particularly on speeders, speeding having been apparently the main problem. The situation there was that U.S. Highway No. 2 ran directly through the town and the highway carried a tremendously increased traffic flow between Williston and Tioga. (SEE PAGE 41)

RESIDENCES—RAY, N.D., SUMMER, 1954
Regular employees of established drilling companies brought their housing with them. This is part of one of the large trailer camps which characterized the oil development area.

---

[4] *Uniform Crime Reports for the United States*, Semiannual Bulletin, Vol. XXV, No. 1, 1954 and Vol. XX, No. 1, 1949.

TABLE LIX
WILLISTON EXPENDITURES AND RECEIPTS, FISCAL YEARS*
1950–51 TO 1953–54, FOR SELECTED ITEMS

EXPENDITURES

Year	Police Magistrate's Courts	Police	Prisoner	Liquor Licenses	Total
1950–	$2,142.00@	$18,113.82	$1,711.50		$97,545.58
1951	$2,142.00@	15,045.76@			63,554.22
1951–	3,173.00@	24,753.53	2,512.00		108,934.76
1952	3,173.00@	19,104.46@			72,729.56
1952–	4,791.30@	42,770.70	4,086.11		164,859.05
1953	4,791.30@	34,119.84@			110,955.17
1953–	3,471.40@	49,176.34	1,892.38		203,984.21
1954	3,471.40@	43,079.81@			144,661.47

RECEIPTS

Year	Police Magistrate's Courts	Police	Prisoner	Liquor Licenses	Total
1950– 1951	8,644.70			14,500.00	94,886.56
1951– 1952	14,499.00			17,500.00	131,426.10
1952– 1953	35,110.50			18,916.67	189,035.30
1953– 1954	27,006.00			19,250.00	178,281.02

@ Salaries
* To get approximate semiannual data, figure 40% for first half, 60% for second half year

Third, drunkenness was prevented from developing to the problem proportions it might have reached by a combination of already existing circumstances. Williston had already put into operation a police technique for controlling excessive drinking prior to the peak in oil development migration. The Williston officials had been considering the migrant farm labor population as a source of the prospective problem and had instituted a system of quick pick-ups in the "skidrow" section.

(In Williston the taverns tended to be concentrated within a 3-block area, thus it was possible to station one or two policemen in the area during the peak periods of activity, particularly Saturday nights.) This system was supplemented by an informal one which was probably unknown to the local officials. One owner-operator of a quiet but fairly popular tavern reported that he had avoided trouble with the police because "once trouble starts in a tavern they will really check on you." His solution was not the curtailment of beer sales, but the personal care of the over-imbiber by sending him home in a taxi at his (the tavern owner's) expense. He had never been bothered by the police because no difficulty had resulted from drinking in his establishment. Another factor which probably helped prevent a drunkenness problem was the attitude of the local judiciary (at least prior to 1955 when a local "revolution" occurred with respect to arbitrary and selective enforcement of the law by Williston police). The police magistrate penalized to the maximum offenders of the drinking laws. (SEE TABLE LIX).

Fourth, a main source of drinking and gambling activity was available immediately outside the area, thus what might have been a problem within the area was removed. An active gambling, drinking, dining and dancing "club" just across the Montana state line attracted a large clientele from the oil development area although it has been restricted since the field survey following a raid in which the gambling devices were confiscated. Any compelling urges to participate in relatively large-scale gambling could be satisfied through this well known channel.

Finally, evidence is lacking that there was a greater inclination among migrants than among "natives" to participate in illegal and "fringe" types of activity, although some of the people interviewed referred to one particular kind of illegality which was attributed exclusively to oil field workers. There were a few instances when, apparently, migratory workers wrote "bad checks" or moved out from under debts. The rural residents in the area were particularly disturbed by this because it resulted in a complete redefinition of the relationship between themselves and the businessmen in small centers. Where formerly they had been able to cash checks at any business place without even considering having to identify themselves, now they could not cash checks at these places at all.

There were no indications available to the researchers that there had been a notable increase in, or even the presence of, organized criminal or immoral activity—gambling houses, theft rings, "protection" or houses of prostitution. There were two known prostitutes in Williston, but in no sense were their activities organized, continuous or flagrant.

These explanations account for the absence of readily observable behaviors in contradiction to the mores and laws, but official statistics show that the "problem behaviors" which were expected did occur.

TABLE LX
WILLISTON POLICE MAGISTRATE'S CASES, SEMIANNUAL,
JULY 1952 TO JUNE 1954

	DRIVING			LIQUOR			
	Reckless	Speeding			Open	Drunk		
Half-Year	Driving	Stop	Drunk	Bottle	and		
		Sign	Driving	in Car	Disord.	Misc.	Total
1952—2nd	49	490	41	50	668	219	1517
1953—1st	80	418	67	28	529	118	1240
1953—2nd	95	287	72	44	529	194	1221
1954—1st	56	101	43	39	329	173	741

GRAND FORKS (a city three times as large—for comparison)

1954—1st	60	120	32	12	286*		

*This does not include 14 cases of disorderly conduct.

COMPARISON OF WILLISTON CASE RATE WITH THAT FOR
THE NATION FOR CITIES OF COMPARABLE SIZE, ON TWO
COMPARABLE TYPE OFFENSES, 1953

Offenses	Williston rate cases/100,000 pop. (computed at Williston 9,500 pop.)	US rate cases/100,000 pop. for cities of 2,500- 10,000 pop.**	Williston Cases
Drunk driving	1454.5@	346.0	139
Drunkenness	11109.0	1714.0	1058

@ This category may not be directly comparable, inasmuch as "drinking and driving" or "driving while having been drinking" might more nearly characterize the Williston situation.
** IBID.

As Table LX indicates, Williston had a large number of cases in which offenders were held for prosecution (and a comparison of the total number of cases in this table with the receipts of the police magistrates court in Table LIX indicates the financial punishment of the offenders). The sample figures for Grand Forks, North Dakota, a city more than twice the size of Williston, and for two comparable offenses nationally for cities of the same size make possible a gross interpretation of the greater frequency of offenses (and/or prosecution) than one would expect of a city like Williston.

The reader might well ask at this point if the researchers had their eyes shut in order to cite these statistics in the same paragraph in which the "absence of readily observable behaviors" was mentioned. In the monthly figures, furthermore, June 1954 (one of the months in which the field research was conducted) exceeds all the months in the biennium except March for the number of offenses, 178 as compared to 202 for these months. The explanation, it appears, is the quick apprehension of offenders (particularly liquor) which was mentioned earlier.

Returning to the conception of social problems with which this analysis was approached, the only situations which were represented as social problems by residents of Williston in the area of immorality and illegality were the drinking-fighting incidents involving, for the most part, immigrant farm labor and the drinking-driving activities of the Williston young people, neither of which could be attributed (except very indirectly through economic change) to the oil development.

3. Welfare Activities

There are a number of institutionally-recognized "social problems" which were little, if at all, affected by the development of oil in the Williston Basin. Old age cases, aid to dependent children cases and the like were simply not changed materially by the situation. There was, however, an increase in the incidence of payments to transients who were temporarily unable to leave the area. The Williams County office of welfare services reported as their biggest new problem the number of transient persons who moved in after hearing about the "big oil boom," who should not have moved and who had become stranded. The Mountrail County office had had an increase in cases involving negligence of children and tracing of people, but payments to cases had not been affected materially by the oil development.

4. The Public Service Situation

Some of the social service or community service agencies encountered problematic situations which were, at least, indirect social problems, that is, situations about which the public through its agencies desired change toward a more acceptable alternative.

a. *Schools.* In all three communities there arose the necessity of expanding school facilities to relieve crowding in both space and time. In Williston, for example, 22 elementary class rooms had been constructed and 26 persons had been added to the staff to accommodate the 36% increase in enrollment between 1950 and 1954 (SEE TABLE LXI). The superintendent has calculated, as nearly as was possible, that about 24% of the total enrollment was "oil-related." In Ray and Tioga emergency measures, such as the split day, had to be taken because of the tremendous expansion in enrollment. All three communities have expanded the physical plants considerably.

TABLE LXI
WILLISTON PUBLIC SCHOOL ENROLLMENT AND EMPLOY-
MENT, OCTOBER, 1950–1954

	1950	1951	1952	1953	1954
Enrollment	1508	1639	1524	1815	2041
Employment	60½	62½	63	73½	86

b. *Library.* An interesting change occurred in the Williston Library service, although the librarian was so pleased that she was more inclined to call it a solution rather than a problem. There was a disproportionate participation in library services by migrants (including children) and a "revival of local interest" following a general revision of the library in 1951. The circulation of library materials had increased 373% from 1950 to 1954 (SEE TABLE LXII). There had been, furthermore, increased monetary contributions by the local citizens and the donation of technical books by a large oil company.

TABLE LXII
WILLISTON LIBRARY CIRCULATION, FISCAL YEARS 1950–1954

1950	1951	1952	1953	1954
7,967	13,925	24,303	32,826	37,679

c. *Post Office.* One of the most serious problems encountered by a specialized public service agency was the situation in the Williston post office. The building was much too small to admit easy handling of the increased volume of business, particularly since much of that increase involved commercial and transient (general delivery) mail. On one Monday alone a special test conducted by the postmaster indicated that one single company had over 1000 pieces of mail. The situation was equally difficult because of the relatively continuous necessity of reorganizing the carrier service and expanding it into new areas. Table LXIII shows the extent of the increase in service that followed the oil discovery.

TABLE LXIII

WILLISTON POST OFFICE; ANNUAL RECEIPTS AND FIRST
CLASS MAIL PIECES HANDLES, 1950–1954

	1950	1951	1952	1953	1954*
Annual Receipts ($)	109,184	114,154	140,192	150,074	......
Pieces of 1st-class	1,594,120	1,720,300	2,121,096	2,281,323	1,078,005*

* January 1–June 30 only.

d. *State Employment Service*. The State Employment Service encountered an increased demand for its services in both directions, for workers and for jobs. It had problems in both directions, finding enough workers in 1952, finding enough jobs in 1954. There was a continuous increase in the use of its facilities despite these labor supply and demand fluctuations because of the increase of total employment.

e. *Newspapers*. The increase in population was accompanied by a corresponding increase in the circulation of newspapers in Williston, local circulation people maintaining that the newcomers did not differ from the older residents in their interest in the coverage of local papers.

TABLE LXIV

WILLISTON NEWSPAPER CIRCULATION, AVERAGE, 1950–1954

	1949	1950	1951	1952 1st half/ 2nd half	1953 1st half/ 2nd half	1954 1st half/ 2nd half
Williston *Herald*	4200[1]	......	5981	5739/6438	6775/7021	7112/......
Williston *Plains Reporter*	......	......	......	....../......	....../......	3200[2]
Minneapolis *Star and Tribune*[3]	......	200	300	450	550	600

1. Circulation manager's estimate for January.
2. Publisher's estimate.
3. Circulation manager's estimates

Summary of Investigated Social Changes in the Williston Basin and Conclusions

Social changes—changes in numbers and kinds of people, in attitudes, in organizations, in personal and agency actions—were general as a consequence of the oil discovery and its development. Certain hypothesized changes, however, did not occur in Williston to any marked extent. Economic and religious organizations made no special attempts to attract migrants into their memberships, although there were no evidences that migrants were unwelcome. Migrants were not disapproved of categorically except by a small number of people in the rural areas. There were value conflicts, particularly in Ray and Tioga, but enough of the "natives" joined forces with the migrants that the opponents tended to be labeled "progressives" and "conservatives" rather than "old" and "new" residents. The opinion was general among both natives and migrants that the latter had been accepted into the community.

Some of the hypothesized changes or failure to change were borne out at least partly. Social groups did not recruit migrant members. At least two groups were organized by Williston migrants—a Southern Baptist Church and a social club for the wives of oil workers. There were social problems but they were far short of the anticipated magnitude. Housing of the "right" type was short, and there were a few indications of general dissatisfaction about it. There were high rates of minor offenses against the law, but there were no indications of organized crime. There were no serious complaints about the migrants being responsible for the increased offenses. Special problems were created for various public service agencies: schools were crowded and additions had to be built; the library, the post office and the state employment service all encountered considerable increases in the demand for their services; the local governments had to provide new and expanded services.

Most of the evidence presented is of the descriptive survey type in keeping with the general purpose of the study. It is, at best, suggestive with respect to any general theory of social change. On the other hand, the description itself could have general usefulness for the officials and interested citizens in any community which is confronted with rapid change in helping them anticipate the kinds of actions which they might have to take. There is no question that the people of the Williston Basin knew little or nothing as to what to expect, consequently many of their actions and reactions contributed little to the solution of their problems or of the general situation. In our *opinion* (the data were not and are not available to express these as facts or as systematic predictions): realtors over-extended themselves into the construction of residences for which there was no continuous, or future, demand; many North Dakotans migrated to the Basin in anticipation of unlimited opportunities only to find no more opportunities than in the areas they left; school officials committed too much permanent building expansion;[5] a general spirit of over-optimism, reflected in expansions, investments, and population estimates, left the citizens unprepared to handle the out-migration and the decrease in economic activity which had already begun in 1954. (One of the unfortunate aspects of a report of this sort is that some of the predictions which are practically useful are not available early enough. We could have predicted fairly accurately the amount of immediate decrease in Tioga's population as we were conducting the fieldwork because of our knowledge that particular individuals already knew the dates on which they were to be transferred. Furthermore, we could have predicted the decrease in activity because of the knowledge we obtained about the relative number of employees needed in exploratory as compared to development activity in the oil fields. The predictions of this sort that we expressed orally tended to be ridiculed as obviously wrong or as attempts to devaluate the importance of the oil development to the state of North Dakota. This reaction, itself, would be an interesting study.)

The total report is, in effect, a case study and as such tends to give the appearance that it is a description of unique situation. The practical usefulness of such a report depends in large measure on the applicability of the results to other situations of the same sort. The following quotation indicates the similarity of the consequences of oil development to those of industrial development in the small community; if North Dakota is successful in its attempts to attract industry the picture will be repeated.[6]

The information in this study illustrates the nature of social changes which are almost certain to occur in a community as a consequence of industrial development in or near its borders. The need for increased and improved trade facilities develops, and the demand for various public-supported services grows. Sewage disposal, street improvements, additional water supply, expanded hospital facilities and more school buildings were problems which

---

[5] It is our prediction that the population of Ray and Tioga will decrease markedly from the 1954 figures, thus tending to leave a surplus of classroom space. This will be no total loss by any means, since the communities will at least have modern buildings which they would not have had otherwise.

[6] C.R. Hoffer and W. Freeman, *Social Action Resulting from Industrial Development*, Michigan State University Agricultural Experiment Station. Special Bulletin 401, September 1955, pp. 29–30.

were present in Mohawk, as they are likely to be in any community which has rapid increase in population.

The ways in which communities deal with these problems are varied. Systematic and scientific planning to take care of needs as they arise would be the ideal course to follow, but many communities are not successful in achieving this goal. In most instances, the need becomes very great—sometimes critical—before a community will act. Mohawk, for instance, did not make definite plans to build a sewage disposal plant until the village was threatened with a court action. Such situations emphasize again the need of city and county planning as a basis for community action in response to social change.

In Mohawk, as in most communities, different points of view emerged in regard to the various action programs proposed to meet community needs. These views varied along a continuum from opposition to change to support for it. Such attitudes are characterized in different ways—conservative or progressive—old or new—reactionary or progressive. The name is not particularly important. The significant point is that in community action such divergent points of view are almost certain to rise.

Many of the old roots in Mohawk, that is the residents who had been in the community for a long time, tended to take the cautious, conservative position in regard to community action. Those who became residents as a consequence of industrial development favored a more aggressive program of community action. As in other similar situations, these points of view had to be harmonized, at least to the extent that some kind of social actions to meet community needs could be accomplished.

Chapter 10
Social Impacts of Oil Development

2018

Rick Ruddell and Heather Ray

North Dakota experienced three oil booms between 1951 and 2008, and while the effects of the 2008–14 boom and the subsequent cycle of slowdown and expansion are still playing out as this book goes to press, each of these expansions in oilfield activities presented a set of distinctive economic, political, and social benefits and challenges for local and state governments. To a large extent these three factors are inextricably connected, economic activities being a key driver of political behavior as well as shaping a boom's social impacts. With respect to economic activity, for example, between 1951 and 1955, oil production in North Dakota increased from less than 30,000 barrels to 11 million barrels per year (North Dakota Industrial Commission 2019). That increased production, however, occurred primarily in Mountrail and Williams counties, and while oilfield activities disrupted the lives of local residents, these effects were generally contained in a relatively small geographic area and for a relatively short period of time.

The 2008 boom, by contrast, saw oil production increase in the Bakken region of North Dakota from less than a half-million barrels per month right before the boom to a peak of over 361 million barrels in December 2014 (North Dakota Department of Mineral Resources 2019). When the June 2014 price of oil reached $112 per barrel, that production represented $44 billion in revenue, a figure that does not count the revenue from natural gas. The 2008 boom was also spread across seventeen counties, although most oil was extracted in four of those (North Dakota Workforce Intelligence 2018). In contrast to what happened during the 1950s and 1980s booms, the economic benefits and the political and social impacts rippled from the Williston Basin throughout the entire state. Not only did the 2008 boom have a significant statewide impact, but extraction activities have waxed and waned since then and peaked in 2019. Thus, when examining the impacts of a resource-based boom, we have to consider the location, magnitude, and duration of the activities. Table 10.1 provides a framework for better understanding resource-based booms based on these three factors.

TABLE 10.1.
LOCATION, MAGNITUDE, AND DURATION OF
NORTH DAKOTA OIL AND NATURAL GAS BOOMS

Boom (Era)	1951–4	1981–6	2007–19
Location	2 counties	4 counties	17 counties
Duration	48 months	60 months	152 months
Magnitude	Minor	Minor	Major

Prior research shows that a common set of social problems emerge after the rapid population growth and industrialization associated with resource-based booms; these outcomes are called boomtown effects or social ills. The Government of New Brunswick (2012, 5) observes how these social ills include increased levels of crime, substance abuse, sexually transmitted infections, a lack of safe and affordable housing, higher levels of community dissatisfaction, growing child welfare, mental health, and social service caseloads, increased hospital admissions, and an inability to meet the need for health, education, public safety, and social services. Although no two booms are the same, Ruddell (2017, 16–18) contends that booms have a life cycle that starts with a rapidly growing population that overwhelms local government services, breaks down community order, and reduces the residents' quality of life.

Despite the existence of a growing body of research highlighting the challenges of resource-based booms, local government officials have often failed to learn from the mistakes their predecessors made, and most rural governments lack the capacity to effectively manage these events (Morrison, Wilson, and Bell 2012). Oil company officials, by contrast, are more familiar with the ups and downs of commodity-based business cycles and have learned to manage the expansion and contractions.

Although studies focusing upon a single boom and bust, such as the conditions described in the 1958 *Williston Report* or North Dakota government reports about the 1981–6 boom (see Heck 1992), provide us with insight into the impacts of booms occurring in the past, we have to be careful consumers of that research. Jacquet and Kay (2014) argue that the findings of research about rapid growth communities prior to 2000 provide limited insight about contemporary booms. They say that the economic and social conditions and demographic makeup in rural America—where most booms occur—have undergone a profound change in the past four decades. For example, booms occurring after 2000 are distinctive because many regions are experiencing cycles of boom, bust, and recovery over periods spanning decades. As oil and natural gas prices decrease, wells are shut down and personnel laid off, but as prices increase, wells are reactivated and workers rehired. Communities in the Bakken are experiencing this cycle, and after the downturn in drilling in the 2008 boom when production bottomed in 2016, there was a subsequent 51 percent production growth by midyear 2019 (North Dakota Department of Mineral Resources 2019).

Most social problems associated with booms are interrelated (Gilmore 1976). Fernando and Cooley (2016) contend that all boomtowns suffer from an inability to provide enough safe and affordable housing to meet demands. High housing costs force those without homes into unsafe, temporary, or undesirable living conditions. Temporary or makeshift housing arrangements can also contribute to crime as living in cramped and unsuitable conditions leads to tension and conflict and can result in increased family violence (Jayasundara, Heitkamp, Mayzer, Legerski, and Evanson 2016). Furthermore, as rents increase and quality of life decreases, some longtime community residents on fixed incomes move to more affordable communities. The presence of these longtime residents, however, is important for building community resiliency through their volunteerism and support of family members, such as providing low-cost child care (Flanagan, Heitkamp, Nedegaard, and Jayasundara 2014).

Moreover, reducing the proportion of established community residents increases antisocial behavior and crime because informal social controls are weakened (see Freudenburg 1986). A lack of safe and affordable housing also leads to other social problems, and some women, for example, may feel forced to stay in dysfunctional or abusive relationships as they rely upon their partner's housing (Jayasundara, Legerski, Danis, and Ruddell 2019). Writing about women in resource-based communities, Amnesty International (2016) has described this problem as a form of precarity, saying that some women are only one argument away from living on the street, as there are so few housing alternatives. Last, a lack of affordable housing makes it difficult to recruit human service personnel into education, health-related, or law enforcement jobs (Jayasundara, Heitkamp, and Ruddell 2016).

Social Impacts of the 1951–4 Boom: A Brief Overview of the Williston Report

The authors of *The Williston Report* describe the social impacts of the 1950s boom and identify the biggest challenge as that of responding to the rapid population increase. From 1950 to 1954, the population of the oil-producing areas in Williams County increased by half (50.5 percent), whereas Mountrail County experienced a 6.1 percent growth (Wills, p. 53). Similar to other booms, the population increase in those counties was driven primarily by men, and in Williston the gain between 1950 and 1954 was 33.6 percent men and 29.8 percent women (Wills, p. 56). One challenge in fully understanding the population changes in a resource-based boom county, however, is that some individuals are missed in the census counts. These so-called shadow populations are often living in nontraditional housing arrangements such as man camps (see Caraher, Weber, and Rothaus, current volume), campgrounds, or other out-buildings in the countryside. Campbell (p. 252) notes, for example, that a very high population of long-term county residents were living in trailers after the boom.

One of the strengths of the analyses presented in the 1958 *Williston Report* is related to the research strategies used by these scholars. Campbell, for example, surveyed newcomers and established residents from the oil-impacted counties about their perceptions of the boom. Moreover, these residents were asked about their behaviors, whether they had met new residents to their community, and what they thought of them (the newcomers were also asked about their perceptions of the community). These researchers also went to community-based organizations such as churches to solicit additional information about the boom. So what did these efforts tell us about the 1950s Williston boom?

Similar to the case in other resource-based booms, the characteristics of these newcomers to the Williston Basin—many of whom were from out of state—may have been threatening to longtime community residents. Some of these newcomers were from minority racial and ethnic backgrounds, and because most of these oilfield personnel were shift workers, it was difficult for them to join local organizations or develop a stake in the community. Interestingly, many newcomers had families, which differentiated this group from similar groups in other boomtowns, where the influx of new residents included primarily young men with few attachments to the community. Despite this influx of families, Campbell writes that few newcomers became members of local churches or joined fraternal organizations.

Researchers found evidence of tension or conflict between the newcomers and longtime residents, and Campbell says these disagreements were sometimes based on the perception that newcomers were "riff-raff" and their presence disrupted existing relationships (p. 250). Other community-level conflicts emerged over disagreements about development, although those disputes did not seem to result in long-term problems. When asked whether newcomers had been accepted into the community, only 3 percent of longtime residents said they had not, while a similar proportion of newcomers (4 percent) expressed the same feeling (Campbell, p. 253).

When it comes to describing the social problems related to the boom, the challenges identified by Campbell are similar to those reported in other studies of rapid growth communities: a severe housing shortage, an uptick in disorder and crime (and especially offenses related to alcohol abuse), a rise in traffic flow and congestion, the challenges of dealing with transients seeking work, and the increased demand on public services and local businesses. With respect to the municipal or county services, for instance, school enrolments increased and the library's book circulation grew fourfold (Campbell, p. 265). Increased demands were also placed on state and federal agencies, and the state employment service was busy during both the boom and the bust, while the post office was overwhelmed with business-related mail.

To accommodate these demands, many human service agencies expanded capacity in terms of increased office space and personnel, although these solutions became problems once oil production waned and county populations dropped. One of the hard lessons learned in the oil-impacted communities was the risk of making long-term investments in physical infrastructure, such as housing, in these places as investors lost money when the population decreased in the bust. This lesson may have reduced interest in investing in housing developments in subsequent booms.

Altogether, a review of *The Williston Report* shows that the rapid population growth led to a severe housing shortage and government services, and local businesses struggled to meet their demands. While the results of surveys revealed the presence of tension between newcomer populations ("outsiders") and the existing residents ("insiders"), Campbell and his colleagues found that most new residents felt accepted. Yet, the 1950s boom was distinctive as it lasted only four years and its impact centered primarily on two counties. One interesting question is the degree to which municipal leaders learned from this experience, and whether the social impacts of the post-2000 resource-based boom were similar to ones that occurred earlier.

Social Impacts of the 2008 Boom

Every resource-based boom is distinctive in regards to its location, duration, and magnitude, but one common factor is the inevitable bust (Marais and Nel 2016). With respect to North Dakota, the 1950s oil and gas boom-and-bust cycle was followed by a similar one in the 1980s. The boom that started in

2008 differed from the prior booms because of the massive scale of the development and duration of the boom, and because extraction activities were being carried out over an entire region, rather than in several out-of-the-way counties. Kelsey, Partridge, and White (2016) describe how the increasing value of oil and natural gas, combined with the introduction of hydraulic fracturing (or "fracking") enabled producers to extract oil from areas where conventional drilling was not profitable. Taken together, these factors resulted in a "perfect storm" that led to unprecedented levels of oil and natural gas production in sparsely populated rural counties throughout the Bakken (Montana and North Dakota), Eagle Ford (Texas), and Marcellus (Pennsylvania and New York) regions. Of all these locations, however, the oil boom in the Bakken had the most significant social impact, especially considering an almost 1300 percent increase in oil production between January 1, 2007, and May 31, 2019 (North Dakota Industrial Commission 2019).

Both the rapid population increase and industrialization in the 2008 North Dakota boom differed from its 1950s counterpart in a number of ways. When it comes to population growth, Scheyder (2016) reports that over 80,000 people came to North Dakota to work in the oil and gas and supporting industries. It is not surprising these newcomers had a disruptive impact, especially considering there were fewer than 660,000 residents in the entire state population before the boom. As was the case during prior expansions in oilfield activities, many of these newcomers were young men, but in contrast to the 1950s boom described in the *Williston Report*, few brought their families to the oil patch. The fastest population growth occurred in the early phase of this boom as a greater number of workers was required to drill the wells and to construct the infrastructure, such as plant structures, railways, and pipelines, that move these commodities.

The stressors placed on the communities affected by a rapid population increase depend upon the community's resiliency and the characteristics of the newcomers. Some of these new residents stay a short time, thus increasing the population turnover. The deployment of the workforce might also influence the social ills experienced in a boomtown. Depending on the location of a boom, many of the out-of-town personnel live in company housing, and either fly (or drive) in and out on a rotating work schedule (e.g., two-weeks on, and two-weeks off). These full-time workers and part-time residents will typically have little investment in community life. Taken together, the rapid growth and population turnover contributes to community instability by reducing informal social controls, which in turn increases disorder and crime. Population growth can also have a corrosive effect on some communities by increasing conflict between different groups of longtime residents as well as the longtime residents and newcomers (Ruddell 2017).

There is a predictable set of outcomes when the population of young men with little stake in a community increases and the informal controls decrease, and these ill effects were reported after the 2008 boom. Incidents of alcohol and drug abuse increased. Women reported being hounded by men and feeling unsafe, and a growing number of them experienced assaults and stalking (Jayasundara, Heitkamp, Mayzer, Legerski, and Evanson 2016). Law enforcement agencies in the Bakken reported a substantial increase in calls for service beyond what could be expected by a population increase (Dahle and Archbold 2105; Montana All Threat Intelligence Center and North Dakota State and Local Intelligence Center 2012).

The second factor common to all resource-based boom towns or counties is the increased level of industrialization that reduces the residents' quality of life. Loh and Loh (2016) describe how noise, light, and water pollution are common by-products of resource extraction. One factor differentiating the 2008 boom from the prior booms was the introduction of fracking, which is a technologically complex undertaking requiring massive investments in material and personnel. For example, Kondash and Vengosh (2015, 276) point out that between 3.6 and 6 million gallons of water are required to frack each well, and this water must be hauled by trucks, which creates traffic-related problems such as congestion, the destruction of roadways, and a rise in the number of collisions. A series of surveys carried out in one boomtown over almost a decade reveals that aggressive, dangerous, and drunk driving are among the greatest concerns of community residents (Britto 2016).

Boomtown Effects after 2008

Every rapid growth community differs in the extent to which social problems affect its residents. The magnitude, duration, and location of the 2008 boom in the Bakken created a situation where the impacts of these factors were many times those experienced in the 1950s. One of the challenges of fully understanding the extent of these social problems was the exaggeration by the media of the impacts of the boom, as news accounts featured sensational headlines such as "crime turns oil boomtown into Wild West" (Ellis 2011), a theme that was repeated in magazine articles, blogs, news reports, and television series over a seven-year period (Ruddell 2017). But were those accounts accurate? In what follows, we provide a short summary of the boomtown effects in the Bakken region by drawing on official government statistics and the perceptions of human service workers and police officers.

One of the challenges of relying upon official statistics to assess the impact of rapid population growth is that booms are often located in out-of-the-way places where local governments have often done an incomplaete job of collecting and reporting statistics about the demand and delivery of human services. Thus, educational or health agencies might not formally track information about their students or patients regarding their origins or other characteristics, such as their histories of special needs. As a result, after the population surges, local agencies frequently scramble to justify additional funding from the state or federal governments to manage the increased demand, but lack accurate pre-boom statistics. Researchers and journalists have consistently reported how the demands for services exceeded the capacity to respond effectively in the health (McChesney 2012), education (Schafft, Glenna, Green, and Borlu 2014), and social services (Weber, Geigle, and Barkdull 2014).

With respect to crime, Ruddell, Jayasundara, Mayzer, and Heitkamp (2014) analyzed the pre- and post-boom crime statistics in Montana and North Dakota counties affected by the expansion in oilfield activities. One of the difficulties in carrying out this type of research is that sparsely populated rural counties did not consistently report their annual crime-related statistics to the Federal Bureau of Investigation for its annual *Uniform Crime Report*. One of the barriers to researchers interested in studying crime in these rural counties is that police departments or sheriff's offices are not required to submit statistics about the crimes reported to them, the number of arrests made by their deputies or officers, or the calls for services their agencies receive. Unless those statistics are accurately reported, our knowledge of crime in these rapid growth communities will continue to be incomplete.

When frontline human service workers from education, health, public safety, and social service agencies were asked about the impact of the boom, they clearly indicated their workloads became overwhelming and their agencies lacked the resources to adequately manage demands. Because these officials work directly with clients, their perceptions and insights are important when considering the social impacts of rapid population growth. In order to better understand the impact of the boom, Flanagan, Heitkamp, Nedegaard and Jayasundara (2014, 93) conducted focus groups with human service workers, and the consensus was that while many North Dakotans benefited from the boom, these workers carried the burden. They found that the boom had the following impacts:

- *Changes in the nature of service delivery*: The workloads and the complexity of cases these workers managed increased, and many of the clients these workers served had serious addictions issues.
- *Difficulties in hiring and retention*: Agencies lost staff members to more lucrative jobs in the oilfield, and it was difficult to replace them as the high costs of living in boom counties made it difficult to recruit. Consequently, the workloads of existing workers increased.
- *Lack of training to meet changing needs*: The increasing complexity and seriousness of cases required additional training, although agency staff had few opportunities to participate in training and their agencies lacked the funds for training.
- *Insufficient services to address needs*: In addition to high workloads, many organizations lacked the physical resources to meet client demands; domestic violence shelters, for instance, did not have enough beds and some abused and vulnerable women were told to seek help in other counties.
- *Economic realities of resource allocations*: Workers reported that their funding agencies were reluctant to expand the capacity of local services because they felt the boom would be short-lived. (Flanagan et al. 2014, 94–100)

Altogether, a lack of resources forced agency staff to exercise creativity in order to meet an almost relentless demand for services with no corresponding increase in funding or staffing. Respondents indicated they engaged in more partnerships, coordinated activities to reduce duplication, and sought donors to fund their efforts (Flanagan et al. 2014). Human service workers made a similar set of observations about the impacts of the oil boom, mentioning a discrepancy between the caseloads they reported to the agencies that funded them and their actual workloads. They also described how shortages in areas such as housing contributed to crime and reported that clients showed up at human service agencies with a greater set of unmet needs (Jayasundara, Heitkamp, and Ruddell 2016, 72). As Everingham, Devenin and Collins (2015) observe about the impact of resource-extraction in Australia, "the beast doesn't stop."

Police scholars have also examined the impact of the oil boom on officers policing North Dakota counties. Dahle and Archbold (2015, 810) describe how police workloads—as indicated by calls for service—increased in oil-impacted North Dakota towns and cities between 2000 and 2013. Although some agencies, such as the Minot Police Department, had relatively modest increases in calls (26.4 percent), Williston, which was the epicenter of the boom, experienced a 857.5 percent increase in calls. While workload demands increased exponentially, these agencies were slow to add additional officers or to receive budget increases that were commensurate with the new demands. The complement of sworn officers in Williston, for example, increased from twenty-one to thirty-eight (81 percent) in those thirteen years, and their annual budget tripled. These results were similar to those published in the Montana All Threat Intelligence Center and North Dakota State and Local Intelligence Center (2012) report. The question that follows those statistics is how officers manage these expanding workloads.

Dahle and Archbold (2015, 811–16) asked three questions about managing the impacts of rapid population growth on crime in North Dakota, and after analyzing the responses of 101 police officers and sheriff's deputies in focus groups, they observe:

- *The impact of rapid population growth on police organizations*: Over two-thirds (67 percent) of respondents reported that their agencies lacked the resources to keep up with workloads, although half of their agencies hired additional personnel. Participants said that the quality of their services decreased as officers were more reactive (and no longer had time to spend explaining their actions with the public) and were not engaging in informal community-building efforts.
- *The impact of changing work environments on police organizations*: Not only did calls for service related to disorder and crime increase, but officers were responding to very high numbers of traffic-related incidents. Officers also reported that there was a cultural change in their communities, and they believed that some outsiders had little stake in them. They were also perceived as having less regard for the law than established residents. Participants said they had less time for informally interacting with teachers, students or business owners due to workload demands. Similar to the results reported by the human service workers in Jayasundara, Heitkamp, and Ruddell's (2016) study, the high workload demands increased the number of collaborative relationships with other law enforcement agencies.

- *The impact of rapid population growth on police resources*: Almost one half of the respondents said their organizations were "stretched thin," and even though most agencies hired additional officers, the recruiting and training of these new officers (in the academies and in the field) placed additional demands on their operations. Although the opportunity to work overtime increased due to the staffing shortages, working longer hours contributed to burnout and fatigue. Participants also reported that the resources needed for their operations, such as office space or jail cells and vehicles, did not meet their needs.

A consistent theme underlying the observations of human service workers and law enforcers is that workload expectations became unreasonable and the ability of their agencies to provide responsive services decreased as the boom progressed. Agencies already criticized for being reactive could no longer engage in preventative activities, and almost all respondents said that the quality of their services suffered. In some cases, the human service agencies did not have the resources to help some clients.

Summary and Conclusions

The 1950s boom in the Williston Basin resulted in a rapid population increase that placed great demands on local businesses and human service agencies. But as Campbell observes, the boom was relatively short-lived, and local governments overcame these shortcomings. The boom starting in 2008, by contrast, had a much greater social impact due to its longer duration and its impact on all aspects of community life, starting in the Williston Basin and radiating throughout the state. Whereas prior booms were contained to several counties, the 2008 boom had a profound effect throughout western North Dakota and eastern Montana. The final chapters about the 2008 boom have not been written, and the oil and gas extraction activities have persisted for over a decade, albeit with a slowdown from 2014 to 2016 before production increased and then peaked in 2019 (North Dakota Department of Mineral Resources 2019). This brings us to the question of what we have learned from this comparison of the booms in different eras.

Thomas, Smith, and Ortiz (2016) contend that if a social problem can be predicted, it can be prevented. For the most part, the social impacts of the rapid population growth and industrialization associated with a resource-based boom can be foreseen, and local and state government officials can act proactively to mitigate the worst aspects of these booms by leveraging resources and participating in intergovernmental collaborations (Smith, Haggerty, Kay, and Coupal 2019). Research from over four decades has provided us with a good understanding of the impact of rapid population changes in sparsely populated rural communities and the interconnectedness of the social problems that emerge during a boom. Based on those observations Ruddell (2017) developed a list of fifteen steps that local governments can take to mitigate the crime-related and other social problems caused by a natural-resource boom. Local government officials can tailor those strategies for the distinctive conditions in their jurisdictions. Regardless of where and when a boom occurs, however, attempts to reduce the social ills occurring in these places must be broad-based, integrated, and start with the assumption that all resource-based booms eventually bust.

References

Amnesty International. 2016. *Out of Sight, Out of Mind: Gender, Indigenous Rights, and Energy Development in Northeast British Columbia, Canada.* London, UK: Amnesty International.

Britto, Sarah. 2016. "Finding the Town Amidst the Boom: Public Perceptions of Safety and Police Priorities in a Boomtown Milieu." *Internet Journal of Criminology* Special Issue on Resource-Based Boomtowns: 9–26. https://docs.wixstatic.com/ugd/b93dd4_88d7e9607fe546d1a9bc4c0441f9c58f.pdf.

Dahle, Thorvald O., and Carol A. Archbold. 2015. "'Just Do What You Can [...] Make It Work!' Exploring the Impact of Rapid Population Growth on Police Organizations in Western North Dakota." *Policing: An International Journal of Police Strategies and Management* 38 (4): 805–19.

Ellis, Blake. 2011. "Crime Turns Oil Boomtown into Wild West." *CNN Money,* October 26. http://money.cnn.com/2011/10/26/pf/America_boom-town_crime/index.htm.

Everingham, Jo-Anne, Veronica Devenin, and Nina Collins. 2015. "'The Best Doesn't Stop': The Resource Boom and Changes in the Social Space of the Darling Downs." *Rural Society* 24 (1): 42–64.

Fernando, Felix N., and Dennis R. Cooley. 2016. "Socioeconomic System of the Oil Boom and Rural Community Development in Western North Dakota." *Rural Sociology* 81 (3): 407–44.

Flanagan, Kenneth, Thomasine Heitkamp, Randall C. Nedegaard, and Dheeshana S. Jayasundara. 2014. "Black Gold and the Dark Underside of Its Development on Human Service Delivery." *Contemporary Rural Social Work* 6 (1): 86–106.

Freudenburg, William R. 1986. "The Density of Acquaintanceship: An Overlooked Variable in Community Research?" *American Journal of Sociology* 92 (1): 27–63.

Gilmore, J. S. 1976. "Boom Towns May Hinder Energy Resource Development." *Science* 191 (4227): 535–40.

Government of New Brunswick. 2012. *Chief Medical Officer of Health's Recommendations Concerning Shale Gas Development in New Brunswick.* Fredericton: Government of New Brunswick.

Heck, Thomas J. 1992. *Oil Exploration and Development in the North Dakota Williston Basin: 1990–1991 Update.* Bismarck: North Dakota Geological Survey.

Jacquet, Jeffrey B., and David L. Kay. 2014. "The Unconventional Boomtown: Updating the Impact Model to Fit New Spatial and Temporal Scales." *Journal of Rural and Community Development* 9 (1): 1–23.

Jayasundara, Dheeshana S., Thomasine Heitkamp, Roni Mayzer, Elizabeth Legerski, and Tracy A. Evanson. 2016. *Exploratory Research on the Impact of the Growing Oil Industry In ND And MT On Domestic Violence, Dating Violence, Sexual Assault, and Stalking*. Grand Forks: University of North Dakota.

Jayasundara, Dheeshana S., Thomasine Heitkamp, and Rick Ruddell. 2016. "Voices from the Front Line: Human Service Workers' Perceptions of Interpersonal Violence in Resource-based Boom Communities." *Internet Journal of Criminology* Special Issue on Resource-Based Boomtowns: 72–93. https://docs.wixstatic.com/ugd/b93dd4_88d7e9607fe546d1a9b-c4c0441f9c58f.pdf.

Jayasundara, Dheeshana, S., Elizabeth Legerski, Fran S. Danis, and Rick Ruddell. 2019. "The Impact of Resource Development on Interpersonal Violence: Survivor Risk Factors and Experiences." *Social Development Issues* 41 (1): 24–48.

Kelsey, Timothy W., Mark D. Partridge, and Nancy E. White. 2016. "Unconventional Gas and Oil Development in the United States: Economic Experience and Policy Issues." *Applied Economic Perspectives and Policy* 38 (1): 191–214.

Kondash, Andrew, and Avner Vengosh. 2015. "Water Footprint of Hydraulic Fracturing." *Environmental Science and Technology Letters* 2 (10): 276–80.

Loh, Hsue-Peng, and Nancy Loh. 2016. "Hydraulic Fracturing and Shale Gas: Environmental and Health Impacts." In *Advances in Water Resources Management*, edited by L.K. Wang, C.T. Yang, and M.S. Wang, 293–338. New York: Springer.

Marais, Lochner, and Etienne Nel. 2016. "The Dangers of Growing on Gold: Lessons for Mine Downscaling from the Free State Goldfields, South Africa." *Local Economy: The Journal of the Local Economy Policy Unit* 31 (1–2): 282–98.

McChesney, John. 2012. "Bakken Boom Fractures North Dakota Health Care." *Stanford Rural West Initiative*. http://web.stanford.edu/group/ruralwest/cgi-bin/drupal/content/bakken-boom-fractures-north-dakota-health-care.

Montana All Threat Intelligence Center and North Dakota State and Local Intelligence Center. 2012. *Impact of Population Growth on Law Enforcement in the Williston Basin Region*. Helena: Montana All Threat Intelligence Center and North Dakota State and Local Intelligence Center.

Morrison, T. H., C. Wilson, and M. Bell. 2012. "The Role of Private Corporations in Regional Planning and Development Opportunities and Challenges for the Governance of Housing and Land Use." *Journal of Rural Studies* 28 (4): 478–89.

North Dakota Department of Mineral Resources. 2019. "ND Monthly Bakken Oil Production Statistics." https://www.dmr.nd.gov/oilgas/stats/historicalbakkenoilstats.pdf.

North Dakota Industrial Commission. 2019. *Oil in North Dakota, 2018 Production Statistics.* Bismarck: North Dakota Industrial Commission.

North Dakota Workforce Intelligence. 2018. "North Dakota's Oil and Gas Economy." https://www.ndworkforceintelligence.com/admin/gsipub/htmlarea/uploads/lmi_ndoilandgaseconomy.pdf.

Ruddell, Rick. 2017. *Oil, Gas, and Crime: The Dark Side of the Boomtown.* New York: Palgrave Macmillan.

Ruddell, Rick, Dheeshana Jayasundara, Roni Mazyer, and Thomasine Heitkamp. 2014. "Drilling Down: An Examination of the Boom-Crime Relationship in Resource-Based Boom Counties." *Western Criminology Review* 15 (1): 1–15.

Schafft, Kai A., Leland L. Glenna, Brandn Q. Green and Yetkin Borlu. 2014. "Local Impacts of Unconventional Gas Development within Pennsylvania's Marcellus Shale Region: Gauging Boomtown Development Through the Perspectives of Educational Administrators." *Society and Natural Resources: An International Journal* 27 (4): 389–404.

Scheyder, Ernest. 2016. "In North Dakota's Oil Patch, a Humbling Comedown." Reuters, May 18. https://www.reuters.com/investigates/special-report/usa-northdakota-bust/.

Smith, Kristin K., Julia H. Haggerty, David L. Kay, and Roger Coupal. 2019. "Using Shared Services to Mitigate Boomtown Impacts in the Bakken Shale Play: Resourcefulness or Over-adaptation?" *Journal of Rural and Community Development* 14 (2): 66–86.

Thomas, Matthew O., Sarah M. Smith, and Natalie R. Ortiz. 2016. "The Boom's Echo: Learning How to Mitigate Boomtown Effects." *Internet Journal of Criminology* Special Issue on Resource-Based Boomtowns: 125–38. https://docs.wixstatic.com/ugd/b93dd4_88d7e9607fe546d-1a9bc4c0441f9c58f.pdf.

Weber, Bret A., Julia Geigle, and Carenlee Barkdull. 2014. "Rural North Dakota's Oil Boom and Its Impact On Social Services." *Social Work* 59 (1): 62–72.

2018

Chapter 11
Making Home in the Bakken Oil Patch

William Caraher, Bret Weber, and Richard Rothaus

If not for the dated photographs, the 1958 *Williston Report's* treatment of housing could apply to the early twenty-first century Bakken boom. Both 1958 and the early twenty-first century witnessed the arrival of temporary workers who impacted the region's older communities even more than the rig counts or the barrels of oil sent to market. In both eras, the influx of a rapidly changing workforce produced high rents, limited housing options, and created a sense of social disruption.

During the Bakken's most recent boom, we led the North Dakota Man Camp Project. Like the authors of the *Williston Report*, we brought a multidisciplinary team to the Bakken oil patch (for a review of this project see Caraher, Weber, Kourelis, and Rothaus 2017; Caraher and Weber 2017; Caraher, Weber, and Rothaus 2016; Barkdull, Weber, and Geigle 2016). Our project focused on documenting the material and social lives of the workers living in the wide range of workforce housing sites across the region. The North Dakota Man Camp Project and the *Williston Report* both captured a moment in the dynamic space of the Bakken. Indeed, the rapid pace of change and the resulting housing crisis and social disruption appear to be a common feature to resource booms around the world (Ruddell and Ray, this volume). Booms can create collisions when they bring the needs and capital of the global center to rural peripheries (Caraher 2016), and when "outside" workers arrive in the region and interact with longer-term, more established residents. Despite these structural similarities, there are differences in terms of the scope of the two Bakken booms, each involving distinct policy reactions and economic and political contexts. As a result, we located the twenty-first century Bakken boom within its particular historical context and framed our attention to workforce housing amid the growing concern for housing in the late modern world (Madden and Marcuse 2016).

This chapter provides a critique of the 1958 *Report's* treatment of housing, a consideration of the emergent perspectives on workforce housing in the present, and an overview of our research of temporary workforce housing. It concludes with a consideration of how economic booms and busts manifest and accelerate changing ideals about domesticity and the political ramifications of these changes for community in the context of global capital.

Summary of the Williston Report *with Special Attention to Housing*

The 1958 *Williston Report* provides an invaluable snapshot of the 1950s oil boom. It describes the scale of the boom, confronts the challenge of counting and documenting a mobile and temporary workforce, and wrestles to measure the impact of social change. In the absence of consistent and high-resolution data, the authors of the *Williston Report* supplemented their study with interviews and more impressionistic readings of the situation. Our work follows similar patterns.

The *Williston Report* is very much a report, and it approached aspects of the 1950s oil boom largely on its own terms. There is little effort to locate the 1950s Bakken boom within the history of the state, the region, or larger conversations about extractive industries and the associated changes in the mobility of the American workforce in the postwar era. As the authors note, their report is a case study rather than a policy brief or an argument for understanding the broader causes and patterns of social change.

That being said, Campbell and his colleagues' observations are not without judgment. They assert that some of the housing in the Bakken, particularly around Tioga was, indeed, "substandard," including tar-paper shacks and structures rough enough to be thought of as "grain bins." Photos from the 1950s showed light-weight, closely-spaced buildings that could be moved two at a time with a farm truck (p. 258–2). Interviews with one resident confirmed their unsuitability, noting, "How can they expect a man to live in something like that? I've come all the way from (a southern state) because of my job and I've never had to live in anything like this before" (p. 258). These temporary houses were not the only solution to the housing boom: communities like Ray and Tioga also subdivided more substantial, existing structures to accommodate workers, and Williston and Tioga built new housing. Additionally, both then and now, as is common in boom areas around the globe, some oil companies provided mobile housing units to accommodate their employees in the oil patch, though this is generally done for more highly skilled workers and management, with the rest of the workforce largely left to find their own way with limited options (Weaver 2010; Van Bueren 2002; Caraher 2016).

In the 1950s, the tight housing market caused by the boom motivated communities and developers to invest in housing, but, ironically, most of it was expensive and high quality, built to attract individuals with higher incomes who already enjoyed stable housing. As a result, new construction did little to alleviate the housing challenges facing workers who only intended to stay in the region temporarily or who did not enjoy high salaries or wages. Further aggravating the immediate situation, new construction motivated policy makers to limit the extent and impact of temporary housing, which further limited available choices for temporary residents. This dynamic has seemingly recurred in each subsequent boom in the Bakken.

The authors of the *Williston Report* hinted at an analysis that considered the social and political dynamics of housing, but, despite the changes taking place across the region, they shied from considering housing to be a genuine "social problem" (p. 257). Instead, there was a tendency to acquiesce. Quotes from longer-term residents suggest a sense that something was wrong with the workers who seemingly *chose* to live in "substandard" temporary workforce housing. One Tioga resident commented that "I don't see how anyone could rent" the available housing, suggesting that there was something wrong with the workers rather than the housing (p. 256). Workforce housing was primarily seen as an individual problem and the responsibility of the workers. Rather than a social responsibility, temporary workforce housing became an inconvenience for longer-term residents to endure. In this regard, the 1958 *Report* echoed many of the sentiments expressed to members of the North Dakota Man Camp Project during our research. Housing remained "disturbing to the researcher" (p. 254), but longtime residents only rarely articulated it as a problem for the workers. Whether the discussion was about RVs or modular crew camps, long-term residents tended to view them as necessary solutions, or even evils, to tolerate and eventually banish, rather than seeing the housing shortage as a social problem to be solved. The *Williston Report* demonstrates what is probably obvious for all who have experienced booms: housing and the resulting tensions between existing communities and new arrivals is a recurring, key dynamic of booms related to extractive industries.

Historiography of Short-term Housing and Home

The *Williston Report* appeared at a transformative time for scholars considering new forms of American housing in the post-war era, particularly in the American west, and the report anticipated a twenty-first century global housing crisis emerging around the time of the Bakken boom. John Bickerstaff Jackson's 1953 study of the "westward moving house" (Jackson 1953), and his late 1950s research on housing in the Four Corners area of the American southwest (Jackson 1960) recognized housing in the west as a distinct phenomenon adapted both to the identity of the owner and to the economic needs of a region. More recent studies on temporary worker housing during World War II (such as Foster 1980; Mitchell 2012), and on the rise of mobile homes and RVs as expressions of the tension between mobility and stability in the American suburbs (Jackson 1984; White 2001), likewise saw the middle of the twentieth century as a period during which housing and concepts of domesticity came to intersect with new materials, plans, and social roles (Berger 1961; Duncan and Duncan 2004). Set against this backdrop, Campbell and his colleagues' ambivalent attitude toward the housing problem in the 1950s Bakken likely reflected the significant changes taking place within American attitudes toward the house and domesticity during the same decade (see Hayden 1984 for the classic treatment of this period; Miller 2010).

Sixty years after the *Williston Report*, United Nations' experts warned of a global housing crisis largely driven by financial speculation (Johnstone 2017). The intense commodification of housing has increased the mobility of global capital in ways that have harmed the housing security of multiple populations. There has been a dramatic expansion of ad hoc housing around urban areas in the global south, worsened challenges associated with housing the growing number of refugees and migrants in the global north, and—as is the case in the Bakken—greater numbers of laborers engaged in precarious manufacturing jobs, construction projects, and other short-term ventures. Activists and scholars alike recognize that the housing needs of workers, migrants, refugees, and urban dwellers are a matter of social, economic, and environmental justice. Recent critiques have made clear, for example, that the *Williston Report's* prescient observation that the tendency of developers to invest in high cost and high profit units at the expense of affordable housing, when multiplied across the global stage, has contributed to the global housing crisis (for example, Madden and Marcuse 2016).

Indeed, for those interested in the housing-related challenges of the twenty-first century, the 1958 *Williston Report* is almost uncannily relevant, even if it might strike the modern readers as calloused. For a start, the *Report*'s nonchalant assertion that in many cases housing problems represented more of a "personal" problem than a larger social one, forecast the tendency of many twenty-first century policy makers to turn a blind eye to the reality that temporary housing represents a compromise negotiated across a dramatic power imbalance. This imbalance separates workers and employers, shapes the attitude of the Bakken counties' longer-term residents, and colors prevailing attitudes of society at large. Attitudes toward domesticity favor home ownership, but the material, economic, and environmental limits present in the industrial wilderness of the Bakken, and the attitudes and policies promulgated by state and local communities, tend to marginalize temporary labor and limit their housing options. Workers, migrants, other marginalized groups find themselves in a social bind where status is tied to a preference for single-family home ownership in an environment where that is largely not possible.

For their part, longtime residents often seek to alleviate the pressure of global and national financial capital that directly impacts their lives (increased housing costs, social disruption, etc.) by leveraging their access to local and regional political and social capital at the expense of temporary workers (for some of this see Olive, current volume). In this context and in this contest, the temporary housing in the Bakken and the conditions that produced it emerge as less than an exceptional response to an unexpected boom and more of a grim model for housing the growing class of precarious workers in the twenty-first century. In other words, the "personal" problem of housing in the *Williston Report* masked deep issues that would come to the fore over the next sixty years.

North Dakota Man Camp Project's Approach to Housing in the Bakken

The NDMCP looked at workforce housing in the Bakken both directly and as a lens on shifting ideals about work and home. We considered the lives of temporary workers and longer-term residents, and how both negotiated the practical realities of housing, home, and community. We looked at the material and social aspects of various forms of workforce housing, and how the resulting constraints and opportunities shaped personal wellbeing amid the intersection of the private and the political. Over the course of five years, we developed a longitudinal sample of workforce housing sites in the Bakken that reflected a wide range of forms, practices, and experience in North Dakota's Williams and McKenzie counties. The resulting archive consists of nearly 10,000 photographs, dozens of hours of video, and interviews with camp residents, managers, owners, as well as local officials in the Bakken.

Neither the *Williston Report* nor our own work ever offered precise counts of workers in relation to available housing. Both numbers were so rapidly fluctuating that such attempts were not practical, and such a count was simply outside the scope of our research focus. However, in the process of disseminating our findings we were often pressed for such data. Some illustrative, point-in-time estimates help to address this. In 2012, the North Dakota Petroleum Council estimated that the boom had created 65,000 jobs, with a state population of just over 700,000. At that same time, the Department of Commerce estimated the number of "available beds" in crew camps at just 15,119, suggesting that fewer than 25 percent of the new workers would have been readily accommodated by temporary workforce housing. These figures also neglect those who came to the Bakken looking for work and housing but then left, usually due to the lack of affordable or available housing. Further, in consideration of the tension between the workers and the longtime residents, many of the camps dwarfed neighboring communities in terms of population. In terms of population alone, several of the worker settlements would have been counted among the state's twenty largest cities.

Like the *Williston Report*, we observed workers living in substandard, overpriced, and cramped housing vulnerable to the vagaries of North Dakota's weather, and we recognized the range of housing options as well as the ways workers modified their temporary accommodations to endure the seasons and to enhance their domestic lives. But we also strove to be more nuanced in capturing the changing conditions throughout the boom and the subsequent slowdown, and to monitor the changes brought on by the increased inventory of permanent housing, the decline in employment opportunities in the oil patch, and the policy-driven legal challenges to the provisional use permits under which many temporary man camps functioned.

The eventual decline in the number of jobs we observed parallels the observations made in the *Williston Report*. For instance, Tioga saw an easing of housing pressures with the completion of a gas plant and other regional projects in 1954 (p. 214). We saw similar outcomes in Tioga and, perhaps most dramatically, in Watford City. The completion of major infrastructure projects (especially roads and pipelines), and the increase in housing inventory, alleviated some of the pressure on workforce housing, and we worked to capture the ways that the end of the most intense phases of booms tend to reveal and even highlight the underlying tensions and flows of capital that the earlier frenetic pace, optimism, and opportunism tend to obscure.

The issues of housing and home in the Bakken oil patch must also be considered in relation to the reality that many of the workers who lived in temporary housing were victims of the housing crisis and the Great Recession of 2008. There were some parallels with the earlier, nationwide, 1952 recession, and the acute, post-World War II housing shortage. But that is where the similarity mostly ends. The earlier period was one where lifetime employment with a single employer was relatively common. That was also the dawn of a burgeoning, suburban domesticity. In contrast, after 2008, many of the workers who came to the Bakken continued to pay mortgages on distant homes in other states, while others had left properties that were underwater, hoping to start anew in the Bakken. These were workers who understood the likelihood of job insecurity and multiple, shifting employers over the course of a career. Indeed, many had weathered previous booms that shaped their attitudes toward housing and home. One woman, a veteran of the Alaska oil boom, warned in an interview in the fall of 2016, "Don't count on the oil field ... when it's good it's great, but when it tanks, it affects an entire community."[1] She described her and her husband's experience:

> When the oil tanked up there, and the oil went away, I lost my job, his overtime got cut. So our primary home ... we couldn't afford the big mortgage on it anymore, so that got foreclosed on, and we had another little rental house that we sold at a huge loss.[2]

Near the end of the interview she wistfully hinted at the long-term nature of booms in extractive industries with a courageous sense of humor: "My dad has seen the oil field rise and fall a couple times, and he kinda tried to warn us, but, you know, we said the oil field is so big, it's going to last forever!"[3]

---

[1] NDMCP Personal Interview FT 12_3 October 28, 2016. A note on citations: those in footnotes indicate interviews conducted by the North Dakota Man Camp Project, the Field Trip (FT) number during which the interview occurred, the randomly assigned number of the interview, and the date when it was conducted. While we have worked to obfuscate the identity of the interview subject, all individuals signed consent forms with the understanding that anonymity was not guaranteed. Those forms are on file with the authors.

[2] NDMCP Personal Interview FT 12_3 October 28, 2016.

[3] NDMCP Personal Interview FT 12_3 October 28, 2016.

Bakken observers have noted the hard reality that families exchanged the stability of a house for a trailer, mobile home, or room in a prefabricated man camp (see Briody 2017; Rao 2018). The juxtaposition of the subprime mortgage crisis and the challenges associated with workforce housing in the Bakken illustrate the changing nature of work and home in the twenty-first century (e.g. Gold 2014).

Making Home in the North Dakota Oil Patch

The *Williston Report* and our research both describe workers dismayed about the high cost and wretched quality of the housing available to them. We might assume that workers in the 1950s, like those we spoke with, struggled to develop domestic norms, worked to transform temporary housing into homelike spaces, and sought other ways to improve their situation. Regardless, our research focused on these dynamics to a much greater degree than did the 1958 *Report*. To facilitate that focus, we utilized a three-level typology to describe the different forms of temporary workforce housing.

The NDMCP started its research at the end of the most hectic phase of the oil boom during which the most ad hoc camps, which we categorized as informal Type 3 camps, emerged and dissipated across the region. These included sites like the infamous Williston Walmart parking lot camp, local city parks, and the sudden overcrowding of recreational camping sites across the region. The temporary shelter created in Williston's Concordia Lutheran church's basement by Rev. Jay Reinke (chronicled in the documentary *The Overnighters* [Moss 2014]), represents a dramatic but not entirely unique variation on the kinds of spontaneous settlements that appeared in the earliest days of the boom (Briody 2017). These existed in the liminal space between official and unofficial policies, the vagaries of law enforcement attitudes, changing housing options, and local goodwill. The precarity of these camps seemed to create a greater degree of interdependence and even an ephemeral sense of community. But as administrative infrastructure and more formal forms of temporary housing slowly developed during the early chaos of the boom, uncertainty tipped against these camps and their number and visibility slowly dissipated.

More persistent than the Type 3 camps, Type 2 camps consisted largely of RVs arranged in lots with electrical and water hookups. These camps presented more conventional opportunities for homemaking and were both a major source of housing for many workers and a particular focus of our research (see

Caraher et al. 2016). Occupants enhanced and expanded their living spaces through the construction of elaborate "mudrooms" which occasionally exceeded the size of the original units and could include bunks, living spaces, and additional storage. There were also outdoor improvements on the small lots including gardens and various features to delineate some semblance of private space. This making of outdoor living spaces was a consequence of the cramped, spatial limits of life in an RV; interestingly, the mudrooms also provided features of traditional suburban life. The construction of elaborate mudrooms expanded the useful space of the RV units but also allowed residents to demonstrate proficiency in building, and created an opportunity to formalize and personalize the entrance to their units. The Type 2 camps had a blurred, suburban look to them, with informal neighborhoods and some limited sense of community. These camps typically had investors from outside the region and local management who worked with residents and nearby communities to create rules that governed the extent to which residents could modify their units. Most importantly, despite the often ramshackle appearance of some of these camps, they offered the closest alternative to late twentieth century U.S. norms of domesticity.

Type 1 camps, often referred to as crew camps or lodges, offered modular, mobile housing typically managed by national or even global logistics companies. These were sometimes fenced in with security gates and prohibitions against alcohol, firearms, or guests. They generally accommodated workers from larger companies that reserved blocks of rooms for time-specific projects. Such workers tended to move through the region in shifts of three or four weeks of relatively constant work, followed by one or two weeks off. In general, these camps had more formal, on-site, management and security. While some offered the convenience of meals, these camps generally offered only minimal amenities akin to economy motels. They also restricted the opportunities to customize spaces. Most residents lived at these facilities for a limited number of weeks and then departed the camp for a week or two. Some took their paychecks and left for mini-vacations or cruises, while others returned home to domestic dynamics strained by distance, work schedules outside of the norm of a forty-hour work week, and chores and other family tensions that had been waiting during their absence. Either way, when they returned to the camp, they were generally lodged in different rooms, with virtually no opportunity for customized spaces or any semblance of private domesticity. Our experience as temporary workers in the Bakken involved repeated stays in one of these camps, which provided a practical alternative to tracking down scarce and overpriced hotel rooms. We rarely stayed for more than one night, and we found them to be eminently convenient. However, the enforced, apolitical existence with little to no sense of continuity or community meant that these offered the least opportunity for human interaction. Type 1 camps offered the most efficient, but the least human, way for temporary workers to be moved in and out of the Bakken like replaceable parts.

Man Camps and the Policy Realm

The majority of policy makers seemed to share the view of E. Ward Koeser, president of the Tioga city commission in Williams County, who regarded "man-camps as being somewhat a necessary evil" (Klimasinska 2013). As such, the state's general policy response was to rely on existing code, impose minimalist safety standards, utilize ad hoc efforts to limit the spread and longevity of man camps, and alter that course only when pressed. State policy makers tended to focus on short-term, financial considerations.

Despite clear distinctions from other forms of lodging, the most directly relevant policies connected either to motel and hotel regulations, or to mobile home and RV parks, and focused almost exclusively on "fire, life, and safety."[4] The origin of policies governing temporary labor housing were coincident with the state's earlier booms, though they were largely driven by federal responses to the development of mobile homes in the 1950s, and federal designations created by the Department of Housing and Urban Development (HUD) in the 1970s, rather than more specific efforts to control or enhance housing during the previous booms.

The major policy revisions during the twenty-first century boom clarified the definition of temporary work camp housing and set five-year time limits with the requirement that owners remove the housing and "all related above-grade and below-grade infrastructure within one hundred twenty days after the temporary work camp housing is vacated" (NDCC 54-21.3-02.8 and 54-21.3-04.3). By 2014, many camps had already outlived the five-year limit, and by September of that year, headlines in the *Williston Herald* announced, "Companies facing millions in fines for temporary housing," with twenty-nine separate housing units approaching locally imposed expiration dates (Bell 2014; Barkdull et al. 2016).

Highly-impacted communities in the heart of the oil boom tried to regulate man camp proliferation, especially in response to overwhelmed infrastructure.

---

[4] NDMCP Personal Interview FT 10_8 August 1, 2015.

For instance, local waste treatment facilities were only able to accommodate so many new toilets flushing into the system. State officials noted marked improvements in the ability of local governments to plan and control these developments, but, despite being awash in oil revenue, the state generally avoided direct assistance, leaving local governmental entities mostly on their own. As described by one long-term state official, "there was no state funding for any of this. The counties and cities came up with their own money to put their own inspection departments in place."[5] Communities such as Watford City, caught in the crosshairs of some of the boom's busiest activity and traffic, had no planning department through the first years of the boom. The speed with which local entities were able to develop local ordinances and administrative staffing and support for inspection and enforcement varied greatly. With generally insufficient funding and policy support—and a lack of housing for newly hired bureaucrats!—local and state officials developed new collaborations and communicated with one another in novel ways to deal with the explosion of temporary labor housing.

State officials, acutely aware of the challenges, largely had their hands tied in terms of providing assistance. As noted by one official, "When this first hit there were a lot of problems because a lot of cities and counties had no oversight and no local building codes."[6]

The typology developed by the North Dakota Man Camp Project, juxtaposed with the framework of policies regulating temporary workforce housing, suggests insufficient state support of local communities. The unfortunate results included overcrowding, price-gouging, dismal living conditions, and attendant social problems that persist in North Dakota's oil patch. In the face of such realities, North Dakota Governor Jack Dalrymple announced with his second biennial "no growth" budget that despite the state having "the nation's strongest economy," government needed to "become more creative and more efficient" (Smith 2014). Almost inexplicably, amid the rapid growth there were calls for austerity, especially in relation to government oversight.

"What can you do?" is a familiar question uttered by both the longtime and newer community residents and government officials when asked about boom-related housing challenges. This oft-repeated question, once unpacked, reveals assumptions nested within the larger cultural, socioeconomic, and political contexts of North Dakota's oil patch that privilege market forces as the best possible means of addressing human wellbeing (for example, Abromovitz

---

[5] NDMCP Personal Interview Admin Interviews March 21, 2014.

[6] NDMCP Personal Interview Admin Interviews March 21, 2014.

2012). And yet, the growing power of global corporate capital increases the difficulty of addressing local issues of social and economic justice when other countervailing forces (such as the governor or the state legislature) cannot or will not act (for example, Sewpaul 2013).

A series of constraints and influences shaped the availability and character of housing during the twenty-first century Bakken boom. A growing apprehension about the informal Type 3 camps led to stricter enforcement of existing ordinances governing casual sleeping in parks. The Williston Walmart, for example, abandoned its support for an informal, chainwide policy that allowed travelers with RVs to stay overnight in their parking lots after public pressure and a spate of police calls (Woods and Brooks 2012). Local camping sites, for visitors to the Theodore Roosevelt National Park or Lake Sakakawea, enforced maximum stays to manage the influx of workers using these sites for housing (see Briody 2017).

Despite the contingency of these sites, it is clear that they played an important role in both housing and creating spaces for community among new arrivals to the region. In 2012, we visited a small Type 3 camp that had accommodated a group of carpenters from Idaho working on a nearby construction site along with some other new arrivals to the Bakken. This group arranged their RVs and tents around a common space, socialized, shared meals and chores, and even helped those who had not found work. As one resident put it: "We're like brothers, like a family." Despite this sense of family, she also admitted, "the living conditions are terrible here. Like people are shitting behind, in the trees, past the trees right there. There's flies everywhere ... It's fricking terrible living conditions."[7] When another resident of the same camp was asked how he survived living in a shelter belt while looking for work, he responded, "Well that's where the camaraderie thing comes in—every night we sit around the fire and joke and carry on, do stuff. They've got these little air pistols and they're all the time shooting each other. A lot of these guys are young and ... full of it ... But that's what breaks the monotony, you know? Because we have each other."[8] In our experience as researchers, the Type 3 camps had the greatest sense of community, but the least comfortable living environment and very little stability.

A few months later we returned to discover that the RVs and tents of the camp had been removed, leaving behind only fresh tire tracks from a tractor in the snow and a full cooler of beer. All indications suggested that law

[7] NDMCP Personal Interview FT 1_21 August 9, 2012.

[8] NDMCP Personal Interview FT 1_12 August 8, 2012.

enforcement or a local landowner removed this camp without much advance notice. By 2014, most cities in the oil patch had enacted, or were more actively enforcing, ordinances limiting the number of RVs on private property within city limits. Rev. Reinke's shelter at Concordia Lutheran Church finally closed when pressure from local residents forced the city to act (Briody 2017; Moss 2014).

Type 2 camps built to accommodate RVs in individual lots have continued to house temporary workers in the region months and years after the apparent bust. Despite their sometimes scrappy appearance, these camps attracted national investors with modest upfront costs, limited staffing expenses, and the opportunity to charge high rents. Ideally, once built, these camps required only limited maintenance, but frozen water and sewage pipes in the winter, the need to add amenities like the internet to stave off competition or playgrounds to address state requirements, and costly updates to sewage and water systems (sometimes accompanied by lawsuits against the builders or previous owners) all suggest that these camps may have had more ongoing costs than owners had anticipated.

One camp owner on the eastern edge of the patch just off Route 2, who had a background in finance and construction, told us that a group of "finance" investors had asked him to get involved because of the trouble that they had been experiencing with contractors. This was a common problem throughout the state at the height of the boom due to the shortage of tradespeople, especially in relation to all the available work. He had arrived in 2012 near the peak of the boom, but noted, "the park's never made money ... here's what happened: the park was built incorrectly to begin with." As a result, "we're working with the state, we're putting in new water lines throughout the whole park ... we're in a litigation issue with the sub [contractor] ..."[9] The camp had fewer residents during each of our subsequent visits. From a peak of nearly one hundred, by April 2018, only two renters had been there through the winter. One had visible water connection problems.

Type 2 camps sprang up along the major thoroughfares and around the major intersections in the Bakken. Like the 1950s boom, the course between Route 2 and the city of Tioga, and then extending through the northern approach to Williston on Route 85, was a busy stretch for temporary workforce housing. Distinct from the 1950s boom, in the more recent boom Watford City also witnessed a significant influx of workers, accommodated through a halo of RV parks extending along the city's western and southern sides. Watford

---

[9] NDMCP Personal Interview FT 10_1 July 31, 2015.

City hosted a variety of camp types ranging from the unique, massive indoor RV park, which offered climate-controlled stalls for individual RVs, to a series of smaller camps lining the slopes of the rolling landscape. In 2016, a tornado ripped through one of these RV parks, demonstrating the fragility of these light-weight aluminum and fiberglass boxes designed more for easy transport than persistent, multi-season habitation.

In interviews with residents of these camps at the height of the boom, we often heard about the sense of community and the freedom available in Type 2 camps, especially in contrast to the institutional-style Type 1 camps. One camp owner described the Type 1 camps as "just the same thing over and over ... there's no community about it. 'Cause you're in there, it's like this big system. [laughs] You come in, you eat, they take everything from you, you shower, you're gone."[10] In contrast, another owner described his Type 2 camp as promoting "families, dogs, kids. So, it's temporary housing, but some of these people bring their families for the summer, and [the families] go back for the winter, but they'll stay here."[11] The degree of community is debatable, though fears about crime in these camps were, in our experience, greatly exaggerated. The lived experience existed somewhere between the hysteria about crime and the hyperbole about community (but see Berg-Burin, current volume; Ruddell and Ray, current volume).

Many had what we playfully called by the neologism "Bakktimism," which referred to the persistent optimism expressed by residents of the Bakken. Despite the dangers and demands of the work, fluctuations in oil prices, the high cost of rent, the dust and heat in the summer, the frozen pipes, snow, and cutting wind of the winter, and the mud of the springtime thaw, residents of Type 2 camps almost universally remained positive about their situation. Maya Rao recently offered the Gramscian observation (Rao 2018) that this optimism represents faith in the long-term power of capitalism and hard work to reward short-term risk and discomfort. One particularly illustrative form of Bakktimism emerged in a conversation with a man who operated a salvage yard that bought and sold RVs and RV parts. When asked if he might make North Dakota his "permanent" home, he replied, "Well, I'm 62 years old, I'm going to do my best to maybe put in another five years ... I hope to ride it out, there's a millionaire dream here, there's great possibilities."[12] He was living in one of the

---

[10] NDMCP Personal Interview FT 10_1 July 31, 2015.

[11] NDMCP Personal Interview FT 4_6 August 21, 2013.

[12] NDMCP Personal Interview FT 4_7 August 22, 2013.

most marginal camps we ever visited, but his story was more common than eccentric and captured a common sentiment.

Many camp owners shared this confidence. While some made back their initial investments in the first year or so, the persistence of these camps demonstrates an ongoing willingness, as the boom retreated, to operate the camps with significantly lower rents and lower occupancy. However, the receding boom also led others to close their camps, usually because of changing local policies or growing competition from hotels and apartments.

The range of optimism among owners and on-site managers also reflected their varying commitments to the neighboring communities. Some were deeply involved in local affairs and lived locally, while the majority lived outside the region. One park owner who had moved to the Bakken from Oregon and built his business a few miles south of Watford City stated:

> We are North Dakotans. We are licensed. My corporation is licensed. My cars are. We moved. My kids started businesses here. We're part of the community ... [W]e broke an acre off here and an acre for my partner, and this is our home ... We vote. We've been to the planning meetings.[13]

Camp owners and, more importantly, managers, also expressed a wide range of attitudes toward the conditions in their camps. Some, for example, took pride in the cleanliness of their facilities, emphasized the family friendly atmosphere, and paid careful attention to infrastructure and upkeep. A manager of a large RV park outside of Williston remarked,

> It's our community. It's not an RV park. When you asked me what it is, it's Williston Fox Run. I did not say it's an RV camp because that's not what we want here. If you notice, our lots for these RVs and trailers are quite large so that they do have a little piece of home for a yard, for whatever they need. Our lot sizes are 30 by 90 feet. You can go to other places and they are 20 by 40. It's almost three times the size.[14]

Other camps appeared to take a more laissez-faire approach with certain camps garnering the reputation for drug use, prostitution, and other illegal and undesirable activities.

---

[13] NDMCP Personal Interview FT 4_6 August 21, 2013.

[14] NDMCP Personal Interview FT 1_2 August 10, 2012.

As policies toward RV parks changed at the municipal level, camp managers tried to enforce the rules, but the dynamic character of the boom made solutions difficult. As a manager of a camp near Ross observed, "There was no one here to train me on everything, so I've had to learn all myself."[15] Camp managers sought to address the rules, but there was only ever limited support or enforcement from state and county workers overwhelmed by the increased workload and the changing policy environment. Indeed, as late as 2011, according to the executive director of the county's Job Development Authority, "McKenzie County had no land use plan or planning and zoning."[16] And even once policies were established, efforts to place inspectors in the field ran up against the same challenges impacting healthcare workers, law enforcement, educators, etc.: as counties developed the necessary social infrastructure to ramp up enforcement, they ironically ran up against the housing shortage.

Specific rules and regulations, much less policies, remain murky on the ground. Williston, for example, enacted ordinances limiting the size and function of mudrooms in RV parks within city limits. In 2012, a camp manager said, "We do check [mudrooms] out and make sure they meet the fire code and that they're not built shoddily, so that if the wind comes up 80 mph, it's not going to blow away. That's what we do."[17] A year later, they required that residents limit their mudrooms to twelve-by-eight feet.[18] Another camp manager claimed that mudrooms could be any size as long as they maintained a ten-foot clearance between the buildings.[19] In other words, just as a camp's policies work only as well as the ability of the manager to enforce them, this same thing extends to the state, county, and city laws.

The fate of Type 1 camps during the receding boom was reported on a nearly weekly basis in 2015 and 2016 as the city of Williston expanded its extraterritorial jurisdiction to include land on which several man camps operated. In response to Williston's requirement that all man camps close by September 1, 2017, Target Logistics, one of the largest man camp operators in the region, sued the City of Williston to prevent having to shut down its large facility at the northern edge of the city. Other Type 1 facilities around Williston and Tioga unsuccessfully requested that their sites be rezoned as hotels. Most of

---

[15] NDMCP Personal Interview FT 10_7 July 31, 2015.

[16] NDMCP Personal Interview FT 5_1 August 11, 2014.

[17] NDMCP Personal Interview FT1_2 August 10, 2012.

[18] NDMCP Personal Interview FT 4_2 August 22, 2013.

[19] NDMCP Personal Interview FT 7_4 December, 2014.

these larger facilities have since closed. The actual physical removal of these Type 1 man camps is a particularly significant aspect of temporary workforce housing during a boom. The units themselves can be removed by a truck and are sometimes sold individually to buyers who pay for removal and transportation. However, the land where they stood will require significant reclamation work to approach pre-camp condition. Since most of the land was leased from local farmers, there is significant tension between out-of-state investors, their local managers, and the landowners. At a camp outside of Alexander, North Dakota, a Type 1 camp removed their units, but left the farmer with electrical, sewage, and water pipes below the ground and a thick level of gravel and dirt. As the camp failed, the farmer stopped being paid and lamented that land would never again be farmable. Elsewhere, a land owner took a camp owner to court after he tried to sell 110 acres of the farmer's land: "I gave them a long-term lease which I shouldn't have done. Then I found out they were trying to sell this 110 acres out from underneath me and I got pissed off and took them to court ... And [now] the only ones making money is the lawyers."[20] Temporary housing may have been a "necessary evil" to address the housing crisis, but the failure to create more effective policies, the insufficient funding, and the lack of enforcement has meant ill effects persisting long after the boom times.

Visions of Home after the Boom

Compared to 2012, housing and related infrastructure in the Bakken region looked very different by 2018. Like in the 1950s, the Bakken boom introduced a ring of new housing to Williston. By 2018, Watford City was surrounded with subdivisions, a new high school, and a four-lane road routing traffic around downtown. On the one hand, these new developments demonstrate that Bakken communities continue to value permanent housing with the benefits of increased tax revenue and a greater sense of community and stability. In many ways, the interest of workers and the Bakken communities intersect in their shared desire for a sense of home. On the other hand, it remains unclear whether residents of these new homes and apartments will stay in Watford City as the workforce needs of the Bakken oil patch ebb and flow with the price of oil, the requirements of drilling and fracking oil wells, and the lure of opportunity elsewhere. The Bakken landscape changes daily by the ongoing removal of Type 1 camps, the gravel scars on the landscape, and the obvious decline in boom and bustle as oil companies shift resources in workforce and capital

---

[20] NDMCP Personal Interview FT 12_2 October 28, 2016.

elsewhere. The role of outside capital in funding the boom, creating temporary housing, and new development remains obvious as well. It remains to be seen whether the post-boom landscape will inform future policies and serve as a reminder of the speed of twenty-first century capital and the vagaries of home in the global economy.

A new subdivision east of Watford City provides a hint. In the spring of 2018, the driveways and front lawns were already filled with work trucks beneath banners advertising units with four bedrooms and four baths. Rather than family housing, this arrangement would accommodate the same temporary workers as the man camps they replaced. Despite bucolic names suggesting suburban domesticity, the frequent architectural references to shipping containers, including corrugated siding and narrow dimensions, do little to hide the likely transient reality. Ironically, the struggles for domesticity represented by decorated mudrooms and desperately planted gardens in the Type 2 camps gave way to an implicit temporary character that shaped much of the "permanent" housing in the same region.

The NDMCP, the 1958 Report, and Other Contemporary Bakken Research

There are certainly commonalities between the housing related issues described in the *Williston Report* and our own observations. Perhaps even more surprisingly, there are echoes from North Dakota's earliest extractive industry boom periods, namely the original agricultural booms that brought large numbers of European immigrants who similarly struggled with the tension between recreating the domesticity they had known and the needs for temporary workforce housing exemplified by the Bonanza farms. Like the Type 1 lodges of the boom we studied, some of the "permanent" housing that was built during the late 1800s and early 1900s was packed up and shipped off to the next boom (as was the case with the Sears kit houses from that period). Also, then as now, there were abandonment processes as technological advances in agriculture meant diminished workforce needs, leaving the elements to slowly erode the physical remnants of communities.

More poignantly, our work is distinct from the *Williston Report* in its consideration of both a more global and historical context. After an initial attempt to simply consider the role of man camps in relation to the current, short-lived oil boom, we struggled to see what the camps might reveal about housing temporary workers in relation to extractive industry booms. Then, as we engaged that work, we came to understand that the phenomenon we were studying might be even more broadly generalizable. We came to see the impact of global neoliberal policies, and the accompanying market for a "just-in-time" work-force. One result is that housing, to a greater degree than has previously been the case, has become a disposable commodity, intentionally serving global capital rather than individuals, families, or communities. One consequence of that economic dynamic is the surrender of political capacity. While interview respondents often concentrated on the tension between the longtime residents of the host communities and the workers living in temporary housing, we came to see the manner by which both "sides" received only limited benefit from the boom, especially in contrast to the great wealth transferred to outside investors, many of whom rarely or never set foot in North Dakota.

Our contribution to Bakken research is that we did not view the workers (and their families!) as feral intruders. Instead, we demonstrate that both the new workers and the longer-term residents were caught in a global struggle outside their control. Instead of seeing mercenary workers in conflict with "genuine," "native" North Dakotans, we saw both groups struggling to exercise their limited agency to either hold on to, or to create and engage, a sense of home and community amid the hectic, even chaotic environment of an oil boom. The decision-making processes impacting their lives was determined less by local and state policy makers, and more by neoliberal policies and the influence of global capital.

Oil booms can simultaneously be a blessing and a curse. Having lost population for decades, many towns in western North Dakota had struggled to keep grocery stores open, let alone schools or medical services. In contrast, Brad Bekkedahl, a Williston City Commissioner declared, "This is a time of opportunity. It's a time of growth. And it's a time of amazing prosperity and wealth coming into our community" (Holeywell 2011). Others simultaneously lamented the challenges brought about by the market-fueled, locally inflationary economy. Dennis Lindahl, a city councilman in Stanley noted that "merchants are able to charge an increased rate. Folks in town sometimes get a little upset from supporting the industry while not receiving benefits."[21] And clearly, even for oil boom boosters like Bekkedahl, the market does not have all the answers. In the fall of 2014, Bekkedahl, as a Republican candidate for state senate, was supportive of a change in the state's oil production tax to address Williston's projected need of more than $1 billion in infrastructure needs by 2020. But, of all the economic struggles and challenges, the nexus issue in the oil patch continues to be housing—part of a global crisis that continues to be framed primarily as a local problem.

---

[21] NDMCP Personal Interview FT 12_2 October 28, 2016.

References

Abramovitz, M. 2012. "Theorising the Neoliberal Welfare State for Social Work." In *The SAGE Handbook of Social Work*, edited by M. Gray, J. Midgley, and S. Webb, 33–51. London: SAGE.

Barkdull, C., B. Weber, and J. Geigle. 2016. "Extractive Industries and Temporary Housing Policies: Man Camps in North Dakota's Oil Patch." In *The Bakken Goes Boom: Oil and the Changing Geographies of Western North Dakota*, edited by William R. Caraher and Kyle Conway, 199–224. Grand Forks: Digital Press at the University of North Dakota.

Briody, B. 2017. *The New Wild West: Black Gold, Fracking, and Life in a North Dakota Boomtown*. New York: St. Martin's Press.

Caraher, William. 2016. "The Archaeology of Man Camps: Contingency, Periphery, and Late Capitalism." In *The Bakken Goes Boom: Oil and the Changing Geographies of Western North Dakota*, edited by William R. Caraher and Kyle Conway, 181–96. Grand Forks: Digital Press at the University of North Dakota.

Caraher, W., and B. Weber. 2017. *The Bakken: An Archaeology of an Industrial Landscape*. Fargo: North Dakota State University Press.

Caraher, W., B. Weber, K. Kourelis, and R. Rothaus. 2017. "The North Dakota Man Camp Project: The Archaeology of Home in the Bakken Oil Fields." *Historical Archaeology* 51: 267–87.

Caraher, W., B. Weber, and R. Rothaus. 2016. "Lessons from the Bakken Oil Patch." *Journal of Contemporary Archaeology* 3 (2): 195–204.

Duncan, James S., and Nancy G. Duncan. 2004. *Landscapes of Privilege: The Politics of the Aesthetic in an American Suburb*. London: Routledge.

Foster, R.H. 1980. "Wartime Trailer Housing in the San Francisco Bay Area." *Geographical Review* 70 (3): 276–90.

Gold, R. 2014. *The Boom: How Fracking Ignited the American Energy Revolution and Changed the World*. New York: Simon and Schuster.

Hayden, D. 1984. *Redesigning the American Dream: The Future of Housing, Work, and Family Life*. New York: W.W. Norton.

Holeywell, R. 2011. "North Dakota's Oil Boom Is a Blessing and a Curse: The State's Oil Boom Is Bringing Unmatched Growth and Unanticipated Problems." Governing the States and Localities, August. https://web.archive.org/web/20120207095623/http://www.governing.com/topics/energy-env/north-dakotas-oil-boom-blessing-curse.html.

Jackson, J.B. 1953. "The Westward-Moving House." *Landscape* 2 (3): 8–21.

Jackson, J.B. 1960. "The Four Corners Country." *Landscape* 10 (1): 20–6.

Jackson, J.B. 1984. "The Moveable Dwelling and How It Came to America." In *Discovering the Vernacular Landscape*, edited by J.B. Jackson, 91–101. New Haven: Yale University Press.

Johnstone, R. 2017. "UN Expert Warns on Global housing Crisis." *Public Finance International*, March 3. http://www.publicfinanceinternational.org/news/2017/03/un-expert-warns-global-housing-crisis.

Klimasinska, K. 2013. "No Kids, No Booze, No Pets: Inside North Dakota's Largest Man Camp." *Bloomberg News*, February 12. http://www.bloomberg.com/news/2013-02-12/no-kids-no-booze-no-pets-inside-north-dakota-s-largest-man-camp.html.

Madden, D., and P. Marcuse. 2016. *In Defense of Housing: The Politics of Crisis*. London: Verso.

Miller, T. 2010. "The Birth of the Patio Daddy-O: Outdoor Grilling in Postwar America." *Journal of American Culture* 33 (1): 5–11.

Mitchell, D. 2012. "La Casa de Esclavos Modernos: Exposing the Architecture of Exploitation." *Journal of the Society of Architectural Historians* 71 (1): 451–61.

Moss, Jesse, dir. 2014. *The Overnighters*. DVD. San Francisco: Mile End Films West.

North Dakota Century Code (NDDC). https://www.legis.nd.gov/general-information/north-dakota-century-code.

Rao, M. 2018. *Great American Outpost: Dreamers, Mavericks, and the Making of an Oil Frontier*. New York: Public Affairs.

Reed, A. 2016. "Unpackaging Boomtown Tropes: Insider/Outsider Dynamics in North Dakota's Oil Patch." In *The Bakken Goes Boom: Oil and the Changing Geographies of Western North Dakota*, edited by William R. Caraher and Kyle Conway, 51–68. Grand Forks: Digital Press at the University of North Dakota.

Sewpaul, V. 2013. "Neoliberalism and Social Work in South Africa." *Critical and Radical Social Work* 1 (1): 15–30.

Smith, N. 2014. "Governor: Hold Even on Budget." *Bismarck Tribune*, May 7. http://bismarcktribune.com/news/local/govt-and-politics/governor-hold-even-on-budget/article_6012380a-d662-11e3-bfc1-0019bb2963f4.html.

Van Bueren, T.M. 2002. "The Changing Face of Work in the West: Some Introductory Comments." *Historical Archaeology* 36 (3): 1–7.

Weaver, B. 2010. *Oilfield Trash: Life and Labor in the Oil Patch*. College Station: Texas A&M Press.

White, R.B. 2000. *Home on the Road: The Motor Home in America*. Washington, DC: Smithsonian Institution Press.

Woods, D., and J. Brooks. 2012. "Campers Forced Out: Walmart Parking Lot Devoid of RVs as New Security Guard Patrols 'Pioneer Square.'" *Williston Herald*, February 9.

2018

Chapter 12
Drinking, Drugs, and Long Waits: Community Members' Perceptions of Living in a North Dakotan Boomtown[1]

Karin L. Becker

Introduction

Unlike the previous oil boom cycles in North Dakota's history, the bust did not immediately follow the boom from 2008–14. It was more of a downturn. While the slowdown has had obvious economic effects on the state's economy, the social effects on communities are not as clear cut. Residents living in the oil-impacted areas of western North Dakota have witnessed firsthand the changes in their community due to population growth, stresses and strains on infrastructure, and use of community services. While numerous national media outlets have devoted resources to cover the boom, they have relied mainly on outsider reporting, where much of the material comes from budget reports, unemployment figures, real estate costs, census data, and oil and gas forecasts. Although these numbers paint a holistic picture of the economic impacts, what is missing is the insider perspective featuring community members' responses in their own words. For that reason, this chapter will look at how community members have perceived the impacts of the oil boom on the health of their community and how their perceptions align with other boomtown communities.

Community member feedback has been gathered in community health needs assessments (CHNAs), which document people's perceptions and concerns regarding community assets. The Affordable Care Act (ACA) requires

[1] An earlier version of portions of this chapter appeared in "Help Wanted: Health Care Workers and Mental Health Services: An Analysis of Six Years of Community Concerns from North Dakota's Oil Boom Residents," *Journal of Rural Studies* 63 (2018): 15–23. Republished by permission of Elsevier.

every nonprofit hospital to conduct a CHNA once every three years, and this assessment cycle provides a systematic data stream to compare and contrast identified community concerns over the years. Part of the CHNA process is to identify community needs, prioritize them, and then address them through an annual implementation strategy. At the time of this writing, two cycles of CHNAs have been conducted by critical access hospitals located in western North Dakota. In this analysis, seven individual CHNA reports are compiled and the aggregated data are examined to better understand local experiences.

Defining Oil Patch Communities and Assessment Cycles

The Bakken Formation lies under five counties in western North Dakota (Dunn, McKenzie, Mountrail, Stark, and Williams). This resource-rich area is known as the oil patch. Five critical access hospitals are located within it. Since community impacts from the oil boom spill out to other counties, this analysis also includes critical access hospitals located in Crosby (Divide County) and Kenmare (Burke County).

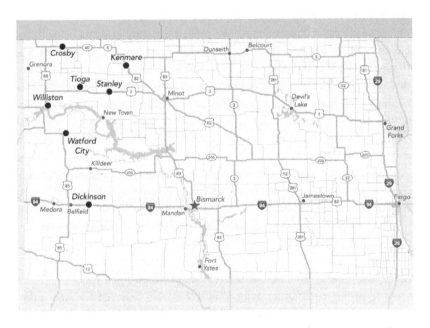

Figure 12.1. Sites where CHNAs were performed (Crosby, Kenmare, Tioga, Stanley, Williston, Watford City, and Dickinson) (image source: David Veller)

The first round of CHNAs was conducted in oil-impacted counties between 2011 and 2013. This cycle coincides with the peak of the oil boom. The second cycle of CHNAs was completed between 2014 and 2016. Now it is time to look at how the prioritized needs have changed against the backdrop of oil's downturn. What community concerns are constant? Which have dissipated as a result of the slowdown? What new concerns are emerging as the oil boom moves from the discovery to the maintenance phase? The lingering effects of the oil boom remain to be determined, and consulting qualitative data from community members living in the boom area provides firsthand accounts about the impacts in people's own words.[2]

CHNA Overview

In order to qualify as a tax-exempt charitable organization, hospitals have long been required to demonstrate a strong commitment to promoting the health of their surrounding communities. Typically, the community benefit has come in the form of charity care where the hospital provides free or reduced cost care to patients who are unable to pay for it (IRS 1956). Due to concerns that hospitals were not adequately contributing to improving their local communities, the ACA increased the community benefit reporting and mandated that all nonprofit hospitals conduct a community health needs assessment or pay an annual fine (IRS 2011).

The purpose of the assessment is to describe the health of the local community, identify needs or service gaps, prioritize concerns, and identify ways to address them. Assessing community health is not new; hospitals have been conducting assessments and identifying health service inequalities for decades (IRS 1969). However, the ACA mandate has institutionalized the routine practice of conducting a CHNA and, as a result, has provided data that are systematically reported and publicly available. The three-year cycle affords a comparative analysis of needs identified at a certain time, needs that remain over the course of the years, and new needs that emerge. With the second cycle of CHNAs completed, we are able to benchmark needs over time. The backdrop of the oil boom and subsequent downturn provide an exciting time to analyze the community health concerns that were prioritized in the two assessment cycles.

---

[2] See the appendix at the end of the chapter for a list of CHNA reports.

Methods to Conduct a CHNA

While the methods to conduct a CHNA are vague, the federal guidelines stipulate that the assessment process involve broad community input, including participation from public health experts and those who interact with medically underserved, low-income, and minority populations (IRS 2011). Although methods differ between assessments, as a whole, the goal of a CHNA is to solicit community input related to health and healthcare. The CHNA process used with North Dakota hospitals derives from National Center for Rural Health Works and Catholic Health Association models. It is informed by both primary data, related to community member interviews, focus groups, and surveys, and secondary data, related to health behaviors, conditions, risks, and outcomes.

The CHNA process is informed by a community-based participatory research framework whereby the researchers enlist community members as co-participants in the research process. In this way, community members are invited to identify not only community problems but also ways to address them. This act of doing research *with*—not *on*—participants is a key characteristic of community-based participatory research and fosters rapport between researchers and participants as they are both unified in a common goal to improve community health (Guba and Lincoln 1994; Ainsworth and Schmidtlein 2013). Moreover, the resulting partnership between community members and academic, organizational, healthcare, and governmental representatives allows for multiple perspectives and expertise to engage and develop solutions to community health concerns (Schulz, Israel, and Lantz 2003).

CHNA Process

Seven out of thirty-six critical access hospitals in North Dakota are located in communities within the oil patch (Crosby, Dickinson, Kenmare, Stanley, Tioga, Watford City, and Williston). In each of these communities, one-on-one key informant interviews were conducted in person or by phone with selected members who were identified as having insights into the community's health needs. Generally, four to nine interviews were conducted in each community. Topics included community assets and challenges, general health of the community, community concerns, and suggestions for improving the community's health. Focus groups consisted of 11–25 community members with representation from schools, faith-based organizations, social service agencies, healthcare services, senior services, and businesses and economic agencies, as well as law enforcement and elected officials. The same questions posed in the key informant interviews were asked during the focus group.

Content analysis of the responses from key informant interviews, focus groups, and open-ended survey questions was conducted using a grounded theory approach. Grounded theory provides order from the plethora of feedback by developing categories through an ongoing process of comparing units of data. This constant comparative method allows for flexibility within the categories; as the analysis continues, themes emerge and an analytical framework takes shape (Lindlof and Taylor 2011). For example, responses such as "shortage of primary care physicians" and "not enough healthcare staff" or "lack of specialists" or "need more docs" were grounded into the category of "healthcare workforce shortage."

Additionally, each community customized a survey that was available at local businesses and health clinics. For broader distribution, an electronic version of the survey was promoted in local media outlets and through social media. The survey tool was designed to gather residents' perceptions about community assets and concerns, understand the attitudes about the overall health of the community and hear suggestions for improvement, and learn how local healthcare services were used. Average survey response rates hovered around 10–15 percent of the county's population, which is slightly lower than the 20 percent average rate for unsolicited surveys (Fink 2003). The survey was not intended to be a scientific or statistically valid sampling of the population, but another tool to gain qualitative data.

Sample Characteristics

The survey asked several demographic questions about gender, race, age, education, employment status, marital status, and annual income. In both assessment cycles, the majority of respondents identified as Caucasian females, with almost twice as many women completing surveys as men. The majority of respondents were married, worked full time, had a technical degree or a bachelor's degree, and were considered longtime residents, living in the community for twenty or more years. Mean annual household income was reported between $100,000 and $149,000. There was a slight change in age between the two cycles. The majority of respondents in the first CHNA cycle were 55–64 years of age, whereas the second CHNA cycle had younger participants, most being 25–34 years of age. Relative to North Dakota state demographics, respondent characteristics were representative of demographics for oil patch counties (U.S. Census Bureau 2010).

Prioritization of Needs

Once the data were analyzed and synthesized, they were presented at a community meeting. After a discussion of the findings, community members were asked to identify on a ballot what they perceived as the top five community health needs. Prioritization criteria included a need's burden on the community, its scope, its severity, or its urgency. The results were totaled and the most frequently cited concerns were included as priority needs in the CHNA report. This prioritized list fulfilled the mandate of the ACA, offered guidance for what the hospital should address in its implementation strategy, and provided an emerging picture of community-articulated concerns.

Oil Patch Concerns: Then and Now

While there was not a systematic documentation of concerns from North Dakota's first oil boom, the effects of oil development as identified in the 1958 *Williston Report* reveal considerable community impacts. If a community-based health needs assessment had been implemented during the 1951–4 timeframe in Williston, the prioritized needs would likely have included transportation, housing, and strains on social and public services. Table 12.1 summarizes needs conveyed in *The Williston Report*.

TABLE 12.1.
SUMMARY OF PRIORITIZED NEEDS: 1951–4

Needs
1. Lack of transportation resources
2. Lack of housing
3. Lack of social services
4. Overcrowded schools
5. Strained communication resources

Transportation needs stemmed from increased wear and tear on the roads from heavy truck traffic and increased traffic. Housing was deemed substandard and rents were high. Social services were taxed, both in welfare and state employment services. Migrants who moved to Williston to capitalize on the oil boom often got stranded there, which increased welfare case management, including a rise in cases of child neglect. Also, increases in population ushered in demand for workers and jobs. Other significant problems included strains on public services such as schools and communication systems. Schools were overcrowded and facilities had to be expanded to accommodate more students. Communication systems like the postal service were overburdened to accommodate the increase in commercial and residential mail (Campbell, current volume).

To compare how the needs of the 2008–14 oil boom compare to those described sixty years earlier, a methodical review of each community's prioritized needs was conducted and individual needs were aggregated with an eye to emerging trends in oil-impacted communities. An inventory of community member concerns voiced in response to the 2008–14 oil boom provides a new perspective on social impacts. Traffic safety and housing are needs shared between then and now. However, the focus on healthcare and mental health shortages, which are largely absent in the 1958 *Report*, received the most attention now.

In the recently conducted CHNAs, similar methodologies were used in both assessment cycles, allowing for a valid comparison with the same seven critical access hospitals in the oil patch. This consistency in methods provides the ability to examine the impact on communities and benchmark change over time. Table 12.2 displays the significant needs that were most frequently ranked as most prevalent, most persistent, and most substantial.

TABLE 12.2.
THE BAKKEN: ASSESSMENT CYCLES

CHNA Cycle 1: 2011–13	CHNA Cycle 2: 2014–16
1. Healthcare workforce shortage	1. Mental health (including alcohol and drug use and abuse)
2. Mental health (including excessive rates of drinking)	2. Healthcare workforce shortage
3. Access to needed equipment/facilities	3. Lack of child care
4. Traffic safety	4. Lack of resources for agin population
5. Lack of affordable housing	5. Rising costs of health insurance

Since the top two needs received significantly more votes than the others, the focus of this analysis is on the top two prioritized concerns from each CHNA cycle. At a glance, the prioritized needs have not changed significantly over the span of the past two assessments, but a closer analysis of how the needs are articulated reveals the nuances and impacts of the oil boom. Healthcare workforce shortage and mental health remain the most pressing community concerns, with alternating order of importance, during the peak of the boom as well as during the downturn. Yet the ways in which these concerns are expressed show granular details of community impact. To better understand the circumstances characterizing the categories of healthcare workforce shortage and mental health, specific responses are provided in community members' own words and are then contextualized against the backdrop of the oil boom.

CHNA Cycle 1 (2011–13), First Prioritized Need: Healthcare Workforce Shortage

In the first assessment cycle, community member feedback indicated a variety of concerns relating to access to healthcare providers, retention and recruitment of providers, and increased burden on emergency medical services. Therefore, the category of healthcare workforce shortage encompasses these needs.

In regards to healthcare availability, the influx of people led to more demand for services. Patients experienced long waits and limited appointments: "There are long waiting times to get in. We have the same number of providers, but probably three times the population."[3] The increase in demand also lessened rapport between providers and their patients; community members perceived this tension as doctors were forced to see more patients and spend less time with each: "My doc doesn't have time to chat with me anymore."

Additionally, the demand for healthcare backlogged appointments so patients either had to wait months or travel to alternate facilities if they couldn't afford to wait: "No appointments are available. An appointment just to get seen is four to five weeks out. There's no walk-in clinic or urgent care." The extent of traveling for healthcare added to the stress and financial impact on patients, in addition to delivering an economic hit on the community: "There's frustration over trying to get in to see a provider. It can be a 3–4 day wait, so they go out of town." For some community members, a visit to the doctor may include expenses for gas, food, and lodging on top of medical bills.

Retention and Recruitment of Providers

The problem posed by the increase in demand for healthcare services was compounded by the challenges communities faced to retain and recruit providers. High turnover among healthcare providers impacted access to services and

---

[3] All unattributed quotations come from community members' responses gathered during the CHNA process.

continuity of care: "The staff is overworked and there are not enough doctors and nurses for the current population to receive a sustainable, high quality of service." Some of the smaller critical access hospitals had only one doctor on staff. The increase in patients strained already limited resources: "We need a second doctor to relieve the on-call burden resting on the sole doctor." Some medical professionals left to take advantage of the handsome pay the oil industry offered: "We don't have the funds to pay our healthcare staff the wages they need to compete with the oil field business. We need to pay the employees that are willing to make this their home competitive wages so that we can focus on keeping workers long term." Others left town due to the extent of change experienced in their community or their inability to afford the skyrocketing rent. During this time, Williston was listed as the most expensive place to rent a home in the United States, with Dickinson positioned as fourth most expensive (McCormick 2014).

Moreover, with the influx of population and the increased need for services, hospitals had little time to focus on recruiting efforts: "Our community is changing very rapidly with the oil industry. Healthcare employee recruitment has not been able to keep up." Rural healthcare recruiting is a consistent challenge; of the primary care physicians who practice in North Dakota, 75 percent practice in urban areas (Center for Rural Health 2017). There are almost twice as many patients per physician in large rural areas than urban areas, and more than five times as many patients per physician in small/isolated rural areas (see Trinity Kenmare Community Hospital 2016). Recruiting specialists is even harder.

Nationally, the healthcare workforce shortage has been widely documented in the United States (Hempell et al. 2016; Derksen and Whelan 2009; Florell 2009; Commonwealth Fund 2017). According to the National Rural Health Association, demand for more healthcare professionals is expected to rise with aging Baby Boomers (Burrows, Suh, and Hamann 2012). With over 20 percent of Americans living in rural areas, yet served by less than 12 percent of the nation's physicians, healthcare workforce shortage is a formidable national problem (Hempel et al. 2016). Rural economic income disparities, smaller numbers of rural health professional training sites, and lower reimbursement rates provide context to this problem (Hart, Salsberg, Phillips, and Lishner 2012).

Emergency Services

A plurality of responses pertained to emergency services that are unique to the oil boom. Typically, the nature of most ER calls prior to the oil boom related to farming and ranching accidents, fires, and traffic accidents. However, the nature and frequency of the calls has changed since the oil boom: "Trauma here can be so diverse—crushed by rig, crushed by equipment, falling off rig, stomped by cattle." The diversity of calls also necessitates specialized training to deal with the chemical and environmental hazards of oil extraction.

Oil work is physical and dangerous, with an increased risk for accidents because of the heavy machinery, hazardous chemicals, long hours, and inclement weather conditions.

From 2009–13, usage of ER services in the Bakken quadrupled. Plus, the increase in wait times to see a doctor prompted greater usage of the emergency room: "It's not uncommon to wait 4–8 hours to get seen in the ER. If the ambulance brings you in, you go to the top of the list, so people are calling 911 for little things." Overuse of the ER taxed personnel, where concerns of quality of care were prevalent: "We need more full time emergency services personnel. I feel that they are overworked. This may cause concerns in patient care, and things may get missed that are clinically significant."

It is important to note that many emergency medical services were provided by volunteer squads. Although in the past volunteer EMS squads may have been able to meet the community's needs, the demand exceeded the supply. Additionally, the amount of ER activity was taking its toll on the volunteers, professionally and personally. Members of the volunteer squads may have been granted leave time from work to attend to a call, but the increase in calls hampered work productivity: "Some employers pay volunteers for when they're on a call, but not all employers do." While communities have considered paying their EMS volunteers a salary, it is often economically unfeasible: "We need to look at professionally staffed EMS. It could take up to $1 million/year to do that appropriately."

Comments from EMS volunteer squad members convey the extent of exhaustion and personal strain:

- "The only way I can get away from the calls is if I leave town."
- "We see daily traffic accidents."
- "I am so, so tired."
- "I don't sleep well anymore."

CHNA Cycle 1 (2011–13), Second Prioritized Need: Mental Health, Including Excessive Rates of Drinking

The second most prioritized community concern during the first CHNA cycle pertained to alcohol abuse and excessive rates of drinking. Embedded in this need is a larger problem of addiction, related to both alcohol and drugs, and the need for counseling and services. While this is classified as a behavioral issue, it is often associated with underlying mental health issues.

One trend to emerge from the community member responses that cannot be ignored is that of ascribing addiction and drug usage to "transients." Almost half of all CHNA comments related to this need referenced transients or oil workers:

- "Addiction and substance abuse are becoming a bigger issue with a larger volume of transient people."
- "It's the nature of oil rig work. Some guy's working 140 hours and it's hard to stay awake so they're reaching for prescription drugs to help stay awake. Our company has had to get rid of multiple employees because of alcohol issues."
- "Substance abuse treatment is a need with the increase in transient population."
- "Addiction and substance abuse has gone up since the oil boom."
- "Addiction and substance abuse is a major problem on reservation and oil fields. We need an addiction counselor."
- "Transient workers transport drugs."
- "Surge in the abuse of bath salts, cocaine and meth."
- "Everyone I talk to in town says there is an increase in drug use because of transient workers and the growing workforce."

This attribution aligns with an ethnocentric attitude where newcomers are viewed as "outsiders." As one oil boom resident said, "The people that come here to work are not the cream of the crop" (personal communication, October 28, 2015). The construction of an "outsider" category differs from longtime residents who are viewed as "locals"; the two groups are perceived to have different values and views which shape their identities and interactions with each other (Matarrita-Cascante et al. 2017). This classification creates an "us" versus "them" dichotomy which works to divide the community and implicates "transients" as being responsible for bringing the problems. The "newcomer" and "longtimer" distinction is common in boomtown studies where fear of crime and drugs is indicative of social disruption experienced in boom communities (Freudenberg 1982). Yet this negative attitude is missing from the 1958 *Report*. While newcomers were called "riff raff" and "alien people," there was little overt antagonism exhibited toward them and they were generally accepted into the community. Once the two groups interacted, their attitudes and opinions of each other were overwhelmingly positive (Campbell, p. 253).

The changes in population may account for some of the differences in intergroup attitudes. With Williams County witnessing a 32 percent population change from 2010–13 and neighboring McKenzie and Mountrail Counties reporting 46 percent and 22 percent population changes respectively, the number of newcomers arriving in the oil patch was overwhelming (U.S. Census Bureau 2010). By comparison, in the 1950s, Williams County experienced a 27 percent population increase whereas Mountrail County reported a decline of 5.5 percent (Willis, p. 53). Rapid population growth can lead to a breakdown in municipal services, intensifying economic costs to provide community services to new residents (Little 1977), and increases in crime, traffic, accidents, and suicide (Kennedy and Mehra 1985; Seydlitz 1993). Previous researchers looking at boomtown communities have concluded that they enter a period of crisis and loss of traditional routines and attitudes, disrupting individuals' mental health, worldview, and social networks (England and Albrecht 1984). The population influx and resulting social disruption may have hindered community organizations' and residents' ability to reach out to new people.

Regardless of perceptual and population differences, addiction and drug use are the symptoms of a larger mental health problem. The emphasis on mental health aligns with boomtown phenomena and extraction scholarship stemming from research conducted in Colorado, Utah, Louisiana, West Virginia, Pennsylvania, and Canada. Rapid changes in population and development are associated with mental health problems (Bacigalupi and Freudenburg 1983). Research on energy boomtowns has shown that the incoming workforce accounts for a substantial portion of the service demand. Many accounts have testified to the characteristics of the initial surge of oil boom workers: mainly men, unskilled but resilient, coming to North Dakota to earn money to make a better life for themselves (Rao 2014). Yet this workforce often lacked housing, health insurance, and money management skills once payday came (Bohnenkamp et al. 2011).

In 2014, when oil was at $100 per barrel and cash flow was high, crime, drugs and prostitution rings flourished (Horwitz 2014; Ruddell and Ray, current volume). The limited infrastructure of these small, rural, western prairie towns and the harsh winter climate may have exacerbated the temptations. As one resident stated, "Once you bought a new truck, there isn't much to spend your money on out here except booze, drugs, and women" (personal communication, December 2, 2015). A report issued to the Center for Community Vitality regarding Bakken oil counties stated, "Most rural communities do not have experience with economic growth, so the real issue is learning how to effectively deal with that growth" (Bohnenkamp et al. 2011, 22).

Entrepreneurs, drug cartels, and organized criminals flocked to western North Dakota to try to capitalize on the emerging market (Valencia 2015). With thousands of men away from home, holed up in remote places with cash in their pockets, the Bakken was a ripe market for sex trafficking (Boyle 2015; Berg Burin, current volume). A rise in narcotics and opiates, such as heroin and methamphetamines, as well as human trafficking had the FBI worried (Valencia 2015). These circumstances provide context regarding the initial mental health concern. Community participants echoed the nationwide concern over the increased distribution and use of heroin. According to the Centers for Disease Control and Prevention (2015), heroin use in the United States has increased among men and women of all age groups and income levels. It has more than doubled among young adults in the 18–25 age bracket in the past decade.

CHNA Cycle 2 (2014–16), First Prioritized Need: Mental Health, Including Alcohol and Drugs among Youth

In the second CHNA cycle, the same focus on addiction emerged, but the concern centered on youths' alcohol and drug use: "Youth mental health is the most important because in my mind, it drives all the other issues. Unwell youth make unwell adults." Some community members attributed teen alcohol and drug usage to broken homes, low self-esteem, new drug mixtures, and depression. A clear theme to emerge among community member comments is the need for more mental health and substance abuse resources and funding: "Mental health and substance abuse needs more resources to hire people. We need early intervention and more dollars for kids."

Of note was the fact that oil field workers or perceived "outsiders" were mentioned only once: "Mental abuse treatment services are needed here. At most of the child protection meetings there [are] addiction issues and also with the oil field workers that is a high rate." This change in perception may suggest that oil field workers are integrating into the community. Length of residence has been associated with fear of outsiders and crime. In boom communities, five years is generally the threshold for when outsiders are perceived as locals

(Freudenberg 1982). This second cycle of CHNAs marks a five-year timespan from the peak of the oil boom and may indicate less division between outsider and longtime residents.

Consistent with oil boom research, mental health problems and clinical case-loads often increase for non-oil boom workers (Bacigalupi and Freudenburg 1983). Age plays a significant factor when assessing quality of life in boom-towns (Finkle 2015). As reinforced by the community member comments above, youths living in boomtowns are found to be more alienated, isolated, and confused than other youth (Freudenburg 1979) whereas longtime residents often retreat as a result of experiencing loss of sense of community (Cortese and Jones 1977). Further research by Freudenburg (1984) indicates adolescents exhibit less satisfaction and greater alienation in post-boomtown communities.

Now, although the oil boom has slowed and much of the workforce has left, it is not necessarily the case that the problems have disappeared. The price of drugs, like the price for oil, has decreased, making them more accessible. The price for meth has dropped 75 percent from the height of the boom, down to $800 per ounce (Monke 2016). "Methamphetamine use in North Dakota is epidemic," according to Stark County State's Attorney Tom Henning; methamphetamine arrests increased 22 percent from 2012 to 2016 (Mook 2017). Use of heroin and other opiates like fentanyl are causing overdoses and deaths, and with so many people addicted to these drugs and unable to hold down a job, there is a rise in burglaries, theft, and traffic violations (Mook 2017).

CHNA Cycle 2 (2014–16), Second Prioritized Need: Healthcare Workforce Shortage, Including Access to Aftercare and Specialists

While healthcare workforce remained an oft-cited concern in the second cycle of CHNAs, it was downgraded to the second prioritized need. The way it was expressed in this period focused on a desire for extended care, in the form of evening and weekend hours, and access to specialists: "We need access to healthcare on weekends without having to go to the ER." Community participants expressed concern over the times during which they were able to see a medical provider outside of the emergency room: "I have gone to the walk-in clinic in town at noon and been told they were not taking any more patients for the day." A clinic's operating hours are similar to the hours worked by an average working adult (for example, 8:00am to 5:00pm, Monday through Friday), which can limit the ability of working adults and school children to access those healthcare providers: "Doctor will not make appointments after 3:00pm. Many people cannot take off work to go to the doctor. I work until 3:45 and need to have late day appointments." Keeping a healthcare appointment may mean taking time off work, which may pose financial and professional consequences.

In terms of specialists, while demand exists, it may not be large enough to warrant a fulltime provider of specialty services. Some specialists are available on a rotating weekly or monthly basis, but that schedule may not be frequent enough for some. Specific requests for specialists included pediatrics, OB-GYN, dermatology, cancer care, and pain management.

What Has Changed in the Last Two CHNA Cycles?

Taking inventory of community member concerns voiced in response to the 2008–14 oil boom provides new perspective on social impacts. While the prevailing concerns from the most recent oil boom are focused on healthcare and mental health, traffic safety and housing are needs that are shared between then and now.

Healthcare Workforce Shortage

In both assessment cycles, the lack of healthcare workers impacted community members' ability to access healthcare. In the first cycle, this need centered on service delivery, recruitment, and emergency services, whereas in the second cycle, it was predominantly expressed as limited access to after-care and specialists. This change in articulation from service delivery and ER services to aftercare and access to specialists highlights a healthcare need that is less acute. With the drop in oil prices during the second assessment cycle, populations declined and development slowed, which may have decreased the need for healthcare providers and ER services.

Mental Health: Addictive Communities

Specific to North Dakota's oil boom, previous research identified the themes of social disruption (due to rapid population influx), loss of identity, and uncertainty and anxiety (Becker 2016). The emphasis on mental health services, including alcohol and drug use and abuse and the need for treatment centers, not only aligns with these themes but also supports the social disruption hypothesis. However, this need is unique to the recent oil booms. The 1958 *Report* claims there was not a remarkable increase in crime or immoral activity and drunkenness was swiftly addressed (Campbell, p. 259; for a contrary view, see Berg Burin, current volume).

As substance abuse was prioritized as a community concern in both assessment cycles, the underlying addictive theme carried over to other facets of oil boom phenomena. North Dakota may be classified by what Freudenburg (1992) calls an addictive economy, which is marked by continual boom and bust cycles. North Dakota is vulnerable to this addictive tendency due to the volatility of oil prices, the uncertainties of employment and development, and the imprecise measures of oil forecasting.

While community members' responses attest to the similarities in experience with community members from other extraction communities, the extent of their disruption may be uniquely their own. Although this author has previously questioned whether the oil boom has been a blessing or a curse for western North Dakota communities (Becker 2016), Freudenburg (1984) has argued that a better question to ask is to what degree communities experience negative change. This question assumes oil boom communities experience adverse conditions and positions the oil boom as a curse. While no two communities experience energy development the same way, characteristics such as population density, history with extractive industries, and type of extraction may affect residents' perceptions (Finkle 2015). In this regard, North Dakota should fare pretty well as longtime residents may recall previous boom and bust cycles.

In addition, there still may be a silver lining if we extend our scope and look at the health of oil patch communities longitudinally. Boomtown research has shown that a recovery phase occurs after the bust, where community members adapt to their new community and experience enhanced levels of community satisfaction and dimensions of wellbeing ten to fifteen years after the boom (Brown, Dorins, and Krannich 2005; Smith, Krannich, and Hunter 2001). This was the case at the tail end of the 1950s boom as it was reported that one year post-boom, community conditions were stabilized and settled (Campbell, current volume).

The prediction by some analysts that oil prices will remain stagnant over the next few years may help North Dakota to transition into a recovery phase (FIBO Group 2017). However, the recent rise in oil prices and production has left Lynn Helms, the Director of North Dakota's Department of Mineral Resources, tentatively optimistic (Hughlett 2018). In fact, the state may be gearing up for another mini-boom, with the increase in oil production projected to be on pace to beat the 2014 record (Hughlett 2018; Flynn, current volume). Either way, the uncertainty of the future can add to the overall anxiety and strain on mental health.

Implications

The CHNA's design emphasis on qualitative data highlights the value of conducting key informant interviews and focus groups as a legitimate data source to help take the pulse of the community. This methodological consideration has special significance in rural areas where there is a dearth of healthcare research (Hart et al. 2002). Moreover, gaining access to rural community members can be difficult for researchers who are often perceived as outsiders and regarded with skepticism (Becker 2015). Outsider bias runs strong in rural areas and is especially acute in the medical profession, where residents prefer to interact with long-established local residents rather than newcomers (Bushy 2006). As Kathleen Norris writes in her book *Dakota: A Spiritual Geography*, "an expert is someone who's fifty miles from home" (1993, 55). This statement attests to the tendency of locals to refuse to accept information that comes from the "outside" world, including accounts published in national media.

Since this analysis stems from community members' views and voices, the hope is that not only will residents listen to the community health concerns, but also accept and act upon them. The inclusion of local voices helps to lend credibility to insider knowledge, and the alignment of their responses with boomtown phenomena on a national scale validates their lived experiences.

Conclusion

The need for more healthcare workforce and mental health resources provides a glimpse of the impacts that the oil boom has caused at the community level. As a research tool, the systematic and cyclical CHNA data can provide meaningful and relevant data that aid in understanding lived experiences. One of the unanticipated outcomes of the Affordable Care Act is that it has produced a data set that adds a humanistic quality to the oil boom story. The prioritized list of community concerns can inform policy makers and stakeholders about places where more resources are needed to target solutions aimed at addressing the needs of North Dakota constituents. While we wait for future CHNA cycles to occur, it is important to compare concerns and benchmark change over time. This longitudinal research sheds light on how contemporary energy development evolves with time and how the ebbs and flows of oil boom activity affect community health.

References

Bacigalupi, Linda M., and William R. Freudenburg. 1983. "Increased Mental Health Caseloads in an Energy Boomtown." *Administration in Mental Health* 10 (4): 306–22.

Becker, Karin L. 2015. "Conducting Community Health Needs Assessments in Rural Communities: Lessons Learned." *Health Promotion Practice* 16 (1): 15–19. http://dx.doi.org/10.1177/1524839914555887.

Becker, Karin L. 2016. "The Paradox of Plenty: Blessings and Curses in the Oil Patch." In *The Bakken Goes Boom: Oil and the Changing Geographies of Western North Dakota*, edited by William Caraher and Kyle Conway, 11–29. Grand Forks: Digital Press at the University of North Dakota.

Bohnenkamp, Shelby, Alex Finken, Emily McCallum, Audrey Putz, and G.A. Goreham. 2011. *Concerns of the North Dakota Bakken Oil Counties*. Fargo: North Dakota State University Center for Community Vitality.

Boyle, Darren. 2015. "North Dakota's Oil Boom Creates 'Emerging Market' for Mexican Drugs and Prostitution Trafficking Gangs." *Daily Mail*, December 15. http://www.dailymail.co.uk/news/article-3361220/North-Dakota-s-oil-boom-creates-emerging-market-Mexican-drugs-prostitution-trafficking-gangs.html.

Brown, Ralph B., Shawn F. Dorins, and Richard S. Krannich. 2005. "The Boom-Bust-Recovery Cycle: Dynamics of Change in Community Satisfaction and Social Integration in Delta, Utah." *Rural Sociology* 70 (1): 28–49. https://doi.org/10.1526/0036011053294673.

Burrows, Elizabeth, Ryung Suh, and Danielle Hamann. 2012. *Health Care Workforce Distribution and Shortage Issues in Rural America*. National Rural Health Association Policy Brief. https://www.ruralhealthweb.org/getattachment/Advocate/Policy-Documents/HealthCareWorkforceDistributionandShortageJanuary2012.pdf.aspx?lang=en-US.

Center for Disease Control and Prevention. 2015. "Today's Heroin Epidemic." https://www.cdc.gov/vitalsigns/heroin/index.html.

Center for Rural Health. 2017. *Demographics of Primary Care Physicians in North Dakota*. Grand Forks: University of North Dakota School of Medicine and Health Sciences. https://ruralhealth.und.edu/assets/623-1802/demographics-of-nd-primary-care-physicians.pdf.

Commonwealth Fund. 2017. "Transforming Care: Reporting on Health System Improvement." March 30. http://www.commonwealthfund.org/publications/newsletters/transforming-care/2017/march/in-focus.

Cortese, Charles, and Bernie Jones. 1977. "The Sociological Analysis of Boom-towns." *Western Sociological Review* 8 (1): 76–90.

Derksen, Daniel J., and Ellen-Marie Whelan. 2009. "Closing the Health Care Workforce Gap." Center for American Progress. https://www. americanprogress.org/wp-content/uploads/issues/2010/01/pdf/health_care_workforce.pdf.

England, J. Lynn, and Stan L. Albrecht. 1984. "Boomtowns and Social Disruption." *Rural Sociological Society* 49 (2): 230–46.

FIBO Group. 2017. "Oil Price to Remain Stagnant." Investing. com, October 11. https://www.investing.com/analysis/ oil-price-to-remain-stagnant-200218166.

Fink, Arlene. 2003. *How to Sample in Surveys*, 2nd edition. Thousand Oaks, CA: Sage.

Florell, Melissa Loftis. 2009. "Rural Health Care Workforce: Opportunities to Improve Care Delivery." *Center for Rural Affairs* 6. http://files.cfra.org/pdf/ HealthCare_Workforce.pdf.

Freudenburg, William R. 1979. "Boomtown's Youth." Paper Presented at the Annual Meeting of the Rural Sociological Society. Burlington, VT.

Freudenburg, William R. 1982. "The Impacts of Rapid Growth on the Social and Personal Wellbeing of Local Community Residents." In *Coping with Rapid Growth in Rural Areas*, edited by B. Weber and R. Howell, 137–70. Boulder, CO: Westview.

Freudenburg, William R. 1984. "Differential Impacts of Rapid Community Growth." *American Sociological Review* 49: 697–715.

Freudenburg, William R. 1992. "Addictive Economies: Extractive Industries and Vulnerable Localities in a Changing World Economy." *Rural Sociology* 57 (3): 305–32.

Hart, Gary L., Edward Salsberg, Debra M. Phillips, and Denise M. Lishner. 2002. "Rural Health Care Providers in the United States." *Journal of Rural Health* 18 (5): 211–32.

Hempel, S., M. Maggard Gibbons, J.G. Ulloa, I. Macqueen, I. Miake-Lye, J. Beroes, and P. Shekelle. 2016. "Rural Healthcare Workforce: A Systematic Review." *Management eBrief* 112. https://www. hsrd.research.va.gov/publications/management_briefs/default. cfm?ManagementBriefsMenu=eBrief-no112.

Horwitz, Sari. 2014. "Dark Side of the Boom." *Washington Post*, September 28. http://www.washingtonpost.com/sf/national/2014/09/28/ dark-side-of-the-boom/.

328

Hughlett, Mike. 2018. "North Dakota Expects to Hit Oil Production Record in 2018." *Star Tribune*, January 16. http://www.startribune.com/north-dakota-expects-to-hit-oil-production-record-in-2018/469580453/.

Internal Revenue Service (IRS). 1956. Rev. Rul. 56-185, 1956-1 C.B. 202, 203.

Internal Revenue Service (IRS). 1969. Rev. Rul 69-545, 1969-2 C.B. 117.

Internal Revenue Service (IRS). 2011. Internal Revenue Bulletin: 2011-30. http://www.irs.gov/irb/2011-30_IRB/ar08.html.

Kennedy, Leslie W., and N. Mehra. 1985. "Effects of Social Change on Well-Being: Boom and Bust in a Western Canadian City." *Social Indicators Research* 17 (2): 101–13.

Lindlof, Thomas R., and Bryan C. Taylor. 2011. *Qualitative Communication Research Methods.* Thousand Oaks, CA: Sage.

Little, Ronald L. 1977. "Some Social Consequences of Boom Towns." *North Dakota Law Review* 53: 401–26.

Matarrita-Cascante, David, Hugo Zunino, and Johana Sagner-Tapia. 2017. "Amenity/lifestyle Migration in the Chilean Andes: Understanding the Views of 'the Other' and Its Effects on Integrated Community Development." *Sustainability* 9 (9): 1–19.

McCormick, Rich. 2014. "A North Dakota Town is the Most Expensive Place to Rent an Apartment in the United States." *The Verge*, February 19. https://www.theverge.com/2014/2/19/5425040/williston-north-dakota-most-expensive-place-to-rent-in-us.

Monke, Dustin. 2016. "Post-oil Boom, Drug Prices Fall in Oil Patch as Gang Trafficking Increases." *Bismarck Tribune*, July 2. http://bismarcktribune.com/bakken/post-oil-boom-drug-prices-fall-in-oil-patch-as-article_92256837-b87d-5f38-8191-58fb1ae00453.html.

Mook, Sydney. 2017. "Drugs Still a Problem in the Bakken Since Oil Boom." *West Fargo Pioneer*, October 21. http://www.westfargopioneer.com/news/4346717-drugs-still-problem-bakken-oil-boom.

Rao, Myra. 2014. "Searching for the Good Life in the Bakken Oil Fields." *The Atlantic*, September 29. https://www.theatlantic.com/business/archive/2014/09/searching-for-the-good-life-in-the-bakken-oil-fields/380677/.

Schulz, Amy J., Israel, Barbara A., and Lantz, Paula. 2003. "Instrument for Evaluating Dimensions of Group Dynamics within Community-based Participatory Research Partnerships." *Evaluation and Program Planning* 26 (3), 249–62.

Seydlitz, Ruth, Shirley Laska, Daphne Spain, Elizabeth W. Triche, and Karen L. Bishop. 1993. "Development and Social Problems: The Impact of the Offshore Oil Industry on Suicide and Homicide Rates." *Rural Sociology* 58: 93–110. http://dx.doi.org/10.1111/j.1549-0831.1993.tb00484.x.

Smith, Michael D., Richard S. Krannich, and Lori M. Hunter. 2002. "Growth, Decline, Stability, and Disruption: A Longitudinal Analysis of Social Well-Being in Four Western Rural Communities." *Rural Sociology* 66: 442–50. http://dx.doi.org/10.1111/j.1549-0831.2001.tb00075.x.

Trinity Kenmare Community Hospital. 2016. *Community Health Needs Assessment Report*. Kenmare, ND: Trinity Kenmare Community Hospital. https://www.trinityhealth.org/wp-content/uploads/2018/09/Kenmare_Report063016.pdf.

U.S. Census Bureau. 2010. "Quick Facts North Dakota." Retrieved from https://www.census.gov/quickfacts/fact/table/nd/PST045217.

Valencia, Nick. 2015. "North Dakota's Oil Boom Creates 'Emerging Market' for Mexico's Cartels." CNN, December 14. http://www.cnn.com/2015/12/14/us/north-dakota-bakken-oil-mexico-drug-cartels/index.html.

Appendix: List of Community Health Needs Assessment Reports

2011–13

Becker, Karin L., and Ken Hall. *Community Health Needs Assessment: Mountrail County Health Center [Stanley]*. The North Dakota Medicare Rural Hospital Flexibility (Flex) Program. Grand Forks: University of North Dakota School of Medicine and Health Sciences, 2013.

Becker, Karin L., and Ken Hall. *Community Health Needs Assessment: St. Joseph's Hospital and Health Center [Dickinson]*. The North Dakota Medicare Rural Hospital Flexibility (Flex) Program. Grand Forks: University of North Dakota School of Medicine and Health Sciences, 2013.

Becker, Karin L., and Ken Hall. *Community Health Needs Assessment: Tioga Medical Center*. The North Dakota Medicare Rural Hospital Flexibility (Flex) Program. Grand Forks: University of North Dakota School of Medicine and Health Sciences, 2012–13.

Hall, Ken and Karin L. Becker. *McKenzie County Healthcare Systems [Watford City]*. The North Dakota Medicare Rural Hospital Flexibility (Flex) Program. Grand Forks: University of North Dakota School of Medicine and Health Sciences, 2012–13.

Hall, Ken and Karin L. Becker. *Mercy Medical Center [Williston]*. The North Dakota Medicare Rural Hospital Flexibility (Flex) Program. Grand Forks: University of North Dakota School of Medicine and Health Sciences, 2012–13.

Trinity Kenmare Community Hospital. *Community Health Needs Assessment and Implementation Strategy*. Kenmare, ND: Trinity Kenmare Community Hospital, 2013. https://ruralhealth.und.edu/assets/340-5608/2016-trinity-kenmare-community-hospital.pdf.

Ward, Jody, Marlene Miller, Shawnda Schroeder, Angie Lockwood, and Shelly Davis. *St. Luke's Hospital [Crosby]*. The North Dakota Medicare Rural Hospital Flexibility (Flex) Program. Grand Forks: University of North Dakota School of Medicine and Health Sciences, 2011.

2014–16

Dickson, Lynette, and Kylie Nissen. *Community Health Needs Assessment: CHI St. Alexius Health, Williston, North Dakota.* The North Dakota Medicare Rural Hospital Flexibility (Flex) Program. Grand Forks: University of North Dakota School of Medicine and Health Sciences, 2016.

Dickson, Lynette, and Kylie Nissen. *Community Health Needs Assessment: Mountrail County Medical Center [Stanley].* The North Dakota Medicare Rural Hospital Flexibility (Flex) Program. Grand Forks: University of North Dakota School of Medicine and Health Sciences, 2016.

Dickson, Lynette, and Kylie Nissen. *Community Health Needs Assessment: St. Luke's Hospital [Crosby].* The North Dakota Medicare Rural Hospital Flexibility (Flex) Program. Grand Forks: University of North Dakota School of Medicine and Health Sciences, 2016.

Dickson, Lynette, and Kylie Nissen. *Community Health Needs Assessment: Tioga Medical Center.* The North Dakota Medicare Rural Hospital Flexibility (Flex) Program. Grand Forks: University of North Dakota School of Medicine and Health Sciences, 2016.

Howe, Melana. *Community Health Needs Assessment: Stark County [Dickinson].* The North Dakota Medicare Rural Hospital Flexibility (Flex) Program. Grand Forks: University of North Dakota School of Medicine and Health Sciences, 2016.

McKenzie County Healthcare Systems. *Community Health Needs Assessment.* Watford City, ND: Northland Health Care Alliance, 2016.

Trinity Kenmare Community Hospital. *Community Health Needs Assessment Report.* Kenmare, ND: Trinity Kenmare Community Hospital, 2016. https://www.trinityhealth.org/wp-content/uploads/2018/09/Kenmare_Report063016.pdf.

2018

Chapter 13
Boomtown Bias: Reflections on the Past, Present, and Future of Prostitution and Sex Trafficking in North Dakota

Nikki Berg Burin

In American public memory, the phrase "boomtown" often brings to mind images of the Old West—a time and place where small, rural communities were transformed by significant and swift economic and demographic growth, as well as by the social problems that accompanied such changes. Boomtown narratives typically follow the same progression. There is a discovery of rich natural resources, followed by a rapid influx of outsiders, especially men, and particularly young, rowdy bachelors. Then there is the building of saloons, pool halls, and brothels, followed by the mayhem of drinking, gambling, violence, and fornication. In such narratives, these changes threaten the stability and safety of otherwise wholesome communities. Among the most prominent villains in such stories are prostitutes who occasionally receive public sympathy, but more often than not experience public condemnation. Also present in boomtown narratives are the victims—typically innocent, chaste girls tricked or forced into a life of vice.

This familiar trope of bachelors, prostitutes, immorality, and crime in boomtowns is not unique to the Old West, but rather transcends time and place. Strikingly similar versions of this story made the rounds during North Dakota's agricultural boom at the end of the nineteenth and beginning of the twentieth century, as well as during the state's oil boom in the early twenty-first century. In both cases residents bemoaned the noticeable presence of bachelors, prostitutes, commercial sexual activity, and the trafficking of innocent girls in their rapidly changing communities. And in both cases the state responded with legislation to crack down on the perceived problems.

Robert Campbell anticipated finding similar problems and discontent in his study of the social impact of North Dakota's oil boom in the 1950s. In his chapter in the 1958 *Williston Report*, Campbell hypothesized that "various kinds of social problems, such as increased crime, immorality, and low grade housing, would arise" as a result of the influx of immigrants into North Dakota (p. 246). Yet upon conducting his research, Campbell found that "there was a surprising absence of social problems" in the Williston area. According to Campbell, "There were no indications available to the researchers that there had been a notable increase in, or even the presence of, organized criminal or immoral activity—gambling houses, theft rings, 'protection' or houses of prostitution." While there were two "known prostitutes" in the area, he argued that "in no sense were their activities organized, continuous, or flagrant" (Campbell, p. 13 and p. 262).

Was 1950s Williston an anomaly among boomtowns? Perhaps, but it is likely that there is more to the story than Campbell uncovered. There are at least four problems with his analysis that collectively demonstrate the need for more research on the topic. First, Campbell did not conduct an in-depth study of commercial sex in boomtown Williston. It was one of several social problems that he touched on in just one chapter of a lengthy report. As such, it is not surprising that his analysis of this particular issue was limited to a handful of surface level observations. Second, it seems that even his cursory analysis was cut short by the influence of the boomtown trope described above. Campbell expected to find rampant prostitution, and when he did not see it, he ceased exploring. Third, his intentionally narrow scope of inquiry into prostitution and unintentional boomtown bias caused Campbell to overlook relevant historical contexts. The anti-vice laws passed in the state legislature during the Progressive Era, which stayed on the books until the late twentieth century, worked to obscure but not necessarily eliminate the presence of prostitution during the time when Campbell was writing. Fourth, Campbell did not have access to the wealth of research on the commercial sex industry that exists today. Given what we now know about the complex nature and intersections of prostitution and sex trafficking, it is likely that Campbell's conclusions were curtailed by a limited analytical framework.

I do not attempt to fill the gaps in Campbell's empirical research with this essay, but instead offer a critical analysis of his observations on prostitution in 1950s Williston so as to provide guidance about the kinds of questions and methods that should be applied to an in-depth historical study of the topic. My analysis has three parts: first, a brief overview of the Progressive Era anti-vice legislation that drove the commercial sex industry underground and perhaps out of Campbell's sight by the 1950s; second, a critique of the indicators he provided as evidence for the lack of social problems during the oil boom—all of which are flawed when applied to prostitution and sex trafficking; and third, an overview of North Dakota's legislative response to prostitution and sex trafficking during the state's twenty-first century oil boom, which reveals the progress and stagnation of the state's understanding of these issues and offers insights into how one might go about a new study of boomtown prostitution and sex trafficking in 1950s North Dakota. In all three periods the nuanced reality of the commercial sex industry and the complex experiences of the people within it have been obscured by the persistent influence of the boomtown trope.

Progressive Era Anti-Vice Laws

In its inaugural session in 1862, the Legislative Assembly of Dakota Territory laid the foundation for the subsequent 150 years of prostitution and human trafficking legislation in North Dakota. Lawmakers determined it was illegal for any person to engage in "open lewdness or other notorious act of public indecency ... or maintain or keep a lewd house or place for the practice of fornication" (Dakota Territory Legislative Assembly 1862, ch. 9, sec. 126). Generally speaking, lewdness was understood to be an indecent sexual act done openly and with the possibility or intent of corrupting the community's sexual morality. The sexual morality at risk of corruption was marital fidelity and the chastity of single women, particularly single white women. The most obvious sites for such corruption were so-called disorderly houses—brothels, saloons, and gambling halls—which meant that such establishments were early targets for legislators. In fact, by the second legislative session in the winter of 1862–3, the legislative body adopted a new penal code that included a separate statute condemning such businesses as seedbeds of lewdness and increasing the penalties for operating them in the communities of Dakota Territory (Dakota Territory Legislative Assembly 1862–3, ch. 10, secs. 4–10). In other words, while it was problematic for an individual to commit an act of lewdness, it was a far more serious crime to promote and facilitate sexual immorality in a public, commercial setting.

Lawmakers added another level of criminality related to the commercial sex industry in 1865 when they passed Dakota Territory's first anti-sex-trafficking laws. The pair of laws criminalized the act of enticing any unmarried female "of previous chaste character" under the age of twenty-five into prostitution and of abducting any female under the age of fifteen for the same purpose (Dakota Territory Legislative Assembly 1864, penal code sec. 328–9). While present-day North Dakotans might applaud territorial lawmakers for taking an anti-trafficking stance at such an early date in the state's history, a closer look at the legislation reveals significant flaws. Only girls and single women under the age of twenty-five were considered legitimate victims of sex trafficking. Married adult women and all women over the age of twenty-five were excluded as potential victims, as well as all boys and men. Also excluded from the ranks of potential victims were girls and women who were not of "previous chaste character." This exception is not surprising, given nineteenth-century sexual scripts and gender prescriptions, which demanded female sexual purity, but this fact makes it no less problematic in terms of practical consequences for victims of sex trafficking. The law validated society's bias against women and girls who fell outside the boundaries of acceptable femininity and female sexuality by choice or otherwise, and, as a result, it directed exploiters to vulnerable prey who would not be protected by the state.

The practice of narrowly defining sex trafficking victims within the law held well beyond the territorial period. While compiling its laws for the first time in 1895, the state of North Dakota amended the territorial trafficking statutes and, in short, expanded by three years the age range of girls who could be trafficking victims in the eyes of the law, but reduced by five years the age range for potential adult victims (North Dakota Legislative Assembly 1895, secs. 7165–6). Both changes reflect the white slavery panic of the late nineteenth and early twentieth centuries, which sensationalized the kidnapping and seduction of those deemed innocents by society—chaste white girls and young women. These were the victims in the commercial sex industry according to turn-of-the-century North Dakotans and Americans more generally. Individuals who performed commercial sex acts for hire and who did not fall within this narrowly defined category of sex trafficking victims were assumed to be willful prostitutes who, whether truly autonomous or not, had no legal protection from or recourse against commercial sexual exploitation or trafficking. The legal marginalization of women who performed commercial sex acts in the state's early years was reinforced when lawmakers passed a statute in 1901 regarding the slander of females. The law stated that it was illegal to expose any female over the age of twelve who was "not a public prostitute" to "hatred, contempt, or ridicule" by disparaging her virtue or chastity (North Dakota Legislative Assembly 1901, ch. 175, sec. 1). While it true that individuals who performed commercial sex acts were not chaste, the law was not about sex per se, but rather about a woman's character. This statute made it clear that in the eyes of the law prostitutes were sullied women and that no one could disparage their virtue (physical or moral), for it was already compromised.

The combination of anti-sex-trafficking laws and the laws against slandering women reveals that at the turn of the twentieth century the state of North Dakota understood all women over the age of twenty who were involved in the commercial sex industry to be willful prostitutes and that all prostitutes were unworthy of protections from the state, at least in terms of slander and commercial sexual exploitation. "Hatred, contempt, and ridicule" of such women was reasonable and legal. This was obviously problematic for adult trafficking victims, but it was also problematic for autonomous sex workers, for women who entered the life because of limited options or out of necessity, and, of course, for those who were prevented by individuals, society, or circumstances from leaving commercial sex work. Legislators' creation of laws that protected "virtuous" women and that degraded or allowed for the degradation of others reinforced society's bias and firmly planted it within the legal system. When force and choice are the only publicly accepted means of entry into prostitution, it becomes easy for lawmakers and society to identify clear-cut villains and victims. By creating laws based on this simplistic understanding of the women and girls who performed commercial sex acts, legislators obscured the various forces that brought individuals of diverse backgrounds into the life, as well as the complex forms of victimization they experienced within it. Such laws also made empowerment within the commercial sex industry much more difficult for consensual sex workers to obtain.

As North Dakota moved into the twentieth century, the legislature continued the trend of protecting "legitimate" victims of sex trafficking and enacted new laws overtly condemning those defined by the state as prostitutes. For instance, the 1895 statute on the abduction of girls for the purpose of prostitution identified as victims only those who were taken from their parents or legal guardians. In 1903 the legislature amended the statute to include "any friendless female under the age of eighteen years" (North Dakota Legislative Assembly 1903, ch. 149, sec. 7166). This suggests an increased awareness among legislators of the vulnerabilities of homeless, abused, and abandoned youth and was a positive step forward. In 1909 the state recognized that *any* unmarried female of previously chaste character could potentially be inveigled into a house of prostitution, not just those under the age of twenty (North Dakota Legislative Assembly 1909, ch. 88, sec. 8899). The legislature also passed a new statute that same year that made it unlawful to "detain any woman against her will by force, threats, putting in bodily fear, or by any other means, at a house of ill-fame, or any other place ... for the purpose of prostitution" (North Dakota Legislative Assembly 1909, ch. 89, sec. 1). In short, by 1909 the state broadened the definition of sex trafficking and expanded the pool of potential victims.

Around the same time, however, legislators passed new vagrancy laws that stigmatized and further marginalized prostitutes and many others. Up to this point, prostitution was not explicitly identified as a crime in the North Dakota Penal Code. Prostitutes could be arrested on charges of public lewdness or as a public nuisance, but unlike those who facilitated prostitution or engaged in human trafficking, prostitutes were not specifically named as criminals in the statutes in the first forty-two years of Dakota Territory and North Dakota history. That changed in 1903 with the introduction of vagrancy laws. The list of people who qualified as vagrants was long and included "common night walkers; lewd, wanton and lascivious persons" (North Dakota Legislative Assembly 1903, ch. 206, sec. 1). Given the limited opportunities for gainful employment by homeless, runaway, and orphaned girls and single women without familial or financial support and given the willingness of exploiters to take advantage of others' vulnerabilities, it is very likely that victims of commercial sexual exploitation could be and were treated as criminals under the vagrancy law. The "friendless female" clause in the statute criminalizing the abduction of girls for the purpose of prostitution and the removal of age limitations in the law criminalizing the deception of females into prostitution would not offer protections for all women and girls reluctantly caught up in the commercial sex industry. Abduction and seduction were not and still are not necessary conditions for those who unwillingly enter the life. For many, entry into commercial sex was and continues to be an issue of survival. What drew them and "friendless females" of all ages to the commercial sex industry? The need for food, shelter, and money. For these women and girls, North Dakota law made it clear there was to be little help or sympathy. Victims deemed worthy of legal protections were those who were forced, coerced, or deceived. Destitution and the lack of options were irrelevant when even a hint of choice was detectable.

And what about the women who willfully chose prostitution—those who envisioned economic independence, an opportunity for sexual freedom, or a way to take control over their lives and bodies? For Progressive-era North

Dakotans and Americans more generally these women were beyond the pale. In 1909, nearly sixty years after the passage of Dakota Territory's first law regulating commercial sex, North Dakota defined and explicitly outlawed prostitution with its own law for the first time. A prostitute was defined as any female who frequented or lived in houses of ill-fame or who was paid for sex (North Dakota Legislative Assembly 1909, ch. 87, sec. 1). Arresting individuals for prostitution when there were few alternative employment opportunities for women only served to increase the social and economic vulnerability of those who labored as prostitutes. Moreover, the 1909 law had little chance of accomplishing lawmakers' objective of stopping the spread of vice in North Dakota, for not only did it fail to address the reasons why women and girls participated in prostitution, but it was also put in place without a companion law that addressed the demand for commercial sex.

Following suit with the rest of the country, early North Dakota lawmakers condemned and punished the women performing commercial sex acts rather than targeting the buyers who fueled the industry. Anti-prostitution activists like the purity reformers of the Women's Christian Temperance Union (WCTU) had long been critical of this sexual double standard and promoted demand-reduction as a strategy for diminishing the commercial sex industry.[1] However, from the state's territorial period up through the end of the Progressive Era, lawmakers did not embrace the WCTU's preventative initiatives or its efforts to advance "one standard of morality for men and women" (WCTU of North Dakota 1895). It wasn't until 1919—a full decade after the state criminalized prostitution—that lawmakers declared it illegal to "receive any person into any place for the purpose of prostitution" (North Dakota Legislative Assembly 1919, ch. 190, sec. 1).[2] This was the state's first law that explicitly targeted buyers of commercial sex acts. Fears about the spread of venereal disease during and after World War I led the legislature to declare the passage of anti-prostitution laws an emergency "necessary for the immediate preservation of the public peace, health and safety" (North Dakota Legislative Assembly 1919, ch. 190, sec. 8).

---

[1] This is not to say that buyers could patronize prostitutes without potential legal risks. In the late nineteenth century they could be charged with lewdness or public indecency and at the turn of the twentieth century habitual buyers could also be arrested on vagrancy charges.

[2] The Legislature also broadened the definition of prostitute by changing the law's gendered language from "female" to "someone" and added individuals who had "indiscriminate sexual intercourse without hire" (North Dakota Legislative Assembly 1919, ch. 190, sec. 2).

As the early legislative history of North Dakota reveals, the driving impulse of anti-vice laws in the territory and then state has been a desire to penalize "deviant" women, to protect some—but not all—victims of commercial sexual exploitation, and to punish some—but not all—exploiters. This approach was adopted during the social, economic, and demographic upheavals of North Dakota's agricultural boom in the late nineteenth and early twentieth centuries and fit well with the common trope of boomtown villains and victims, which was part of public discourse at the time. The collection of early anti-vice laws set the stage for those engaged in or on the periphery of the commercial sex industry for decades to come, including Robert Campbell, who expected to find a visible rise in the number of prostitutes and customers in the western part of the state during the 1950s oil boom. By this time, though, the state's anti-vice legislation had been in place for over fifty years and had effectively driven the business of commercial sex underground and generally out of plain sight. It's not surprising, therefore, that Campbell's surface level study uncovered "no indications" of "immoral activity" in the Williston area. Taking this historical context into consideration, as well as what we now know about the commercial sex industry, we can see that some of Campbell's observations about the lack of social problems during the oil boom—namely prostitution—are problematic.

Crime and Immorality During the 1950s Oil Boom

Campbell writes in the 1958 *Report*:

> As soon as one hears that a particular place is a "boom" area, he is likely to think of a general laxity of law enforcement or, at least, of a greater incidence of loose spending for illegal and barely legal pleasures. Couple that conception with the idea that there has been a considerable increase in population composed largely of unmarried men in "rough" occupations and the ingredients are complete for a common-sense prediction that criminality and immorality will be greatly increased. (p. 259)

Campbell's prediction was indeed common sense, for it reflected some historical realities of past boomtown experiences around the country and beyond. The problem, however, is that there is far more nuance to the commercial sex industry and prostitution specifically than such common sense predictions capture. While Campbell acknowledged that there were likely "some exceptions to [this] generally useful theory," he proceeded to outline five indicators that explained "why some [crime and immorality] did not occur as well as why some did" (Campbell, p. 259). As we'll see, these indicators do not provide sufficient explanation or evidence for what appeared to Campbell to be a lack of commercial sexual activity in the Williston area. Instead, his indicators serve as an invitation for more research on the topic than Campbell was able or interested in conducting at the time.

Indicator 1

> First, the assumption that a large proportion of the increased population was composed of unmarried men was contrary to the facts. The bulk of the oil field workers not only were married but had children. (Campbell, p. 259)

As discussed earlier, a key component of the boomtown trope is the presence of sexually charged, unattached bachelors driving the demand for commercial sex. While a thriving bachelor culture often does support a thriving commercial sex industry, the lack of bachelors or, rather, the abundance of married fathers, does not mean there is no demand for commercial sex in a community. As recent studies have shown, the buyers of commercial sex come from all backgrounds and engage in the practice for a wide variety of reasons, including not feeling comfortable asking their wives to perform certain sexual activities.[3] In fact, in their 2017 report on buyers, a research team funded by the Women's Foundation of Minnesota found that the predominant buyers of commercial sex in the state were married, middle-aged, white men (Martin, Melander, Karnik, and Nakamura 2017). While the marital and parental status of new or old residents in Williston during the 1950s oil boom is not irrelevant to a study of prostitution, it is also not a reliable marker of increased morality or immorality in the community.

Indicator 2

> Second, there was a general provision of increased law enforcement facilities ... Ray had employed a full-time policeman who was reported by the citizens as being "tough" on violators of any sort but particularly on speeders, speeding having been apparently the main problem. (Campbell, p. 260)

---

[3] For research on the buyers of commercial sex, see Bernstein (2001) and Durchslad and Goswami (2008).

Campbell's implication is that the expansion of law enforcement kept immoral crimes at bay. That may very well have been the case in terms of prostitution during the 1950s boom. The laws were certainly unfriendly to those engaged in prostitution and the presence of extra officers to enforce those laws might have given pimps, prostitutes, and buyers pause before engaging in the trade in the Williston area. However, it is unclear whether officers of the law had any particular incentive to look for and disrupt acts of prostitution. Even if there wasn't a special incentive, doing so would require extra work. Speeding was a socially tolerable and visible crime that was committed and punished with frequency. Prostitution, on the other hand, was covert and stigmatized, which made it more difficult for law enforcement officers to locate and for researchers to quantify. Perhaps law enforcement knew what to look for in terms of underground acts of commercial sex, went looking for it, and found few or no cases of crimes being committed. Campbell suggests, though, that something else might have been going on. He noted that there were "two known prostitutes in Williston, but in no sense were their activities organized, continuous, or flagrant" (p. 262). Without more evidence it is difficult to know the extent to which the activities of these individuals were organized, but it is fair to suggest that at this historical moment they couldn't risk their own well-being or livelihood with continuous or flagrant acts of commercial sex. That Campbell describes these individuals as "known prostitutes" raises the question of whether there was a communal acceptance of prostitution so long as prostitutes kept to themselves and kept moving. If this kind of behavior was acceptable and not pursued by law enforcement, it is probable that there were more than two prostitutes making their way in and out of the region during this time and even more buyers.

Indicator 3

> Third, drunkenness was prevented from developing to the problem proportions it might have reached by a combination of already existing circumstances. (Campbell, p. 261)

Campbell points to various techniques to control drunkenness that Williston had in place prior to the boom. For example, law enforcement placed extra officers in the areas of town where seasonal laborers resided so as to make quick arrests for public intoxication, and tavern-owners often called taxis for intoxicated patrons. While there is no reason to doubt these efforts helped control the rates or potential damage of drunkenness, they likely had little effect on the commercial sex industry in the region. At this point in time brothels were not operating in taverns (at least not openly) and drunkenness is not a necessary element for the purchase of commercial sex.

Indicator 4

Fourth, a main source of drinking and gambling activity was available immediately outside the area, thus what might have been a problem within the area was removed. An active gambling, drinking, dining and dancing "club" just across the Montana state line attracted a large clientele from the oil development area ... (Campbell, p. 262)

Of all the indicators provided by Campbell as to why there was not a "notable increase in, or even the presence of ... immoral activity" in the Williston area, this may be the most problematic. More research is needed on the nature of the club mentioned by Campbell and its surrounding community, but the fact that North Dakota residents crossed state lines to engage in certain frowned-upon (if not illegal) activities raises the question whether procuring commercial sex was also easier there. If so, this means that even if there were no prostitutes in the Williston area (aside from the two who were known), there were likely buyers. Since Campbell puts prostitution under the umbrella term of immoral activities, the presence of buyers in the community must also be identified as part of the problem even if their purchases were being made elsewhere. Like many late nineteenth and early twentieth century North Dakota lawmakers, Campbell seems at risk of dismissing as inconsequential the demand side of the issue.

Indicator 5

Finally, evidence is lacking that there was a greater inclination among migrants than among "natives" to participate in illegal and "fringe" types of activity ... (Campbell, p. 262)

With this statement Campbell challenged the accuracy of the boomtown trope in which outsiders are typically blamed for the problems that often arise in boom areas. Criminal or immoral activity is never exclusive to newcomers. The increased presence of a new population of people and especially unattached men might exacerbate or shine a light on existing problems, but the new arrivals are not necessarily the cause of those problems. When it comes to prostitution in the Williston Basin during the boom, it appears few people—newcomers or longtime residents—were arrested for buying commercial sex. Does this mean it wasn't for sale there and so they went elsewhere? Does it mean the residents and newcomers alike weren't interested in commercial sex? Does it mean that law enforcement looked the other way when it came to buyers or perhaps to prostitution as a whole? Or does it mean that by this time the longstanding laws and social norms had driven the practice so far underground that it ceased to be perceptible to the untrained eye? A combination of some or all of the above is likely.

Campbell conducted his study at a time when prostitution and sex more generally were not discussed in public (at least not in small town North Dakota). Prostitution was an underground activity in every sense of the word and had been driven there as a result of the panic launched by the state's first population boom at the end of the nineteenth century. Campbell understandably expected to find an increase in prostitution during the 1950s oil boom, but it appears that his analysis fell sway to the boomtown trope of brothels and deviant women. When he did not see either in the form he expected, his analysis came to a close. What he didn't account for was the influence of the laws penalizing prostitution, which had long been on the books. His surface-level observations may ultimately be proven correct, but for now they raise more questions than they answer and, as such, they serve as a terrific springboard for further research about prostitution during North Dakota's oil boom in the 1950s. However, as the state's twenty-first century oil boom reveals, such a study must also include the topic of sex trafficking. This issue, which caused much hand-wringing in the Progressive Era and informed many of the anti-vice laws for the first half of the twentieth century, was entirely absent in Campbell's analysis. Yet given the presence of sex trafficking and prostitution in the state's first and most recent booms, it was likely present in the 1950s as well. While the Progressive Era residents, anti-vice activists, and lawmakers engaged in a fair amount of sensationalism regarding so-called "white slavery," the recent boom in North Dakota's Bakken region and the anti-trafficking efforts (both promising and problematic) of activists and lawmakers provide some guidance not only for tackling human trafficking, but also for tackling a renewed study of prostitution and sex trafficking in Campbell's Williston.

Prostitution and Trafficking Laws During the Twenty-first Century Oil Boom

As news outlets around the state, the country, and even the world began reporting on the enormous boom in oil production and population in western North Dakota in the first decades of the twenty-first century, they also began to report on what appeared to be a simultaneous surge in prostitution, especially in areas surrounding the man camps near the Bakken oil fields. American society had changed considerably since the time of Campbell's report, with sex and even prostitution being common parts of popular culture and discourse. As such, it's no surprise that the presence of the commercial sex industry was more readily apparent to residents in the twenty-first century than in mid-twentieth century. However, the response of the general public to the seeming rise of commercial sex in their community harkened back to that of their nineteenth century ancestors, for many residents complained about the sordid influence of prostitutes on their communities. Such complaints were soon followed by concerns about high rates of sex trafficking and the threat of innocent girls being kidnapped by traffickers (Berg Burin 2016). As was the case 120 years earlier, these concerns were not baseless. There was an increase in prostitution and sex trafficking in the Bakken. Like their nineteenth century ancestors, lawmakers responded to these developments.

By the time of North Dakota's twenty-first century oil boom, human trafficking had long since been on the radar of national and global lawmakers. The United Nations took over international anti-trafficking efforts from the defunct League of Nations in 1949 with the Convention for the Suppression of the Traffic in Persons and of the Exploitation of the Prostitution of Others. The UN's Commission on the Status of Women had also been monitoring and advocating for international action against sex trafficking and exploitation within prostitution since the 1940s. This work was continued by the UN's Committee on the Elimination of Discrimination Against Women (CEDAW) during the 1960s and beyond. As awareness of modern day slavery spread across the globe in the late twentieth and early twenty-first century, the UN gathered in Palermo, Italy, in 2000 and passed the Protocol to Prevent, Suppress and Punish Trafficking in Persons, Especially Women and Children (a supplement to the 2000 Convention Against Transnational Organized Crime).[4] As the world's "first global legally binding instrument with an agreed definition on trafficking," the protocol was intended to protect the human rights of victims

---

[4] For a fulsome description of the United Nations' efforts to address human trafficking in the twentieth century, see Reanda (1991).

of trafficking and help coordinate international efforts to combat the crime (UNODC 2000). At the same time the United States passed its first federal comprehensive anti-trafficking legislation with the Trafficking Victims Protection Act of 2000, which has been reauthorized four times (most recently in 2013) and which seeks to prevent severe forms of trafficking, protect victims, and prosecute exploiters. The federal government also passed the Justice for Victims of Trafficking Act in 2015, which strengthened the government's assistance for victims, created a survivor-led U.S. Advisory Council on Human Trafficking, and made buyers of commercial sex from trafficking victims culpable for trafficking offenses (United States Department of State 2018). In addition, many local, national, and international NGOs were organized in the late twentieth and early twenty-first century dedicated to combating human trafficking. As a result of these developments, sex trafficking had become a hot topic in news and entertainment media. While increased media attention led to increased public awareness, much of the coverage included (and still does include) sensationalized images and stories of scantily clad girls in chains. Such images are reminiscent of the white slavery panic and perpetuate the false assumptions of a bygone era.

North Dakota residents and lawmakers were not blind to these developments and in the face of the demographic changes of the oil boom they were compelled to take action. As it turned out, the Uniform Law Commission (ULC, a nonprofit organization dating back to the nineteenth century, which promotes consistency across states in various areas of law) created a Uniform Act on Prevention of and Remedies for Human Trafficking in 2013. As the ULC states, the model legislation "provides the three components necessary for ending human trafficking: comprehensive criminal penalties; protections for human-trafficking victims; and public awareness and prevention methods" (Uniform Law Commission 2018). Through the persistent efforts of anti-trafficking advocates and supportive lawmakers, the North Dakota state legislature adopted the ULC's Uniform Act on trafficking in 2015 and, as a result, took its strongest stance on human trafficking in 153 years of lawmaking (North Dakota Legislative Assembly 2005, ch. 117). The most significant changes from the previous anti-trafficking legislation include the following provisions:

- The past sexual behavior of victims is not admissible in court.
- Minors who provide commercial sex for hire are presumed to be children in need of protective services and are immune from prostitution charges. (This is known as Safe Harbor legislation).

- Adult trafficking victims have the opportunity to vacate and expunge convictions for crimes that they committed as a result of being a victim of human trafficking.
- Victims are eligible for state-funded services.
- The Attorney General is authorized to make a grant or contract with government units, tribal government units, and non-governmental organizations to expand and develop services for victims.
- Organizations and units that receive grants or make contracts with the Attorney General must provide numbers and demographic information for the purpose of data collection.
- Enhanced penalties will apply to people who purchase commercial sex from a minor, from a known trafficking victim, and from all others, including the possibility of required participation in an offender education program on the negative consequences of the commercial sex industry.

With its adoption of the Uniform Act on Human Trafficking, the North Dakota Legislature took an important step forward in the fight against sex trafficking. In addition to putting increased responsibility on exploiters—both traffickers and buyers—the statutes set the foundation for data collection so that the state can better understand and address the problem as it exists in North Dakota. Moreover, by attaching a fiscal note to the legislation, legislators empowered organizations to proactively combat human trafficking. The legislation would reek of insincerity without the provision of funds for training legal system professionals and enhancing support services. By creating the opportunity for survivors to vacate and expunge convictions for crimes committed while a victim a trafficking, lawmakers revealed their increased awareness of the various forms of manipulation and exploitation that victims can endure in a trafficking situation. Finally, the legislation emphasizes the lack of consent for minors providing sex for hire regardless of their personal, criminal, and sexual history. The legislature reinforced this new approach to minors in the commercial sex industry by changing the definition of prostitute from "individual" to "adult" (North Dakota Legislative Assembly 2015, ch. 109, sec. 12.1-29.02).

While these significant legal changes reflect a renewed and more critical approach to combating sex trafficking in North Dakota, the state still has a way to go in shedding its outdated and harmful "boomtown" approach to sex trafficking and prostitution. For example, much like the state's early anti-trafficking laws, the Uniform Law protects only certain victims of trafficking. Safe harbor provisions are for minors. Adult victims of trafficking must present evidence of force, fraud, or coercion to prove they are indeed victims of trafficking and not consenting prostitutes who can still be charged as criminals under the state's prostitution laws. As victims of trauma and complex manipulation, providing such evidence can be incredibly difficult. Even getting survivors to recognize their victimization can be difficult. Moreover, while a sex trafficking victim can apply to have prostitution charges vacated, this can be a grueling and retraumatizing process for many individuals. Law enforcement officers who have received training on sex trafficking are encouraged to take a victim-centered approach when encountering adults engaged in prostitution and to use their discretion when deciding whether to charge them with a crime or direct them to services. But the law still provides a narrow definition of legitimate victims, which has the effect of shaming and putting at risk those who fall outside that definition.[5]

North Dakota state law continues to see the selling of commercial sex as a black and white issue represented by the binary of criminal prostitutes and trafficking victims. The reality, though, is that many adults engaged in the labor of prostitution move back and forth along a spectrum between consent and force, empowerment and oppression. This large gray area is something the law does not yet fully recognize, much to the detriment of autonomous and reluctant sex workers, as well as adult trafficking victims. By looking at the issue through a human rights lens rather than that of criminal justice alone, the legislature could enhance protections for all individuals who engage in prostitution and reduce the rates of those who do so reluctantly or by force.

At the heart of a human rights approach to prostitution and sex trafficking is attentiveness to the social, economic, and political conditions that contribute to one's vulnerability to commercial sexual exploitation.[6] Legislators need to address poverty, housing insecurity, affordable healthcare, and job opportunities in their communities. Many individuals in the life "choose" to engage in that line of work out of economic necessity and a lack of viable alternatives. Exploiters are also quick to capitalize on the vulnerabilities of those experiencing economic and housing insecurity by providing the basics of survival

---

[5] It is also notable that the North Dakota legislature added a section to the Uniform Law on Human Trafficking that prevents service providers from informing victims of their full reproductive healthcare choices, which can be seen as a form of state control over victims' bodily autonomy. See North Dakota Legislative Assembly (2015, ch. 109, sec. 12.1-41-20).

[6] For a discussion of a human rights approach to human trafficking, see O'Connell Davidson (2015) and Kempadoo (2015).

and reaping the economic benefits of their victims' unfree labor. Legislators must also address discrimination on the basis of one's race, sexual orientation, and gender identity, for across the nation girls and women of color, as well as individuals of all sexes who identify as LGBTQ+, are overrepresented among sex trafficking victims and sex workers. Exploiters feed off the marginalization of these groups. Legislators must also provide funding for mental health and social services, including the child welfare system, substance abuse programs, and domestic and sexual violence services. Victims of sex trafficking and commercial sexual exploitation frequently come into the life already having experienced violence, emotional abuse, or neglect.[7] Legislators must also fund education and support services within schools so as to prevent and detect trafficking and exploitation and, of course, to provide better opportunities in life for all children. When education budgets are slashed, the vulnerabilities of at-risk youth increase. Legislators who take a human rights approach must also address the humanity and rights of sex workers who have been and continue to be dehumanized by the public, a portion of their customers, and the legal system. Criminalizing their labor without sufficiently addressing the above issues does nothing but put them at greater risk for exploitation and marginalization. If legislators are serious about increasing public safety and decreasing sex trafficking and the negative effects of prostitution, they need to address the conditions that create these problems and the human rights of all those who perform commercial sex for hire, regardless of the reason.

A Human Rights Approach to Campbell's Study

A human rights approach to prostitution and sex trafficking would not only help legislators take meaningful steps to solve the problems associated with these issues, but it would also help guide scholars who seek to uncover and make sense of the history of sex trafficking and prostitution in North Dakota and beyond. Campbell wrote at a time in which prostitution had been driven underground by the laws of an earlier era. Those laws reinforced society's condemnation of false villains (all prostitutes) and disregard of many hidden victims and exploiters all the way up through the twenty-first century. While the state's legislative history illuminates North Dakotans' willingness to engage with social problems, as well as the advances the state has made on the issues of sex trafficking and exploitation within prostitution, it also reveals the

---

[7] For a discussion of the abuse and neglect many victims of sex trafficking experience before being trafficked, see Lloyd (2011).

historical and continued bias and blind spots of lawmakers, their constituents, and even researchers.

The impact of late nineteenth-century anti-vice laws on prostitution during Campbell's time and his own expectations about what he would find in 1950s boomtown Williston undoubtedly contributed to what he observed to be the absence of prostitution. As the state's first and most recent economic booms reveal, prostitution and sex trafficking are present and always have been in the state. Moreover, where there is one, the other can usually be found. A human rights approach to these issues will allow new researchers to look back at the 1950s Williston area in Campbell's study and ask questions that are better suited for recovering the stories of people and activities relegated to the margins of society and history, no matter how few or many there are. A renewed study will take the boomtown trope for what it is—a historical stereotype with some truth and lots of fiction—and dig into the nuances of the complex problems and people associated with prostitution and sex trafficking. Doing so will bring the experiences, needs, and rights of victims, survivors, and autonomous sex workers into the light.

References

Bernstein, Elizabeth. 2001. "The Meaning of the Purchase: Desire, Demand, and the Commerce of Sex." *Ethnography* 2 (3): 389–420.

Berg Burin, Nikki. 2016. "Public Discourse on the Rise and Regulation of the Illicit Sex Trade During North Dakota's Economic Booms." In *The Bakken Goes Boom: Oil and the Changing Geographies of Western North Dakota*, edited by William Caraher and Kyle Conway, 117–28. Grand Forks, ND: Digital Press at the University of North Dakota.

Dakota Territory Legislative Assembly. 1862. *General Laws and Memorials and Resolutions of the Territory of Dakota Passed at the First Session of the Legislative Assembly.* Yankton, Dakota Territory: Josiah C. Trask.

Dakota Territory Legislative Assembly. 1862–3. *General Laws, and Memorials and Resolutions of the Territory of Dakota, Passed at the Second Session of the Legislative Assembly.* Yankton, Dakota Territory: Kingsbury and Ziebach.

Dakota Territory Legislative Assembly. 1864–5. *General and Private Laws, and Memorials and Resolutions, of the Territory of Dakota, of the Fourth Session of the Legislative Assembly.* Yankton, Dakota Territory: G.W. Kingsbury.

Durchslag, Rachel, and Samir Goswami. 2008. "Deconstructing the Demand for Prostitution: Preliminary Insights from Interviews with Chicago Men Who Purchase Sex." Chicago: Chicago Alliance Against Sexual Exploitation. https://www.issuelab.org/resources/1190/1190.pdf.

Kempadoo, Kamala. 2015. *Trafficking and Prostitution Reconsidered: New Perspectives on Migration, Sex Work, and Human Rights*, 2nd edition. New York: Routledge.

Lloyd, Rachel. 2011. *Girls Like Us: Fighting for a World Where Girls are Not for Sale.* New York: HarperCollins.

Martin, Lauren, Christina Melander, Harshada Karnik, and Corelle Nakamura. 2017. "Mapping the Demand: Sex Buyers in the State of Minnesota." https://uroc.umn.edu/sites/uroc.umn.edu/files/FULL%20REPORT%20Mapping%twentiethe%20Demand.pdf.

North Dakota Legislative Assembly. 1865. *The Revised Codes of the State of North Dakota.* Bismarck, ND: Tribune Company.

North Dakota Legislative Assembly. 1901. *Laws Passed at the Seventh Session of the Legislative Assembly of the State of North Dakota.* Fargo, ND: Satterthwaite and Knight.

North Dakota Legislative Assembly. 1903. *Laws Passed by the Eighth Session of the Legislative Assembly of the State of North Dakota.* Grand Forks, ND: Herald.

North Dakota Legislative Assembly. 1909. *Laws Passed at the Eleventh Session of the Legislative Assembly of the State of North Dakota.* Bismarck, ND: Tribune.

North Dakota Legislative Assembly. 1919. *Laws Passed at the Sixteenth Session of the Legislative Assembly of the State of North Dakota.* Bismarck, ND: Tribune.

North Dakota Legislative Assembly. 2005. *Laws Passed at the Fifty-ninth Session of the Legislative Assembly of the State of North Dakota.* Bismarck, ND: North Dakota Legislative Council. https://www.legis.nd.gov/assembly/64-2015/session-laws/documents/crmlc.pdf.

North Dakota Legislative Assembly. 2015. *Laws Passed at the Sixty-fourth Session of the Legislative Assembly of the State of North Dakota.* Bismarck, ND: North Dakota Legislative Council. https://www.legis.nd.gov/assembly/64-2015/session-laws/documents/crmlc.pdf.

O'Connell Davidson, Julia. 2015. *Modern Slavery: The Margins of Freedom.* New York: Palgrave Macmillan.

Reanda, Laura. 1991. "Prostitution as a Human Rights Question: Problems and Prospects of United Nations Action." *Human Rights Quarterly* 13 (2): 202–28.

Uniform Law Commission. 2018. "Prevention of and Remedies for Human Trafficking." https://my.uniformlaws.org/committees/community-home?CommunityKey=0c541796-903d-450a-bb0e-84856 50bf360.

United States Department of State. 2018. "U.S. Laws on Trafficking in Persons." https://www.state.gov/j/tip/laws/.

UNODC (United Nations Office on Drugs and Crime). 2000. "United Nations Convention against Transnational Organized Crime and the Protocols Thereto." https://www.unodc.org/unodc/en/organized-crime/intro/UNTOC.html.

Women's Christian Temperance Union (WCTU) of North Dakota. 1895. Minutes of the Woman's Christian Temperance Union (WCTU of North Dakota Sixth Annual Meeting). Fargo, ND: Grant and Cook. State Historical Society of North Dakota, Bismarck, ND, MSS 10133, Box 1, Folder 2.

2018

Chapter 14
Conclusion: Reading *The Williston Report* Sixty Years Later

Kyle Conway

In their chapter about the social effects of North Dakota's most recent oil boom, Rick Ruddell and Heather Ray warn that although studies such as the 1958 *Williston Report* "provide us with insight into the impacts of booms occurring in the past, we have to be careful consumers of that research" (p. 272). The change communities undergo now is more intense than in the past, the boom-bust cycle faster, and the effects more widely spread. Direct comparisons are useful, but they do not tell us everything.

There are other reasons to read the 1958 *Report* critically or even skeptically. William Caraher, Bret Weber, and Richard Rothaus, for instance, identify aspects of housing that the authors of *The Williston Report* did not see. Longtime residents appeared to suggest that "something was wrong with the workers who seemingly *chose* to live in 'substandard' temporary workforce housing," and consequently, "Rather than a social responsibility, temporary workforce housing became an inconvenience for longer-term residents to endure" (Caraher et al., p. 289). This blindspot was a result of the failure by the authors of the 1958 *Report* to reflect critically on their categories of analysis. As Caraher and his coauthors point out, they defined a social problem as "any situation which is reported by people involved in it as undesirable and, therefore, about which they express a negative opinion, possibly indicating a tendency to act to change the situation" (Campbell, p. 254). In effect, they took as their only point of reference the perspective of the people they surveyed or interviewed, people who—understandably enough—were concerned primarily with their own lives and the local effects of the boom. The closest they came to questioning this definition was to remark, "From this point of view a situation may not be a problem to the participants despite the fact that the observer is disturbed by it" (Campbell, p. 254). In other words, they saw the definition's shortcomings in reference only to their own *personal* frames. They did not ask about systemic problems, nor did they examine structural causes and effects.

Historian Michel-Rolph Trouillot (1995) provides a useful framework for describing this shortcoming. He speaks of "silences" or omissions that are introduced into the historical narrative at different places, in particular,

> the moment of fact creation (the making of *sources*); the moment of fact assembly (the making of *archives*); the moment of fact retrieval (the making of *narrative*); and the moment of retrospective significance (the making of *history* in the final instance). (1995, 26)

The different silences build on each other: a gap in sources affects the way historians assemble facts and then weave them into a story. Put another way, the authors of the 1958 *Report* asked only about residents' personal opinions about housing but neglected the structural dimensions of housing, such as the role of preexisting social networks embedded in a specific historical context, in helping people find and maintain homes (fact creation). They then incorporated this selective set of facts into their report (fact assembly), leading them to tell a story where inadequate housing was—to their surprise!—not the problem they thought it would be (fact retrieval). Readers six decades later encounter a history of relative harmony among new and longtime residents, despite the occasional minor conflicts (retrospective significance). By identifying these silences, Caraher and his coauthors make them "speak"—that is, they use them to reveal something about the original authors' situation that they themselves might not have recognized, namely their assumptions about the individual, rather than social, causes and effects of social problems.

This is a useful exercise, one that Nikki Berg Burin undertakes in her chapter about human trafficking in the Bakken. The 1958 authors write,

> There were no indications available to the researchers that there had been a notable increase in, or even the presence of, organized criminal or immoral activity—gambling houses, theft rings, "protection" or houses of prostitution. There were two known prostitutes in Williston, but in no sense were their activities organized, continuous or flagrant. (Campbell, p. 262)

Berg Burin suggests, however, that the authors missed something—the facts they assembled were incomplete because, she argues, when they did not find what they expected to find, they stopped looking. They looked for public examples of prostitution when they were more likely to be hidden from view, and they presumed that if the single men who flocked to Williston were not buying sex, then no one was, neglecting the likelihood that married men might buy sex, too.

Of course, this exercise is not free of ambiguity. Making silences speak is not the same as finding new facts. Its value lies in the way it raises questions about why silences exist in the first place—what forces, that is, work together to produce and maintain them. That is the question the conclusion explores. What did *The Williston Report* leave out, and what social or political forces contributed to that exclusion? It considers two silences in particular: Native Americans are absent from the text, as is almost any discussion of the environment. The conclusion ends by asking about future readers. If reading about an oil boom sixty years after it took place can shed new light on the era in which people wrote it, what will readers in 2078 think of *this* book?

Native Americans

Native Americans are completely absent from the 1958 *Report*. In some ways this is surprising: part of the Fort Berthold Reservation, for instance, home to the MHA Nation (the Mandan, Hidatsa, and Arikara), is in Mountrail County not far from Tioga, one of *The Williston Report*'s areas of focus. In other ways, it is not surprising at all: *The Williston Report* is a product of its time, where the dominant mythology was that of the frontier. In fact, the *Report* opens by evoking that myth, framing (non-Native) residents' presence as the result of struggle by generations of settlers to tame the land:

> Directly or indirectly, almost every resident had relied primarily upon the thin cover of soil, upon the vagaries of a capricious weather and upon the biological rhythm of plant and animal life for his livelihood and for his welfare ... Several generations in that place had brought about a pattern of living, an adjustment of man to land which was established and mature. (Wills et al., p. 7)

This myth is of a piece with the dominant narrative of the era. For instance, the American Petroleum Institute, a trade association formed after the First World War, produced a series of movies about oil exploration to supplement the other "educational" materials it published (as mentioned by Talbot, p.

151). One film, *American Frontier* (API 1953), was even about Williston.[1] It tells the heroic story of a self-described "wheat farmer and school teacher" named Nils Halverson, who is willing to take risks in the name of progress. Much like *The Williston Report*, it opens with the myth of the frontier, as its title suggests. Over swelling music and images of empty highways blown over with snow (Figure 14.1),[2] the narrator says,

> Not so long ago, this was frontier. Listen closely, and you'll hear the old ghost-echo of covered wagons, the phantom shadows of pioneers, fighting for their lives against the wilderness. Lean men, hard as hickory, lonely women, wearing their dreams like a bit of bright calico. They began with nothing—with their bare hands and a bucket of hope, breaking the land of freedom's plow, planting towns with names as American as a banjo tune: Fargo, Stampede, Blue Grass, Beaver Lodge, Lincoln Valley, Williston.

The plot revolves around the oilmen coming to Nils's farm to persuade his family to lease their mineral rights. Companies are exploring the area, but nothing happens until one day when Nils comes home from teaching and his wife says the oilmen are drilling a well on a neighbor's farm. Curious, they go to see it and talk to the man in charge of drilling. Staring out at the prairie, admiring the derrick putting in the well, the oilman says it will cost half a million dollars, but with only a slim chance of success: "That's the oil business, a real gamble. One out of nine, with half a million riding on the play" (Figure 14.2).

"Pretty tough odds," Nils says.

"Plenty a man willing to take it," the oilman replies, "especially when there's a chance of profit." He pulls an arrowhead out of his pocket.

"Indian arrowhead?" Nils asks.

"Yeah," he says, "found it right over there, where we put the rig. It's for luck—we're going to need it!" (Figure 14.3)

---

[1] At least ostensibly. The very first sentence of the film, meant to situate the action for the viewer, is nonsense: "The wind blows west from the Great Lakes." Anyone who has lived in Williston knows, first, that the wind comes from the west and blows toward the east, and, second, that the closest Great Lake is 700 miles away.

[2] *American Frontier* is in the public domain. All screenshots come from archive.org.

Figure 14.1. "The old ghost-echo of covered wagons, the phantom shadows of pioneers…" (source: *American Frontier*, API 1953)

Figure 14.2. "That's the oil business, a real gamble. One out of nine, with half a million riding on the play." (source: *American Frontier*, API 1953)

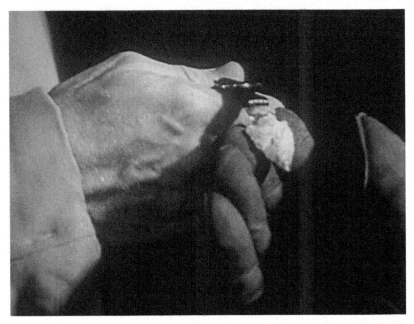

Figure 14.3. An arrowhead for good luck. (source: *American Frontier*, API 1953)

The arrowhead is the only indication of Native Americans in the film. Its function in the plot, not to mention the broader social narrative shaping the plot, is twofold: it relegates Native Americans to history, and it transforms their historical presence into a token of luck, which ultimately serves the interests of the oil business. The film, like *The Williston Report*, erases Native Americans at the moments of fact creation and assembly (they are present only in the token of the arrowhead), fact retrieval (except for this token, they are otherwise absent), and finally, if we take this film at face value, retrospective significance.

It is important, in that respect, to remember, as Sebastien Braun (2016, 95) reminds us, that "frontiers exist as *frontiers* for outsiders, on the same land that is home to locals." Despite the absence of Native Americans in *The Williston Report* (and *American Frontier*), they *were* living in the Williston Basin during the 1950s oil boom, just as they live in the Bakken region now (see Rundquist and Vandeberg, p. 77, and Olive, p. 164). Their perspective, absent in *The Williston Report*, is present in other places. For instance, during the fight against the Dakota Access Pipeline in 2016, David Archambault (2016), chair of the Standing Rock Sioux tribe, explained his opposition to the pipeline by placing it in the context of other historical injustices committed against the people he represented. One of these, the creation of the Garrison Dam to control the flow of the Missouri River in the 1950s, occurred at roughly the same time as the 1950s boom. Archambault (2016, par. 8) explains that it "took our river-front forests, fruit orchards and most fertile farmland," and he shows how its creation was part of an ongoing cycle of broken promises.

In this way, he helps fill in the gaps in *The Williston Report*, whose authors started from a different set of epistemological assumptions. Where they treated problems caused by oil as distinct from other problems, Archambault did not, showing instead how the damming of the Missouri River and the construction of the Dakota Access Pipeline were part of a broader pattern. Put another way, *The Williston Report* seeks to explain social problems, such as they were, as symptoms of the oil boom. Archambault, in contrast, explains both the destruction caused by the Garrison Dam and the risks associated with oil exploration as symptoms of the U.S. government's failure to deal fairly with Native Americans (Conway and Duguay 2019). For him, these events fall into the same category, and his account of the Garrison Dam helps with the production of historical narrative (that is, the moment of fact retrieval) by making it possible to reconstruct those facts about Native communities during the 1950s oil boom to which contemporary non-Native scholars do not have direct access.

It also brings into sharp relief the different ways Native and settler communities organize their accounts of history. The authors of *The Williston Report* treated problems caused by the oil boom as independent of other problems, whose causes they saw as unrelated to oil. So did non-Native leaders during the conflict over the Dakota Access Pipeline, in contrast to Archambault. That compartmentalization was politically expedient in that it allowed North Dakota's political leaders in 2016 to argue in favor of the pipeline and against the protests (and protestors) (Conway and Duguay 2019). In a similar way, it made it possible for the authors of *The Williston Report* not to ask about the effect of the 1950s boom on Native communities, a decision that contributed—indirectly, at least—to the conditions in which the conflict over Dakota Access took place six decades later.

The Environment

Another silence in *The Williston Report* concerns the environment. In fact, the word *environment* appears in only one place, where it refers to the state's economic environment (Kelley, p. 190), although ideas related to the physical environment do appear in the authors' descriptions of the impact of the boom on roads (Wills, p. 44–50). They also appear in their discussion of pipelines (Wills, p. 50, and Talbot, p. 121) and flaring, or the burning of excess natural gas (Wills, p. 51), but again in the context of politics (in the case of pipelines crossing state borders) or the economy (in the case of flaring).

Simply put, the authors of *The Williston Report* are not concerned with the effect of the boom on the air people breathe or the water they drink. They differ in this respect from the authors of the chapters that update the 1958 *Report*, some of whom do address these concerns, albeit in works not included in this volume. Both William Caraher and Bret Weber in *The Bakken: An Archaeology of an Industrial Landscape* (2017) and Rick Ruddell in *Oil, Gas, and Crime: The Dark Side of the Boomtown* (2017) address the pollution caused by oil development, related not just to fracking but also to flaring, wastewater, oil spills, and the illegal dumping of toxic waste, as well as light and noise pollution, all of which affect residents' quality of life (Ruddell 2017, 108–11; Caraher and Weber 2017, 21–2).

What accounts for this silence in the 1958 *Report*? Here, as above, the proximate cause is the authors' reliance on their informants (who were concerned with their immediate circumstances) to identify and define social problems. Although the conservation movement in the United States had existed since the nineteenth century, led by people like Henry David Thoreau and later John Muir, concerns about conservation had not entered the public consciousness to the degree they would even a few years later when Rachel Carson published *Silent Spring* (1962). In other words, although this omission might appear strange to contemporary eyes, environmental issues did not yet have the urgency they have since come to have. Atmospheric rates of the greenhouse gas carbon dioxide (CO_2), for instance, which had held more or less steady at about 280 parts per million (ppm) since biblical times, had risen, but only to 313 ppm in 1951 (IAC 2016; see Figure 14.4).[3] Their rise since then has been more dramatic, reaching nearly 400 ppm by 2014 and 407 ppm by 2018 (IAC 2016; Harvey 2018).

To explain this silence in greater detail would require an exercise of intellectual archeology that is beyond the scope of the concluding chapter of an edited volume. It would involve, for instance, digging down to the unspoken

---

[3] Note that the turning point after which CO_2 rates rose without falling again came in the 1780s, at the beginning of the geological epoch that Paul Crutzen and Eugene Stoermer (2000, 17) describe as the Anthropocene, a term they choose to designate "the central role of mankind in geology and ecology." For them, the symbolic beginning of the Anthropocene is 1784, the year James Watt invented the steam engine. Although change was still gradual at that point, it seems well chosen nonetheless.

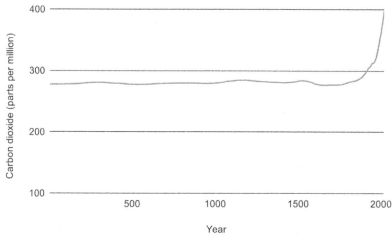

Figure 14.4. Global rates of atmospheric carbon dioxide concentration, Year 1–2014 (data source: IAC 2016)

assumptions shaping the decision by the 1958 authors to privilege informants' notions of social problems: what were the social and intellectual conditions that made their decision appear self-evident? How did those conditions affect the moments of fact creation, assembly, and retrieval?

Still, the idea that environmental consequences are greater now is clear in many places, not just rising CO_2 levels. Pipelines are a concern because people are acutely aware of the risks involved in transporting oil, after the explosions of trains carrying Bakken oil in Lac Mégantic, Quebec, and Casselton, North Dakota, in 2013. They are also a concern because of the threat they pose to water supplies, as the protests against the Dakota Access Pipeline showed. More broadly, the end of 2018 was marked by the publication of two reports, one from the U.S. Global Change Research Program (USGCRP 2018), the other from the United Nations' Intergovernmental Panel on Climate Change (IPPC 2018), that sounded the alarm about the risks of climate change and the need for immediate action. They describe a cascading series of effects if CO_2 emissions go unchecked: sea levels will rise and extreme weather events such as hurricanes and wildfires will become more frequent, leading to greater rates of poverty in affected areas and causing mass migration as people lose their homes or seek homes that are more secure (see Dennis and Mooney 2018; Watts 2018). Even North Dakotans, many of whom have resisted the idea that climate change is happening or is human-caused, have begun to recognize that it is indeed taking place and that it is affecting things they value, especially in agriculture (Baumgarten 2018). Some have even begun to speak against the oil industry in North Dakota, especially in relation to the Dakota Access Pipeline (Ruddell 2017, 111–13; Brorby 2017).

How Will People Read this Book Sixty Years from Now?

The nature of the social sciences is such that the authors of a book like *The Williston Report*—or *Sixty Years of Boom and Bust*—assume a certain amount of authority with respect to their readers and the people they write about. They claim to see things that the people they write about might not see, insight they have gained through the tools they use—surveys, interviews, statistical analysis, and so on, all designed to provide a broader perspective or ferret out hidden patterns.

But their claim to authority does not go untested. The test they face is simple: do their readers, including the people they write about, recognize the situations they have described? In other words, do their descriptions ring true? In addition, as they describe what they have observed, they also make predictions about the future, at least implicitly, in the trends they use to explain how the current situation came to be. Those too can be tested as time passes and new readers engage with their work.

In this respect, Robert Campbell makes a revealing comment at the end of his chapter on social change in the Williston Basin. The authors of the 1958 *Report* saw themselves as being a bit like Cassandra, the figure from Greek mythology whose predictions about the future always fell on deaf ears:

> One of the unfortunate aspects of a report of this sort is that some of the predictions which are practically useful are not available early enough. We could have predicted fairly accurately the amount of immediate decrease in Tioga's population as we were conducting the fieldwork because of our knowledge that particular individuals already knew the dates on which they were to be transferred. Furthermore, we could have predicted the decrease in activity because of the knowledge we obtained about the relative number of employees needed in exploratory as compared to development activity in the oil fields. The predictions of this sort that we expressed orally tended to be ridiculed as obviously wrong or as attempts to devalue the importance of the oil development to the state of North Dakota. (Campbell, p. 268)

Might the same be true of *Sixty Years of Boom and Bust*? This book has covered a wide range of topics—changes in physical geography, changes in politics and the economy, and social changes—over a span of sixty years. The chapters describing the 1950s boom covered a lot of ground, and those describing the boom in the first decades of the 2000s covered more, addressing issues that were not as salient in 1958, such as hospital access and drug use. At the same time, this book shares blind spots with *The Williston Report*. Although some of the 2018 authors write about Native Americans, for instance, they focus on those aspects most relevant to the questions they are asking, such as Native Americans' role in governance (Olive, p. 164), without going further.

So, how will people read this book sixty years from now? What patterns are likely to affect the social fabric of western North Dakota, and what, consequently, will become salient for future readers? In answer to the first question, two patterns stand out, at least for the near future. The first relates to climate change. The predictions by the Global Change Research Program (USGCRP 2018) and the Intergovernmental Panel on Climate Change (IPPC 2018) are dire, but few countries have succeeded in cutting their CO_2 emissions. In fact, despite the agreement reached in Paris in 2015 to limit emissions to prevent global temperatures from rising by more than 1.5°C beyond pre-industrial levels, global CO_2 rates rose to record levels by 2018 (Storrow 2018). The pattern is one of missed goals. The demand for oil remains high because it makes economic growth possible. It might not be the only energy source, but it is more readily accessible than many others.

The second pattern relates to the contradictory logics shaping how people interact with and relate to one another. One trend in the United States (and elsewhere) is that of the development of diffuse political and social movements with loosely related goals, made possible through online social networks that allow people to affiliate with each other in ever-evolving ways. Another related, occasionally conflicting trend is that of increased political polarization, as the networks people join draw them away from those with whom they disagree. Oil will continue to shape these logics directly, by bringing people together either in support of or in opposition to oil extraction, and indirectly, by shaping the conditions in which they meet and the ways they understand their relationships to each.

It is risky, however, to make anything more than short-range predictions. The authors of the 1958 *Report* could not have foreseen the controversies about pipelines, for instance, because the scale of oil production in the first decade of the 2000s was beyond anything they might have imagined. Here is where the question of salience matters. What will be salient for future readers will depend on a social situation resulting from changes that the authors of this book can only imagine. If society has split irreversibly into warring camps that refuse to recognize each other's claims to humanity, perhaps what will be clear is our undue investment in tribal identities. If it has not, perhaps it will be our ability to overcome the institutional forces that benefit from dividing people into groups. Similarly, if global temperatures have risen more than 1.5°C above pre-industrial levels, perhaps what will be clear is the depth of our naivety and the height of our hubris. If they have not, perhaps it will be a collective sense of determination that is not yet apparent in 2018. Tribalism and oil consumption are related, of course, as the competition for resources prompts people to divide themselves into groups to gain advantage over their adversaries. Those and other factors interact in complex ways. Thus, if this book has shown anything, it is that to understand the impact of oil in North Dakota, we must be attentive to the play between the global and the local, as western North Dakota has become a nexus point in the global flows of oil, capital, people, and ideas, through cycles of boom and bust over the past sixty years.

References

American Petroleum Institute (API). 1953. *American Frontier*. [Los Angeles?]: Affiliated Film Producers. https://archive.org/details/0007_American_Frontier_07_30_37_00.

Archambault, David, II. 2016. "Taking a Stand at Standing Rock." *New York Times*, August 24. https://www.nytimes.com/2016/08/25/opinion/taking-a-stand-at-standing-rock.html.

Baumgarten, April. 2018. "Impacts of Climate Change Being Felt in Region, but Uncertainty Lingers On the Causes." *Grand Forks Herald*, December 16. https://www.grandforksherald.com/news/weather/4543524-impacts-climate-change-being-felt-region-uncertainty-lingers-causes.

Braun, Sebastien. 2016. "Revisited Frontiers: The Bakken, the Plains, Potential Futures, and Real Pasts." In *The Bakken Goes Boom: Oil and the Changing Geographies of Western North Dakota*, edited by William Caraher and Kyle Conway, 91–116. Grand Forks: Digital Press at the University of North Dakota.

Brorby, Taylor. 2017. *Coming Alive: Action and Civil Disobedience*. North Liberty, IA: Ice Cube Press.

Caraher, William, and Bret Weber. 2017. *The Bakken: An Archaeology of an Industrial Landscape*. Fargo: North Dakota State University Press.

Carson, Rachel. 1962. *Silent Spring*. Greenwich, CT: Fawcett Publications.

Conway, Kyle. 2018. "Passing Through: Migration, Class, Crime, and Identity in the Oilfields of North Dakota." *Great Plains Quarterly* 38 (4): 425–32.

Conway, Kyle, and Maude Duguay. 2019. "Energy East and Dakota Access: Pipelines, Protest, and the Obstacles of Mutual Unintelligibility." *Journal of Canadian Studies* 53 (1): 27–47.

Crutzen, Paul J., and Eugene F. Stoermer. 2000. "The 'Anthropocene.'" *IGBP Newsletter* 41: 17–18. http://www.igbp.net/download/18.316f18321323470177580001401/1376383088452/NL41.pdf.

Dennis, Brady, and Chris Mooney. 2018. "Major Trump Administration Climate Report Says Damage Is 'Intensifying across the Country.'" *Washington Post*, November 23. https://www.washingtonpost.com/energy-environment/2018/11/23/major-trump-administration-climate-report-says-damages-are-intensifying-across-country/.

Harvey, Chelsea. 2018. "CO_2 Emissions Reached an All-Time High in 2018." *Scientific American: E&E News*, December 6. https://www.scientificamerican.com/article/co2-emissions-reached-an-all-time-high-in-2018/.

Institute for Atmospheric and Climate Science (IAC). 2016. *Global CO_2 yearly dataset*. Zurich, Switzerland: Eidgenössische Technische Hochschule. ftp://data.iac.ethz.ch/CMIP6/input4MIPs/UoM/GHGConc/CMIP/ yr/atmos/UoM-CMIP-1-1-0/GHGConc/gr3-GMNHSH/v20160701/ mole_fraction_of_carbon_dioxide_in_air_input4MIPs_GHGConcentrations_CMIP_UoM-CMIP-1-1-0_gr3-GMNHSH_0000-2014.csv.

Intergovernmental Panel on Climate Change (IPCC). 2018. *Global Warming of 1.5°C: An IPCC Special Report on the Impacts of Global Warming of 1.5°C above Pre-industrial Levels and Related Global Greenhouse Gas Emission Pathways, in the Context of Strengthening the Global Response to the Threat of Climate Change, Sustainable Development, and Efforts to Eradicate Poverty*. Geneva, Switzerland: IPCC. https://www.ipcc.ch/report/sr15/.

Trouillot, Michel-Rolph. 1995. *Silencing the Past: Power and the Production of History*. Boston: Beacon Press.

Ruddell, Rick. 2017. *Oil, Gas, and Crime: The Dark Side of the Boomtown*. New York: Palgrave Macmillan.

Storrow, Benjamin. 2018. "Global CO_2 Emissions Rise after Paris Climate Agreement Signed." *Scientific American: E&E News*, March 24. https://www.scientificamerican.com/article/ global-co2-emissions-rise-after-paris-climate-agreement-signed/.

U.S. Global Change Research Program (USGCRP). 2018. *Impacts, Risks, and Adaptation in the United States: Fourth National Climate Assessment, Volume II*, edited by D.R. Reidmiller, C.W. Avery, D.R. Easterling, K.E. Kunkel, K.L.M. Lewis, T.K. Maycock, and B.C. Stewart. Washington, DC: USGCRP. http://dx.doi.org/10.7930/NCA4.2018.

Watts, Jonathan. 2018. "We Have 12 Years to Limit Climate Change Catastrophe, Warns UN." *The Guardian*, October 8. https://www.theguardian.com/environment/2018/oct/08/ global-warming-must-not-exceed-15c-warns-landmark-un-report.

Appendix A
Methodology Note

1958

The information on which this report is based was compiled from the results of a census of Williams and Mountrail Counties, from interviews with numerous officials, businessmen and local leaders, and from a variety of publications and governmental records.

The census of population characteristics and of local opinions was conducted during the summer of 1954 in the areas affected by the oil development. Because of practical considerations, the affected area was divided into the following parts, within which interviews were conducted on a sample basis: Williston, Ray, Tioga, "Tioga Environs" (a new residential area outside the town itself), Stanley, and the rural impact townships (the 22 townships which encompassed or adjoined the field development). Interviews with adult members of the households—a total of 1,313 interviews—were conducted by the research staff using standard schedules designed to obtain information about the demographic, social, economic and political characteristics of the inhabitants.

Samples were drawn on a random and stratified basis in the following proportions: Williston—25% of the platted areas; Ray—33% of the residences; Tioga—50% of the residences; Tioga Environs—50% of the residences; Stanley—33% of the platted areas; rural impact townships—25% of the farm areas. Although the remaining areas of the two counties were excluded on the assumption that they were not directly affected by oil development activity, they were surveyed informally by mailed questionnaires in the farm areas (total of above 200) and by personal inspection in the nonfarm population centers to check (and demonstrate) the validity of the assumption.

All the available supplementary information (such as the U.S. Census of Agriculture, records in local offices of state and federal agencies, various indices of population growth) indicates that the samples were highly representative of the survey areas and that the projections of population numbers and characteristics are accurate within a very few percent. In every area which was sampled a double-check was made to determine that every household which belonged in the sample was represented and that the number of households represented was accurate on the basis of a total residence count.

Additional information on employment, gross sales or receipts, gross weekly payroll, value of inventories, gross change in investment, and proprietors' estimates of the impact of oil upon their businesses were obtained from 187 businesses in Williston and from 29 businesses in Tioga, the two centers most directly affected by the oil development. Bank data relating to the general level of economic activity and to financial transactions immediately related to oil development were collected in Williston, Ray, Tioga and Stanley. Institutional data concerning the membership, policies, plans, and influence on and by the oil development were obtained from the agents of 30 organizations and institutions representative of the social structure of Williston.

No less important than the data obtained in formal interviews involving the use of schedules were the impressions gained and the observations made by the research staff as "participant observers," as residents in the area for three months. The staff was rewarded by an apparently mutually satisfying relationship with local citizens which made possible an almost perfect response to the population and opinion census (only 7 refusals in the total 1,313) and a general willingness to discuss local problems and developments in almost every office and store which staff members entered. The informal, "unstructured" discussions over coffee, across counters and on the sidewalks were what gave real content and meaning to the local "boom" and "bust" psychology, to the excitement and to the anxiety attached to individual oil wells and housing developments and business expansions.

Appendix B
Supplementary Table

1958

1. WILLISTON: TOTAL POPULATION—AGE AND SEX

	Male	Female	Male & Female
0–4	785	713	1498
5–9	548	598	1146
10–13	341	330	671
14	40	77	117
15–19	262	354	616
20–29	805	665	1470
30–39	736	718	1454
40–49	533	440	973
50–64	451	493	944
65 and over	346	297	643
TOTAL ALL AGES	4936	4781	9717
No Data	89	96	185

SOURCE: Projections from sample census.

2. WILLIAMS COUNTY: TOTAL POPULATION—AGE AND SEX

	Male	Female	Male & Female
0–4	76	52	128
5–9	92	80	172
10–13	60	28	88
14	4	4	8
15–19	60	48	108
20–29	88	52	140
30–39	96	76	172
40–49	68	64	132
50–64	112	64	176
65 and over	60	40	100
TOTAL ALL AGES	724	512	1236
No Data	8	4	12

SOURCE: Projections from sample census.

3. MOUNTRAIL COUNTY: TOTAL POPULATION—AGE AND SEX

	Male	Female	Male & Female
0–4	28	48	76
5–9	32	20	52
10–13	12	24	36
14	8	4	12
15–19	0	16	16
20–29	36	56	92
30–39	36	16	52
40–49	48	20	68
50–64	52	24	76
65 and over	24	24	48
TOTAL ALL AGES	276	252	528

SOURCE: Projections from sample census.

4. TIOGA ENVIRONS: TOTAL POPULATION—AGE AND SEX

	Male	Female	Male & Female
0–4	124	129	253
5–9	23	41	64
10–13	5	14	19
14	9	0	9
15–19	14	19	33
20–29	133	125	258
30–39	88	51	139
40–49	27	18	45
50–64	28	10	38
65 and over	0	0	0
TOTAL ALL AGES	506	425	931
No Data	55	18	73

SOURCE: Projections from sample census.

5. TIOGA: TOTAL POPULATION—AGE AND SEX

	Male	Female	Male & Female
0–4	92	133	225
5–9	108	89	197
10–13	56	43	99
14	14	14	28
15–19	60	61	121
20–29	130	111	241
30–39	142	116	258
40–49	134	80	214
50–64	50	31	81
65 and over	39	31	70
TOTAL ALL AGES	897	711	1608
No Data	72	2	74

SOURCE: Projections from sample census.

6. RAY: TOTAL POPULATION—AGE AND SEX

	Male	Female	Male & Female
0–4	166	138	304
5–9	98	62	160
10–13	49	34	83
14	7	15	22
15–19	55	28	83
20–29	151	174	325
30–39	132	86	218
40–49	49	47	96
50–64	46	30	76
65 and over	50	46	96
TOTAL ALL AGES	816	663	1479
No Data	13	3	16

SOURCE: Projections from sample census.

7. STANLEY: TOTAL POPULATION—AGE AND SEX

	Male	Female	Male & Female
0–4	125	118	243
5–9	89	84	173
10–13	39	64	103
14	22	16	38
15–19	55	61	116
20–29	142	145	287
30–39	117	81	198
40–49	67	67	134
50–64	82	65	147
65 and over	45	70	115
TOTAL ALL AGES	822	823	1645
No Data	39	52	91

SOURCE: Projections from sample census.

8. MARITAL STATUS FOR THOSE 14 YEARS OF AGE AND OVER, 1954

	Williston	Ray	Tioga	Tioga Environs	Stanley	Williams County	Mountrail County
MALE:							
Married	2401	367	359	229	402	272	112
Single	672	108	185	76	144	200	80
Divorced/ separated	13	3	11	......	......	......	......
Widowed	140	9	19	......	23	16	12
No Data	36	16	67	49	......	8	......
TOTAL	3262	503	641	354	569	496	204
FEMALE:							
Married	2236	343	352	232	361	264	108
Single	575	49	60	9	100	60	32
Divorced/ separated	44	9	......	......	3	......	4
Widowed	267	25	31	......	53	24	16
No Data	18	3	3	......	40	4	......
TOTAL	3140	429	446	241	557	352	160
MALE & FEMALE:							
Married	4637	710	711	461	763	536	220
Single	1247	157	245	85	244	260	112
Divorced/ separated	57	12	11	......	3	......	4
Widowed	407	34	50	......	76	40	28
No Data	54	19	70	49	40	12	......
TOTAL	6402	932	1087	595	1126	848	364

SOURCE: Projections from sample census.

9. RELATION TO HEAD OF FAMILY, 1954

	Williston	Ray	Tioga	Tioga Environs	Stanley	Impact Areas: Williams & Mountrail
Head	2672	394	404	267	466	460
Wife	2186	354	349	222	380	353
Son	2118	387	339	175	357	504
Daughter	2021	274	325	194	345	328
Lodger—						
Hired Worker	205	52	142	60	61	12
Relatives	204	18	35	5	31	95
No Data	311	......	14	8	5	12
TOTAL	9717	1479	1608	931	1645	1764

SOURCE: Projections from sample census.

10. INHABITANTS BY 1950 AND 1954 RESIDENCE

1950 Residence				1954 Residence			
	Williston	Ray	Tioga	Tioga Environs	Stanley	Williams County	Mountrail County
MALE:							
Same	2769	239	283	......	412	544	212
Within Area	203	31	79	39	70	31	8
Other ND	473	55	205	93	112	4	20
Contig. States	232	15	68	25	24	19	4
All Other	474	310	170	225	79	50	4
Total	4151	650	805	382	697	648	248
FEMALE:							
Same	2717	227	196	......	444	353	159
Within Area	240	30	75	23	89	43	26
Other ND	529	51	135	106	89	6	15
Contig. States	207	9	47	14	21	19	4
All Other	375	208	125	153	62	39	......
Total	4068	525	578	296	705	460	204
MALE & FEMALE:							
Same	5486	466	479	......	856	897	371
Within Area	443	61	154	62	159	74	34
Other ND	1002	106	340	199	201	10	35
Contig. States	439	24	115	39	45	38	8
All Other	849	518	295	378	141	89	4
Total	8219	1175	1383	678	1402	1108	452

SOURCE: Projections from sample census.

11. LABOR FORCE STATUS—14 YEARS OF AGE AND OVER

	WILLISTON			RAY			IMPACT COUNTIES			STANLEY			TIOGA & ENVIR.		
	Male	Female	Total	M	F	T	M	F	T	M	F	T	M	F	T
Employed	2548	868	3416	424	59	483	612	20	632	462	123	585	824	86	906
Unemployed	57	25	82	3	6	9	4	......	4	6	5	11	17	8	29
TOTAL LABOR FORCE	2605	893	3498	427	65	492	616	20	636	468	128	596	841	94	935
Keeping House	8	2025	2033	......	326	326	0	423	423	......	338	338	4	534	538
In School	147	216	363	21	28	49	33	56	89	28	50	78	41	61	102
Unable to Work	155	98	253	21	7	28	20	4	24	43	35	78	27	12	39
Retired	145	......	145	29	......	29	4	8	12	15	......	15	31	......	31
Other	21	17	38	4	......	4	20	......	20	3	......	3	3	......	3
No Data	44	28	72	1	3	4	4	4	8	13	5	18	31	3	34
TOTAL NOT IN LABOR FORCE	520	2384	2904	76	364	440	81	495	576	102	428	530	137	610	747
TOTAL IN AGE GROUP	3125	3277	6402	503	429	932	697	515	1212	570	556	1126	978	704	1682

SOURCE: Projections from sample census.

12. PERCENT DISTRIBUTION OF LABOR FORCE—14 YEARS OF AGE AND OVER

	WILLISTON			RAY			IMPACT COUNTIES			STANLEY			TIOGA & ENVIR.		
	Male	Female	Total	M	F	T	M	F	T	M	F	T	M	F	T
Employed	97.8	97.3	97.7	99.3	90.8	98.2	99.4	100	99.4	98.8	95.7	98.2	98.0	90.9	97.0
Unemployed	2.2	2.7	2.3	0.7	9.2	1.8	0.6	......	0.6	1.2	4.3	1.8	2.0	9.1	3.0
TOTAL LABOR FORCE	100	100	100	100	100	100	100	100	100	100	100	100	100	100	100
Keeping House	1.6	84.9	70.7	......	89.6	74.0	......	85.5	73.4	......	78.9	63.7	2.2	87.6	72.0
In School	28.2	9.1	12.5	27.6	7.6	11.1	40.8	11.3	15.4	30.9	11.6	14.8	31.1	10.0	13.8
Unable to Work	29.8	4.0	8.7	27.6	1.9	6.3	24.7	0.8	4.2	42.4	8.2	14.8	20.0	2.0	5.3
Retired	28.2	......	5.0	38.2	......	6.6	4.9	1.6	2.1	12.1	......	2.8	22.2	......	4.1
Other	4.0	0.4	1.3	5.3	......	1.0	24.7	......	3.5	3.0	......	0.6	2.2	......	0.4
No Data	8.1	1.2	2.5	1.3	0.9	1.0	4.9	0.8	1.4	12.1	1.3	3.3	22.2	0.4	4.5
TOTAL NOT IN LABOR FORCE	100	100	100	100	100	100	100	100	100	100	100	100	100	100	100

SOURCE: Projections from sample census.

13. INDUSTRY GROUP FOR EMPLOYED PERSONS, 1954

	Williston	Ray	Impact Counties Williams & Mountrail	Stanley	Tioga and Tioga Environs
Agriculture	239	58	524	30	72
Mining and Construction	611	237	60	186	498
Manufacturing, Durable	21	......	......	......	......
Manufacturing, Non-Durable	89	......	......	5	......
Transportation, Communications, Public Utilities	513	46	16	57	66
Trade	929	83	20	147	130
Finance, Insurance, Real Estate	130	5	......	16	9
Service	581	31	4	88	72
Public Administration	165	5	......	36	17
No Data	138	18	8	20	42
TOTAL	3416	483	632	585	906

SOURCE: Projections from sample census.

14. PERCENT DISTRIBUTION OF INDUSTRY GROUP FOR
EMPLOYED PERSONS, 1954

	Williston	Ray	Impact Counties Williams & Mountrail	Stanley	Tioga and Tioga Environs
Agriculture	7.0	12.1	82.9	5.1	8.0
Mining and Construction	17.9	49.0	9.5	31.8	55.0
Manufacturing, Durable	0.6	......	......	......	......
Manufacturing, Non-Durable	2.6	......	......	0.9	......
Transportation, Communications, Public Utilities	15.0	9.6	2.5	9.8	7.3
Trade	27.2	17.2	3.2	25.2	14.4
Finance, Insurance, Real Estate	3.8	1.3	......	2.8	1.0
Service	17.0	6.4	0.6	15.0	8.0
Public Administration	4.8	1.3	......	6.1	1.9
No Data	4.0	3.1	1.3	3.3	4.5
TOTAL	100.0	100.0	100.0	100.0	100.0

SOURCE: Projections from sample census.

15. OCCUPATION GROUP FOR EMPLOYED PERSONS, 1954

	Williston	Ray	Impact Counties Williams & Mountrail	Stanley	Tioga and Tioga Environs
Professional	260	6	12	46	17
Farm	205	37	479	28	55
Managers	533	31	4	74	81
Clerical	383	25	8	44	87
Sales	335	31	4	71	24
Crafts	447	49	12	52	130
Operatives	348	197	52	97	315
Services	328	25	8	52	46
Farm Laborers	27	22	40	3	17
Other Laborers	294	34	4	96	101
No Data	256	26	9	22	33
TOTAL	3416	483	632	585	906

SOURCE: Projections from sample census.

16. PERCENT DISTRIBUTION OF OCCUPATION GROUP FOR EMPLOYED PERSONS, 1954

	Williston	Ray	Impact Counties Williams & Mountrail	Stanley	Tioga and Tioga Environs
Professional	7.6	1.3	1.9	7.9	1.9
Farm	6.0	7.6	75.8	4.7	6.1
Managers	15.6	6.4	0.6	12.6	8.9
Clerical	11.2	5.1	1.3	7.5	9.6
Sales	9.8	6.4	0.6	12.1	2.6
Crafts	13.1	10.2	1.9	8.9	14.4
Operatives	10.2	40.8	8.3	16.8	34.8
Services	9.6	5.1	1.3	8.9	5.1
Farm Laborers	0.8	4.5	6.4	0.5	1.9
Other Laborers	8.6	7.0	0.6	16.4	11.2
No Data	7.6	5.7	1.3	3.7	3.8
TOTAL	100.0	100.0	100.0	100.0	100.0

SOURCE: Projections from sample census.

Contributors

Karin L. Becker is the director of Reading, Learning, and Communications at the United States Air Force Academy. Her research focuses on understanding communication preferences and generational differences among marginalized groups in healthcare and workplace settings as a way to improve rapport and foster inclusivity.

Nikki Berg Burin is an assistant professor of history and of women and gender studies at the University of North Dakota. She earned her PhD in history from the University of Minnesota in 2007 and specializes in American women's history, with a focus on slavery, sex trafficking, commercial sexual exploitation, and prostitution in North Dakota. Her research has been published in *Family Values in the Old South* (University Press of Florida, 2010) and *The Bakken Goes Boom: Oil and the Changing Geographies of Western North Dakota* (Digital Press at the University of North Dakota, 2016). In addition to her scholarly and pedagogical pursuits, she is actively engaged in collaborative efforts to combat human trafficking in North Dakota. She served on the original advisory committee for North Dakota's anti-human trafficking organization FUSE and has partnered with and served as a consultant for the North Dakota Human Trafficking Task Force.

Robert B. Campbell earned his PhD in sociology at the University of Wisconsin after serving in the U.S. Navy during the Second World War. He taught at the University of North Dakota for eleven years before joining Southern Illinois University-Edwardsville in 1962, where he taught until his retirement in 1986.

William Caraher is an associate professor in the Department of History at the University of North Dakota. He specializes in field archaeology, Early Christian and Byzantine architecture, material culture and settlement in the Bakken oil patch of western North Dakota, and the history of Late Antique Cyprus and Greece. He's the co-author of *Pyla*-Koutsopetria *I: Archaeological Survey of an Ancient Coastal Town* (with David Pettegrew and R. Scott

Moore, American Schools of Oriental Research, 2014) and *The Bakken: An Archaeology of an Industrial Landscape* (with Bret Weber, North Dakota State University Press, 2017). He co-edited *Punk Archaeology* (Digital Press at the University of North Dakota, 2014), *The Bakken Goes Boom: Oil and the Changing Geographies of Western North Dakota* (with Kyle Conway, Digital Press at the University of North Dakota, 2016), and the *Oxford Handbook of Early Christian Archaeology* (Oxford University Press, 2019). He currently edits the literary journal *North Dakota Quarterly*.

Kyle Conway is an associate professor of communication at the University of Ottawa, but his family is from Williston. He studies people's experiences of talking across different types of borders—linguistic, cultural, religious, and geographic. His also writes about oil and modernity. His books include *The Art of Communication in a Polarized World* (Athabasca University Press, 2020) and the edited collection *The Bakken Goes Boom: Oil and the Changing Geographies of Western North Dakota* (with William Caraher, Digital Press at the University of North Dakota, 2016). His current book project, *Boomtown Hospitality: Feeling at Home in Petromodernity*, is about the 2008–14 Bakken boom.

David T. Flynn is Clow Fellow and professor of economics in the Nistler College of Business and Public Administration at the University of North Dakota. He is also the chair of the Department of Economics and Finance and research director for the Business, Economics, and Population Analytics Division of the Institute of Policy and Business Analytics, both in the Nistler College.

Samuel C. Kelley, Jr., directed the Bureau of Business and Economic Research at the University of North Dakota until 1957. He left to join the Department of Economics at Ohio State University, where, as head of the Center for Human Resource Research, he contributed to reports such as *Manpower Forecasting in the United States: An Evaluation of the State of the Art*.

Andrea Olive is an associate professor of political science and geography at the University of Toronto Mississauga. Her area of research is Canada-U.S. environmental policy, especially conservation and land-use policy. She was awarded a grant from the Social Science and Humanities Research Council of Canada to examine the political ecology of the Bakken Formation in Saskatchewan and North Dakota.

Heather A. Ray, a Mount Royal University faculty member since 2002, is a leader in the field of integrative and community health. Her work is multidisciplinary, crossing the fields of health promotion, disease prevention, emotional well-being, and mindful-based interventions. Ray is a high-energy professor, researcher, and speaker, and she has been a personal development coach specializing in stress and health promotion for over twenty-five years. As a physical and mental trainer and associate professor in the Department of Health and Physical Education at Mount Royal University, she combines years of academic and consulting experience to facilitate mind, body, and spiritual transformations with her students, clients, and audiences.

Richard Rothaus is dean of the College of Liberal Arts and Social Sciences at Central Michigan University in Mt. Pleasant, Michigan, where there is no mountain, although it is quite pleasant. He holds a PhD from The Ohio State University and has been a faculty member, a private business owner, and a university administrator. His early fieldwork began at a Roman bath in Greece and expanded to regional archaeological surveys in Greece and Turkey. Since those early years, Rothaus has been involved in various projects studying vibracores in lakes and lagoons, post-earthquake field surveys in Turkey and India, the battlefields and peoples of the U.S.-Dakota War of 1862–5, and the man camps of the Bakken. He currently is applying his interests in the material culture of peoples forced to live where they do not want to in a study of the Minidoka Japanese-American Concentration Camp.

Rick Ruddell, the Law Foundation of Saskatchewan Chair in Police Studies, joined the Department of Justice Studies at the University of Regina in September 2010. Prior to this appointment, he served as director of operational research with the Correctional Service of Canada and held faculty positions at Eastern Kentucky University and the California State University, Chico. His research has focused upon policing, criminal justice policy, and youth justice, and he recently published *Oil, Gas, and Crime: The Dark Side of the Boomtown* (Palgrave Macmillan, 2017)

Brad Rundquist is currently a professor of geography and dean of the College of Arts and Sciences at the University of North Dakota. Much of his career has been spent at the University of North Dakota, where he held several positions, including College of Art and Sciences associate dean for research, the chair of the Department of Geography, interim chair of the Department of Philosophy and Religious Studies, and interim chair of the Department of American Indian Studies. He has led initiatives on budget, research, curriculum, strategic planning and the creation and direction of UND's graduate certificate in geographic information science. He previously worked for Lockheed-Martin at the Johnson Space Center in support of NASA's Earth Observation (astronaut photography) Program and as an editor and reporter for the *Fort Dodge (Iowa) Messenger* daily newspaper. He earned his PhD and MA degrees in geography from Kansas State University and his bachelor of journalism in news and editorial-writing from the University of Nebraska-Lincoln. His primary research area is ecological applications of remote sensing and GIS, having authored or co-authored more than forty peer-reviewed publications. He is the managing editor of the Taylor and Francis journal *Geocarto International*. He served on the governing board of the American Association of Geographers and as president of the St. Louis Region of the American Society for Photogrammetry and Remote Sensing.

Ross B. Talbot earned his PhD at the University of Chicago in 1949. Although he began his career at the University of North Dakota, he took a position in 1957 at Iowa State University, where he worked until his retirement. In his scholarship, he focused on agricultural politics and policy, publishing books such as *The Policy Process in American Agriculture* and *The Chicken War: An International Trade Conflict between the United States and the European Economic Community*.

Gregory S. Vandeberg is a professor at the University of North Dakota, where he has been on the faculty in the Department of Geography and Geographic Information Science since 2004. His main research interests are surface water resources, water quality, and the development of landscapes from water and glacial processes. His areas of study include the northern Great Plains and the intermountain west. He received a BA in geology from the College of St. Thomas, St. Paul, Minnesota, in 1985, an MS in earth science (geology) from Montana State University in 1993, and a PhD in geography from Kansas State University in 2005.

Bret Weber joined the University of North Dakota in 2009. He works at and studies the intersection of social justice and housing-related issues, including urban programs from the War on Poverty, alternative housing programs, and temporary workforce housing. Weber currently serves on the Grand Forks

City Council, chairs the city's Jobs Development Authority, sits on the Board of Commissioners for the Grand Forks Housing Authority, and is a founding member of the board of the High Plains Fair Housing Center. Among other topics, he has published on environmental justice and social work, as well as various pieces related to his work as the co-PI of the North Dakota Man Camp Project.

Bernt L. Wills began teaching at the University of North Dakota in 1943. He served in the U.S. Navy from 1944 to 1946, and upon his return to UND, became chair of the Department of Geography. He published two books, *North Dakota: The Northern Prairie State* and *North Dakota Geography and Early History*, and was recognized with a UND Alumni Association Award for teaching in 1976.